"Hugh Thomas reminds us that China has a long, rich history of innovation, and provides a historical account of China's modern approach to innovation and its future ambitions. He then offers a range of cases that gives the reader a detailed look at businesses and institutions that together exemplify the innovation landscape in China. Prof Thomas's expertise in innovation and experience in China are aptly demonstrated in this unique and insightful book."

Donna Kelley, PhD
Professor of Entrepreneurship
Frederic C Hamilton Chair of Free Enterprise
Chair of the Entrepreneurship Division
Babson College

"Those with an interest in modern China will find this book an accessible and intriguing introduction to understanding how China has developed to become the world leader it is now. It covers the rise, the fall, and the rise again of innovation in China, from the tradition of Confucianism and Daoism in ancient China, to the transformation towards today's market-based mixed economy under the CPC.

This book merges both insightful case studies and an in-depth view of China. Meticulously researched, Hugh Thomas has drawn from sources both in the east and the west, which provide a multidimensional picture of the renaissance of modern China."

Edward Tse, PhD
Founder & CEO, Gao Feng Advisory Company
Author of the book China's Disrupters (2015),
published by Portfolio/Penguin (Random House)

"The saga of innovation in China is a roller-coaster of ups and downs, stretching from such fabled innovations as paper, gunpowder, printing, and the compass, through long periods of stagnation, to emergence as a global innovation powerhouse today. Endlessly interesting, the Chinese experience provides a multitude of insights into how innovation works, and the roles that government and industry play. *Innovation in China* is an up-close and personal view of the innovators and their organizations. Few scholars are as well prepared to interpret China's innovation story as Hugh

Thomas. This is a must-read book. Here, truly, is innovation with Chinese characteristics."

William Fischer, PhD
Senior Lecturer, Sloan School, MIT;
Emeritus Professor at IMD, Lausanne, Switzerland;
Past Executive President and Dean, China-Europe International Business School (CEIBS),
Shanghai, Peoples' Republic of China

Innovation in China

A Strategic Management Casebook

Innovation in China

A Strategic Management Casebook

HUGH THOMAS

Chinese University of Hong Kong, Hong Kong

World Scientific

NEW JERSEY • LONDON • SINGAPORE • BEIJING • SHANGHAI • HONG KONG • TAIPEI • CHENNAI • TOKYO

Published by

World Scientific Publishing Co. Pte. Ltd.
5 Toh Tuck Link, Singapore 596224
USA office: 27 Warren Street, Suite 401-402, Hackensack, NJ 07601
UK office: 57 Shelton Street, Covent Garden, London WC2H 9HE

Library of Congress Cataloging-in-Publication Data
Names: Thomas, Hugh, 1952– author.
Title: Innovation in China : a strategic management casebook / Hugh Thomas, Chinese University of Hong Kong, Hong Kong.
Description: Hackensack, NJ : World Scientific, 2022. | Includes bibliographical references and index.
Identifiers: LCCN 2021045246 | ISBN 9789811245886 (hardcover) | ISBN 9789811245893 (ebook) | ISBN 9789811245909 (ebook other)
Subjects: LCSH: Industrial management--Technological innovations--China. | Information technology--China--Management. | Strategic planning--China. | Globalization--China.
Classification: LCC HD70.C5 T426 2022 | DDC 658.00951--dc23/eng/20211001
LC record available at https://lccn.loc.gov/2021045246

British Library Cataloguing-in-Publication Data
A catalogue record for this book is available from the British Library.

For any available supplementary material, please visit
https://www.worldscientific.com/worldscibooks/10.1142/12518#t=suppl

Desk Editors: Balamurugan Rajendran/Nicole Ong

Typeset by Stallion Press
Email: enquiries@stallionpress.com

To Joanna

The Love of My Life

About the Author

Hugh Thomas was born and raised in western Canada, living in Edmonton and Winnipeg. He received his Bachelor of Arts, Honors, in History from the University of Alberta, postgraduate diplomas in Chinese language from the Beijing Language and Culture University and history from Nanjing University, an MBA from The Chinese University of Hong Kong (CUHK), and a PhD in International Business and Finance from the Stern School of Business, New York University. He participated in founding China's first business school, the National Center for Industrial Science and Technology Management at Dalian in 1980 and subsequently worked in banking and consulting in Hong Kong for seven years. He was tenured at McMaster University in Canada and then at CUHK, and has most recently been on the faculty of CUHK-Shenzhen. He has taught courses in corporate finance, commercial and central banking, international finance, leadership, strategy, entrepreneurship, and management. He has over 40 publications including cases at Harvard Business Publishing, academic articles, and a textbook on banking. He is married to Joanna Hsiung Kai Chau and has two sons, Owen and Jason. He enjoys cross-country skiing, windsurfing, walking and singing.

IVEY | Publishing

CUHK BUSINESS SCHOOL
CUHK Business School
The Chinese University of Hong Kong

Acknowledgments

I am deeply grateful to many people who have made this book possible.

My father Alun Lloyd Thomas and my mother Elizabeth Jean MacDonald were both great story tellers. And the stories they told reflected their clear visions of truth and beauty. I pray that I can live up to their standards telling the stories in this book.

I am greatly indebted to Joanna Hsiung Kai Chau, my wife of 36 years who welcomed me into her life and blessed me with two sons: Owen Hsiung Thomas and Jason David Thomas. They have found their voices and, God willing will continue the bardic tradition.

Cases are snippets of history. I thank my University of Alberta professors who taught me historical scholarship, particularly Pat Prestwich and Brian Evans.

The story of China has fascinated me for as long as I can remember but during my youth China was mysterious. I thank my teachers and school mates at Beijing Language Institute, Nanjing University and CUHK who brought that distant land close.

My first finance teacher, John Lee Espy, showed me the power of cases in business education. As a devotee of the Harvard Case Method, he gave selfless service to his students and colleagues through three decades.

I am indebted to my masters and PhD thesis supervisor and case co-author Ingo Walter of New York University. Thank you for your steady, insightful scholarship, and warm support. I sincerely thank Bill Dill who hired and led me as a case-writer at the National Center for Industrial Science and Technology Management at Dalian. There I was trained in the art. And there I learned much from my senior co-authors Linda Sprague and Bill Fischer.

I enjoyed working with each case co-authors in this book: Kevin Au, Andrew Chan Chi Fai, Du Gang, Vernon Hsu, Howard Lam Pong Yuen, Robert P. Lee, Liu Mingkang, Icy Ngai Fong Ling, Joyce Wang, Keith Wong Chi Ho, and Wu Yuhui. I received especially valuable help from three. Without Kevin's appreciation of entrepreneurship, I would not have learned the perspective of the start-up. Without Howard's persistence, I would not have written so many cases. Without the grace of Liu Mingkang, I would not have seen the view from the top. And without the many years of support from the many unmentioned friends and colleagues at the School of Management and Economics of The Chinese University of Hong Kong, Shenzhen and The School of Business of The Chinese University of Hong Kong, I would not have enjoyed the career in research and teaching that made this book possible.

I sincerely thank the many business executives that freely gave their time to help my case writing efforts. There is little that entrepreneurs and managers can gain from opening their companies for case research. Yet they did with patience and good humor.

I owe an incalculable and accumulating debt to my students who continue to study and discuss our cases. Thank you for giving me the joy of teaching and learning from you.

Thank you reviewers: David Ahlstrom, Bill Fischer, Donna Kelly, Li Chen and Edward Tse. You took time from your busy schedules to help me: a friend in need is a friend indeed!

Thank you to David Sharp, Nicole Ong Shi Min, Balamurugan Rajendran and the team at World Scientific and to Nour Youseff, Jasmine Gao, Kira Harnett, Sara Martinali, Amber McCutcheon, and the double-blind academic referees at Ivey Publishing. Your professional and patient reviewing, editing, and publishing is inspiring. Without you this book would never have seen the light of day.

I have been fascinated by management of innovation in China for 40 years. Yet I have not systematically studied it. This book cites over 500 researchers who have. Thank you for your scholarship.

Finally, you, the reader. Please accept my appreciation for spending your time on my work and my sincere apologies for the misstatements, omissions, and misconceptions that I have unwittingly left in it. I ask not only for your forgiveness but also for your comments, criticisms, and complaints. Contact me. I look forward to learning from you.

Hugh Thomas
The Chinese University of Hong Kong

Contents

Acronyms

AG	auto glass
AGC	Ashai Glass Company Ltd.
AI	artificial intelligence
ANN	artificial neural network
AR	augmented reality
ARD	American Research and Development Corporation
ARG	auto repair glass
ASCO	American Society for Clinical Oncology
BGI	Beijing Genomics Institute
BMC	business model canvas
BYOD	bring-your-own-device
CBDC	central bank digital currency
CBPBS	cross border payments blockchain system
CCIE	Cisco certified internetwork expert
CDIC	Central Discipline Inspection Commission (of the CPC)
CIA	Central Intelligence Agency
CKD	complete knock down kits
CMB	China Merchants Bank
CMG	China Merchants Group
CNIPA	China National Intellectual Property Administration
CNR	China Northern Railway
CNTK	Microsoft Cognitive Toolkit
CNTVIC	China New Technology Venture Investment Corporation
COD	Central Organization Department (of the CPC)

COVID-19	coronavirus disease of 2019
CPC	Communist Party of China
CR	China State Railway Group
CRC	China Railways Corporation
CRRC	China Railway Rolling Stock Corporation
CSCO	Chinese Society for Clinical Oncology
CSR	China Southern Railway
CUHK	The Chinese University of Hong Kong
DARPA	Defence Advanced Research Projects Agency
DEC	Digital Equipment Corporation
DNA	deoxyribonucleic acid
DPI	distributions to paid-in capital [ratio]
EMU	electrical multiple unit
FDI	foreign direct investment
FET	fish embryo toxicity
FGA	Fuyao Glass America Inc.
FI	financial institution
GDP	Gross domestic product
GE	General Electric Appliance
GII	Global Innovation Index
GP	general partner
GPI	global payments innovation
GPS	global positioning system
GPU	graphics processing unit
HBR	Harvard Business Review
HKMA	Hong Kong Monetary Authority
HKSTP	Hong Kong Science and Technology Parks Corporation
HSR	high-speed rail
IC	integrated circuit
ICBC	Industrial and Commercial Bank of China
ICE	Inter-city Express
ICO	initial coin offering
ICT	information and communications technologies
IoT	internet of things
IP	intellectual property
IPO	initial public offering
IPR	intellectual property rights
IT	information technology
ITF	Innovation and Technology Fund

JV	joint venture
KMT	*Kuo Min Tang* [国民党 *Guo min dang*]
KPI	key performance indicator
KYC	know your customer
LP	limited partner
MIT	Massachusetts Institute of Technology
MNC	multinational company
MoE	Ministry of Education
MoR	Ministry of Railways
MOU	memorandum of understanding
Mt. Gox	Magic: The Gathering Online Exchange
NAFTA	North American Free Trade Association
NB	narrow band
NGO	non-government organization
NSA	National Security Agency
NSF	National Science Foundation
NSG	Nippon Sheet Glass Co., Ltd.
OECD	Organization for Economic Cooperation and Development
OEM	original equipment manufacturer
OSHA	Occupational Safety and Health Administration
OSI	Open Source Initiative
P2P	peer-to-peer
PBOC	People's Bank of China
PBX	private branch exchange
PC	personal computer
PCT	Patent Cooperation Treaty
PE	private equity
PLA	People's Liberation Army
PRB	Patent Re-Examination Board
PRC	People's Republic of China
PSTS-SPC	Public Sector Trial Scheme for Incubatees and Graduate Tenants-Science Park and Cyberport
QR-code	quick response code
R&D	research and development
RMB	*Renminbi* [人民币]
SAR	special administrative region
SARS-CoV-2	severe acute respiratory syndrome coronavirus 2

SASAC	State-owned Assets Supervision and Administration Commission
SCM	supply chain management
SEZ	special economic zone
SIPO	State Intellectual Property Office
SMART	specific, measurable, achievable, realistic, timely
SOE	state owned enterprise
STAR Market	Science and Technology Innovation Board
SWIFT	Society for Worldwide Interbank Financial Telecommunication
TEA	total early entrepreneurial activity
TGF	*trains a grande vitesse*
TRIPS	Trade Related Aspects of International Property Rights Agreement
TSMC	Taiwan Semiconductor Manufacturing Company
UAW	International Union, United Automobile, Aerospace and Agricultural Implement Workers of America
USAID	United States Agency for International Development
USPTO	United States Patent and Trademark Office
USSR	Union of Soviet Socialist Republics
VC	venture capital
VHS	very high speed
WFOE	wholly foreign-owned enterprise
WIPO	World Intellectual Property Organization
WTO	World Trade Organization
ZZJYT	*Zizhujingyingti* [自主经营体]

Introduction

This book is about innovation in the largest country in the world by population and real GDP — China.[1] "Innovation" means the introduction of something new with the hope of *creating value*. Humanity directs its future through innovation. Each person, organization, and society chooses how to manage innovation. Understanding how China manages innovation is critical to understanding humanity's future. Whatever corner of the world we live in, we should examine which innovations work, how they work, and whether we should apply, adapt, or reject them.

Innovation is a Fact of Life

All living things, from the simplest to the most complex, innovate. At one end of the spectrum are viruses, the world's most prolific life form with about 10^{31} individuals on earth.[2] Viruses are so simple that they even outsource reproduction. Viruses impact society through their innovations like 2019-nCOV, first identified in China.[3] Viruses' sloppy copying of their

[1] World Bank, "GDP, PPP (constant 2011 international dollars)", 2019. https://data.worldbank.org (accessed May 13, 2020).

[2] Katherine J. Wu, "There are more viruses than stars in the universe. Why do only some infect us?" *National Geographic Science*, April 15, 2020. https://www.nationalgeographic.com/science/2020/04/factors-allow-viruses-infect-humans-coronavirus/ (accessed May 13, 2020).

[3] Nanshan Chen, Min Zhou, Xuan Dong, Jieming Qu, Fengyun Gong, Yang Han, Yang Qiu, Jingli Wang, Ying Liu, Yuan Wei, Jia'an Xia, Ting Yu, Xinxin Zhang and Li Zhang,

own genetic code from generation to generation drives evolution: if a "strict match" criterion of novelty is applied, every virus holds the random promise of innovation.[4]

At the other end of the innovation spectrum of life are humans. Long-lived and genetically fairly consistent from generation to generation, a human of half a million years ago would be recognizable as a human by us today.[5] Yet in those half million years, humanity and its models of innovation have changed. Unlike hunter-gatherer tribes of the past millennia, we live in societies where hundreds of millions of people interact through evolving infrastructures. Moreover, unlike viruses, and unlike human society over most of the last half a million years, we are blessed with self-awareness about our own evolution and how it is driven by innovation. Not only do we and the world around us change, but we view and can understand those changes as they occur. We appreciate, to an extent greater than any previous generations, that the world is a single society for which we write the rules of our own game, affecting how society will innovate and, hence, evolve.

Globalization is a Fact of Life

China is, and always has been, part of a single humanity. The Western notion of a Middle Kingdom sealed off from the rest of the world and developing a 5,000 year, continuous, unique, homogenous, civilization has more to do with western European and North American myopic

---

"Epidemiological and clinical characteristics of 99 cases of 2019 novel coronavirus pneumonia in Wuhan, China: A descriptive study", *The Lancet* 395:10223 (February 15, 2020) 507–513. https://www.thelancet.com/journals/lancet/article/PIIS0140-6736(20)30211-7/fulltext (accessed May 13, 2020).

[4]Alexander E. Gorbalenya, Susan C. Baker, Ralph S. Baric, Raoul J. de Groot, Christian Drosten, Anastasia A. Gulyaeva, Bart L. Haagmans, Chris Lauber, Andrey M. Leontovich, Benjamin W. Neuman, Dmitry Penzar, Stanley Perlman, Leo L.M. Poon, Dmitry Samborskiy, Igor A. Sidorov, Isabel Sola and John Ziebuhr "Severe Acute Respiratory syndrome-related coronavirus: The species and its viruses — a statement of the Coronavirus Study Group", *bioRxiv,* February 11, 2020. https://www.biorxiv.org/content/10.1101/2020.02.07.937862v1 (accessed May 13, 2020).

[5]Aida Gómez-Robles, "Dental evolutionary rates and its implications for the Neanderthal–modern human divergence", *Scientific Advances*, May 2019 https://www.ncbi.nlm.nih.gov/pmc/articles/PMC6520022/ (accessed May 13, 2020).

empire-building, Chinese imperial propaganda and the universal human urge to simplify, than with objective reality.

This book presents recent cases of innovation: Chinese managers making strategic decisions for their organizations. To succeed, they must have a global perspective. They use concepts of design, production, and distribution of goods and services which, even if they are not sold internationally, are impacted by world-wide flows of physical resources, raw materials, intermediate goods, finished products, labor, capital, ideas and data. They play the games of business according to rules set by local, national and, increasingly, global society.

Few of the models of management of innovation presented in this book are uniquely Chinese. The vocabulary of modern Chinese management today is Western, to an extent unimaginable a scant 40 years ago. In those days, the language of management in China was taken from Marxist-Leninism-Mao Zedong Thought. Marxism itself was manufactured in the West before being exported to the rest of the world. Few would have imagined, 170 years ago, that Confucianist China would become its most avid buyer of Marxism in the 20th century. Few would have imagined, 50 years ago, that Marxist, isolated China would fervently subscribe to market economics and the global prescriptions of the World Trade Organization (WTO).

In this book, the reader will recognize a Harvard Business School-style of managerial cases. The reader sometimes may be disappointed to find few vestiges of either traditional Chinese culture or Marxism-Leninism-Mao Zedong Thought. But taken together modern Chinese models of innovation present differences from those of Western management.

China today is perceived by the rest of the world as a possibly threatening alternative to Western European and North American core values. Differences in values are not genetic. They can be traced to China's tradition prior to 1911, its embrace of Communism following 1949, its relative isolation from the Western world prior to 1976, its rapid integration with the rest of the world over the last forty years, and global interplays through the whole process. The world fears China because China could become the world leader, bringing in a system different from the Western models that seemed so inevitable during the second half of the 20th century. Both the differences and the threats argue for serious analysis of the Chinese alternatives, if not to embrace them, then to adapt them, or to challenge them with plausible alternatives.

The Chapters

Chapter 1 looks at the historical context of management of innovation in China, a country that fell from the most innovative society on earth for most of the last 2.5 millennia to an also-ran by the turn of the 20th century. Chapter 2 looks at how the Communist Party of China (CPC), from its founding 100 years ago to present, has shaped the modern Chinese approach to innovation and government. Chapter 3 introduces intellectual property (IP): copyright, patents, and trademarks. How IP is defined, developed, stimulated, protected, and shared constitutes a major part of the rules of the game of innovation. Chapter 4 examines the largest, most successful, single, state-engineered acquisition of foreign technology to stimulate innovation in history: China's high-speed rail (HSR) initiative. Incubators are the subject of Chapter 5, which looks at Hong Kong's Science Park. Incubators, developed in the West and embraced by China, are part of a policy to break with Hong Kong Kong's *laissez faire* past. Chapter 6 looks at the US technology company that was briefly the largest company in the world at the turn of the 21st century, Cisco Systems. In the case presented, Cisco seeks to promote its products in China through innovation and co-ordination with Chinese government policy.

Chapters 1 through 6 look primarily at the role of government in management of innovation in China. But the story of the modern Chinese miracle is as much the story of private enterprise as it is of government *dirigisme*. Chapter 7 looks at two private entrepreneurs, Zhang Ruimin and Ren Zhengfei, who used strikingly different philosophies to build from nothing two major industrial enterprises: Haier and Huawei respectively.

Chinese private companies with technology, branding, and comparative advantage can succeed in international markets. Chapter 8 examines how the leading global producer of auto glass, Fuyao, innovates to minimize the distance to the customer in the North American auto producer market. Chapter 9 highlights the regulatory component of innovation, as it describes ofo, one of the two private, dockless, bike-sharing companies founded to solve the last kilometer problem of the urban, public transit commuter.

Artificial intelligence (AI), fed by the mobile revolution's troves of digital data, processed by innovative algorithms and largely unrestrained by a single party state, epitomizes the West's increasingly Orwellian vision of China. Chapter 10 looks at the business model of a private, profitable unicorn, a leader in Chinese AI, SenseTime. The book concludes with two cases of innovation in finance. Chapter 11 describes a start-up venture capital (VC) company, Redhill Capital and its foray into biotechnology and medical services, raising money for its second fund in the midst of the COVID-19 pandemic. And the final chapter describes how China Merchants Bank's blockchain team, funded by the bank's incubation fund, innovates in cross border payments advice.

Each case can stand alone. The cases are listed on the Richard Ivey and the Harvard Business Schools' case publishing websites, where instructors can access detailed teaching notes. Each case can be used as teaching material for instructors in business school courses. In each, the instructor can ask his or her students to place themselves in the position of the decision maker, to analyze the situation, and to make a strategic decision.

Each case is also a description of how actual managers in China confront issues of innovation. Each case is preceded by a short discussion on how the company and the decision illuminate Chinese management of innovation. Taken together, the cases and the commentaries present a mosaic of innovation, fully understandable to Western managers and academics, yet subtly different. And in the differences lie the food for thought.

In our world, from the simplest life forms to the most complex societies, the only true constant is change. To meet successfully the challenges of our age, we must innovate. I hope that the innovations presented in the book may inspire new approaches that will create value for our future global society.

Chapter 1

The Rules of the Old Game

> How the entrepreneur acts at a given time and place depends heavily on the rules of the game — the reward structure in the economy.
>
> William Baumol[1]

China, throughout most of the last two and half thousand years, has been an innovative civilization. The official Confucian rules of the game encouraged innovation relative to other contemporary cultures. Imperial governments were staffed by scholar-bureaucrats, recruited through examinations and keen to acquire technical knowledge. Medieval China rose to world innovation leadership. However, in early modern times, China fell behind and, in the 19th century, the Chinese Empire crumbled in the face of dynastic decline, foreign invasion, and the modern failure of the Confucian tradition.

Early Innovations

Innovation drives progress. The innovation of the Neolithic Revolution, about 10,000 years ago, was the domestication of farm animals and grain. Occurring only slightly later, in what is now China, than in the Middle

[1]William J. Baumol, "Entrepreneurship: Productive, Unproductive and Destructive", *Journal of Political Economy* 98:5 (1990), 893.

East, the "Chinese"[2] Neolithic Revolution domesticated pigs and poultry, millet and rice, to support larger human settlements in the river basins of the Liao, Yellow and Yangzi, than previous hunter gatherer societies.[3] "Chinese" innovation *lagged* the West in the area that *culturally* became Chinese some 7,000 years later.

Each civilization's origin is shrouded in mist, illuminated by myth. The three sovereigns and five sages at the start of mythical Chinese society about five thousand years ago are striking. All eight linked heaven and earth in their righteous rule. All eight governed unitary, ideal, stable societies. And all eight brought technological innovations to their people: fire, construction, fishing, farming, sericulture, medicine, the calendar, writing, etc.[4]

But myth yields to history. The beginning of historical civilization is often marked by writing. Using this benchmark China's civilization is thousands of years ***younger*** than the Middle Eastern Sumerian and North African Egyptian civilizations on which the West was founded. But unlike Sumerian cuneiform and Egyptian hieroglyphics, Chinese characters, dating from about 1200 BC in the Shang Dynasty (circa 1600–1046 BC), can be traced in an unbroken line to modern Chinese. Therefore, China legitimately claims to have the longest, proven, *continuously living* civilization in the world.[5]

---

[2]The quotation marks are used because if "Chinese" is a linguistic or cultural concept, Neolithic societies in what is now China were only "Chinese" in a geographic sense.

[3]Kwang-Chih Chang, "China on the Eve of the Historical Period", in Michael Loewe, *The Cambridge History of Ancient China*, Cambridge University Press, 1999.

[4]The expression "Three sovereigns and five sages" or "three emperors and five sovereigns" (三皇五帝) identifying the start of Chinese civilization has been in the Chinese language for over 2500 years. So has the controversy over *exactly who were these three sovereigns and five sages*. See, for example, Xu Shunzhan "The interpretation of three emperors and five sovereigns" 许顺湛"三皇五帝解读" *重庆文理学院学报 (中国知纲)*, 30:6 (2011), 1–8.

[5]The Shang (商) is the earliest indisputable Chinese dynasty. There are no contemporary records of China's first mythological Xia Dynasty (夏), although impressive archeological sites of urban cultures that existed within the age ascribed to the Xia (from the end of the third millennium to the middle of the second millennium BC) have been excavated. See "Shimao: A Stone-Walled Settlement of the 2nd Millennium BC in Northern China", *Chinese Archeology* September 1, 2013. http://www.kaogu.cn/en/Research_work/Settlement_archaeology_and_arch/2013/1025/30309.html (accessed August 10, 2020)

The Shang Dynasty marks the starting point of the Chinese ***written language***. Yet the full Chinese ***cultural*** starting point is ***not*** Shang. Centered on the royal family at Anyang, in today's Henan province, the Shang Dynasty was an empire that held military power over many surrounding societies of very different cultures. In the oracle bones that record the genesis of the Chinese language, Shang emperors sought, in question after question, guidance from heaven concerning what futures the emperors faced and what policies they should adopt. The oracle bones give insight into a society focused on ritualized ancestor veneration and divination: caring for the dead of the ruling class was one of the empire's great enterprises requiring large burials of possessions and human sacrifice.[6]

The Shang was overthrown by what the Shang considered to be barbarians of the northwest, the Zhou. The Zhou Dynasty (1046–221 BC) introduced a feudal structure[7] and a novel claim to power that persists to the present day: the mandate of heaven.[8] According to the mandate of heaven, rulers hold the divine right to rule as long as they look after the welfare of the people. Once the dynasty breaks that contract, the rulers lose the right to rule.[9]

---

and "China finds 3,600-year-old palace", *People's Daily Online*, December 13, 2011. http://english.peopledaily.com.cn/90782/7675375.html (accessed July 25, 2020).

[6]Oracle bone script (甲骨文), was text inscribed on ox and turtle bones, cracked by applying heat, and read by priests interpreting the cracks. Troves of oracle bones were excavated at Anyang, Henan. The script is the antecedent of Chinese characters. Robert Bagley "Shang Archeology" in Michael Loewe, *The Cambridge History of Ancient China*, Cambridge University Press, 1999.

[7]"Feudal" in Western historiography means a stratified system where a king bestows land on vassal (and the vassal bestows land on his vassals) in exchange for military service. Vassals let tenants till the land in return for service and payment in kind. Marxist historiography, believing that primitive society gives way to slave society that gives way to feudalism, capitalism, and finally socialism, calls the dynastic, imperial, scholar-bureaucracy-ruled China after Qin Shihuang (221 BC) "feudal". It sets the starting of the transition from "slave society" to "feudalism" as the Spring and Autumn period (722 BC). See Ministry of Education of the People's Republic of China, *Secondary Vocational School History Curriculum Standard* (*2020 version*). http://www.moe.gov.cn/srcsite/A26/s8001/202002/W020200226602560031438.pdf (accessed July 10, 2020).

[8]The Chinese 天命 (the mandate of heaven) could also be translated as "The will of God".

[9]Robert Tignor, *Worlds Together Worlds Apart*, 4th edition. Volume 1, Norton, 2014.

Although ancestor veneration from the Shang and the mandate of heaven from the Zhou are part of traditional Chinese beliefs, it was only as the Zhou Dynasty's feudal structure and power crumbled, when the Western Zhou (with its capital near present day Xi'an) gave way to the Eastern Zhou (with its capital near present day Luoyang), that a fully recognizable *Chinese* society arose.[10]

Chinese technology during the Eastern Zhou drew abreast of, and in some areas surpassed, Europe and the Middle East. Table 1.1 gives 35 global innovations which occurred first in Eastern Zhou China.

Technological advances were accompanied by social, philosophical, and religions innovations: the rules of the game were in flux.

Innovation in the Axial Age: Religion

Religion underlies the rules of the game in society by answering life's basic questions. Where did we come from? Where we are today? Where are we going? What should we do with our lives?

Max Weber, one of the fathers of sociology, in studying why certain nations excelled in early modern development, noted that "…religious forces … are the decisive influences in the formation of national character".[11] His work explained the rise of capitalism with ascetic 17th century Protestantism. In that system, one should do gladly, within ones calling, productive work, acquiring wealth as long as its acquisition does lead to the enjoyment of wealth in greed, gluttony, sloth, pride, lust, or envy. One should use God-given wealth, discretely, humbly and morally to benefit society. To do so is a sign of God's grace.

If religion promoted early modern capitalism in the West, as Weber said, then we might profitably examine religion to understand innovation in imperial, and indeed modern, China.

The Eastern Zhou of the Spring and Autumn Period (722–476 BC) and the Warring States Period (476–221 BC) was a multistate milieu of

---

[10] China's early historian, Sima Qian (145–86 BC) writing in the late 2nd and early 1st century BC, gives the starting date of Chinese history as 842 BC the year that King Li of Zhou was forced by invaders to move the capital east. See Michael Loewe, "Introduction", *The Cambridge History of Ancient China*, Cambridge University Press, 1999, p. 21.

[11] Max Weber, *The Protestant Ethic and the Spirit of Capitalism*, Routledge, London, 2005 (first published 1930), Chapter 5, p. 102 and following.

Table 1.1: Innovations of the Eastern Zhou

Acupuncture
Anemometer
Anti-malarial drugs
Bellows, piston
Belt drive
Bio-geochemical prospecting for minerals
Blast furnace
Bowl, bronze, water spouting (that spouts water through rubbing induced wave action)
Breast strap horse harness
Cast iron
Chess
Chopsticks
Collapsible umbrella
Crossbow
Distillation of mercury
Dujiangyan irrigation system
Fumigation
Gabions (cage filled with rocks for civil engineering)
Great Wall of China
Hand-carts
Kites
Ladders, extendable
Mangonel (counter-weight catapult siege engine)
Maps, topographical
Metals to oxides
Mine ventilation using differential pressure of different depth shafts
Paper
Piston bellows (double acting)
Planting in rows
Refraction
Simple trebuchet siege engine
Sluices for mining ore separation
Soil science (Ecology)
Spinning wheel
Square set mining vertical shaft supports

Source: The author from indices of Joseph Needham, *Science and Civilization in China*, Cambridge at the University Press, 1954–2004.

consolidating countries,[12] nominally venerating the waning Zhou Dynasty while actually engaged in recurring wars and shifting alliances for power. Integrating formerly distinct cultures into what was becoming a single Chinese cultural community of states, the period included the greatest intellectual flowering of competing philosophies in Chinese history[13] with *one hundred flowers blooming and one hundred schools of thought contending.*[14]

The 7th and 6th centuries BC experienced flowering of philosophies, not just in China, but in other parts of the Eurasian continent as well. Simultaneously in Europe, The Middle East, and South and West Asia, the world was in philosophical and religious flux. Joseph Needham comments,

> The close coincidence in dates between the appearance of many of the great ethical and religious leaders has been remarked on: Confucius c –550, Gautama (Buddhism) c –560, Zoroaster (if a historical person) c –600, Mahavira (Jainism) c –560 and so on, but the [Spring and Autumn] period was also contemporary with many important political events such as the taking of Nineveh by the Medes in –621 , the fall of Babylon to Cyrus in –621 and the invasion of the Punjab by Darrius in –512, all examples of Iranian expansion.[15]

It *was not* a coincidence. In the 7th and 6th centuries BC, Eurasia was being integrated as never before. Ideas were spreading through that integration. It was, in the words of the German philosopher Karl Jaspers, an *axial age*:

---

[12] Cho-Yun Hsu, "The Spring and Autumn Period", in Michael Loewe, *The Cambridge History of Ancient China*, Cambridge University Press, 1999, p. 565.

[13] See David Nivenson, "The Classical Philosophical Writings", in Michael Loewe, *The Cambridge History of Ancient China*, Cambridge University Press, 1999.

[14] In modern usage, the phrase "let 100 flowers bloom and 100 schools contend" (百花齐放 百家争鸣) means intellectual ferment. It can be used ironically because Mao Zedong, in the 1950s, first invited intellectual debate with that saying, but then followed with the anti-rightest suppression of intellectual dissention. See Chapter 2.

[15] Joseph Needham, *Science and Civilization in China. Volume I: Introductory Orientations*, Cambridge University Press, London, 1954, p. 99.

> In the years centering around 500 BC — from 800–200 BC — the spiritual foundations of humanity were laid simultaneously and independently in China, India, Persia, Palestine, and Greece.[16]

China was importing iron technology from the West through Central Asia along trade routes.[17] But more than metallurgy was spread. The rules of the game — how society is organized — were literally being written down for the first time.[18]

The Achaemenid Dynasty (the first Persian Empire (550–330 BC)) centered on modern day Iran, was the greatest empire the world had ever seen. Its eastern extent included present day northwestern India. Its western borders enclosed northeastern Greece. Its northern limits included the shores of the Black Sea, the Caucuses, the Caspian Sea, modern day Turkmenistan and Afghanistan. And it included Egypt in the south. It did not border on any part of China, but it bordered on the Scythian, Xiongnu or Hun lands[19] and they bordered on China.

The Achaemenid Empire introduced the innovation of constitutionalism. Cyrus the Great, the founder of the Empire, has been lionized as an ancient champion of human rights evidenced by the cuneiform inscriptions on the *Cyrus Cylinder*, which appear to grant his subjects rights to be implemented through his empire's bureaucracy.[20] Even though

---

[16]Karl Jaspers, (translated by Ralph Manheim), *The Way to Wisdom: An Introduction to Philosophy*, Yale University Press, 1954, p. 98.

[17]Lothar Von Falmenhausen, "The Waning of the Bronze Age", in Michael Loewe, *The Cambridge History of Ancient China,* Cambridge University Press, 1999 mentions technology adaptation from Western Asia and Chinese bronzes being made for export to the central Asian steppe market (pp. 468, 481, 494). Nicola di Cosmo, "The Northern Frontier in Pre-imperial China", in Michael Loewe, *The Cambridge History of Ancient China,* Cambridge University Press, 1999, pp. 890, 892 and 913 says that iron objects in China first appeared in Xinjiang in the ninth century and Inner Mongolia in the mid-7th century before spreading later to the rest of the country.

[18]Cleisthenes, 570–508 BC, could be added to this impressive list. He wrote the constitution of ancient Athens, in what can be seen as the rules of the game of Greek democracy.

[19]The term "Scythian" is western Asian and comes from Herodotus the fifth century BC Greek father of history. It, along with proto-Xiongnu and other terms applying to the pastoral people of central Asia at the time represents an over-simplification, lumping many Asian steppe peoples together. See Nicola di Cosmo, *op. cit.*

[20]In addition to Iranian propagandists, particularly Mohammad Reza, the last Shah of Iran, who was deposed by the Islamic State Revolution in 1979, modern western philosophers

projecting modern human rights onto an ancient civilization is anachronistic, Cyrus certainly set up satraps. The satrapies, constituent states of his empire, under his protection and owing him tribute, were disparate societies he had conquered. But the satraps ruled according to the traditions of the conquered societies not Cyrus'. The satrapies codified their own rules of the game. Among the satrapies was Palestine. The Jews in Palestine codification the oral Mosaic Laws and traditions in the Jewish Tanakh (the Christian Old Testament)[21] as part of the Achaemenid innovation of constitutionalism, siring self-conscious religion.

Religion has texts, traditions, beliefs, behaviors, ethics, eschatology, social structures, and more. They codify for each of us where we came from, where we are today, where we are going, and what we should do with our lives. Religion is the *ultimate* basis of the rules of the game by which a society operates. So religion is as old as human society. But ***self-conscious*** religion is much younger, dating from the axial age.

One cannot prove that self-conscious religion was a Persian innovation that spread to China, India, Palestine, Greece, and elsewhere. Indeed, given the way people communicate, the spread the ideas could have been in the *opposite* direction or, more likely, fitfully, over many years, in both directions. Yet the simultaneous arising of self-conscious religion constitutes at least, "… another example of important events occurring almost simultaneously in Eastern Asia and Western Europe".[22]

Self-conscious religion and philosophy ***were*** major innovations of the axial age. Sets of beliefs ***were*** catalogued for the first time. Because they were catalogued, they were available to foreigners (those who were not born into such beliefs) as well as to locals (those who were). Debate and innovation ensued as locals and foreigners, adherents and detractors analyzed comparative belief systems.

China's *hundred flowers blooming and hundred schools of thought contending* form the rich defining experience of Classical Chinese culture.

---

such as William Talbott also make this claim. W. Talbott, *Which Rights Should Be Universal*, Oxford University Press, New York, 2005, p. 40.

[21]As *The Bible* reports, Cyrus the Great liberated the Jews from Babylonian captivity and was a "Messiah" (meaning "anointed one") Isaiah 45:1. See Dariush Borbor, *"Iran's Contributions to Human Rights, the Rights of Women and Democracy"*, *Iran and the Caucasus*, January 1, 2008, 12:1. https://doi.org/10.1163/157338408X326235 (accessed July 4, 2020).

[22]Needham, *op. cit.*, p. 95.

Confucianism, unique among all of the hundred schools of thought contending in China's axial age, became the ethos of the bureaucratic empires of Han, Tang, Song, Yuan, Ming, and Qing Dynasties, surviving more or less intact for almost two and a half millennia, from the life of the Sage into the 20th century.

Confucianism

"Confucius say… ." Those are the first words of a huge compendium of one-liner, American jokes, laced with pidgin English.[23] "Confucius say" humor reflects the truth that for over 2000 years, every educated Chinese could ***and did*** quote, word for word, the philosophy of the Sage *in Chinese*. Educated Chinese with less than perfect English, living in the middle of the last century in the United States, must have found it almost impossible to translate Confucian ideas into English for their family, friends, and acquaintances. Their futile efforts became the butt of jokes.[24]

But let's leave the jokes aside. An understanding of the rules of the game of classical, Chinese society, influencing management of innovation, requires a modest understanding of Confucian beliefs. Those beliefs underlaid imperial China, and they still influence China today.[25]

---

[23] See Ora Matushansky, "Confucius Say, Top 100". http://www.trees-and-lambdas.info/matushansky/confucius.html (accessed July 15, 2020).

[24] Initiated into American culture by columnist Walter Winchell in the 1930s. See Tom Connolly, "Why Do Americans Say 'Confucius Say'", *Warp, Weft and Way*, October 5, 2014. https://warpweftandway.com/why-americans-confucius (accessed July 20, 2020).

[25] As Chapter 2 describes, at the founding of the CPC, Confucianism was seen as an old belief system to be eradicated. This continued in the 1950s, 1960s, 1970s where adherence to Confucianism was a charge to attack political enemies. Recently, Confucius has enjoyed a restoration. No longer a threat, he is now seen as a representative of Chinese civilization. Confucianism has become a part of the Harmonious Society (和谐社会) government philosophy of Xi Jinping. More than 80 Confucius Institutes, set up and financed by the Ministry of Education of China, are an instrument of the Chinese soft power to promote culture and beliefs to non-Chinese universities around the world See www.english.hanban.org. The 55 Confucius Institutes in the United States, 48 of which are located on university campuses are consequently the target of U.S. legislation seeking to restrict the influence of the CPC. Caitlin Mcfall "Bill limiting China-backed Confucius Institutes passed unanimously by Senate" *Fox News*, March 5, 2021. https://www.foxnews.com/politics/bill-limiting-confucius-institutes-passed-unanimously-senate (accessed March 9, 2021).

Confucius (551–479 BC) was born into an emerging class of civil servants and administrators between aristocracy and commoners in the late Spring and Autumn period. A descendant of Shang nobility and the son of a general in the State of Lu in what is today the province of Shandong, he based his philosophy on what he believed existed in, and was accountable for, golden periods of Chinese history from the Xia and Shang through the end of the Western Zhou, 220 years prior to his birth. He was a lower level official at the court of Lu and an itinerant scholar, attempting to attract disciples to teach his philosophies.[26] Confucianism, which was fully systematized by Zhu Xi in the Sung Dynasty over 1,500 years after the Sage died,[27] is most accessible through the short book "The Great Learning" within *The Classic of Rites*. Its words were memorized by more than 100 generations of aspiring Confucian scholars:

> The way of Great Learning; to understand clear morality; to touch the people; to rest in perfection.
>
> Knowing, one is stable; stability brings calm; calmness brings peace; peacefulness brings thought; thoughtfulness brings success.
>
> Things begin and end: knowing their sequence; approaches Great Learning.[28]

---

[26]A simple, standard introduction is in Michael Burgan, *Confucius: Chinese Philosopher and Teacher* Compass, Point Minneapolis, 2009.

[27]"Zhu Xi (Chu Hsi, 1120–1200)", *Internet Encyclopedia of Philosophy.* www.iep.utm.edu/zhu-xi (accessed July 18, 2020).

[28]This translation, which may recall a "Confucius Say" joke, is my own, as I try to mimic the cadence of the Chinese 大学之道, 在明明德, 在亲民, 在止于至善。知止而后有定, 定而后能静, 静而后能安, 安而后能虑, 虑而后能得。物有本末, 事有终始, 知所先后, 则近道矣. The most accepted translation of the Great Learning is that of the Scottish missionary, sinologist and first professor of Chinese at Oxford University, James Legge (1815–1897). He translates the same passage as "What the Great Learning teaches is to illustrate illustrious virtue; to renovate the people; and to rest in the highest excellence. The point where to rest being known, the object of pursuit is then determined; and, that being determined, a calm unperturbedness may be attained to. To that calmness there will succeed a tranquil repose. In that repose there may be careful deliberation, and that deliberation will be followed by the attainment of the desired end. Things have their root and their branches. Affairs have their end and their beginning. To know what is first and what is last will lead near to what is taught in the Great Learning". See "Confucianism: The Classic of Rites: Da Xue", in *The Chinese Text Project* 2006–2020. https://ctext.org/liji/da-xue (accessed July 10) (礼记 — 大学). The entire compendium of the Chinese Classics

"The Great Learning" says learning is absolutely essential and is based on knowledge of society and nature.

"The Great Learning" goes on to assert that the political order of the state is founded on the cultivation of order in the family, based in each person's clear heart and sincere thoughts. Clarity and sincerity come from assiduously learning how nature operates. Everyone, from the emperor down to the masses of the people, must first cultivate himself if the state is to prosper. Mindfulness is the key to self-cultivation. Passion, terror, regret, sorrow, or distress interrupts mindfulness and, if allowed to dominate, will bring about looking but not seeing, hearing but not understanding, and eating but not tasting.

Confucianism asks adherents to become gentlemen — as opposed to petty people. "The Doctrine of the Mean" (also known as "The Middle Way") in *The Classic of Rites* defines a gentleman as a relativist, acting according to his situation, not reaching beyond his station in life, but doing what is proper for a person in that station. If he is at the top of society, he should behave in a lofty manner. If he is at the bottom of society, he in should behave in a lowly manner. When among barbarians one must do what is proper for barbarians. One always should be fitting in, neither contemptuous of inferiors, nor courting favour with superiors. One should complain neither to God nor one's fellow man. One is not born a gentleman. One is not a gentleman because of one's riches or social status. One becomes a gentleman through study and self-cultivation.[29]

Empathy (or benevolence) characterizes the gentleman. In the book "Li Ren" or "Neighborhood of Empathy", in *The Analects,* Confucius is quoted as saying

> It is virtuous manners which constitute the excellence of a neighborhood. If a man, in selecting a residence, does not fix on one where such prevails, how can he be wise?[30]

---

is highly accessible in translation and through the annotated original Chinese at *The China Text Project* (http://ctext.org) maintained by Donald Sturgeon. In subsequent quotes, I use Legg's translation as reported in the *China* Text *Project.*

[29] *Ibid.,* https://ctext.org/liji/zhong-yong (礼记 — 中庸). The "gentleman" (君子) can be translated as "the superior man" and is contrasted with"the common man" (庶人) and "the mean man" or "the little man"(小人). The male gender is accurate because ancient Chinese society was, outside of the family, male dominated.

[30] *Ibid.,* https://ctext.org/analects/li-ren (论语 — 里仁). Empathy (仁) can be also translated as "benevolence" or "perfect virtue".

"Li Ren" further says that a gentleman does not sacrifice morality for success, but is relentlessly empathetic. Although one should abhor poverty and low social standing, if one cannot avoid them while behaving properly, one should behave properly and accept poverty and low social standing.

Confucianism links the Mandate of Heaven to empathy. In the book of "Li Lou I", Mencius (385–303 BC), Confucius' most famous disciple, born almost a century after the Sage died, is quoted as saying

> It was by benevolence that the three dynasties [the Xia, The Shang and the Zhou] gained the throne, and by not being benevolent that they lost it. It is by the same means that the decaying and flourishing, the preservation and perishing, of States are determined. If the sovereign be not benevolent, he cannot preserve the throne from passing from him. If the Head of a State be not benevolent, he cannot preserve his rule. If a high noble or great officer be not benevolent, he cannot preserve his ancestral temple. If a scholar or common man be not benevolent, he cannot preserve his four limbs. Now they hate death and ruin, and yet delight in being not benevolent — this is like hating to be drunk, and yet being strong to drink wine![31]

Confucius was a teacher and scholar-bureaucrat in a militarized body politic. Loyalty was important. "Li Lou I" says that the official should respect the powerful and be loyal to the king. Yet Confucian loyalty is conditional. If the sovereign "… outrages the benevolence proper to his nature" then ***the official must rebel***.[32]

One becomes empathetic through self-control (mindfulness) and propriety. Propriety is adhering to the proper customs, conventions, practices, ceremonies, and rituals of society: the rites.[33] Propriety extends from simple inter-personal, polite interaction to approaching the Higher Powers through religious ceremonies. Propriety is practiced naturally by the gentleman. He is not stilted in performing the rites.[34] He performs ceremonies simply and with sincerity. Confucius says that if a society respects its

---

[31] *Ibid.*, https://ctext.org/mengzi/li-lou-i (孟子 — 離婁上) "Propriety" (礼) can also be translated as "rites" and should be thought of as a set of practices encompassing everything from proper conventions of society to "holy ritual".

[32] *Ibid.*, https://ctext.org/mengzi/liang-hui-wang-ii (孟子 — **梁惠王下**).

[33] *Ibid.*, https://ctext.org/analects/yan-yuan (论语 — 顏淵).

[34] *Ibid.*, https://ctext.org/analects/xue-er (论语 — 学而).

ceremonies, it is more cohesive than if society is held together by rigid laws and punishments.[35] The rites and ceremonies sincerely performed are the proper restraint of scholarship.[36]

Finally, social relationships permeate Confucianism. On one hand, one should practice reciprocity, through the Chinese Golden Rule: "What you do not want done to yourself, do not do to others".[37] On the other, one should be mindful of and deferential to superiors. In feudal society and in bureaucratic government, superior-subordinate relationships dominate. And, returning to "The Great Learning", Confucianism says that the most basic relationship is familial: between parent and child. The child has a lifelong requirement to practice filial piety towards his parents,

> … that parents, when alive, be served according to propriety; that, when dead, they should be buried according to propriety; and that they should be sacrificed to[38] according to propriety.[39]

Was Confucianism a religion? Yes: it answered the fundamental questions: where did we come from? Where we are today? Where are we going? And what should we do with our lives?[40] In terms of religious

---

[35] *Ibid.*, https://ctext.org/analects/ba-yi (论语 — 八佾).

[36] *Ibid.*, https://ctext.org/analects/yong-ye; https://ctext.org/analects/xue-er (论语 — 学而); https://ctext.org/analects/ba-yi (论语 — 雍也). The admonition to broaden learning and respect propriety (博文约礼) is seen by many to be the heart of the Chinese tradition of scholarship. It is also the motto of my university, The Chinese University of Hong Kong.

[37] *Ibid.*, https://ctext.org/analects/wei-ling-gong (论语 — 卫灵公). Reciprocity (恕) or perhaps more accurately, forgiveness, can also be translated as showing consideration for others.

[38] The "sacrifice" referred to here is sacrifice of wine, food and animals, not humans. Notwithstanding his Shang ancestry, Confucius apparently was ignorant of the Shang rites of human sacrifice.

[39] https://ctext.org/analects/wei-zheng (论语 — 为政). Filial piety (孝) and loyalty to the king were the relationships emphasized by Confucius. Confucianism emphasized full five relationships: father and son, ruler and minister, husband and wife, older brother and younger brother and between friends. Note that only the last is between equals. The five relationships, however, is stressed in neo-Confucianism, rather than by the Sage himself. See Hsu Dau-lin, "The Myth of the Five Human Relations of Confucius", *Momenta Serica*, 29 1970–1971, pp. 27–37.

[40] Confucianism is a religion by the broad definition. If religion is a specific set of beliefs about the sacred, transcendental, spiritual, eternal aspects of life as opposed to beliefs about the secular, immediate, physical, and temporal one would conclude the Confucianism

ceremonies, Confucius "prescribed" the traditional rites of the Zhou Dynasty. But the fact of adherence to a set of rites was more important to Confucius than the actual rites themselves. Confucianism was not doctrinal about the transcendent, God, heaven, and the beginning and end of the world. Confucianism's vagueness on these matters allowed Confucians to embrace concurrently faiths including Daoism, which is traditionally associated with the philosopher Laozi, a contemporary of Confucius,[41] and Buddhism, which originated at the time of Confucius in India, entered China from Central Asia in the Han Dynasty, and was the state religion of the short lived Sui Dynasty of the 6th century.

Both Daoism and Buddhism strongly influenced the rules of the game of imperial Chinese society and both were formally integrated into the neo-Confucian synthesis of the Song Dynasty in Medieval China. The co-existence of the three teachings of old China — Confucianism, Daoism and Buddhism — may be explained partly by the fact that Confucian scholars were not in service of a deity, but in service of the state. Imperial China adopted a pluralistic attitude to the transcendental where Daoist and (later) Buddhist priests could intercede. Confucian scholars were able, without contradicting the Confucian texts, to defer to Daoist rites and philosophies and Buddhist beliefs in the cosmos and man's role in it.

Innovation in the Han Dynasty and the Imperial Examination System

Ironically, the winner of the contention among the *hundred schools* of the Eastern Zhou that ended abruptly in 221 BC was not Confucianism. It was

---

it is not a religion, as life's fundamental beliefs can be bifurcated. Brent Nongbri, *Before Religion: A History of a Modern Concept*, Yale University Press, New Haven, 2013 rejects the concept of bifurcated religion as a fundamentally flawed, western conception (p. 155).

[41] Daoism (also transliterated into English as "Taoism") was expounded in the Axial Age by Laozi (also Romanized as Lao-tzu). But Daoism's roots are in divination, harking back to the classic divination textbook, the *Book of Changes* (also called the *Yi Jing* (易經) or *Zhou Yi* (周易) see *Book of Changes*, China Text Project https://ctext.org/book-of-changes) (accessed August 10, 2020). This handbook of 64 numerological binary hexagrams can be traced back to oracle bones divination. See A. Schwartz, "Between Numbers and Images: The Many Meanings of Trigram Li 離 in the Early Yijing" *饒宗頤國學院院刊* 5: 47, 2018, 47–85. http://www.global-sci.com/intro/article_detail/jas/17078.html (accessed August 20, 2020).

Legalism, the philosophy favored by the Qin emperor, Shi Huang Di (259–210 BC). As part of his strategy to control China, he unified the rules of the game. He executed and exiled competing scholars and burnt contenders' books to impose a single philosophy on the new empire. Legalism was a tough-minded philosophy, based on strict rule by law, under a centralized state authority. Legalism had been forged in an age that merged statecraft with war craft. Legalism distrusted scholars, like Confucius, who lacked absolute allegiance to the emperor. But Qin Shi Huang Di's dynasty lasted little longer than the first emperor himself. The Han Dynasty (206 BC–220 CE), which followed the Qin Dynasty, chose *Ru,* the teachings of Confucius, his disciple, Mencius and their followers, as the ultimate winner, establishing the rules of the imperial game.[42]

Staffing the vast empire of the Han was a challenge. Starting from the Warring States Period, China met the challenge by developing a professional, elite, meritocratic, scholar-bureaucracy, serving the emperor. During the Han Dynasty social classes were ranked as follows: the scholar was at the top, followed by the farmer, the tradesman and finally the merchant. By that ranking, maintained for most of the next 2,100 years, the greatest rewards of prestige, power, and wealth went to the scholar bureaucrats — the mandarins. Their understanding of the Confucian classics was honed to perfection by that quintessential Chinese innovation, that harbinger of modern society: the examination.

[42]The received wisdom of Confucian historiography is that an amoral, anti-humanist, virulently anti-Confucian, Legalist philosophy was embraced by a quasi-fascist Qin. Yet the truth is more nuanced. See Lanny Fields, "The Ch'in Dynasty: Legalism and Confucianism", *Journal of Asian History* 23:1, 1–25 who argues that Legalism was not diametrically opposed to Confucianism and that the persecution, censorship and book burning was largely to achieve political, not philosophical ends. Fields shows that Confucianism (and Daoism and others in the hundred schools) not only survived through the Qin but in the Qin. Other scholars see the Confucian philosophy of scholar bureaucracy of the Han and subsequent dynasties to be a *synthesis* of original Confucianism and Legalism. See Dingxin Zhao, *The Confucian-Legalist State: A New Theory of Chinese History*, Oxford University Press, New York, 2015. Zhao notes that the exaggeration of the Confucian Legalism divide continued into the Cultural Revolution of modern China. For an institutional management perspective on the ultimate long-term Chinese synthesis, see Fan Zheng, Tong Xiner, Fan Peihua, Fan Qingli, "A Glacier Model of Chinese Management: Perspectives from New Institutionalism", *Chinese Management Studies* 13:4 (2019), 742–759.

The imperial examination system was a device to select one among ten thousand. Whereas two or three millions might aspire and take the examinations to be mandarins, only the two or three hundred who passed biannual examinations would enter the privileged ranks. To pass, the scholar had not only to master the classics, but to be able to recall and reorganize passages from them in terse, elegant, original, examination essays. Starting in the second century BC, a thousand years before the exam system was copied in Vietnam and Korea and two thousand years before civil service exams were implemented in Western Europe, the Han Imperial exams were extremely competitive. In theory anyone could take the exams, so society offered upward mobility to the ruling class. But in practice only those who could afford an education could succeed.

The effect of the exams on innovation was paradoxical. On one hand, the exams formalized China's humanistic Confucianism, with statecraft deferring to interpersonal relationships founded on the family. The bureaucracy was charged with harmoniously administering, with moral rectitude, a stable agrarian society. The system generated conformity, loyalty, and a cultural hollowing out, reducing creativity and retarding innovation and social progress.[43] On the other hand, although Confucius had claimed to look back to uphold the ideals of the early Zhou and Shang Dynasties, his stress on social wellbeing predisposed the scholar bureaucracy to valuing merchants and artisans whose advances in technology could benefit society.[44]

Yet the examinations also fostered predatory behavior that marred imperial Chinese social development. Most scholar-bureaucrats came from the literati, a landed class who preserved their wealth and power by success in the bureaucracy, which their best and brightest entered by examination. A newly minted scholar bureaucrat, however, assigned to administer a geographic area for a typically low salary but with substantial power and facing pressure from family, would and did "…purloin from society what the state failed to provide.…"[45] The stability of China's

[43] Kwan Hyun Ko, "A Brief History of Imperial Examination and Its Influences", *Society*, New York, 54:3, 2017.

[44] See Wellington K.K. Chan, "Chinese Entrepreneurship Since Its Late Imperial Period", Chapter 16 in Landes, Mokyr and Baumol [eds], *The Invention of Enterprise*, Princeton University Press, New Jersey, 2010, pp. 469–500.

[45] Etienne Balazs, *Chinese Civilization and Bureaucracy: Variations on a Theme*, Yale University Press, New Haven, 1964, p. 10.

ruling literati is testament to the success of the system[46]; however, the dominance of the landed literati supporting and supported by scholar bureaucracy no doubt suppressed private business and led entrepreneurs into unproductive rent seeking behavior, as opposed to innovative value creation.[47]

With all its faults, however, the imperial Chinese system ushered in by the Han Dynasty was among the most effective on earth *at that time* in terms of innovation. During the Han, the number of world-beating innovations of China rose, as Table 1.2 shows.

The comparative success of the Han Dynasty in the management of innovation was more of an indictment of the competition in the West than a triumph of Chinese social engineering. As Baumol comments concerning the Western Roman Empire, which ruled Europe, North Africa and the Middle East at the same time as the Han Dynasty ruled China

> … [In Rome] they had no reservations about the desirability of wealth or about its pursuit as long as it did not involve participation in industry or commerce. Persons of honorable status had three primary acceptable sources of income: landholding, …"usury" and what may be described as "political payments".

Relatively speaking, the scholar bureaucracy of Ancient China was conducive to innovation.

Medieval China: Innovation Brilliance of the Sui, Ming, Song, and Yuan Dynasties

The contemporaneous decline and fall of two ancient empires, the Western Roman Empire and the Chinese Eastern Han Empire, can be attributed

---

[46]Benjamin A. Elmen, *Civil Examinations and Meritocracy in Late Imperial China*, Harvard University Press, Cambridge, 2013.

[47]William Baumol, "Entrepreneurship: Productive, Unproductive and Destructive", *Journal of Political Economy*, 98(5), 893–921, 1990 gives imperial China as an example, alongside ancient Rome and early middle ages Europe, as societies whose rules of the game channeled entrepreneurs into unproductive and destructive endeavors particularly theft and rent seeking from monopolies.

Table 1.2: Innovations of the Han Dynasty

Innovation	Approximate Year of Innovation
Abacus	190
Air-conditioning fan	180
Algorithm for square and cube roots	50
Astronomical clock drive	120
Axial rudder	50
Ball bearings	150
Balloon principle	–150
Bean curd	100
Callipers	9
Cardan suspension (gyroscope)	–140
Coal as a fuel	50
Deep drilling and use of natural gas as a fuel	–150
Diabetes association with sweet and fatty foods	–50
Dragon kiln	150
Draw loom	50
Drum carriage (surveyers wheel or odometer)	–110
Dyked fields	–50
Edge runner mills	–150
Ephedrine (methamphetamine precursor)	150
Fermented soybean paste	–150
Fertilizers	–150
Gear wheels	50
Grid technique in cartography	130
Hygrometer to measure RH	–129
Interconvision of rotary and longitudinal motion	31
Lodestone compass	83
Magic squares (recreational math)	190
Malt sugar	–50

Table 1.2: (*Continued*)

Innovation	Approximate Year of Innovation
Mat and batten sails	50
Mouldboard in ploughshare to turn sod	–150
Negative numbers' mathematical operations	50
Noodles	100
Pearl fishing conservancy	150
Polar equitorial coordinates	–50
Pre-treatment of seeds (to prevent rot)	–50
Propellor oar, self-feathering	100
Reverberatory or downdraft furnace	–50
Seawalls	80
Seed drill (multiple tube)	155
Seismograph	132
South-pointing carriage (geer wheel based)	120
Square pallet chain pump	186
Tea as a drink	–150
Teadle operated spinning wheel	50
Thyroid treatment	–50
Toxic smoke-screens for seige warfare	178
Trip hammer (cam)	–150
Trip hammer (cam) powered by water	20
Water wheel, horizontal	31
Waterwheel mountings horizontal and vertical	50
Weather vane	–120
Well windlass (crank and shaft)	–120
Wheelbarrow (central mount)	–30
Winnowing fan machine	–50
Wrapping paper	–150
Zeotrope mixtures (substances with different boiling points)	180

partly to pressures of invasion from central Asian nomadic peoples. The collapses of these empires brought about, if not Dark Ages, at least, in the words of George Modelski:

> … localized "dark spots"…. Innovations produce concentrations of metropolitan power…. Forming in opposition to them are the hinterlands … that from time to time organize themselves to effect a system levelling.[48]

The levellers in both cases were nomadic peoples invading developed empires. For Rome, the invaders were Germanic tribes and Huns of the West Asia's steppes. For Han China, the invader was the Xiongnu of Central Asia.[49]

China fragmented into numerous warring countries: the northern kingdoms were overwhelmingly non-Han central Asian and nomadic[50] while the southern kingdoms were combinations of local southern Han, refugee Han fleeing the invasions of the north and non-Han indigenous peoples. China's "Dark Period" was shorter than Western Europe's Dark Ages.[51] After four centuries China was re-united[52] by the short-lived Sui Dynasty (581–605). The Sui revived the examination system and the Confucian scholar bureaucracy, fusing Han culture with foreign elements. As Charles W. Holcombe comments regarding the Tang Dynasty (618–907):

> Tang culture was actually notable for its originality. Much as Medieval Europe sprang from a mixture of Roman legacies with Christian and

---

[48] George Modelski, "Ages of Reorganization", *Nature and Culture* 1:2 Autumn 2006, 213.

[49] Ongoing scholarship suggests that the Huns and Xiongnu were the same people. See Jingyi Gao, "Huns and Xiongnu Identified by Hungarian and Yeniseian Shared Etymologies", *Central Asiatic Journal* 56, 41–48.

[50] Charles W. Holcombe, "Southern Integration: the Sui-Tang (581–907)", *The Historian* 66:4 (2004) 749–771.

[51] The misconception that the "dark period" in the West was long neglects the shifting of the Roman Empire capital to Constantinople in the fourth century and the rise and flowering of the Islamic Umayyad and Abbasid Caliphates of the 7th to 13th centuries which flourished alongside Eastern Roman (Byzantine) Empire.

[52] I neglect the separation of Han into Eastern and Western Han with the short-lived Xin Dynasty and omit entirely the Three Kingdoms, Jin, 16 Kingdoms and Northern and Southern Dynasties, not because of their lack of importance to Chinese history but to keep the focus on the rules of the old game and innovation in imperial China.

> German overlays, Sui-Tang China was a similarly novel combination of ancient tradition, Indian Buddhism and the contributions of semino-madic conquerors.[53]

The originality was fertile ground for innovation. Advances in agricultural technology — particularly multi-crop paddy rice cultivation in south China — greatly increased productivity. The imperial government actively promoted and diffused new technologies and improved inter-provincial transportation fostering the development of a national market economy. Peasants increasingly specialized in production of products for sale, allowing each to become profit-oriented, petty entrepreneurs.[54]

Moveable type for printing was invented in China in the 11th century, four hundred years before Guttenberg re-invented it. But unlike Guttenberg's printing press, movable type in China did not displace woodblock printing. That earlier printing technology, requiring less capital than moveable type for the numerous Chinese characters, was in common use in China in 6th century and continued through the 19th century.

Successive governments in Medieval China appreciated the importance of printing, not only for imperial edicts and laws, but also for promoting official versions of the Confucian Classics. By the Song Dynasty (960–1279), official printing had become an important, regulated, function of government centered on the Directorate of Education. Roughly half of all imprints in Song China were printed by state-owned enterprises (SOEs) of the central government and roughly half of the imprints of commercial printers were classics and histories, largely catering to the examination culture. Private printing, while undertaken to promote religious texts and literary pursuits, was less important. This might be ascribed partly to the dominance of Confucian ideology and the entry-by-examination-system that dominated the scholar bureaucracy. And little economic incentive lay in printing: copyright did not become a part of Chinese law until the last year of the Qing empire, in 1910.[55]

---

[53] Charles W. Holcombe, "Southern Integration: the Sui-Tang (581–907)", *The Historian* 66:4 (2004), 760.

[54] Greg Clydesdale, "Economic Declines and the Failure of Chinese Entrepreneurs", *The Quarterly Journal of Austrian Economics* 10:2 (2007), 160–179.

[55] Seung-Hwan Mun, "Printing Press Without Copyright: A Historical Analysis of Printing and Publishing in Song, China", *Chinese Journal of Communication* 6:1 (2013).

Innovations in other technologies benefitted from printing. During the Song, the theoretical basis and the therapeutic practices of Chinese traditional medicine were standardized. Reprints of classic medical texts, some with the support of central government departments like the Imperial Pharmacy, became cheaply available helping the spread of knowledge of drugs, anatomy, acupuncture, and moxibustion.[56]

Medieval China was never far from war. Central Asian steppe people harried the northern borders. The Sui Dynasty fought to achieve Chinese unification. The Tang Dynasty fought to expand into the south and Central Asia. The country disintegrated for most of the 10th century into the strife of the Five Dynasties and 10 Kingdoms. The Liao (916–1125), Jin (1115–1254), and Xia (1215–1233) Dynasties militarily challenged the Song Dynasty. And the largest military event in Medieval China was the invasion of the Mongols under Kublai Khan to create the Yuan Dynasty (1271–1368).

As one would expect from successful empires at war, a large part of medieval China's innovations — over 15% in Table 1.3 — were military. These innovations evolved around the discovery and state development of gunpowder. Initially springing from medical research to purify chemicals, gunpowder in munitions evolved through time from being an incendiary compound to being an explosive. The imperial government of Song Dynasty recognized the need for centralized research, development, and manufacture of gunpowder-based munitions to increase effectiveness on the battlefield. The Song maintained an SOE at its capital in Kaifang, Henan, with thousands of artisans and laborers capable of manufacturing hundreds of thousands of fire-arrows. By the beginning of the 13th century, the freelance (an early gun) and the iron bomb (an exploding shell launched by a catapult) had been effectively deployed in battle.[57] The technology was "stolen" by the Mongols and successfully used in siege warfare against its developers.

The Mongols united China with central Asia, Eastern Europe, and Iran forming the largest contiguous empire that has existed, before or since, in the world. For China, the century-long Mongol Yuan

[56]Asaf Goldschmidt, "The Song Discontinuity: Rapid Innovation in Northern Song Dynasty Medicine", *Asian Medicine* 1:1 (2005) 53–90.

[57]Tonio Andrade, "Chapter 2: Early Gunpowder Warfare", *The Gunpowder Age: China, Military Innovation and the Rise of the West in World History*, Princeton University Press, Princeton, 2016.

Table 1.3: Medieval Chinese Innovation

Innovation	Approximate Year of Innovation
Anatomy	1100
Artificial vaccination inoculation for smallpox	950
Astronomical clock	725
Beri-beri recognition	1330
Binomial expansion (Pascal's triangle)	1100
Bomb thrown from a trebuchet	1161
Camera obscura	1086
Cast iron bomb	1221
Chain drive	976
Color moveable type printing	1150
Compass	1027
Dating of trees by rings	1150
Dominoes	1120
Earthenware moveable type printing	1050
Economical oil-saving oil lamps	850
Erosion — knowledge of and sedimentary deposition	1070
Firelance (gunpowder propeller spear)	950
Fireworks	1150
Flame thrower (double acting force pump)	919
Government monopoly of gunpowder	1350
Grafting	806
Gravimetry	712
Gunpowder formula described	850
Hand-gun	1128
Leeboards and centerboards in sailboats	751
Light penetration mirrors	1050
Magnetic declination noted	1040
Magnetism used in medicine	970
Metal amalgams to fill tooth cavities	659
multiple spindle silk twisting frame	1313

(*Continued*)

Table 1.3: (*Continued*)

Innovation	Approximate Year of Innovation
Multiple spindle spinning wheel	1050
Numerical equations of higher orders solutions	1250
Observation of comet tails	635
Paper money	850
Parachute principle	750
Pasteurization of wine	1117
Pearl cultivation in oysters	1086
Placenta used to source oestrogen	725
Planisphere star maps or describing stars visible at specific latitudes	940
Playing cards	969
Printed book	868
Printing, woodblock	650
Rain and snow gauges (tianchi)	1247
Relief maps	1086
Rocket arrow	1250
Rocket arrow launchers	1367
Roller-harrow (churning farm implement)	880
Rotary knife for cutting jade	1150
Seedling horse (for pulling rice seedlings for transplanting)	1050
Silk reeling machine	1090
Silk spooling frame	1313
Silk twisting frame (multiple spindle water powered)	1313
Silk twisting frame (multiple spindle)	950
Silk warp doubling and throwing machine	950
Sluices with riffles for ore separation	1050
Standard parts for interconversion of rotary and longitudinal motion	1313
Sterilization by steaming	980
Still for distilling alcohol	650
Tian yuan algebraic notation	1248
Tilt hammer water-powered spoons	1145

Table 1.3: (*Continued*)

Innovation	Approximate Year of Innovation
Toothbrush	850
Two-stage rocket	1360
Underwater salvage	1064
Urinary steroids	1025
Water powered spindle frames	1313
Wet copper precipitation of copper from iron	1050
Winged rocket arrow	1350

Note: Medieval China refers to the Sui Dynasty (581–618), Tang Dynasty (618–907), Five Dynasties (907–979), the Sung Dynasty (960–1279), and the Yuan Dynasty (1271–1368).
Source: The author from indices of Joseph Needham, *Science and Civilization in China*, Cambridge at the University Press, 1954–2004. Indices.

Dynasty — considered by traditional Chinese scholarship to be a dynasty of invaders — was a time of great cultural importing from the Middle East and Tibet. Cartography, clothing, food, language, medicine, metallurgy, munitions, music, philosophy, printing, religion, and textile production were all affected.

The Yuan Dynasty was highly cosmopolitan. The young Venetian merchant, explorer, and travel adventure writer, Marco Polo, at the end of the 13th century served for over 17 years in the court of Kublai Khan. Polo's book, *The Description of the World,* written in a Genoese jail on his return home, was a European best seller. Of course, "best seller" is an anachronism: Polo's book was a manuscript, first written by hand and then, by the hands of countless successive scribes, edited, embellished, translated, and subject to errors, one copy at a time. It was 300 years after its writing that it become a printed book.[58]

Yet, again, Medieval China's record of innovation was only brilliant in comparison with the record of the rest of the world. Innovation was limited. It faced a scarcity of innovative entrepreneurs. Science and labor was abundant, but for ambitious, bright, resourceful young people who

[58] Marco Polo [translated by Sharon Kinoshita], *The Description of the World*, Hackett, Indianapolis, 2016.

wished to achieve power, wealth and prestige, the career of choice was ***still*** the imperial bureaucracy, entry to which was obtained by passing state examinations. Such were the rules of the game.[59]

Early Modern China: Relative Decline in the Ming and Qing

Medieval China was the high point, relative to the rest of the world, of imperial Chinese innovations. As Table 1.4 shows, major innovations made first in China and then copied in the rest of the world dwindled to a trickle in the Ming Dynasty (1368–1644) and then stopped altogether at the dawn of the Qing Dynasty (1644–1911).

The decline in innovations occurred at the same time as China was growing more rapidly than Europe both in population and gross domestic product (GDP) See Table 1.5. Parallel growth would continue until the 1820s: over 5 fold in four centuries. At the same time, Western European GDP grew only three fold. Yet because population *and* GDP in China grew at roughly the same rates, GDP per capita in China remained roughly constant. In Western Europe, GDP grew faster than population. By the start of the Ming Dynasty, European GDP per capita exceeded Chinese GDP per capita and the distance between the two widened for the next four and a half centuries.

Table 1.4: Early Modern Ming and Qing Innovations

Innovation	Approximate Date
Sand clocks	1370
Moveable bronze type printing	1403
Esculentist movement for famine foods	1406
High temperature firing of clay	1500
Piece moulding for bronze casting	1500
Wall paper	1550
Sailing carriage	1550
Hot streak test for metallurgy	1596
Ginning machine for cotton	1650

Source: The author from indices of Joseph Needham, *Science and Civilization in China*, Cambridge at the University Press, 1954–2004. Indices.

[59]Ying Lowrey and William Baumol, "The Entrepreneur in Medieval China", *Proceedings of the American Philosophical Society* 157:1 (2013), 1–21.

Table 1.5: Historical Population and GDP in China and Western Europe

Population (millions)	Year	China	West Europe
	1	59.6	24.7
	1000	59.0	25.4
	1300	100.0	58.4
	1400	72.0	41.5
	1500	103.0	57.3
	1820	381.0	133.0
	1913	437.1	261.0
	1950	546.8	304.9
	2001	1,275.4	392.1
Per capita GDP (1990 int. $)			
	1	450	450
	1000	450	400
	1300	600	593
	1400	600	676
	1500	600	771
	1820	600	1,204
	1913	552	3,458
	1950	439	4,579
	2001	3,583	19,256
GDP (billion 1990 int $)			
	1	26.8	11.1
	1000	26.6	10.2
	1300	60.0	34.6
	1400	43.2	28.1
	1500	61.8	44.2
	1820	228.6	160.1
	1913	241.3	902.3
	1950	239.9	1,396.2
	2001	4,569.8	7,550.3

Source: Maddison, *The World Economy*, 2006, p. 249.

This GDP disparity was partly innovation driven. Why did imperial Chinese innovation decline in the early modern world?

Joseph Needham, a mid-20th century, talented British biologist, with a great love of history, an amazing gift for languages, and unparalleled research determination, devoted his life to describing and answering that question. Needham, in the 1930s, while writing a history of embryology from the ancient Egyptians to modern times, learned classical Chinese from graduate students at Cambridge. Shortly after World War II broke out, he was posted by the UK government to Chongqing, the wartime capital of the Republic of China, where he was scientific counselor to the British Embassy. He returned to post-war UK, burdened with crates of classical Chinese texts detailing scientific works spanning centuries and, more importantly, burdened with a puzzle:

> Why did modern science, the mathematization of hypotheses about Nature, with all its implications for advanced technology, take its meteoric rise only in the West at the time of Galileo [but] had not developed in Chinese civilisation or Indian civilisation?

This is "The Needham Puzzle".

In 1954, the first volume in Needham's epic series *Science and Civilization in China*, cataloguing imperial Chinese innovation, was published. The research, which continued even after Needham's death in 1995, now spans 25 large volumes numbering over 10,000 pages.[60] The more recently completed *Volume 5 Part 12: Chemistry and Chemical Technology: Ceramic Technology*[61] — details china. Fine ceramic chinaware, for centuries of global maritime trade, has been synonymous with the country China. The craft achieved its height in SOEs at Jingdezheng, Jiangxi, during the Ming and Qing Dynasties. Not only is China the land of china. It was known by the ancient Greeks and Romans as "the land of silk or *Serika.*[62] The West has, *through most of recorded history*, associated technological innovations with China.

The Renaissance in Western Europe, a period of rebirth of humanism and science, paralleled the Ming Dynasty in China. During the Renaissance,

[60]Needham Research Institute website: http://www.nri.cam.ac.uk (accessed July 17, 2020).

[61]Rose Kerr and Nigel Wood, with additional contributions by Ts'ai Mei-fen and Zhang Fukang, *Science and Civilization in China,* Cambridge at the University Press, 2004.

[62]For a discussion of the "silk road", a term that has entered modern Chinese from the neologism of 19th century German geographer Baron Ferdinand von Richthofen looking back to the maps of the classical Greek geographer Ptolemy and projecting it on 19th century Western imperial railway dreams in the central Asian great game, see Tamara Chin, "The Invention of the Silk Road, 1877", *Critical Inquiry*, Chicago University Press, 40:1, (Autumn 2013), 194–219. https://www.jstor.org/stable/10.1086/673232 (accessed June 16, 2020).

Europe first equalled and then exceeded China in innovation. The Renaissance gave the West what Needham called "… the mathematization of hypotheses about Nature …", *the scientific method.* As the father of the scientific method, the British statesman and philosopher, Francis Bacon,[63] in the early 17th century noted

> … it is well to observe the force and virtue and consequences of discoveries; and these are to be seen nowhere more conspicuously than in those three which were unknown to the ancients, and of which the origin, though recent, is obscure and inglorious; namely, ***printing, gunpowder, and the magnet.*** For these three have changed the whole face and state of things throughout the world; the first in literature, the second in warfare, the third in navigation; whence have followed innumerable changes; insomuch that no empire, no sect, no star seems to have exerted greater power and influence in human affairs than these mechanical discoveries.[64]

For Bacon, the origins of printing, gunpowder, and the magnet were "obscure and inglorious". By the 18th century, however, all of educated Europe knew that those inventions and more were Chinese. Together with paper, "The Four Great Inventions of Ancient China" were widely credited with helping European advancement the most.[65] The 18th century was the European age of Enlightenment, when *Chinoiserie* — infatuation with all that was Chinese — was in European vogue. Not only was architecture, art, fashion, food and beverage from China being embraced. Chinese thought was entering the West. Confucianism was seen by the *philosophes* of 18th-century Europe as an ideal, Deist, lay, moral, humanist form of

---

[63] The title refers to Bacon's book *Novum Organum Scientiarum.* See *The Philosophical Works of Bacon*, Routledge, 2013.

[64] Francis Bacon in John M. Robertson [editor] "Aphorisms Concerning the Interpretation of Nature and the Kingdom of Man Book I", CXXIX *The Philosophical Works of Bacon*, Routledge, 2013.

[65] *Beijing Review* points out that the top four inventions of ancient China were a moniker applied by Europeans during the Age of Discovery (15th to 17th century) to the four Chinese inventions that helped those Europeans leading the Age of Discovery the most. See "Do We Need to Redefine the Top Four Inventions?", *Beijing Review* No.35 August 28, 2008. http://www.bjreview.com.cn/special/txt/2008-08/26/content_146777.htm) (accessed June 16, 2020).

government administered by the benevolent despotism of the emperor and his highly educated civil service.[66]

Ironically, as Europe was falling in love with China, China was turning away from the rest of the world. The Qing Dynasty was founded by a non-Han people, traditionally nomadic Manchurians from the recently sinocised, north-eastern areas bordering on Korea and Siberia. The Qing doubled the area of China, bringing Manchuria, Xinjiang, Tibet, Mongolia, and Taiwan under the direct rule of Beijing. In so doing, they "solved" the age-old Chinese military problem of fighting off the steppe people. But that expansion naturally focused most of their attention on central Asia, not on the distant regions across the seas, who were experiencing the Renaissance and the Enlightenment.

China was increasingly for the Chinese only. Laws restricted the activities and residence of non-Chinese. The court of the Ming Dynasty had been relatively cosmopolitan. The Italian Jesuit priest, Matteo Ricci (1552–1610), respected by the Ming Emperor for his knowledge of mathematics, geography, and astronomy, was employed as a scholar at the Ming court for eight years. But the Jesuits and other Roman Catholic missionaries in the early Qing Dynasty, had a mission: they planned nothing less than the total conversion of China into a Christian kingdom. And they were making inroads into China. The Kang Xi emperor (who reigned from 1661 to 1722, the longest in Chinese imperial history) initially welcomed the missionaries for their technology and benevolence, officially recognizing Roman Catholicism as a state-approved religion. But the honeymoon did not last. Rivalry between the Jesuit and Dominican priests led to a Christian doctrinal fight over the nature of Confucianism. Was Confucianism a religion in conflict with Christianity? The Rites Controversy, lasting 60 years, was resolved by Pope Clement XI's decision in 1704 that the rites of veneration of ancestors in general and of Confucius in particular constituted idolatry.[67] Initially the Rites Controversy was a doctrinal dispute taking place in Europe with little effect on China. But in 1715 the Pope decreed that Chinese Catholics essentially had to decide whether they were Catholics or

---

[66] Donald Lach, "China and the Era of the Enlightenment", *The Journal of Modern History* 14:2 (1942), 209–223.

[67] Paul Rule, "The Chinese Rites Controversy: Confucian and Christian Views on the Afterlife", *Studies in Church History* 45 (2009), 280–300.

Chinese. In reaction, Kang Xi's successor expelled all Christian missionaries in 1724.[68] They would not return again for over a century.

The Dynasty Crumbles

The 19th century saw imperial China crumble. Three crises coincided: dynastic decay, military defeat, and domestic Chinese loss of faith in the rules of the old game.

Since the Zhou, each dynasty based its legitimacy on the mandate of heaven. Mencius, embellishing the doctrines of Confucius, charged gentlemen, the scholar-bureaucrat literati, to rebel if the sovereign outrages "the benevolence proper to his nature". Chinese historians weaved their stories of the rise and fall of past dynasties using a corollary to the mandate of heaven, the dynastic cycle.[69] Each new dynasty ascends to power with the mandate of heaven, bringing peace and good governance to the people; it rises to a peak of political and economic power and then succumbs to corruption and internal decay. Losing the mandate of heaven, it is displaced by the next dynasty. The stories of the dynastic cycle themselves were parables, quasi-myths, instructing each generation in governance to maintain the mandate of heaven. And a major task of each new dynasty was to write the history of the last.[70]

By the late 18th century, the dynastic cycle of the Qing was entering its decadent phase. Standards of living were declining. Peasant unrest, especially in border areas was increasing. Corruption was rife. China was facing an opium epidemic. And foreigners were worming their way into the empire.

The First British Chinese Opium War of 1839–1842 was about free trade, property, sovereignty, morality, status, and power. By the early 19th century, the sun did not set on the British Empire which, relying on its superior naval and military technology and industrial might, had become the greatest empire in the world. The British championed free trade, yet

---

[68] Lawrence Fouraker, "Historical Legacy of Jesuits in China" *Verbum* 6:1 (2008). https://fisherpub.sjfc.edu/cgi/viewcontent.cgi?article=1145&context=verbum (accessed July 23, 2020).

[69] In Chinese the dynastic cycle is 朝代循环 *chaodai xunhuan.*

[70] The contrast between the traditionalist, liberal, and Marxist historiography is captured by Wang, Q. Edward, *Inventing China Through History: The May Fourth Approach to Historiography*, State University of New York Press, Albany, 2001.

the Qing dynasty restricted trading access to foreigners: they could reside only in the Portuguese colony of Macao and their ships could call only at the wharfs of Shamian in Guangzhou. The Qing refused to deal with foreigners as equals: all countries wishing to have relations with China did so as inferior states, paying tribute. Their emissaries literally had to kowtow to the emperor.[71]

Foreign traders had chronic, massive, balance of trade deficits with China: silk, tea, and ceramics were highly valued by the West but little of the West's output was demanded by China. For three centuries, traders addressed the problem by shipping silver from the New World to China. In the early 19th century, British traders increasingly shipped opium (illegal in China but legal in Britain and British-ruled India) from India to China to profitably solve the balance of trade problem. Local corrupt officials in Guangzhou were happy to take their share of profits from the drug trade. But appointments of an upright mandarin, Lin Zixu,[72] who seized the traders' opium, and an assertive British superintendent of trade in China, Charles Elliot, who took possession of the seized opium on behalf of the British Crown — changed the seizure from a trader's dispute into a national affront, igniting the First Opium War.[73]

The British won the war based on military technology — naval, munitions, and organizational.

China had fallen far since being the largest military power in the world under the early Ming Dynasty. Half a century before Columbus discovered the New World with his three small ships commissioned by the Spanish Crown, Zheng He (1371–1433), an admiral of the Ming Yongle Emperor's court, in seven expeditions, some with over 350 vessels, each vessel many times larger than Columbus' boats, mounted expeditions to the East Indies, India, Arabia, and the east Coast of Africa. But this policy of exploration to align tributaries with the Middle Kingdom proved a too expensive long-term policy for the Ming, which had continental threats to address. The Qing Dynasty, a non-Han,

[71] The word "kowtow" comes from 磕头, pronounced *ketou* (in pinyin romanization) and means a full prostrating bow involving knocking ones head on the ground. In greeting the Qing emperor, it would involve knocking the head nine times on the ground.

[72] Lin Zixu in Chinese is 林则徐.

[73] Harry G. Gelber, *Opium, Soldiers and Evangelicals: Britain's 1840–1842 War with China and Its Aftermath.* Palgrave, 2004.

"foreign" northeast Asian former nomadic power, was not inclined to pursue naval innovation. After decisively defeating the Mongols, it rested on its laurels, ushering in the Great Military Divergence as Chinese military stagnated during the following centuries of the Qing Dynasty peace.[74]

The might of European imperialism flowed from the Industrial Revolution, unleashing a tremendous creation of wealth that started in Western Europe and would eventually flow to every part of the world.[75] In the 19th century, Western European economic growth vastly exceeded China's.[76] Western innovations — especially coal and the steam engine — plus the relaxing of land constraints through the opening of the Americas and the windfall of the colonies introduced successful political and economic models of extraction, coercion, trade, and entrepreneurship.[77]

The First Opium War opened the curtain on gunboat diplomacy. Steam-powered, shallow draft, heavily armed boats could deliver both concentrated shelling and small, well-armed, and disciplined soldiers rapidly to successfully attack large, slow moving, ill-disciplined, and ill-equipped forces. The winning gunboat diplomacy formula — which inflicted unacceptable pain to extract economic and political concessions, but not to occupy large areas[78] — also worked in the Second Opium War of 1856–1860 and the Boxer Rebellion of 1898, fully opening China to the West.

To the Qing Dynasty, however, the foreign threat through most of the 19th century was less existential than domestic threats. In 1837 Hong

---

[74] Tonio Andrade, "Chapter 16: The Opium War and the Great Divergence", *The Gunpowder Age: China, Military Innovation and the Rise of the West in World History*, Princeton University Press, Princeton, 2016.

[75] McCloskey, D., "The Great Enrichment: A Humanistic and Social Scientific Account", *Social Science History*, 40:4, (2016).

[76] For statistics of ancient and early modern GDP, see Angus Maddison, *The World Economy*, OECD, Paris, 2001 and the Maddison Project. https://www.rug.nl/ggdc/historicaldevelopment/maddison/releases/maddison-project-database-2018.

[77] For a discussion of the Great Divergence, see Kenneth Pemerancz, *The Great Divergence: China, Europe and the Making of the Modern World Economy*, Princeton, New Jersey, 2000.

[78] Gelber, *op. cit.*, "Chapter 6: Fighting and Talking", pp. 102–124 describes the devastating effect of the iron paddle-steamer *Nemesis.*

Xiuquan, an ambitious, Guangdong province school teacher who had tried and failed four times to become a mandarin in the imperial exams and had read Christian missionary tracts, had a vision: he ascended to heaven where he met God the Father and Christ the son, who told him that he was the second son, Christ's brother. They charged Hong with a mission: establish the Kingdom of Heavenly Peace[79] on earth. The Kingdom of Heavenly Peace was eventually defeated in 1864 by the Qing, but not before it had become the largest peasant rebellion in modern history, inciting revolution in every province of the country, occupying more than 600 walled cities, establishing itself in most of South China, setting up its capital in Nanjing and, notwithstanding the fact that Hong was at least as Confucian as Christian,[80] introduced for the first time a "Western" religion on a truly national scale in China.[81]

In the face of these challenges, the late Qing Dynasty attempted the reform. The Self Strengthening Movement of the 1860s to 1880s focused on technological and military modernization. The Jiangnan Arsenal, the largest in East Asia at the time, undertook a massive translation of industrial treatises and technical engineering papers. The government saw not only the military as a national concern. Steamships were too important to be left to private sources, so the Qing set up a new SOE: China Merchants' Steam Navigation Company in 1872.[82] Foreign missionary-sponsored technical, scientific, and liberal arts colleges sprouted around the country and the Qing government sent promising graduate students overseas to study. Japan, itself recently forced open by American gunboat diplomacy, looked to China for inspiration, translating Chinese texts, that had recently been translated from Western languages, into Japanese.

But inertia, dynastic decay and foreign intervention in Qing China triumphed over reform. China's loss of the Sino-Japanese war 1894–1895 and the Boxer Rebellion of 1898–1900, ended when the

[79] In Chinese, 太平天国 or *Taiping Tianguo*.

[80] Given Hong Xiuquan's background, it's not surprising his kingdom was not particularly innovative: it attempted to replicate an idealized scholar-bureaucracy state. Much modern Chinese Marxist history concerns the role of peasant rebellions in modern history. See, for example, Liu Kwang-Ching, "World View and Peasant Rebellion/Reflections on Post-Mao Historiography", *The Journal of Asian Studies* 40:2 (1981), 295–326.

[81] Fairbank, Reischauer and Craig, "Chapter 2: Invasion and Rebelling in China", *East Asia: the Modern Transformation*, Houghton Mifflin, Boston, 1965.

[82] China Merchants survives as an SOE to the present day — see Chapter 12.

armies of the Eight Nations Alliance (Austria-Hungary, Britain, France, Germany, Italy, Japan, Russia, and the United States) entered Beijing, showing that the Qing was financially, militarily and intellectually bankrupt. Imperial China was the sick man of Asia and was extinguished 11 years later in the Republican Xinghai Revolution of 1911. The rules of the old game were gone but what would replace them?

When the revolution broke out, the new republic's first president, the Hong Kong- and Japanese-educated medical doctor Sun Zhongshan rushed back from San Francisco where he had been raising money from overseas Chinese. He planned to implement nationalism, democracy, and socialism in China. But he and his party, the *Guomindang*[83] were ultimately unsuccessful. Four decades of war and revolution were to rock China before the country achieved peace and unification under the CPC.

---

[83]The *Guomindang* (国民党) or Nationalist Party is also known by an alternate Romanization *Kuomintang* or KMT.

Chapter 2

Communism, Government, and Innovation

Innovation has always been central to Chinese development. China's greatest, modern, political innovation occurred in 1949 when the CPC won the civil war and came to power. Since then the CPC has proved to be the world's most successful communist party. This chapter summarizes how the CPC came to power and how it stimulates innovation. I describe the control exercised over the Chinese state by the CPC and how the one-party-directed state leads a market-based economy. This "socialism with Chinese characteristics"[1] is the environment for business innovation in China.

Historical Background

In 1911, after the last Qing emperor was deposed in the Xinghai Revolution, China slipped into factional fighting between warlords while

[1]The term was coined in the early 1980s and appeared in the organ of the CPC *The People's Daily* since 1982. See "The Draft Amended Constitution Exemplifies Socialism with Chinese Characteristics" (宪法修改草案是部有中国特色的社会主义宪法), *People's Daily*, November 16, 1982 and Deng Xiaoping, "Building Socialism with a Specifically Chinese Character", 1984 in translation *New Learning*. http://newlearningonline.com/new-learning/chapter-4/deng-xiaoping-socialism-with-chinese-characteristics (accessed June 29, 2019).

the foreign concessions remained in the hands of the European and Japanese imperial powers. A fragmented, weak, Republican China entered the First World War on the side of the Allies but Allied victory brought humiliation to China. The Treaty of Versailles in 1919 awarded the former German concessions in China to the Japanese, who were also among the Allies.

On May 4, 1919, educated, young Chinese reacted with mass demonstrations. They protested against the Treaty of Versailles, but they also opposed old Chinese customs, the classical language which had served the scholar bureaucracy for over 2000 years and the teachings of Confucianism, Taoism, and Buddhism. The demonstrators embraced Mr. De (democracy) and Mr. Sai (science).[2] Those demonstrators looked back on a century of Chinese decay, disorder, invasion, and rebellion. They found most inspiration not in the parliamentary or presidential democracies of the United Kingdom or the United States. They turned to the Russian communist model of clandestine, militarized, socialism.

In October 1919, the *Guomindang* (National Party) was formed in Guangzhou. Two years later the CPC was formed in Shanghai. Both parties were more inspired by the successful Russian Revolution and its Union of Soviet Socialist Republics (USSR) than by liberal democracies of the West. For the next 30 years, both parties would compete, cooperate, and fight to defeat each other, the warlords, the colonialists, and the Japanese invaders, to re-unite their country and to restore Chinese greatness.

The CPC's Philosophy

The first quarter of the CPC's century-long life was dedicated to taking power by revolution. Often outlawed and persecuted, it waged war — against both foreign invaders and domestic opponents. To win a war one needs an army. The CPC founded the People's Liberation Army (PLA) six years after the party's birth and thereafter effectively led it "... to defend the Motherland and to participate in the socialist

[2]Although "democracy" and "science" for over a half a century have recognized translations in Chinese as 民主 (pronounced *minzhu*) and 科学 (*kexue*), in 1919, they were novel, western concepts, and were often referred to by their transliterations 德莫克拉西 (*de-mo-ke-la-xi*) and 赛因斯 (*sai-en-si*).

modernization drive".[3] That integration of party with army continues to the present.

Following its victory of against the *Guomindang* in 1949 the CPC has been the only party of power in China. Although the Constitution the People's Republic of China vests top authority in the National People's Congress (NPC) which elects the State Council, the top of China's executive-led system of government, the Constitution cedes leadership to the CPC. For every part of the government, there is a parallel, leading, CPC organization. The personnel in both government and CPC organizations typically overlap, and at higher levels of government, almost all positions are held by CPC members.

Today, the CPC has 90 million members[4]: just over one adult in 12.[5] The CPC is open to new recruits from all walks of life. It is a self-perpetuating organization. Anyone 18 or over ***can*** apply for membership to a local CPC cell, but CPC leadership at each level decides whether to accept or reject the application.

The CPC is politically conservative, deferring to the *status quo* at home and abroad. In China, it is highly suspicious of any person or organization who may usurp its power. Internationally, it scrupulously seeks to pose no threat to any friendly or neutral foreign regime: it does not espouse violent, peasant, or proletarian revolution of the type by which it gained power in the first half of the 20th century. The CPC ***does not*** export revolution and, since the end of the Cultural Revolution in 1976, does not even claim to have political formulae that should be applied in other countries of the world.

---

[3] *Constitution of the Communist Party of China* 17th National Congress, October 21, 2007, p. 9.

[4] CPC has nearly 89.5m members according to the Xinhua News Service, see Xinhua, "The Communist Party of China (CPC) Had a Total of 89.447 Million Members at the End of 2016", *China Daily*, June 30, 2017. This ranks the Party as the second largest political organization in the world. Since 2015, it has had fewer members than the much younger Bharatiya Janata Party of India. Manu Balachandran and Saptarishi Dutta, "Here's How the BJP Surpassed China's Communists to Become the Largest Political Party in the World", *Quartz India*, March 31, 2015. https://qz.com/india/372466/heres-how-the-bjp-surpassed-chinas-communists-to-become-the-largest-political-party-in-the-world/ (accessed February 21, 2019).

[5] Given that the population of China is about 1.4 billion in 2019 and approximately 79% of the population is 18 or over, the minimum age for CPC membership.

The CPC is staunchly nationalistic. It is ***not*** internationalist. Although the CPC sprang from the communist international movement dating back to Marx's and Engles' Communist Manifesto of 1848 and led by the USSR after 1917, Comintern (the heir to the international communist movement following the Russian Revolution) did not survive the Second World War. The Sino-Soviet alliance did not survive the 1950s and the CPC's international influence over Marxist–Leninist–Maoist parties abroad did not survive its abandonment of Maoism after the end of the Cultural Revolution. Today, the CPC Central Committee maintains a foreign department having active relations with over 200 political parties worldwide, many of them communist parties. But it adheres to the principles of independence, equality, mutual respect, and non-interference.[6]

Managing innovation in China is one major task of the CPC. To understand how its leaders approach the task, one should understand the philosophy of the CPC. The CPC is idealist, humanist, atheist, and futurist. In the words of the CPC's constitution, "the realization of Communism is the highest ideal and ultimate goal of the CPC".[7] The standard, current, Chinese definition of communism is

> ... a political viewpoint and ideology. Today's communism is based on Marx and Engels. Communism advocates the elimination of private ownership of the means of production, and the establishment of a society without class system, without exploitation, without oppression, and realizing a full individual freedom. It is a society in which large scale production is collectivized and which will unite when confronted by evil forces. Communists believe that in future all class based societies will eventually transition to a communist society where each member of society will contribute to society according to his ability receive from society according to his need, and in which the ideology will enter an advanced stage.[8]

---

[6]See International Department of the Party website: http://www.idcpc.org.cn (accessed February 19, 2019).

[7]*Constitution of the Communist Party of China*, Chapter II the Party's Organizational System Article 10.1, 17th National Congress, Preamble, October 21, 2007.

[8]The current Chinese accepted definition of communism is taken from the search engine Baidu. https://baike.baidu.com/item/共产主义 (accessed February 26, 2019). It is taken from Karl Marx, *Critique of the Gotha Programme Part I*, Marxists Internet Archive. https://www.marxists.org/archive/marx/works/1875/gotha/ch01.htm (accessed September 15, 2020).

The CPC's constitution says that China's economy will evolve, like the economies of every country in the world, into communism — eventually. How long will that evolution take?

> "China is in the primary stage of Socialism and will remain so for a long time to come.... It will last for over a hundred years".[9]

Because those words were written in 2007, the arrival of communism currently is expected to be after 2107.

Although the CPC believes, in theory, in the inevitable triumph of global communism, the CPC does not claim to know *how* socialism will evolve eventually into communism. But the CPC believes it is responsible, today and in the future, for discovering and facilitating that evolution. The difference between a correct and an incorrect CPC policy is found in the effectiveness of facilitating the socialist transformation process. So, in the absence of a policy blueprint, policy innovation takes the form of "... crossing the river by feeling stones".[10]

Is communism a religion?

The economist most widely recognized for proposing that (1) innovation is *the* force of economic development and (2) the entrepreneur is *the* driver of innovation, Joseph Schumpeter (1883–1950) has no doubt:

> Marxism is a religion. To the believer it presents, first, a system of ultimate ends that embody the meaning of life and are absolute standards by which to judge events and actions; and, secondly, a guide to those ends which implies a plan of salvation and the indication of the evil from which mankind, or a chosen section of mankind, is to be saved.[11]

---

[9] *Constitution of the Communist Party of China*, Chapter II the Party's Organizational System Article 10.1, 17th National Congress, Preamble, October 21, 2007.

[10] The expression is taken from an old saying, "When crossing a river by feeling the stones, you make sure one foot is steady and then take another step", and was used in central Party statements on agricultural and industrial policy in the late 1950s and mid 1960s, and to describe Deng Xiaoping's strategy for reform and opening up in the late 1970s and 1980s where reform was necessary but how that reform was to be achieved was not clear. But Deng Xiaoping did not actually use the expression. See "The History of Crossing the River by Feeling the Stones", *Deng Xiaoping's Memorial Web* from *Guang An Ri Bao*, April 12, 2018. http://cpc.people.com.cn/n1/2018/0412/c69113-29921565.html (accessed February 25, 2019).

[11] Joseph Schumpeter, *Capitalism, Socialism and Democracy* (originally published 1943), Routledge, New York, 1992, p. 5.

Communism is a religion in the same way that Confucianism is a religion. It is made up of the texts, traditions, beliefs, behaviors, ethics, eschatology, social structures, etc. that tell believers where they came from, where they are today, where they are going, and what they should do with their lives.

However, if religion is a specific set of beliefs about the sacred, transcendental, spiritual, eternal aspects of life as opposed to beliefs about the secular, immediate, physical, and temporal, one would have to conclude — as indeed the CPC concludes — that communism is not a religion. It is, after all, Marxist. And Marxism is at its heart, dialectical materialism. It is stridently opposed to organized religion as Marx oft-quoted words emphasize:

> Religious suffering is, at one and the same time, the expression of real suffering and a protest against real suffering. Religion is the sigh of the oppressed creature, the heart of a heartless world, and the soul of soulless conditions. It is the opium of the people. The abolition of religion as the illusory happiness of the people is the demand for their real happiness.[12]

Notwithstanding the CPC's Marxist roots, it's not actively atheist. The CPC constitution requires members to fully implement China's policy on religion, encouraging religious believers to contribute to China's development.[13] This policy reflects the protection, in China's constitution, of freedom of religious belief. Religions organizations must be registered. No organizations may question the authority of the CPC or the government. Moreover, the constitutional requirement that "religious groups and religious affairs shall not be subject to control by foreign forces"[14] is strictly observed. Suspicion of foreign interference runs deep. As the sole, legitimate political power in the country, the CPC currently warmly embraces Confucianism and mainstream Buddhism, but calibrates various

---

[12] Karl Marx, "A Contribution to the Critique of Hegel's Philosophy of Right: Introduction", *Works of Karl Marx* 1843 in Marxists Internet Archive: https://www.marxists.org (accessed July 30, 2020).

[13] *Constitution of the Communist Party of China 17th National Congress of the Communist Party of China*, October 21, 2007, p. 9.

[14] *Constitution of the People's Republic of China*, Article 36 clause 4. See Chapters 7 and 8 for religious beliefs of three famous Chinese entrepreneurs.

levels of toleration and suppression of different denominations of Christianity and Islam, religious with strong foreign ties.

The CPC's Organization

The CPC is organized on the principle of democratic centralism, outlined by Vladimir Ilyich Ulyanov, better known as Lenin, the Russian communist leader and revolutionary founder of the USSR.[15] Lenin's words clearly distinguish between broad, bourgeois democracy and socialist (i.e., communist party) democratic centralism:

> no revolutionary organization has ever practiced, or could practice, broad democracy, however much it may have desired to do so.[16]

The CPC continues to subscribe to Lenin's maxim. Democratic centralism requires that members of the CPC debate policy and vote on policy implementation, but once a decision is made, all members are required to implement the decision, with no dissention.

The CPC is structurally democratic but effectively autocratic. Authority is vested in CPC congresses, held every five years. Delegates to the CPC congresses are elected by secret ballot of all CPC members.

CPC authority is centralized. At the top of the national hierarchy, daily decisions are made by various standing committees of the Central Committee. The Central Committee itself is elected, by secret ballot, by the CPC congress. The elected General Secretary of the Central Committee is the highest authority in the CPC. And since the CPC dominates the government, the General Secretary is also the highest authority in China. Today, Xi Jinping is the General Secretary.

The CPC is disciplined: no externally visible vying for votes based on different platforms occurs. While factions exist, they are not organized in

---

[15]The principle is outlined in V. Lenin *What Is To Be Done? Burning Questions of our Movement*, 1901 and February 1902, *Lenin's Selected Works*, Foreign Languages Publishing House, 1961, Moscow, Vol. 5. https://www.marxists.org/archive/lenin/works/download/what-itd.pdf (accessed February 21, 2019). The answer to the question "what is to be done" given by Lenin is to set up and support at the heart of the social democratic (i.e., communist) party in Russia a national, clandestine, newspaper, *Iskra*, organized by professional revolutionaries.

[16]*Ibid.*, p. 89.

intra-party elections. Centralized power flows down from the CPC General Secretary. In the words of the CPC constitution:

> Individual CPC members are subordinate to the CPC organization, the minority is subordinate to the majority, the lower CPC organizations are subordinate to the higher CPC organizations, and all the constituent organizations and members of the CPC are subordinate to the National Congress and the Central Committee of the CPC.[17]

Commenting on discipline, Lenin said,

> the only serious organizational principle for the active workers of our movement should the strictest secrecy, the strictest selection of members, and the training of professional revolutionaries … which sternly and ruthlessly punishes every departure from the duties of comradeship".[18]

In the 120 years since Lenin wrote those words, the "duties of comradeship" have been considerably diluted, but the ideal still remains within the CPC.

The CPC is self-organizing throughout society. Its constitution explains how this works:

> Primary CPC organizations are formed in enterprises, rural areas, government organs, schools research institutions, communities, social organizations, companies of the PLA and other basic units where there are at least three full CPC members.[19]

This "rule of three", that every organization with at least three CPC members in it should form a primary CPC organization (i.e., a CPC party cell) means that party cells permeate society. At the grassroots level, each CPC party cell is democratic in that it elects its government committee and reports to the next higher CPC organization. Remembering that there

---

[17] *Constitution of the Communist Party of China*, Chapter II the Party's Organizational System Article 10.1, 17th National Congress, October 21, 2007. Note that the Party did not have a constitution for the first 86 years of its life. The constitution approved in 2007 was its first.

[18] V. Lenin, *What Is To Be Done? op. cit.*, p. 90.

[19] *Constitution of the Communist Party*, Article 29.

Table 2.1: Penetration of the CPC

Type	Number of Administrative Units	Number of CPC Organizations	Rate of CPC Penetration (%)
Townships and towns	32,756	32,753	99.99%
Urban street administrations	7,567	7,565	99.97%
Communities	93,018	92,581	99.53%
Villages	5,77,336	5,77,273	99.99%
State owned enterprises	2,13,000	1,94,000	91.08%
Private enterprises	2,97,300	1,57,900	53.11%
State administrative organs	2,37,000	2,36,000	99.58%
Public institutions	5,46,000	5,06,000	92.67%
Social organizations	4,39,000	1,84,000	41.91%

Source: Lance L. P. Gore, The Communist Party-Dominated Governance Model of China: Legitimacy, Accountability, and Meritocracy Polity, Volume 51, Number 1, January 2019, pp. 161–194.

are 90 million CPC members in a country of 1.4 billion people where about 80% are 18 or older, roughly 8% of Chinese are CPC members. So, in China, roughly speaking, you could expect *any* organization with 40 or more people in it to contain a CPC party cell.

Table 2.1 shows that the rate of penetration of the CPC party cells in organizations in China is overwhelming in government units (including military educational and research organizations) and SOEs and is considerable in private enterprises and NGOs.

The CPC's permeation of society and feedback mechanisms gives it a high degree of responsiveness to social pressure. A CPC party cell in an organization may have formal power if the organization recognizes it (as, e.g., an SOE or government department would), or it may not have formal power (as, e.g., in some private enterprises or non-government social organizations). However, even if a given CPC party cell has no formal power within its organization, it can enjoy authority, simply because the CPC controls the government. Therefore, opinions of the CPC party cell members in the organization count. Moreover, the CPC impels each CPC party cell to seek power in the organization within which it formed:

> The primary CPC committees [i.e., CPC party cells] … provide leadership for work in their localities and assist administrative departments economic institutions and self-government mass organizations.... In a

> state-owned or collective organization, the primary CPC organization acts as the political nucleus and works for the operation of the enterprise.... In a non-public economic institution, the primary CPC organization carries out the CPC's principles and policies, provides guidance to and oversees the enterprise in observing the laws and regulations of the state, exercises leadership over the trade union, the Communist Youth League organization and other mass organizations, rallies the workers and office staff around it, safeguards the legitimate rights and interests of all quarters and stimulates the healthy development of the enterprise.[20]

The CPC differs fundamentally from most political parties elsewhere in the world in that the CPC is the ***only*** legitimate source of political power in the country.[21] It believes that as long as it stays true to its principles and pursues its goals, it will continue to be the only legitimate power holder in China. Its principles can be summarized as

> the guidance of Marxism-Leninism, Mao Zedong Thought, Deng Xiaoping Theory, the important thought of Three Represents, the Scientific Outlook on Development, and the Xi Jinping Thought on Socialism with Chinese Characteristics for a New Era.[22]

These principles are less a unified ideology and more an evolving set of strategies to effect the continued economic and social development of China under CPC leadership as it "... crosses the river by feeling the stones".

---

[20] *Ibid.*, Article 32.

[21] It is not, however, the only political party in China. China has nine officially recognized political parties, although the non-communist parties operate under the direction of the United Front Office of the CPC. See website of the United Front, http://www.zytzb.gov.cn/html/index.html (accessed February 25, 2019).

[22] Amendment to the Constitution of the People's Republic of China (2018) Adopted at the First Session of the 13th National People's Congress on March 11, Website of the National People's Congress http://www.npc.gov.cn/englishnpc/constitution2019/201911/36a2566d029c4b39966bd942f82a4305.shtml (accessed December 13, 2021). The important thought of Three Represents refers to General Secretary Jiang Zemin's thought expressed in 2002 that the CPC succeeded in the past by representing advanced productive forces, advanced culture and the overwhelming majority of the Chinese people and should continue to do so.

The CPC and the Government

Following the founding of the People's Republic of China in 1949, the CPC copied the Russian model and established a Soviet style government with a centrally planned economy in which the CPC set and re-set standards of political purity and economic organization. During the first 30 years, under that model, the CPC was broadly successful: China achieved an average annual real (after subtracting inflation) rate of GDP growth of over 4%. However, economic growth was plagued by volatility and, in the early 1970s, by stagnation.

Since 1978, the CPC has directed China's reforming and opening up, setting and implementing market-oriented policies that have facilitated China's emergence as a global economic, social, political, and military power. In the 40 years from 1978 to 2018, real annual rates of GDP growth have exceeded 7%.[23] In the 70 years since the CPC achieved power, both before and since China's reform and opening up, China's GDP growth rates have been higher than for any other large country in the world. Measured by the CPC's power, and by China's tremendous socio-economic progress and peace under its leadership, the CPC has been highly successful.

The relationship between CPC and government organizations has ebbed and flowed. The 1950s saw the CPC exert very tight, often extremely violent[24] control to consolidate power. That was followed in the early 1960s by increased emphasis on professionalizing government and reducing the role of ideology. The Cultural Revolution of 1966–1976 was a reaction against that professionalization to reassert ideological purity both in the CPC and in the country and to consolidate the power of

---

[23]The growth rates from the early 1950s to 2018 are based on the U.S. Federal Reserve data base FRED. Real growth rates subtract off the inflation rate. Typically, GDP growth uses nominal, not real growth. Inflation varies from year to year and country to country but using US dollars, one could add roughly 3% to the numbers quoted to get nominal GDP growth.

[24]The early 1950s in China saw the centrally mandated, locally implemented open execution of more class enemies of the state than any other classicide or genocide in history, when up to 30 million rich peasants especially under the directives of Kang Sheng. See Byron and Pack, *The Claws of the Dragon: Kang Sheng — The Evil Genius Behind Mao — And His Legacy of Terror in People's China*, Simon & Schuster, New York, 1992. The Great Leap Forward and creation of the People's Communes precipitated the death of 15 million in the three years of natural disasters from 1959 to 1961.

Chairman Mao Zedong. And the triumph of reform and opening up in the late 1970s was an admission of the bankruptcy of the Cultural Revolution's ideology.

The mid to late 1980s marked the highest commitment to separating the functions of the CPC from the state that China has known since 1949. This was the period of the nominal leadership of CPC General Secretary Hu Yaobang.[25] It was nominal because real leadership at the time was held by Deng Xiaoping, the party elder who had engineered the reform and opening up policy. In 1987, Deng concluded that political liberalization had gone too far and replaced Hu as General Secretary with the then Premier Zhao Ziyang. Hu's death in April 1989 triggered student protests culminating in hunger strikes in Beijing's Tiananmen Square. The students called for an end to CPC and government corruption and demanded an increase the pace of reform, separating the CPC further from the government. As students increasingly called for liberal democracy and ending the CPC power monopoly, Deng quashed the protest. On June 4, 1989, the army occupied Tiananmen Square, causing substantial loss of life. The June 4 incident coincided with the replacement of Zhao Ziyang by Jiang Zemin as CPC general secretary and the tightening of the CPC's control over government. That tightening continued through the early 1990s.

In the later years of Jiang's CPC leadership, and under the government policies of Premier Zhu Rongji, China deepened its economic reforms and prepared for entry into the WTO in 2001. Under General Secretary Hu Jintao, who succeeded Jiang and Wen Jiabao who succeeded Zhu, CPC control over government was gradually relaxed. But following Xi Jinping's rise to the role of General Secretary in 2012, CPC control has tightened again. Notwithstanding this ebb and flow, even at times of maximum relaxation of CPC control over the government, the CPC and the government of China have never questioned that the CPC has the exclusive right to rule China.

The people of China generally share the belief in the CPC's right to rule China. This confidence in the system is demonstrated by the strong support Chinese people express for all the major institutions of society: the CPC, national, provincial and local governments, the civil service, universities, the press, labor unions, the army, the police, and the judicial

[25] Zhao, Ziyang, "关于党政分开" (On separating the Party from government), Xinhuanet, October 14, 1987.

Table 2.2: Confidence of Percent of Population in Social Structures

Country or Region	Armed Forces	Government	Universities	Civil Services	Justice Systems	The Police	The Press	Labor Unions	Average
USA	80	33	54	41	57	68	30	33	49
Australia	82	30	72	48	59	80	17	29	52
Taiwan	63	52	72	65	57	82	26	55	59
Germany	53	44	76	62	72	86	36	45	59
Hong Kong	54	55	74	57	79	67	53	41	60
Japan	81	40	56	45	78	79	69	38	61
China	95	95	91	86	86	84	68	67	84

Source: "Results in Percent by Country", World Values Survey Wave 7 (2017–2020) accessed January 29, 2021, pp. 171–206, http://www.worldvaluessurvey.org/WVSDocumentationWV7.jsp.

system. Relative to the support expressed by people in other countries for the institutions of society, Chinese people lead the world.[26]

Table 2.2 shows the percent of the population in seven parts of the world who expressed a great deal or quite a lot of confidence in eight key structures of society.

The CPC's legitimacy and power make it ***the*** organization for ambitious and talented people to join to advance their careers in government and business. They do so not as a cynical strategy but as a matter of course.[27]

The CPC, with its future-based philosophy and scientific socialist ideology, is fully committed to development, using the word 53 times in its 43-page constitution. From its founding a century ago until today, the CPC has believed in democratic centralism and scientific progress. The CPC naturally sees innovation as a wellspring of development and has always considered that the effective management of innovation is essential not only to the CPC's continued success but also to its survival and the eventual

[26]Popular Chinese support for the military, police, legal system, central government, ruling party, national legislature, and civil service exceeded that of most other countries of the world, see Lance L. P. Gore, "The Communist Party-Dominated Governance Model of China: Legitimacy, Accountability, and Meritocracy", *Polity*, 51:1 (January 2019), 166.

[27]*Straits Times*, Having Chinese Communist Party membership is like having "a diploma", "opens doors", October 21, 2017. https://www.straitstimes.com/asia/east-asia/having-chinese-communist-party-membership-is-like-having-a-diploma-and-opens-doors (accessed February 21, 2019).

achievement of communism. In managing innovation, the relationship between the CPC, the government and companies in China is critical.

The CPC's Levers of Control

The CPC relies on four levers to control China[28]:

- The appointment of leaders through the Central Organizational Department (COD);
- Anti-corruption and disciplinary force;
- Residual mobilization;
- Institutional and policy entrepreneurship.

The COD

The COD (中国共产党中央委员会组织部)[29] is the personnel department of the Central Committee of the CPC. Dating from 1924, three years after the founding of the CPC, the COD's first director was Mao Zedong, who effectively used the power of appointment to further the CPC's (and his own) rise to power.

The COD handles all of the senior appointments of the CPC, the government, and the central government-controlled SOEs. This dominance of senior appointments means that senior officials' career paths frequently move smoothly between the government, the CPC, and the SOEs. Under Hu and Zhao in the mid-1980s, there was a drive, culminating in the 13th CPC Congress, to separate the functions of the CPC from the government. Although direct control of SOEs was removed from the CPC control, there has never been a transfer of personnel appointment authority over the centrally controlled SOE senior management from the COD to the State Council (i.e., from the CPC to the government). Today, as in the

[28]The levers framework draws heavily on Li Chen, "Holding 'China Inc.' Together: The CCP and The Rise of China's Yangqi", *The China Quarterly* 228 (December 2016), 927–949 who identifies three (the COD, anti-corruption discipline, and residual mobilization). He also discusses policy innovation which I classify as a fourth lever.

[29]The COD is often referred by western scholars as leading the *nomenklatura* system of China. The term *nomenklatura* is a Russian term meaning "list of names" and was applied to the appointment system of senior cadres in the USSR.

past, the concept of separating CPC from government means government independence *under the supervision of the CPC*. Although the actual number of annual appointments made directly by the COD is just in the hundreds (counting the centrally controlled SOEs and top-ranked government officials), these relatively small numbers of appointments ensure effective indirect control.[30] As Chen observes, concerning the *yangqi*:[31]

> "… the CPC gave up direct control of lower level managers within *yangqi* allowing them to pursue business goals under strategies determined at the (personnel) controlled level of top management. This depoliticized (and professionalized, technically competent and market oriented) intra-group management of *yangqi*".[32]

Today the centrally controlled SOEs, through the appointment system under the COD are both a talent pool for CPC recruitment into politics and a well-trodden path on the career developments of the leaders of Chinese society.

Anti-Corruption

China has a full, multi-level legal and judicial system. It is a system, however, where, the rule of law is unevenly applied. Beyond the legal and judicial system, the CPC through the Central Discipline Inspection Commission (CDIC or 中央纪律检查委员会, often called the 纪委 or *jiwei* for short) exercises extra-judicial authority over CPC party members being investigated for corruption. Since 1949, the CDIC has been ***the*** vehicle to attack corruption both on a continuous basis and in anti-corruption campaigns. Corruption erodes the reputation of the CPC, so the CPC believes that effective fighting of corruption is necessary for the long-term viability of the CPC. And that fighting of corruption itself is an instrument of control within the CPC.

---

[30] Provincial and local SOEs have similar appointing systems controlled by CPC provincial and local organization departments.

[31] The term *yangqi* is often used interchangeably with SOEs, but they are not equivalent. *Yangqi* (央企) means "central enterprises" in Chinese. So *yangqi* are SOEs that are owned by the central governments. There are other SOEs that are owned by provincial and local governments that are not *yangqi*.

[32] Li Chen, *op. cit.*, p. 944.

The long-term viability of the CPC as China's leading party is based on its legitimacy. To the extent that corruption erodes that legitimacy, it threatens the CPC's future. Part of the CPC's success comes from the fear that the CDIC instills in CPC members. Among CPC members, *shuang gui* (双规 or "double appointed", refers to an appointed place at an appointed time at which the member must present him- or herself) is a much feared form of extra-legal detention in which, without formal charges or the chance of a trial, a person of interest is held against his or her will until he or she provides the evidence that the CDIC considers necessary to implement its disciplinary activities. For CPC members, *shuang gui* is double jeopardy, for the CDIC acts as a law unto itself.[33]

But fear is only one weapon in the fight against corruption. Moral suasion is at least as important as fear. In the words of Wang Qishan, the former chief disciplinary official of the CPC,

> We must stick with the principle of "Four Supervision and Discipline Forms", which is to say, light disciplinary punishment and small rank adjustments must be used in the majority of cases to deal with mistaken [CPC] members; heavy disciplinary punishment and significant position adjustment must be used in the minority of cases; and cases that require legal proceedings must become extremely rare. The supervision within the Party must take discipline as the first resort, often carry out criticism and self-criticism during democratic life meetings and often interview problematic individual officials. We must ensure that practices of officials [being] "red face[d] and sweating" becomes the norm [for those found to be corrupt].[34]

---

[33] Leadership of the CDIC conferred on Wang Qishan the mantle of being the most feared man in China, second in power only to Xi Jinping. See "The Devil, or Mr Wang: China's Second Most Powerful Leader Is Admired and Feared", *Economist*, March 26, 2015. Since the end of 2016 there have tests in Beijing, Zhejiang, and Shanxi of harmonizing the double appointment system so that it applies to non-CPC officers as well as CPC officers. See The Twenty-fifth Meeting of the Standing Committee of the 12th National People's Congress adopted the "Decision of the Standing Committee of the National People's Congress on the Pilot Work of National Supervision System Reform in Beijing, Shanxi, and Zhejiang Provinces".

[34] Wang Qishan 把握运用监督执纪 "四种形态" (Grasp "The Four Forms of Supervision and Discipline") XinHua Web September 26, 2015 http://www.xinhuanet.com/politics/2015-09/26/c_1116687031.htm (accessed December 13, 2021).

Disciplinary punishments, meted out by the CPC, if accompanied by a sincere change in behavior of the offending official, are far more effective in asserting CPC legitimacy than legal proceedings which are themselves an embarrassment to the CPC. If CPC members are seen as morally upright, the CPC strengthens its own legitimacy.[35]

Residual Mobilization

Political campaigns have been a recurring part of Chinese life since 1949. While the Campaign to Exterminate the Landlords, the Campaign to Suppress Counter-Revolutionaries, the Hundred Flowers Campaign, the Anti-Rightest Campaign, the Great Leap Forward, the Four Pests, the Learn from Lei Feng, the Party Rectification and the Cultural Revolution of the 1950s and 1960s may seem far away, the CPC can still mobilize its members. In recent years, Xi Jinping's Anti-Corruption Campaign, the China Dream and appeals to patriotism to achieve domestic self-sufficiency in high technology discussed below are echos of the movements of the 1950s, 1960s, and 1970s. The CPC can mobilize. It can rapidly and effectively influence public opinion around specific, directed issues that resonate with the public.

Institutional and Policy Entrepreneurship

It may seem incongruous that the CPC, outwardly a conservative organization, can be described as innovative, but if one looks at the structural changes in government which have continued since 1949, it is hard to conclude otherwise. China is a large country and the CPC has allowed in different areas of the country the process of "… crossing the river by feeling the stones …" to go forward by exploration, experimentation, collecting feedback and allowing that feedback to inform institutional innovations and policy reforms. Because members of the CPC tend to be risk-averse, however, innovations are typically incremental and reversible. In this respect, the CPC combines

[35] Shaoying Zhang and Derek McGhee, "Regaining Honour and Regaining Legitimacy: Shame, Obedience and Risk Practices amongst Chinese Communist Officials", *Economy and Society*, 47:3 (2018), 453–476.

> ... top-down design and guidance ... with bottom-up experimentation and feed-back. The CPC can be seen as a meta-organizational entrepreneur in the policy and institutional domain, one that sets up goals, incentivizes innovations, and restructures assets in China's large state enterprise sector.[36]

The Evolution of the Chinese Economy from Soviet Planning to a Mixed Market Economy

Although in theory, pure market economies and pure planned economies could exist, in fact, every country in the world has a mixed economy. Even countries that have not been through a communist revolution have SOEs and state planning. Even the most planned, socialist economies in history have had some markets with price signals determined by supply and demand. Moreover, the degree of state versus market control evolves in each country over time.[37]

China also has always had a mixed economy. But China has been preceding monotonically over the last 40 years from a very high degree of state ownership, control, and planning to the current moderate level. One can debate the degree of state control, but the Organization for Economic Cooperation and Development (OECD) considers the Chinese economy to be less subject to state control than India or Indonesia and on par with Turkey's earlier in this century.[38] The shift of China from an extreme outlier of centralized planning to a mixed, 21st century moderately high state-controlled market economy represents a considerable change from the beginning of the reform and opening up period.

The reform and opening up is commonly dated from the passing of the report of the Third Plenum of the 11th CPC Central Committee on

---

[36]Li Chen, *op. cit.*, p. 943.

[37]For a discussion of the motives and modalities of mixed economies, see OECD, *State-Owned Enterprise Governance: A Stocktaking of Government Rationales for Enterprise Ownership*, OECD Publishing, Paris, 2015. http://dx.doi.org/10.1787/9789264239944-en (accessed March 6, 2019).

[38]OECD Stats. "Product Market Regulation 2013". https://stats.oecd.org (accessed March 20, 2019). OECD rates India and Indonesia in 2013 as more state controlled than China. And the degree of state control in Turkey is 2.48. According to this index, Turkey's degree of regulation in 1998 and 2003 exceeded China 2013 level of stage control.

December 22, 1978.[39] But like most CPC Central Committee decisions, that official date was, in fact, the *end* of a process of discussion. The jockeying for fundamental change started on September 9, 1976, with the death of Mao Zedong, and progressed through the purge of the leaders of the Cultural Revolution in October 1976, the rehabilitation of Deng Xiaoping in July 1977, and the liberalization of the official media in China through 1978.[40] On December 22, 1978, the CPC officially started to pivot away from the Soviet-style planned economy.

At the start of the pivot, there were only three forms of ownership: SOEs owned and operated by the central government, collectively owned enterprises (controlled by local governments) and single-worker enterprises (single individuals in handicrafts and repair industries). The SOEs were the stars of the planning system launched by the first five-year plan of 1953 to 1957 and continued without substantial change through to the last year of the fifth five-year plan of 1976–1980. In that system, production targets for the SOEs were centrally set and passed down. SOEs purchased raw materials for production from single allocated sources and sold their output to guaranteed buyers — SOEs, collectively owned enterprises and state controlled distributors. And the state allocated to SOEs capital goods for production.

Prices were centrally set and foreign trade was handled by central government ministries. But even in those years, the market was not completely dead: collectively owned enterprises and single worker enterprises legally carried on production, distribution and sales in fragmented markets on the edges of the planned economy. And members of the rural population had some control over at least a part of the land they tilled, the produce of which also satisfied (fragmented) market demands. The rural population, the individual enterprises and the collectively owned enterprises formed the nucleus of what has become, since the late 1970s, by far the most important part of the Chinese economy.

The Old Planning System

The center of the Soviet style economy was the national economic plan. In its purest original form, the national plan was a single state-run,

---

[39]The Report of the Third Plenum of the 11th CPC Central Committee. http://cpc.people.com.cn/GB/64162/64168/64563/65371/4441902.html.

[40]See Hugh Thomas, *Comrade Editor: Letters to the People's Daily*, Commercial Press, Hong Kong, 1980.

input-output matrix for the economy, or at least the SOEs in the economy. In the words of the Chinese State Economic Commission in 1980 the interface between the national economic plan and each SOE was

> … two downs, one up. This process starts with the responsible government agency, (industrial ministry or bureau) giving the enterprise a control figure. The enterprise, combining the control figure with the concrete conditions of the enterprise, works out a plan which it submits to the responsible agency. Then the agency after synthesizing and balancing, sends down the final plan. The control figure used by the enterprise's responsible agency comes from the planning agency, which itself performs a balancing function before giving each individual ministry or bureau its quota. In general, that process between the planning and the industrial agencies is also "two downs one up". The system has many abuses, has very little flexibility and takes into account few of the tens of thousands of market factors …. Now [in mid-1980, a year and a half into the reform and opening up] we are in the process of investigating reforms to achieve a mutual adjustment of plans to market. The initial idea is for the state to moderate its practice of autocratic planning, to change gradually into a system where enterprises would submit plans in accordance with centrally conceived long term goals, and where those plans after balancing would be passed down for implementation….[41]

From this statement, we can see that, at the beginning of the reform and opening up, the Chinese government had no wish to reduce the role of either the SOEs or the five-year plans. The Planning Commission (计划委员会 or *"jiwei"* for short) was one of the three "super commissions" at the ministerial level (along with the Economic Commission and the Science and Technology Commission). But today, the Planning Commission is gone. When one says *jiwei* in Chinese, the listener hears a homonym (纪委) which is the CDIC of the CPC — the second method by which the CPC exercises its control discussed above.

The Planning Commission in 1998 was folded into the Development and Planning Commission. In 2003 its name was changed to Development

[41] Office of Enterprise Management of the Chinese State Economic Commission, "A Brief Introduction to China's Enterprise Management Conditions", June 9, 1980. Introduction to Hugh Thomas (ed.), *A Chinese Managerial Casebook*, National Center for Industrial Science and Technology Management Development at Dalian. Unpublished manuscript 1981.

and Reform Commission. The Planning Commission's successor is no longer a super commission and no longer is concerned with microeconomics. Although the tradition of five-year plans continues to the present — with the most recent being the 14th Five-Year Plan of 2021 to 2025 — the plans no longer entail ***any*** grand input-output matrix or "two downs and one up". The successor to the Planning Commission is essentially a macroeconomic development policy commission, setting development policies and goals not dissimilar to development policies in other, market based countries of the world. It sets broad goals and specific targets, but the only people who are directly answerable to the plan's targets are government officials. And government officials do ***not*** run companies.

The SOEs

Starting in the early 1990s, reform and opening up included gradual listing (on stock markets) of some of the equity, but not controlling interests, of many SOEs. Shares were publically listed in order to improve corporate performance through market discipline, develop capital markets to improve capital allocation efficiency, improve SOE access to capital, increase economic transparency and efficiency, free enterprises from public ownership constraints, and raise governance standards.[42]

The shift away from the planning system corresponded to the implementation of the campaign to "grasp the large and let go of the small" (抓大放小) which started in 1996 in the 9th Five-Year Plan (1996–2001) under Premier Zhu Rongji: the government "grasped" (supported) several hundred large SOEs and let go (allowed to be privatized, consolidated, or dissolved) of thousands of subsidiary and smaller enterprises. The large were consolidated into what has become just under 100 SOEs under the control of the State-owned Assets Supervision and Administration Commission (国务院国有资产监督管理委员会 or SASAC). As of the end of 2017, these *yangqi* SOEs had assets of ¥54.5 trillion, annual operating income of ¥26 trillion and profits of ¥1.4 trillion.[43] The companies are listed in Table 2.3.

---

[42] OECD, *Broadening the Ownership of State-Owned Enterprises: A Comparison of Governance Practices*, OECD Publishing, Paris, 2016, p. 24. http://dx.doi.org/10.1787/9789264244603-en (accessed March 6, 2019).

[43] Reported in SASAC 2017 Annual Report. http://www.sasac.gov.cn/n2588025/n2643314/c8492129/content.html (accessed April 1, 2019).

Table 2.3: Non-Financial Centrally Owned SOEs Managed by the SASAC as of Year End 2017

Number	English	Number	English Name
1	China Nuclear Industry Group Co., Ltd.	50	China Energy Conservation Environmental Group Co., Ltd.
2	China Aerospace Science and Technology Corporation	51	China International Engineering Consulting Co., Ltd.
3	China Aerospace Science and Industry Group Co., Ltd.	52	China Chengtong Holding Group Co., Ltd.
4	China Aviation Industry Corporation	53	China China Coal Energy Group Co., Ltd.
5	China Shipbuilding Industry Corporation	54	China Coal Science and Technology Group Co., Ltd.
6	China Shipbuilding Industry Group Co., Ltd.	55	Mechanical Science Research Institute Group Co., Ltd.
7	China Ordnance Industry Group Co., Ltd.	56	China Steel Group Co., Ltd.
8	China Ordnance Equipment Group Co., Ltd.	57	China Steel Research Technology Group Co., Ltd.
9	China Electronic Technology Group Co., Ltd.	58	China National Chemical Corporation
10	China Aviation Engine Group Co., Ltd.	59	China Chemical Engineering Group Co., Ltd.
11	China National Petroleum Corporation	60	China Salt Industry Group Co., Ltd.
12	China Petrochemical Group Co., Ltd.	61	China National Building Material Group Co.
13	China National Offshore Oil Corporation	62	China Nonferrous Mining Group Co., Ltd.
14	State Grid Corporation	63	Research Institute Group Co., Ltd.
15	China Southern Power Grid Co., Ltd.	64	Beijing Mining Technology Group Co., Ltd.
16	China Huaneng Group Co., Ltd.	65	China International Technology Intelligence Cooperation Co., Ltd.
17	China Datang Group Co., Ltd.	66	China Academy of Building Research Ltd.
18	China Huadian Group Co., Ltd.	67	China CRRC Group Co., Ltd.
19	National Power Investment Group Co., Ltd.	68	China Railway Communication Signal Group Co., Ltd.
20	China Yangtze River Three Gorges Group Co., Ltd.	69	China Railway Engineering Group Co., Ltd.
21	National Energy Investment Group Co., Ltd.	70	China Railway Construction Group Co., Ltd.
22	China Telecom Group Co., Ltd.	71	China Communications Construction Group Co., Ltd.
23	China United Network Communications Group Co., Ltd.	72	China Putian Information Industry Group Co., Ltd.
24	China Mobile Communications Group Co., Ltd.	73	China Information and Communication Technology Group Co., Ltd.

25	China Electronic Information Industry Group Co., Ltd.	74	China Agricultural Development Group Co., Ltd.
26	China First Automobile Group Co., Ltd.	75	China Zhongsi Group Co., Ltd.
27	Dongfeng Motor Group Co., Ltd.	76	China Forestry Group Co., Ltd.
28	China Yizhong Group Co., Ltd.	77	China Pharmaceutical Group Co., Ltd.
29	China Machinery Industry Group Co., Ltd.	78	China Poly Group Co., Ltd.
30	Harbin Electric Group Co., Ltd.	79	China Construction Technology Co., Ltd.
31	China Dongfang Electric Group Co., Ltd.	80	China Metallurgical Geology Bureau
32	Angang Group Co., Ltd.	81	China Coal Geology Bureau
33	China Baowu Iron and Steel Group Co., Ltd.	82	Xinhua International Group Co., Ltd.
34	China Aluminum Group Co., Ltd.	83	China Civil Aviation Information Group Co., Ltd.
35	China Ocean Shipping Group Co., Ltd.	84	China Aviation Oil Group Co., Ltd.
36	China Aviation Group Co., Ltd.	85	China Aviation Equipment Group Co., Ltd.
37	China Eastern Airlines Group Co., Ltd.	86	China Power Construction Group Co., Ltd.
38	China Southern Airlines Group Co., Ltd.	87	China Energy Construction Group Co., Ltd.
39	China Sinochem Group Co., Ltd.	88	China Aneng Construction Group Co., Ltd.
40	COFCO Corporation	89	China Gold Group Co., Ltd.
41	China Minmetals Corporation Limited	90	China General Nuclear Group Co., Ltd.
42	China General Technology (Group) Holding Co., Ltd.	91	China Hualu Group Co., Ltd.
43	China Construction Group Co., Ltd.	92	Shanghai Nokia Bell Co., Ltd.
44	China Reserve Grain Management Group Co., Ltd.	93	Overseas Chinese Town Group Co., Ltd.
45	National Development Investment Group Co., Ltd.	94	Nanguang (Group) Co., Ltd. [China Nanguang Group Co., Ltd.]
46	China Merchants Group Co., Ltd.	95	China Xidian Group Co., Ltd.
47	China Resources (Group) Co., Ltd.	96	China Railway Materials Group Co., Ltd.
48	China Travel Group Co., Ltd. [Hong Kong China Travel (Group) Co., Ltd.]	97	China Guoxin Holdings Co., Ltd.
49	China Commercial Aircraft Co., Ltd.		

As noted above, the COD directly appoints top management of centrally controlled SOEs, including chairman of the board, the CPC Party secretary and Chief Executive Officer. In addition to these *yangqi* SOEs, the largest banks of China are also SOEs. These include the Industrial and Commercial Bank of China, the Postal Savings Bank of China, the Bank of China, The Construction Bank of China, the Agricultural Bank of China, and The Bank of Communications. The majority of the shares of these SOEs are owned by the Central Huijin Investment Company, directly under the State Council of China. Other SOEs (which are not *yangqi*) are owned by provincial and local governments and legal persons that are themselves owned by SOEs.

China's SOEs are less efficient, less innovative and more endowed with access to government and financial resources than China's private enterprises. They have a soft-budget constraint through their access to funding and top management and board members concerned political and career goals external to and sometimes in conflict with maximizing shareholder wealth.[44] Chinese seldom debate whether the SOEs' position in the economy is "fair" probably because the SOEs' reduced position and increased efficiency relative to the past already represents substantial progress in the reform and opening up. They accept that SOEs (and indeed privately owned companies) can act to advance national government interests (rather than for its own shareholders' interests) whether in the domestic or in the international market.[45]

Notwithstanding the critical role played by SOEs, if one divides the Chinese economy into the SOE sector and the private sector, the private sector, following 40 years of reform and opening up, is more important than the SOE sector. In the words of a leading CPC official:

> At present, there are nearly 25 million private enterprises in China. Their role and contribution can be summarized by the number "56789". "5" means that private enterprises contribute more than 50% to the state in taxes. "6" means that domestic private enterprises' share of GDP output, fixed assets investment and share of outgoing foreign direct investment

---

[44] Xiaojie Liu, Jim Huangnan, Kent Deng, *A Rational Path towards A Pareto Optimum for Reforms of Large State-Owned Enterprise in China, Past, Present and Future*. London School of Economics Economic History, Working Papers No. 244, 2016.

[45] OECD, *State-Owned Enterprises as Global Competitors: A Challenge or an Opportunity?* OECD Publishing, Paris, 2016. http://dx.doi.org/10.1787/9789264262096-en.

all exceed 60%. "7" means that private enterprises account for more than 70% of high-tech enterprises. "8" means that private enterprises account for more than 80% of employment. "9" means that the contribution rate of private enterprises to new employment has reached 90%.[46]

Because none of these figures is below 50%, one can characterize the Chinese economy as being more market-based than plan-based. Moreover, each passing year increases its market-basis.

Economic Planning for Innovation in China Today

As described above, China is a mixed economy where the private sector is more important than the public sector. Both SOEs and private enterprises, as well government departments, non-government organizations (NGOs) and private citizens, purchase and sell goods and services whose prices are largely determined by market mechanisms. The Soviet style planning system of input-output matrices is dead. Yet the five-year "planning" cycle is very much alive.

Every five years, the CPC takes the opportunity to express its mission and vision in the five-year plan. Every five years, the CPC Politburo draws up an exhaustive set of policy exhortations, which it gives to the NPC and which the NPC then passes without amendment. The plan is not detailed. It is rather a set of exhortations, slogans, maxims, and principles, demonstrating broadly what the CPC wishes to achieve in all parts of the economy. The plan is short. The 14th Five-Year Plan (2021–2125) contains only 60 sections occupying 142 pages and can be comfortably read in a day.[47] But CPC members do *not* comfortably read it in a day. They intently study it, as religions people may study a sacred text. The plan contains few hard targets, few key performance indicators (KPIs). Most of it is

---

[46]Qi Wanxiang, Vice Minister of the United Front Work Department of the CPC Central Committee in answer to a question at the press conference of the 19th National Party Congress on October 21, 2017. *Xinhua Net News* 冉万祥：民营企业的作用和贡献可以用"56789"来概括. http://www.xinhuanet.com/politics/19cpcnc/2017-10/21/c_129724207.htm (accessed March 3, 2019).

[47]"National Economic and Social Development of the People's Republic of China Outline of the Fourteenth Five-Year Plan and Vision 2035" ["中华人民共和国国民经济和社会发展第十四个五年规划和 2035 年远景目标纲要"] March 2021 accessed August 17, 2021 https://www.ndrc.gov.cn/xxgk/zcfb/ghwb/202103/P020210323538797779059.pdf.

qualitative, not quantitative. And the 65 sections can lead to different interpretations. So they must be *carefully* studied to be a useful guide for daily decision making. The need to study the plan exists both for national and (the far the greatest number of) provincial and local government officers. The more than 90 million CPC members spread throughout society need to study the plan. And all others who, in anticipation of the direction of CPC policy, make decisions to capitalize on society's development should also study the plan. Thus a relatively short document reverberates across the country, affecting countless decisions.

This chapter concludes by briefly reviewing two plans, Made in China 2025 and the 14th Five-Year Plan.

Made in China 2025

Made in China 2025 was ***not*** a five-year plan. Its targets, laid out in 2015, explicitly stretched beyond a five-year horizon. It had far more KPIs than a "regular" five-year plan. And it caused considerable consternation in the West, where it was perceived as China's challenging Western technological superiority.

By 2015, China had become the dominant manufacturing country in the world in terms of output but lagged far behind leading industrial powers such as the United States, Germany, and Japan in terms of quality. Rather than projecting China's rise based on past growth as an inevitability, however, China's planners looked anxiously at innovations in the West. Rapid increases in 3D printing, the mobile internet, cloud computing, big data, bio-engineering, smart manufacturing re-industrialization initiatives, new energy, new materials, integrated intelligent manufacturing, crowd-sourcing, mass customization, collaborative design, e-commerce, wearable smart products, and smart cars, these and more alarmed the Chinese as did western national calls to innovation action, exemplified by the German Industry 4.0 initiative of 2012.[48]

---

[48] Bonner, Mike. "What is Industry 4.0 and What Does it Mean for My Manufacturing?" March 2, 2017. https://blog.viscosity.com/blog/what-is-industry-4.0-and-what-does-it-mean-for-my-manufacturing (retrieved July 2, 2019) and Bernard Marr, "Why Everyone Must Get Ready For The 4th Industrial Revolution", *Forbes*, April 5, 2016. https://www.forbes.com/sites/bernardmarr/2016/04/05/why-everyone-must-get-ready-for-4th-industrial-revolution/#1b652e0c3f90 (accessed July 2, 2019).

These innovations occurred as the Chinese growth model of the previous decades — increasing application of investment capital, export-led production, reliance on proven technologies, and cheap labor from the countryside — was increasingly perceived as unsustainable. Chinese leaders feared that China was becomes a strong manufacturer with a weak technological base, inefficient, polluting, and poor in globally popular brands. Economic studies revealed stagnant factor productivity. With the country's aggregate labor pool peaking in 2015 and going into decline many felt that a crisis loomed.[49]

The fear that China faced a middle income trap led the premier, Li Keqiang and his State Council, to conclude that massive domestic innovation was urgently needed to effect a transformation of the manufacturing base. Hence, in early 2015, the State Council published Made in China 2025[50] *between* the 12th Five-Year Plan of 2011 to 2015 and the 13th Five-Year Plan of 2016–2020. Its paragraphs contained modern industrial management slogans but most importantly, it emphasized innovation. The word "innovation" occurred 101 times in the 26-page plan.

Made in China 2025 expressed the desire for the economy to be:

- Driven by innovation
- Placing quality first
- Ecologically friendly
- Optimized to develop a strong manufacturing country and
- Oriented towards developing required talents

And Made in China 2025 had specific numerical KPIs as given in the Table 2.4.

It also included general goals, stretching into the future. For example, by 2025 the quality of Chinese manufacturing will be greatly enhanced, achieving industrialization and informationalization and international standards in pollution control, and by 2035 Chinese manufacturing will be at the mid-level of advanced countries with major breakthroughs in key areas. These general goals are both aspirational and difficult to measure.

---

[49]Hongbin Li, Lei Li, Binzhen Wu, and Yanyan Xiong, "The End of Cheap Chinese Labor", *Journal of Economic Perspectives* 26:4 (Fall 2012), 57–74.

[50]Notice of the State Council on Printing and Distributing, "Made in China 2025" No. 28 国务院关于印发《中国制造2025》的通知国发 (2015) 28号国务院2015年5月8日 http://www.gov.cn/zhengce/content/2015-05/19/content_9784.htm (accessed July 1, 2019).

Table 2.4: Quantitative KPIs of Made in China 2025

Category	Standard	2013	2015	2020	2025
Innovative ability	R&D as a percent of company income	0.88	0.95	1.26	1.68
	patents per ¥100 million of income	0.36	0.44	0.7	1.1
Quality efficiency	Manufacturing Quality Competitiveness Index*	83.1	83.5	84.5	85.5
	Increase in manufacturing value added	—	—	Increase 2% from 2015	Increase 4% from 2015
	Manufacturing labor productivity growth rate (% per year)	—	—	7.5% during the 13th 5-year plan	6.5% during the 14th 5-year plan
Dual goals of industrialization and informationalization	Broadband penetration rate (%)**	37	50	70	82
	Digital R&D design tool penetration rate %***	52	58	72	84
	The numerical control rate of key processes is (%)****	27	33	50	64
ECO development	Decrease in energy consumption of industrial added value of units above designated size	—	—	Decrease 18% from 2015	Decrease 34% from 2015
	Decrease in CO2 emissions per unit of industrial added value	—	—	Decrease 22% from 2015	Decrease 40% from 2015
	Decrease in water consumption per unit of industrial added value	—	—	Decrease 23% from 2015	Decrease 41% from 2015
	Comprehensive utilization rate of industrial solid waste (%)	62	65	73	79

Notes: *Produced annually by the General Administration of Quality Supervision, Inspection and Quarantine of the PRC.
**Installed fixed broadband households / total Chinese households.
***Ratio of design companies surveyed using digital design/substantial size design companies.
****Average percent of key processes that are numerically controlled in manufacturing companies surveyed.
Source: Notice of the State Council on Printing and Distributing "Made in China 2025" No. 28, May 8, 2015.

The final goal that, by 2049, the hundredth anniversary of the founding of the People's Republic of China, China will be among the leading manufacturers, foremost in innovation with the leading industrial and technology system is simply the desire that China will become the number one industrial and technological power in the world, a producer of quality goods in an environmentally friendly economy.

Specific industries for development included integrated circuit (IC) fabrication and design, 5G technologies, security operating systems, high-end industrial software, high-end numerically controlled machine tools and robots, aerospace, marine engineering equipment, and high-tech ships, advanced rail transit equipment, energy saving and new energy vehicles, power equipment, agricultural machinery and equipment, new materials and biomedical and high performance medical devices. In short, the industries span the entire space of high technology.

The CPC can enforce some hard KPIs in SOEs by the methods that it uses to implement its policies described above. The CPC has no such levers to control privately owned enterprises; however, the existence of such written KPIs establishes a moral obligation which, given the omnipresence of the CPC in large private as well as SOEs and government organizations, can be considerable. On the other hand, aspirational targets, such achieving reduction of costs, production times and substandard products in smart manufacturing by 50% by 2025 are clearly not enforceable, even within SOEs.

Made in China 2025 called for 80% of "the four basics" — core basic components, advanced basic processes, key basic materials and industrial technology foundations — in 80 advanced industries to be supplied domestically. Promoting this goal is at odds with promoting an integrated world of free trade in goods and services. Because Made in China 2025 represented a strident, credible, call for Chinese self-sufficiency and leadership in technology, it further inflamed anti-Chinese reactions from the rest of the world.[51]

---

[51] See Wübbeke, J., M. Meissner, M. J. Zenglein Jaqueline Ives, B. Conrad, "Made in China 2025 The Making of a High-Tech Superpower and Consequences for Industrial Countries", 2016 and Lorand Laskai, "Why Does Everyone Hate Made in China 2025? China's Grand Plan to Bolster Hi-Tech Industries at Home Is Not Receiving Much Love Abroad". *Net Politics*, March 28, 2018. https://www.cfr.org/blog/why-does-everyone-hate-made-china-2025 (accessed July 2, 2019).

The 14th Five-Year Plan

One can get the flavor of the 14th Five-Year Plan simply by reading the titles its 19 chapters:

1. Start the new journey of building a modern socialist country in an all-round way
2. Persist in innovation-driven development and fully shape new development advantages
3. Accelerate the development of a modern industrial system and promote the optimization and upgrading of the economic system
4. Form a strong domestic market and build a new development patterns
5. Accelerate digital development and building digital China
6. Comprehensively deepen reforms across the board and build a high-level socialist market economic system
7. Prioritize the development of agricultural and rural areas, and fully promote rural revitalization
8. Improve the new urbanization strategy and the quality of urbanization development
9. Optimize regional economic design to promote regional coordinated development
10. Develop advanced socialist and enhance national cultural soft power
11. Promote green development, and the harmony between people and nature
12. Achieve a high degree of openness to the outside world, opening up new prospects for win-win cooperation
13. Improve the quality of the people and promote their all-round development
14. Enhance people's livelihood and well-being, raising the levels of shared construction, governance and enjoyment
15. Coordinate development and safety to build a more peaceful and safe China
16. Speed up the modernization of national defense and the military achieving prosperous civilian-military integration
17. Strengthen the construction of socialist democracy and rule of law, improving the party and state supervision system

18. Adhere to "One Country, Two Systems" and promote the reunification of the Motherland
19. Strengthen commitment to plan implementation.

Among the quantitative targets are an increase in the GDP per capita to the level of US$ 30,000 per person by 2035, a realization of maximum carbon emissions by 2030 and carbon net zero emissions by 2060 and strengthening intellectual property and the securitization of IP rights.

Innovation dominates the plan.[52] Chapter 2 identifies development as being led by innovation, and lists the areas where cutting-edge research should be carried out: artificial intelligence, quantum information, integrated circuits, life and health sciences, brain science, genetic engineering, aerospace technology, deep earth studies, deep sea studies, etc.[53] The plan identifies the three areas for building global research centers as Beijing, Shanghai and the Greater Bay Area.[54] And it gives much advice about how China should increase innovation.

Concluding Remarks: The Great Renaissance of the Chinese People

Since the founding of the CPC, its members have earnestly studied its directives. Whether it be the words of Chairman Mao on class struggle or Chairman Xi on building an innovative, modern economy, pages of slogans are patiently dissected for understanding and implementation at local levels. The process can seem anachronistic and stifling. Rote reciting of Marx and Mao today has largely been replaced by earnest citing of modern western management jargon, the five-year plans and statements

[52] The term "innovate" is used 181 time in the plan, less than "develop", "construct" and "strengthen" (which occur 518, 478 and 253 times respectively) but more than other terms.

[53] "National Economic and Social Development of the People's Republic of China Outline of the Fourteenth Five-Year Plan and Vision 2035" ["中华人民共和国国民经济和社会发展第十四个五年规划和*2035* 年远景目标纲要"] March 2021 accessed August 17, 2021 https://www.ndrc.gov.cn/xxgk/zcfb/ghwb/202103/P020210323538797779059.pdf 2:4:2 page 12.

[54] *Ibid* 2:4:4 page 13.

of Chairman Xi. Yet the CPC led system in China has yielded impressive results. The CPC is a strong, and surprisingly popular, flexible organization that continues to deliver economic performance and effectively to implement innovation in China.

One important aspect of the CPC's popularity and success is its goal recurring over the last 20 years: the great renaissance of the Chinese people.[55] The goal of communism does not inspire: it recedes into the mists of a future where time is measured in centuries. It is a utopia in which few fervently believe, even within the CPC. Deng Xiaoping's "crossing the river by feeling the stones" and "building a modestly prosperous society"[56] is the reality of today. These realities are good, but they are *not* particularly inspiring. But the great renaissance, raising China to a status no less than ***any*** power on earth, economically, socially, culturally, environmentally, politically, diplomatically, and militarily does capture the imagination. The Chinese dream[57] is achievable within the lifetimes of most people alive today. It can become reality by the hundredth anniversary of the birth of the People's Republic of China in the year 2049. The seamless pursuit of this nationalist goal with socialist ideals led by a trusted government in a mixed market economy is the greatest triumph of the CPC today.

---

[55] The expression was first used in the 16th CPC Congress in 2002 by Hu Jintao and was embraced by Xi Jinping in the 18th CPC Congress in 2012. It continues to surface in CPC organs. See Xie Fuzhan, "An Important Milestone in the Great Renaissance of the Chinese People", *People's Daily*, July 15, 2020.

[56] Achieving a "moderately prosperous society" (小康社会), has been a medium term CPC goal since Deng Xiaoping launched the reform and opening up. The term refers to the Confucian Classic, *Book of Rites: Ceremonial Usages:* 2 ((礼记：礼运:2) also translated as the period of "small tranquility" and used by Confucians to characterize the idealized time of the early Western Zhou Dynasty. See *China Text Project*. https://ctext.org/liji/li-yun (accessed September 3, 2020). The CPC believes that it has already largely achieved a moderately prosperous society, in time for the 100th anniversary of the CPC, and will achieve the great renaissance, in time for the 100th anniversary of the PRC. For a description of the achievements of the moderately prosperous society, see Xie Fuzhan, *op. cit.*

[57] "The China dream" (中國夢) is a term coined by Xi Jinping in 2012 in referring to the road to renaissance, dating from the Song Dynasty and often used in the 20th century. See Wang Qiangan, "The Origin of the Words 'China Dream'", *Contemporary China History Studies* 20:6 (2013), 110–116.

Chapter 3

Intellectual Property

All essays under heaven are nothing but copying. It's just whether or not you know how to copy … After reading carefully 300 Tang Dynasty poems, even if you can't recite, you can recite.

— old Chinese sayings[1]

Patent law is … a quintessential expression of the assumptions and values of Western society. As such, it is highly objectionable to communist theory.

— Hsia Tao-tai and Katheryn A. Hsia[2]

[1]The first saying, 天下文章一大抄, 就看你会抄不会抄, is spoken in modern Chinese, and is sufficiently well known that, in front of any college class, an instructor need only speak the first four words and the class will gleefully complete it, often following with the second. The second saying 书读唐诗 300 首不会吟诗也会吟 comes from the foreword to a Qing Dynasty 18th century text by Sun Zhu entitled *300 Tang Dynasty Poems.* See Huang Liang, "The Origin After Reading Carefully 300 Tang Dynasty Poems, Even If You Can't Write Poetry, You Can Recite" *Zhi Hu* 熟读唐诗三百首, 不会作诗也会吟。这句诗是谁写的? https://www.zhihu.com/question/38100912.

[2]Tao-tai Hsia and Katheryn A. Hsia, "Laws of the People's Republic of China on Industrial and Intellectual Property", *Law and Policy in International Business*, 5:3 (1973). https://scholarship.law.duke.edu/cgi/viewcontent.cgi?article=3409&context=lcp (accessed August 22, 2020).

Heavens are high. The emperor is far away. People are few. Our friends are many.

— old Chinese saying[3]

IP laws are "rules of the game" enacted by countries to reward innovation. In a single generation, China has evolved from a Soviet-style planned regime, averse to private property, including IP, into a country with an IP regime, headed by the China National Intellectual Property Administration[4] (CNIPA), compatible with international norms. Today, Chinese produce, take pride in, register, violate, and litigate more IP than citizens of any other country in the world.

Knowledge is a public, great, global, good. New knowledge benefits society through valuable innovation. Knowledge is hard to produce but easy to store and share. In sharing knowledge, the giver loses no knowledge and indeed may gain more knowledge by the interaction with the receiver. As a teacher, I confess that I only really learned many theories through the process of teaching them. Sharing knowledge can be a pleasure: an instructor enjoys lecturing to a student; a mentor finds pleasure leading a mentee; a parent loves teaching her child.

Making new knowledge can be fun, but it's also hard, expensive work.

If every potential producer of a good or service perfectly shared all relevant knowledge, creating new knowledge would be profitless. If you spend time and money on research and development (R&D), if you produce new knowledge, and if that new knowledge is immediately made available to all competitors, you can never recoup your R&D costs.

[3] 天高皇帝远, 民少相公多. The current version is more often "mountains" rather than "heavens". The old saying dates from an old saying from the waning days of the Yuan Dynasty, when it was associated with the growing resistance in southern China against the Mongols. See the explanation in Baidu, "Mountains Are High and the Emperor Is far Away." https://baike.baidu.com/item/天高皇帝远/3098735?fromtitle=山高皇帝远&fromid=4616239#reference-[4]-171504-wrap. Even though China is and, in most of imperial times, was a unitary state, in fact the power of local customs and local authorities means that the will of the central government can be and is often flouted. Today the expression is used in any large organization, where local power centers can arise in spite of central policies.

[4] CNIPA was called, before 2018 the State Intellectual Property Office (SIPO). For annual reports, regulations and statistics, see the CNIPA website http://www.cnipa.gov.cn.

In such a world, new knowledge would only come from those who did it for fun. Fun is unlikely to be the main motive for corporate R&D, although it may be one motive. Economists have long recognized this, and the consequent tendency of free markets to *underproduce* knowledge.[5]

Free market economists, who find fault with monopolies for the inefficiencies they engender, typically advocate for the creation of monopolies to solve the problem of underproduction of knowledge. Confronted by the appropriability problem concerning IP, they prescribe the following.[6] Define the new knowledge created as IP. Allow the creators to hold limited monopolies over the IP excluding others from selling products (or services) that the IP impounds. With the monopoly the creators of the IP can sell, rent, and/or charge higher prices for the IP than had it not been protected. They will then engage in more knowledge production, R&D and innovation.[7] Moreover, the legally protected IP can be pledged to lenders, allowing it to be used as collateral, increasing liquidity, and helping to finance innovation.

Principles are clear. Implementation is complex.

One has to define what constitutes IP. What is a valid IP monopoly. Who should be awarded exclusive rights? Who should be excluded? How should the monopoly be run and for how long? How is IP to be registered?

---

[5] Underproduction or overproduction is relative to an economic optimum, which must be derived from analysis of an equilibrium model. For an introductory rigorous treatment, see William Nordhaus "The Optimal Life of a Patent", *Cowles Foundation Discussion Paper* Number 241, 1967. http://cowles.yale.edu/sites/default/files/files/pub/d02/d0241.pdf (accessed August 10, 2020). The design of an optimal patent system dependent on the structure of the economy, the nature of progress, the utility of the inventor, etc., is suggested succinctly by Northaus in Nordhaus, "The Optimum Life of a Patent: Reply", *American Economic Review* 62:3 (1972), 428–431.

[6] The problem was explained by Joseph Schumpeter and modeled by Kenneth Arrow and David Teece. See Sidney G. Winter "The Logic of Appropriability: From Schumpeter to Arrow to Teece", *Research Policy* 35:8 (2006), 1100–1106. https://doi.org/10.1016/j.respol.2006.09.010 (accessed September 13, 2020).

[7] Joseph E. Stiglitz, "Knowledge as a Global Public Good", *Global Public Goods*, UNDP, New York, 1999. https://www.researchgate.net/profile/Eugenio_Bobenrieth/publication/46440722_The_Political_Economy_of_International_Environmental_Cooperation/links/55ddb07308ae79830bb531ed/The-Political-Economy-of-International-Environmental-Cooperation.pdf#page=346, pp. 308–325 (accessed August 10, 2020).

How should it be disclosed? How should it be defended? How should abuses of the IP system be detected and challenged? These are complex moral and legal issues. Each country of the world has the sovereign authority to set up institutions, pass laws, introduce regulations and execute actions concerning IP.

But international standards exist. Today, all members of the WTO[8] subscribe to the Trade Related Aspects of International Property Rights Agreement (TRIPS), which sets standards for IP laws and administers some aspects of global IP protection through the World Intellectual Property Organization (WIPO).[9]

This chapter will consider copyright, patents, and trademarks and how they relate to IP policy and strategy in China.

Copyright

Copyright protects the original expression of an idea, its recording, broadcasting, performing and reciting in public, and its adapting and translating into other languages. As the WTO *Agreement on* TRIPS states,

> Copyright protection shall extend to expressions and not to ideas, procedures, methods of operation or mathematical concepts as such.[10]

Copyright applies to writing (including translations), art, music, videos, computer programs (source and operating codes), compilations of data (but not the data itself), etc. Under TRIPS, copyright is an automatic right: there is no need for its legal assertion or regulatory permission or formal registration. The act of original expression itself generates

---

[8] There are 164 members and 25 observers of WTO. Members include all major countries of the world. China has been a member since 2001. Hong Kong and Macao, both special administrative regions of China are separate members, having joined prior to China. Taiwan is neither a member nor an observer, but its IP rules of the game are largely in line with the rest of the world.

[9] WIPO website: https://www.wipo.int/portal/en/index.html (accessed August 20, 2020).

[10] WTO *Agreement on Trade-Related Aspects of Intellectual Property Rights*, p. 245. https://www.wto.org/english/docs_e/legal_e/27-trips.pdf (accessed August 20, 2020).

copyright.[11] And copyright protects regardless of the nationality or location of the expresser.[12]

Chinese copyright law protects the expresser for his or her lifetime plus 50 years. Thereafter, the idea's expression enters the public domain: anyone can copy it free of charge. The United States, Russia, and much of Europe protects copy for the life of the expresser plus 70 years. Canada protects for life plus 60 years. So IP of an expresser's work would first expire in China, and would expire 10 years later in Canada and another 10 years later in the United States, Russia, and much of Europe.

Does copyright IP protection "work" in China? Yes, with some important caveats. But copyright has seen dramatic changes which are currently accelerating, eroding the strength of copyright.

Historical Background

A cultured person in China, since the dawn of China, has been able to spice discourse with appropriate quotations — from the philosophers of the Axial Age, from Tang and Song poetry, from the Marxist-Leninist classics, from Mao Zedong, from Xi Jinping, from western philosophers, and from modern entrepreneurs. The tradition is old. In imperial China, scholars taking civil service examinations would quote classics in their meticulously crafted essays. Those quotations were generally without reference. The scholars who marked the exams knew the sources, and would understand the wit of well-placed allusions.

China, the culture with the oldest printing tradition in the world, had no copyright laws until the last year of the Qing Dynasty, 1910. That lack of copyright, coupled with the imperial examination tradition which included unattributed yet understood allusions, and the fondness for citing the classics may account for what non-Chinese often see as a sloppy tradition of casual plagiarism that pervades Chinese writing. The tradition is

[11]And there is no need to use the copyright symbol ©, which was required under the U.S. system prior to the late 1980s.

[12]If a country is a member of the Berne Convention for the Protection of Literary and Artistic Works of 1886, the country accepts the copyrights of other members to its jurisdiction and extends its copyrights to other members' jurisdictions. China has been a Berne Convention member since 1992, pre-dating its WTO/TRIPS compliance. The Berne Convention is administered by WIPO. See https://www.wipo.int/treaties/en/ip/berne/.

exacerbated by the cultural divide of language. Massive technology transfer accomplished by translating foreign texts into Chinese, with no thought to giving royalties back to non-Chinese originators of text, started in the 19th century and has continued, largely unscathed, down to the present.

Popular literature protected, at least in theory, by copyright, enjoyed a great flowering in early 20th century Republican China. Yet with the founding of the People's Republic of China, there was a literary clamp down. Copyright stayed in place[13] but the newly empowered CPC, intent on the culturally remoulding the country, took control of print media. Propaganda was important. The nationalized SOE publishing companies devoted their copy to promoting Marxism and building new, pure, proletarian, socialism. And in the New China, Mao Zedong's works were best sellers.

Between 1949 and 1965, Mao's works sold about 64 million copies. Then, during the Cultural Revolution from 1965 to 1976, sales really boomed: over 13 billion copies of his works sold. These included selected works, collected works, poems, and single essays in pamphlet form. Of course, the biggest sellers were the *Works of Chairman Mao*, selling 2.8 billion and *Quotations of Chairman Mao*, which had over 3,200 editions and sold 965 million copies.[14] Even with royalties at pennies per copy (and royalty waivers for single-essay pamphlets and PLA editions) it all added up. His bank account balance swelled to ¥75 million by the time of his death. Notwithstanding the protests of his fourth and final wife, Jiang Qing, however, the CPC Central Committee determined that

[13]The continuance of copyright was by default and administrative action, not by new legislation. See Tao-tai Hsia and Katheryn A. Hsia, *op. cit.*, p. 275.

[14]The best-selling book, worldwide, in history, according to the *Guinness Book of Records*, is *The Bible*, with more than five billion copies sold. Mao's best-selling single book, *Quotations of Chairman Mao*, affectionately known as "the little red book", is in second place. See "Best Selling Book", *Guinness Book of Records,* 2020. https://www.guinnessworldrecords.com/world-records/best-selling-book-of-non-fiction accessed August 20, 2020) Note, however, that the Mao's *Works* (a multi-volume set, not a single book) would beat *The Bible* in terms of bound *volume* sales. The total all of the book publication sales of Mao (a single author) are several times the total sales of *The Bible* (written by several authors).

his works were the IP of CPC; hence, that bank balance and further accumulating royalties have, since then, accrued to the CPC.[15]

Starting from 1978 China has seen considerable relaxation of CPC control over traditional print channels. Privately owned newspapers and publishing houses compete, sometimes gingerly, with SOE publishing houses. The SOEs, to survive, publish popular works to reap revenue from competitive markets. Today, there are over 900 publishing houses, up from just over 60 during the Cultural Revolution. They publish over six times the output of forty years ago. With the rise in standards of living, books sold per capita have also risen, from slightly less than one book per capita per year in the late 1990s to about 2.5 in 2019.[16]

But today, books are ***not*** where the publishing action is.

Digital Communication and Copyright

Digital communications and content have exploded. As of 2019, China has over 850 million mobile phone users, about half the users on the planet.[17] Four of the six million 4G base stations worldwide are located throughout China and the remaining two million are spread over the rest of the world. Chinese mobile data volume will increase by an order of magnitude as 5G is rapidly rolled out[18] and China is in the forefront of 6G

---

[15]陈昌喜, "毛泽东亿万稿酬的争议" *民间历史*, 香港中文大学中国研究服务中心, http://mjlsh.usc.cuhk.edu.hk/Book.aspx?cid=4&tid=4121 (accessed August 20, 2020). The CPC central committee gave ¥2 million each to Mao's two daughters by his third marriage to He Zizhen. Jiang Qing was imprisoned shortly after Mao's death and committed suicide in 1991.

[16]Zhao Yushan and Xing Zixing, "From Big Data Looking at 70 Years of Publishing Development in New China", *Media People*, September 30, 2019, 赵玉山 邢自兴 "从大数据看新中国70年出版成就与发展历程" 中国新闻出版广电报. http://media.people.com.cn/n1/2019/0930/c40606-31381950.html (accessed August 22, 2020).

[17]S. O'Dea, "Smartphones — Statistics & Facts", *Statistica*, June 26, 2020. https://www.statista.com/statistics/748053/worldwide-top-countries-smartphone-users/ (accessed August 22, 2020).

[18]The CPC has required that the SOE telecommunications companies to provide coverage virtually *everywhere* in China where people live. This policy helps address the digital divide relative to a fully for profit model, typically found elsewhere in the world. Zhang Chi, "Why China's Mobile Coverage Is Superior to That of the US", *Global Times*, December 12, 2019. https://www.globaltimes.cn/content/1172513.shtml (accessed August 22, 2020).

satellite research.[19] The creative content that Chinese consume is mostly, and increasingly online.

The digital explosion impacts copyright. Today, digitally delivered blogs, videos, novels, music, movies, video games, etc. occupies the time, entertains the minds, and molds the thoughts of young and old, rich and poor, rural, and urban. With the exception of anti-CPC content, anti-Chinese content and pornography, all of which are censored, digital content in China is completely free to meet market demand. The growth is unprecedented. Millions of amateur authors compete to provide romances, fantasy, martial arts, history, military, suspense, science fiction, and lesser genres. Payment follows various models including pay by the word, freemium, and advertising based.[20]

A leader in the domain is Tencent, a major global video games company, that burst into life in 1999 with its messaging app. Tencent has become one of the largest retail payments providers in the world.[21] Management at Tencent uses AI and several thousand employees to comb user posts, culling out inappropriate content.

Tencent's 80 person strong IP team is mainly concerned with defending its copyrights. It advises those posting content to be vigilant and to report to Tencent any copyright violations. But tens of thousands of pirate websites provide content with rampant plagiarism, looking to generate advertising revenue from views regardless of IP. The government audits tens of thousands of sites, shutting down thousands each year, but replacements continue to spring up.

China's IP policy is frequently cited as causing tremendous losses to non-Chinese companies with by far the largest losses to Chinese IP

---

[19]"China Sends 'World's First 6G' Test Satellite into Orbit" BBC, November 7, 2020. https://www.bbc.com/news/av/world-asia-china-54852131 (accessed April 30, 2021).

[20]R. Cheung, "China's Online Publishing Industry — Where Fortune Favours the Few, and Sometimes the Undeserving", *South China Morning Post,* May 6, 2018. https://www.scmp.com/magazines/post-magazine/long-reads/article/2144610/chinas-online-publishing-industry-where-fortune (accessed August 20, 2020).

[21]See the "Connecting People, Social, Enterprises to Build our Future", Tencent website. https://www.tencent.com/en-us (accessed August 22, 2020). The instructor who wishes to feature Tencent in courses has a wealth of cases to choose from, with new cases being published every year. See, for example, John R. Wells and Gabriel Ellsworth, "Tencent", Harvard Business School, 2017, HBSP 9-718-426. As Tencent is listed in Hong Kong, one can use selections from the annual report to stimulate discussions.

property theft coming from copyright violations — particularly software.[22] If code can be hacked, hackers seeking to place product at the lowest cost tend to hack. Those who suffer are predominantly domestic Chinese companies. They react less by defending their code copyright in the courts than by devising and placing new content, increasing turnover and innovation.

Copyright has existed continuously in China since 1910. But as anyone with access to a photocopier or a smart phone can attest, copyright is often honored in the breech. Only when substantial sums of money from lost royalties are involved, and when the accused is sufficiently easily identifiable and wealthy is it worthwhile for the copyright holder to take legal action against the alleged violator. There are in China, and indeed everywhere in cyberspace, too many who reproduce expressions of ideas without permission: publishers, copy-paste enthusiasts, concert producers, DJs, programmers, downloaders and hackers. But the sheer size of China and the fast speed with which the digital revolution is advancing has made the phenomenon more striking in China than in any other country of the world.

The human mind's creativity is based on bending, breaking and blending existing concepts.[23] It is not from nothing that we create. Moreover, that creativity can be and is increasingly being modeled with AI. AI is increasingly capable of producing, if not good art, at least passable expressions of ideas. The speed at which this will be accomplished begs the question as to whether copyright should be applied to AI IP — especially given the sheer volume that will shortly be produced by those

---

[22]United States International Trade Commission, *China: Effects of Intellectual Property Infringement and Indigenous Innovation Policies on the U.S. Economy,* May 2011. https://www.usitc.gov/publications/332/pub4226.pdf I have been unable to find similar studies of the losses to Chinese companies of Chinese copyright violations but suspect that they are not less than U.S. copyright holders losscs. Nor am I aware of studies of losses to U.S. companies of U.S. copyright violations, which are also probably high.

[23]Anthony Brandt and David Eagleman, *The Runaway Species: How Human Creativity Remakes the World* Catapult, New York, 2017. For a video introduction to bending, blending, and breaking, see Eagleman, David, "How the Mind Makes New Ideas", Big Think, August 4, 2018. https://bigthink.com/videos/david-eagleman-how-the-mind-makes-new-ideas-spider-goats-mario-bros-dick-cheney-david-eagleman (accessed June 12, 2019).

possessing the computing power.[24] Copyright was a game rule written in the Western Enlightenment that matured during the 19th century Industrial Revolution before reaching China 111 years ago. Perhaps the next generation will witness the dawn of a post-copyright era.

Patents

Background of European and American Patents

Patenting is more a nuanced, complex and controversial form of IP protection than copyrighting. WIPO says that patents are *available* to protect IP

> … whether products or processes, in all fields of technology, provided that they are new, involve an inventive step and are capable of industrial application … [where] … the terms "inventive step" and "capable of industrial application" may be deemed by a Member to be synonymous with the terms "non-obvious" and "useful" respectively.[25]

Unlike copyright, patents are *not* automatic. The prospective patentee applies to a patent-granting authority. The authority then reviews the application and, subject to acceptance, grants the patent to the patentee. Far more so than copyrights, patents in China (and the rest of the world) are today active instruments of the management of innovation.

Patents to protect the IP of inventors were originally, in Europe, one type of "letters patent" issued by a monarch. The word "patent" means "open". Letters patent were open royal decrees, addressed to subjects at large, rather than sealed letters, meant only for the eyes of the receiver. In a letter patent, the sovereign decreed that the patentee had the rights of a monopolist to exclude others from specific activities.[26] During the era of early modern European imperialism — the mercantilist phase of capitalism — the decrees of letters patents had many functions. They could be

---

[24] He Tianxiang, "The Sentimental Fools and the Fictitious Authors: Rethinking Copyright Issues of AI-Generated Contents in China", *Asia Pacific Law Review* 27:2 (2019), 218–238.

[25] TRIPS, *op. cit.*, p. 331. "Member" refers to a country or a non-national territorial entity with separate WTO membership such as Hong Kong.

[26] Shannon Lee Dawdy and Joe Bonni, "Towards a General Theory of Piracy", *Anthropological Quarterly* 85:3 (Summer 2012), 673–699.

tools of patronage, sources of royal revenue or instruments of policy. They were not granted on request. There were no codified procedures for application. Letters patent decreed aristocratic titles, offices, and lands. They were used to create exclusive rights to sell specific products (e.g., tea, salt), to carry out activities in certain areas (e.g., Virginia, India, Hudson's Bay) and to take part in certain activities (including privateering rights against enemy states outside of the confines of war).

The first industrial patents granting monopoly rights over inventions were in Renaissance Venice, during the 15th century, concerning inventions in making glass, silk, medicines, and construction machinery, but these patents were to protect existing Venetian guild knowledge, to maintain the technological edge of the city, to stop industrial espionage and to prevent artisans from being enticed to foreign competitors. They involved no definitions of novelty or invention and no publication of the art — two important features of modern patents.[27] Letters patent were even used by competing sovereigns to grant monopolies to talented foreign artisans who had technologies the sovereign wished to foster. In a foreshadowing of the 1,000 Talents Program implemented by Beijing to attract persons with outstanding technological prowess in 2008,[28] letters patents were used by Renaissance European states to stimulate new industries by attracting skilled immigrants.[29]

Monopolies granted by letters patent could be phenomenally profitable to the patentee. They also could be highly unfair to those not granted the monopoly. And when the systems protecting the inequalities were challenged, contradictions could split societies. The revolutionaries of the 17th century English Civil War who decapitated their king, and the revolutionaries of the 13 British North American Colonies who declared

---

[27] J. Kostylo, "Commentary on the Venetian Statute on Industrial Brevets (1474)", in L. Bently and M. Kretschmer [editors] *Primary Sources on Copyright (1450–1900)*. www.copyrighthistory.org, 2008, accessed August 10, 2020. Hence, the English antecedent of modern patenting is only the first in the American direct legal line of decent, not the first in history.

[28] Jenny Leonard, "China's Thousand Talents Program Finally Gets the U.S.'s Attention", *Bloomberg Business Week*, December 12, 2019. https://www.bloomberg.com/news/articles/2019-12-12/china-s-thousand-talents-program-finally-gets-the-u-s-s-attention (accessed August 22, 2020).

[29] Christine MacLeod, *Inventing the Industrial Revolution: The English Patent System,* 1660–1800, Cambridge University Press, Cambridge, UK, 2002.

independence in 1776, both railed against the monopolies granted by letters patent.

1776 was the year that Adam Smith published his *Wealth of Nations*. Smith shared the optimism of the 18th century Enlightenment, that invention came not from the almighty provenance of God but from the applied ingenuity of man. And man's ingenuity could be stimulated by acts of government. Smith said that patents for inventors were

> … the easiest and most natural way the state can recompense them for hazarding a dangerous and expensive experiment…[30]

The fathers of the American revolution agreed. They wrote into the U.S. Constitution

> The Congress shall have the Power … To promote the Progress of Science and useful Arts, by securing for limited Times to Authors and Inventors the exclusive Right to their respective Writings and Discoveries.[31]

Shortly after that, the United States became the first country in the world to define and protect IP in a permanent national patent office[32] which evolved — through twists and turns[33] — into the U.S. Patents and Trademarks Office (USPTO) whose objective was explicitly (and democratically) to stimulate innovation. By the middle of the 20th century, the USPTO system, well patronized by the United States and foreign

---

[30] Adam Smith, *An Inquiry into the Nature and Causes of the Wealth of Nations*, ed. R.H. Campbell, A. S. Skinner, and W. B. Todd (2 vols., Oxford, 1976), vol. 2, p. 754.

[31] Constitution of the United States of America Article 1, section 8, clause 8.

[32] The British industrial patent "system" predated the American, but it was, until the mid-19th century, a system of royal conferrals of monopolies. The application process was complex, legalistic, and opaque until well after the Americans established their patent office.

[33] In 1793, the need for the patent board to review for novelty and usefulness was abolished until re-established by the patents act of 1843, which put in place the current USPTO system. The difficulties and changing definitions encountered with invention, usefulness, novelty, non-obviousness, the prior art, subsequent improvements, filing, awarding and defending industrial patents are put into 17th to 19th century context in Kenneth W. Dobyns, *History of the United States Patent Office*, 1994. http://www.myoutbox.net/popstart.htm (accessed August 22, 2020).

inventors and enforced by the U.S. courts, had become the invention protection standard of the market economies of the world. The inventor applied to a neutral but informed office (the USPTO) who determined whether the invention was new, useful and not obvious to one versed in the *prior art*. The prior art was a legal term meaning all publically available information concerning the area of knowledge advanced by the invention that was available prior to the date of filing the patent with the USPTO.[34] The grant of the patent conferred a monopoly to the patentee to use the IP for a limited time. The patent was published, giving a full enough description of the innovation to allow anyone versed in the prior art to replicate the invention. Thus the patent advanced the state of the art, granted a monopoly and encouraged progress through innovation.

By the mid-20th century, most western political philosophers agreed with most Americans that any inventor should have the right to apply for a patent. The inventor as patentee could then freely sell, license, or keep for exclusive use the protected IP.

Patents in China since the Revolution

The revolutionaries who established the People's Republic of China,[35] however, had a different opinion. Marxists believed patents were an appropriation of IP by those whose social class gave them the resources necessary for invention. And they believed that the state of the art was a

---

[34]As a legal term "prior art" is defined separately (but not necessarily independently) by each country which separately issues patents. WIPO lists 116 different definition of prior art (see "Prior Art", *Certain Aspects of National/Regional Patent Laws*, WIPO. https://www.wipo.int/export/sites/www/scp/en/national_laws/prior_art.pdf, accessed August 25, 2020) one for each patenting jurisdiction. Some countries (like China) have multiple jurisdictions (China, Hong Kong, and Macau), while others such as the European Patent Organization serve multiple countries. For a summary of the *principles* of prior art, see Yumiko Hamano, "Use of Patent Information for Technology Management", Innovation and Technology Transfer Section, Patent Division, WIPO, 2009 (accessed August 27, 2020). https://www.wipo.int/edocs/mdocs/aspac/en/wipo_ip_cm_09/wipo_ip_cm_09_topic7_01.pdf.

[35]Prior to the revolution, there had been Chinese patent laws. In 1889, the Guangxu Emperor protected some shipping inventions and in Republican China, western style IP legislation was passed from 1928 to 1944. See Chris Devonshire-Ellis, Andy Scott, and Sam Woollard [eds.] *Intellectual Property Rights in China*, Asia Briefing Ltd. 2011.

public commons that should be available freely to all. They looked to the USSR for inspiration.

Following their victory over Germany in the Second World War the allies split. The USSR confronted the West in a new, cold, war. In 1950, the CPC and the USSR formed Sino-Soviet alliance. A key project of that alliance was the largest state-to-state transfer of technology in world history with

> the transfer of entire designs; shipment of manufacturing technology and equipment; deployment of experts to instruct Chinese during construction, installation, and debugging of equipment; and training and instruction of Chinese technical and administrative cadres and workers during trial production. Thus, the Soviet Union provided China with designs and manufacturing or processing technology for such industries as alloy steel and petroleum products, heavy machinery, machine tools, measuring and cutting tools, power plants, electric generators, mining machines, oil extracting and oil refining devices, trucks, caterpillar tractors, locomotives, instruments, bearings, switches, rectifiers, films, heavy artillery, tanks, tank engines, fighter jets, airplane engines, and rockets.[36]

The scale was massive — over 7% of USSR national income from the 1950s through the early 1960s, paid for with loans to and commodity exports from China.

And the cost of the IP acquisition? Zero! There were no patents or copyright involved. The only costs for IP transfer were for the ***physical copying and translating*** of blueprints, drawings, designs, specifications, data, manuals, textbooks, research studies, etc. More than 10,000 Soviet experts moved to China to effect the transfer while 10,000 elite Chinese moved to the USSR to study.[37]

The Chinese implemented Soviet models of social-political organization. The party–government structure and the successive five-year centralized planning system were also imported. And so were Soviet rules on patenting. Notwithstanding ideological Marxist resistance to patenting — based on a general distrust of private property — the Soviets

[36] Zhang Baichun, Zhang Jiuchun and Yao Fang, "Technology Transfer from the USSR to the People's Republic of China 1949–1966", *Comparative Technology Transfer and Society*, 4:2 (2006), 115.

[37] *Ibid.*

believed that knowledge producers — both physical and intellectual workers — should be incentivized to innovate. Their compromise was adopted by China.

The rule was to let the inventor choose between receiving from the government either a patent or a certificate of authorship. The patent gave the patentee the right to exclude others from using the IP. The certificate of authorship surrendered the IP to the state, but gave the inventor prestige, privileges, and some pecuniary benefits. In practice, the choice was illusory. In a regime where the rules for exclusive use of patented IP were unclear, where hording private property was an anathema, where the practice of donating private property to the cause of building New China was common, and where policies could change rapidly with potentially devastating consequences, the great, glorious, and correct choice was the certificate of authorship.[38] In 1960 the Sino-Soviet alliance came to an abrupt end. Yet Soviet structures and IP rules set up in the 1950s stayed in China for the next two decades.

China Adopts World Standards of Patents

The reform and opening up of the 1980s shifted China to a market orientation that naturally led to implementing market economy models of IP protection, starting with the first patent law of 1985. Amendments in 2000 to facilitate Chinese entry into WTO aligned Chinese legislation with TRIPS. Since the 10th Five-Year Plan (2001–2005), the Chinese central government has urged local governments to stimulate innovation by encouraging patent filing, a call that has led the vast majority of provincial level governments to subsidize parts of the patent application process.[39] Since WTO entry, there have been two additional amendments, in 2008 and 2019, keeping abreast of international IP developments.

---

[38] Tao-tai Hsia and Katheryn A. Hsia, *op. cit.*

[39] The rules, timing of implementation, amounts, fees, whether they are domestic or domestic and foreign, reimbursement procedures, etc. vary by province. Jia Lin, Ho-mou Wu, and Howei Wu, "China's Patent Subsidy Policy and Its Impacts on Invention and Patent Quality", CEIBS Working Paper, April 5, 2019. https://www.ceibs.edu/sites/portal.prod.dpmgr.ceibs.edu/files/import_images/seminar/patent_lww_2019april_ver3_3.pdf (accessed September 9, 2020) demonstrate that both the quantity *and quality* of patents have been positively affected by implementation of the subsidy policies.

China has two patent durations: 10 years and 20 years. The utility patent, modeled on the German concept to protect innovations that concern a product's shape, structure, or combination of both, and the design patent that protects innovation in a product's aesthetics (i.e., shape, design, color, etc.), give patentees 10-year monopoly use of IP. These 10-year life patents have a relatively low threshold of novelty and CNIPA may (but is not obliged to) conduct a search to verify the applicant's claims. The invention patent gives the patentee 20 years' IP protection and requires a higher threshold of novelty: CNIPA conducts a full patent search to verify technical validity of claims before granting the patent. Recent amendments allow up to 5-year extensions to invention patents applied to pharmaceuticals based on the post-filing regulatory approval period which would otherwise shorten the effective life of IP protection for new drugs.[40]

About half of the approximately 3 million invention patents filed in the world each year are filed in China.[41] Moreover, the annual increase of Chinese patent filings (11%) is greater than its nearest competitors: India (7.5%) and the European Patent Office (4.7%). In terms of patent filing intensity — patents filed per dollar of GDP — China is second in the world to Korea, followed by Japan, Germany, Switzerland, the United States, and Finland in that order. However, because of its early lead and the up to 20 lifespan of patents, more patents are in force today in the United States (3.2 million) than in China (2.4 million) or third place Japan (2.1 million).[42] Figure 3.1 shows the breakdown of national patent filings in 2019.

Patenting in a Global Environment

There is no such thing as an international patent. There are, however, international standards of patenting which are adhered to by WTO-compliant

[40]Drug trials typically take from three to six years. See "How Long to Clinical Trial Phases Take", *Antidote*. https://www.antidote.me/blog/how-long-do-clinical-trial-phases-take (accessed August 27, 2020). With the extension, a drug company whose patented drug took six years to complete clinical tests could apply for its patent to last 25 years from filing, instead of 20, to compensate for not receiving royalties during the clinical trial years. This is based on the U.S. Hatch-Waxman Act of 1984.

[41]These figures refer only to invention (i.e., 20 years) patents, ignoring design and utility patents, which are not subject to PCT described below. Different jurisdictions treatment of design and utility patents differ and their standard of innovation is lower, so they are typically ignored in international comparisons.

[42]WIPO, *World Intellectual Property Indicators 2019*, Geneva, 2019, pp. 16–19.

Figure 3.1: Patents Applied

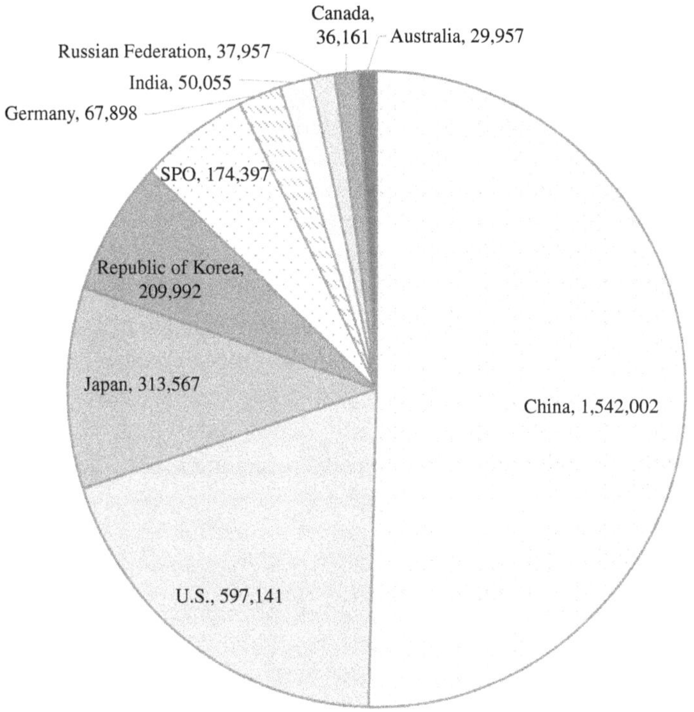

Source: "Facts and Figures" *WIPO Website* accessed September 4, 2020. https://www.wipo.int/edocs/infogdocs/en/ipfactsandfigures2019/.

jurisdictions. China's patent system, administered by CNIPA, is a WTO-compliant jurisdiction.

The lack of international patents presents a problem to the inventor. The prior art, on which the inventor must demonstrate novelty when applying for a patent, is global. The prior art incorporates ***all*** relevant, prior, publicly available knowledge (including previously patented IP) in ***all*** parts of the world.[43] Yet each patent grants the patentee monopoly rights only in the country of patent issue. A Chinese patent gives no protection in Europe or the United States or any other of the more than

[43] This requirement can be extremely onerous and is at the core of the inequitable conduct defense of patent infringement leading to many patents being invalidated. If the defendant in an infringement lawsuit can show that the patent application omitted relevant prior art then the patent is deemed to be fraudulently obtained and is therefore invalid. See Eric Johnson, "The Case for Eliminating Patent Law's Inequitable Conduct Defense", *Columbia Law Review*, New York 117:1 (2017), 1–21.

150 patent granting jurisdictions of the world. And a U.S. patent similarly gives no protection in China (or elsewhere).

Take the case of an inventor who files a patent in the US but does not file in China.[44] Say a Chinese manufacturer, well versed in the state of the art, reads the granted US patent — which is extremely easy because all approved USPTO patents are posted online.[45] If the Chinese manufacturer then uses the invention from the USPTO patent in a product manufactured and sold in China, the US inventor has no legal recourse against the Chinese manufacturer because, from the Chinese point of view, the IP in China is in the public domain. No theft occurs: the information in the US patent is simply part of the freely available current state of the art. If, however, the Chinese manufacture exports that product to the US, and if the US patent has not yet expired, the US inventor has legal recourse. He may ask his lawyer to write a cease and desist letter and, if the Chinese manufacturer-exporter does not desist, the patentee can sue the Chinese manufacturer for patent infringement — in U.S. courts for the U.S. infringement.

Similarly, if a Chinese inventor patents her invention in China with CNIPA but does not file with USPTO in the United States, the Chinese inventor has no recourse against a U.S. company using the invention in the United States, without the Chinese patentee's permission. The Chinese invention is simply part of the unprotected state of the art in the United States. Any American can freely go to the CNIPA website and read the contents of any patented Chinese invention.[46] But the U.S. businessperson cannot legally sell products that rely on that patented IP in China if the CNIPA patent has not expired.

---

[44] This is not unusual. As C. Devonshire-Ellis et al. notes in *Intellectual Property Rights in China*, Asia Briefing Ltd., 2011, pp. 1–2 notes, "Surveys conducted by national chambers of commerce reveal that companies throughout the United States and Europe do not use existing legal measures to protect and defend their IPR [intellectual property rights] in China. Although the risk of IPR infringement is widely known, a vast majority of companies doing business in the country have not filed their IP rights here, citing high costs as one of the main reasons". But note below that costs, while considerable, are no greater than in European and U.S. jurisdictions.

[45] See USPTO Full Text and Image Database. http://patft.uspto.gov/netahtml/PTO/search-bool.html (accessed August 22, 2020).

[46] See China National Intellectual Property Administration China Patent Registry http://pss-system.cnipa.gov.cn/sipopublicsearch/inportal/i18n.shtml?params=902F004CA61084A284089435EAAEA94F59CC921A916ADCEB (accessed December 14, 2021).

Effective patents are expensive to file. Filing fees are shown in Table 3.1.

Far more expensive than the filing fees, however, are the legal fees for the patent practitioner which range from about a thousand U.S. dollars to well over US$20,000 per patent, based on the hours spent by the lawyer or patent practitioner. At large firms, legal fees range from ¥ 2,200 per hour for a junior associate to ¥ 6,000 per hour for a managing partner.[47]

An inventor can file for a patent herself, but the vast majority use lawyers/practitioners, because self-filers are unlikely to succeed in their applications and, if they do succeed, are likely not to sufficiently protect the very IP that constitutes their inventions.[48] The lawyer/practitioner is familiar with not only patent law and filing practice, but with the state of the art. This familiarity requires substantial expertise and research on existing patents, not only in the country of filing but (at least in theory) in every other country in the world active in advancing the art. An inventor increases the cost of patenting in more than one jurisdiction because of multiple filing and legal fees. The decisions of whether or not to file, what to file, and where to file are critical to a company's IP strategy.

Timing of filing with a patent authority is important. The inventor must file before the invention enters the public domain (for example by publication or by the secret leaking out of the company) and before any-one else files the same invention. Yet in a rapidly changing market, the inventor may not know if the value of the invention exceeds the cost of filing. And because the world has more than 150 patent jurisdictions, holding an option to file in any of those different jurisdictions while delaying payment of filing costs is valuable. The TRIPS Patent Cooperation Treaty (PCT) application procedure establishes that option.

The PCT application is not an international patent. It is a global *option* to file national patents. The inventor reserves the right to file anywhere in the world within the next 30 months and receives from the PCT authority

---

[47] "Survey of Law Firm Billing Rates in China", *China Business Law Journal*, December 13, 2017. https://www.vantageasia.com/law-firm-billing-rates-china-2017/ (accessed September 13, 2020). This places Chinese legal fees at less than 60% of U.S. fees. See "2020 Attorney Hourly Rate Report", *Business Wire*. https://www.businesswire.com/news/home/20191219005415/en/2020-Attorney-Hourly-Rate-Report---2019.

[48] See Jon J. Lee, "An Empirical Study of Patent and Trademark Discipline", *Boston Law College Review* 61:5 (2020).

Table 3.1: Patent Filing Fees in Four Jurisdictions

		Fees							
Jurisdiction	Currency	Transmittal	International Filing	Search Fee	Preliminary Examination	Handling Fee	Sum in Domestic Currency	Exchange Rate to USD	USD
China	CNY	—	9,975	2,100	1,500	200	13,775	0.1500	2,066.25
European Union	EUR	135	1,217	1,775	1,830	183	5,140	1.1800	6,065.20
Japan	JPY	10,000	1,43,200	70,000	26,000	21,500	2,70,700	0.0094	2,544.58
US	USD	240	1,337	2,080	600	201	4,458	1.000	4,458.00

Notes: does not include discounts offered for small and micro entities International filling of China stated in CHF not CNY converted at CNY 7.5 per CHF gives cost for domestic language; foreign language may double costs as in Japan PCT Fee Tables (amounts on August 27, 2020, unless otherwise indicated) *https*://www.wipo.int/export/sites/www/pct/en/fees.pdf.

Source: WIPO PCT Fee Table, 2020. https://www.wipo.int/export/sites/www/pct/en/fees.pdf (accessed September 9, 2020).

(which is the national patent office) an opinion on patentability. Both the report and the lapse of time are valuable to the inventor planning his patenting strategy.

China leads the world in PCT filings with 58,990 in 2019 (edging out the United States for the first time since PCT was set up in 1978). Huawei Technologies of Shenzhen was the largest filer of PCTs in the world, with 2661 applications followed, in order, by Mitsubishi Electric of Japan, Samsung Electronics of Korea, and Qualcomm of the United States.

Chinese and European patentees are far more likely to use the PCT option when filing overseas than Americans. While less than 40% of Americans enter Japan, China, and Korea through the PCT route, over 60% of Chinese enter the United States through the PCT.

Issues Concerning Patenting

Rules of the game change. Patenting is no exception. Philosophies, theories, norms, practices, institutions, and technologies evolve challenging those trying to write fair and effective IP rules. Below I discuss three issues in current patent law evolution: commercializing technology developed in publicly funded university/research labs, balancing public welfare with private profits in pharmaceuticals, and stemming the rising tide of frivolous patents. These issues are familiar to those both in China and the rest of the world.

Commercializing Publicly Funded Technology: The Bayh–Dole Act. Chinese universities and state-sponsored research institutes have risen over the last forty years to rough equivalence with Western universities and state-sponsored research institutes in terms of PCT filings. Of the top 50 universities in the world filing PCTs in 2019, 20 were in the United States while 14 were in China. The top two were Chinese, Shenzhen University and Tsinghua University, followed by University of California, MIT and South China University of Technology in that order. In terms of state-owned research organizations, China's Shenzhen Institute of Advanced Technology is in second place behind Germany's Fraunhofer-Gesellschaft zur Förderung der angewandten Forschung. France's Commissariat à l'Énergie Atomique et aux Énergies Alternatives and

Singapore's Agency for Science, Technology and Research are in third and fourth place.[49]

A PCT filing is one measure of successful innovation and at least a *step* in the direction of global commercialization. This rise to the top of innovation in the world *by this one measure* is an amazing achievement for a country ridiculed just a few years ago by leading Harvard academics as being unable to innovate.[50] How does China motivate government-employed researchers to use inventions made in state-owned facilities to innovate, patent, and create value in the economy?

China follows the United States lead. In the United States prior to 1980, only a very small percent of research patented by universities and state-owned research institutes was transferred to the economy because the IP belonged to the government that owned the university or research institute. Large portfolios of unused patents built up. In 1980, U.S. senators Birch Bayh (a Democrat) and Bob Dole (a Republican) co-sponsored the Bayh–Dole Act, allowing individuals and corporate entities that developed technologies with federal funding to enjoy the patent rights of their inventions, sharing non-exclusive rights of usage with the government.[51] This small but important innovation was replicated in China in 1998 with the passage of the Science and Technology Advancement Law — Chinese version of the Bayh-Dole Act. In the first five years after the law was passed over 100,000 science and technology researchers from over 1,000 research institutes moved into the private sector, founding private companies to commercialize their newly acquired IP.[52]

Health Policy Exemptions for Drugs. Although the principle of patenting was generally established more than 250 years ago, its application to

[49] WIPO *Patent Cooperation Treaty Yearly Review 2020*, Geneva, 2020 https://www.wipo.int/publications/en/details.jsp?id=4508 (accessed September 4, 2020).

[50] Regina Abrami, William Kirby and Warren McFarlan, "Why China Can't Innovate", *Harvard Business Review*, 2014 https://hbr.org/2014/03/why-china-cant-innovate (accessed May 1, 2021).

[51] General Office of Accounting of the US Government, *Technology Transfer: Administration of the Bayh-Dole Act by Research Universities* 1998 https://www.gao.gov/products/rced-98-126 (accessed December 14, 2021).

[52] Keith E. Maskus, "China's Uneasy Engagement with Intellectual Property Reforms during Its Globalization", *The Brown Journal of World Affairs*, Providence 22:2 (2016), 137–159.

pharmaceuticals and medical equipment occurred much later. Medical doctors in Europe and North American, through the 19th and the first half of the 20th century considered it ***immoral*** to profit from patenting drugs and medical equipment for the simple reason that reaping monopoly profits from alleviation of suffering compounded the suffering. In those simpler times, medical associations shared this view.[53] Notwithstanding the Western medical profession's current acceptance, if not welcoming, of patents, distaste for big pharma's profits from patents remains widespread, blending into fringe conspiracy theories.[54] The rules of the game have evolved to support the changing ethics.

The manufacture and sale of a generic drug — a drug identical to a patented drug, but produced by a company different from the patent holder and bearing a different name — would generally violate a valid, unexpired, patent in the same jurisdiction. Yet the generic drug, like any drug, needs to obtain regulatory approval prior to being sold. That regulatory approval may take years to obtain. And such a lapse of time would give the patent holder an effective extension of the patent period. To forestall this free, unintended monopoly, Bolar exemptions[55] are granted to allow companies to manufacture *and test* generic drugs prior to patented drugs' patent expiry. Chinese patent law incorporated Bolar exemptions in the third amendment of 2008. More generally, in most countries of the world, including China, if health emergencies justify it, patents can and

---

[53] See Gabriel, Joseph M. "Pharmaceutical Patenting and the Transformation of American Medical Ethics", *BJHS* 49:4 (December 2016), 577–600. Salk was advised by his lawyer that he could not patent the polio vaccine and justified it on moral grounds by asking "could you patent the sun", Jane Smith *Patenting the Sun*, Zero Vector, 1990.

Banting, Collip, and Best, the inventors of insulin in 1923, did patent it, but then sold the patent to University of Toronto for $1.00. See Banting, Best, and Collip "Q10013_0001: Assignment to the Governors of the University of Toronto", University of Toronto Archives, 1923. https://insulin.library.utoronto.ca/islandora/object/insulin%3AQ10013 (accessed September 20, 2020).

[54] Robert Blaskiewicz, "The Big Pharma Conspiracy Theory", *Medical Writing* 22: 4, 2013.

[55] Named after Roche Products, Inc. Appellant, v. Bolar Pharmaceutical Co., U.S. Court of Appeals for the Federal Circuit — 733 F.2d 858 (Fed. Cir. 1984), April 23, 1984. https://law.justia.com/cases/federal/appellate-courts/F2/733/858/459501/ (accessed September 20, 2020).

will be set aside in the public interest. Private property, including IP, is a right granted by the state. The state gives. The state can take away.

COVID-19 brings into relief public health concerns and the incentive structure of patenting. The global pandemic brought companies into the vaccine race — the biggest race for innovation in drugs that the world has ever seen. And public health and political issues, far more than the market for IP, drives the distribution of successful vaccines. Of the over 30 vaccines in human trials worldwide as of August 2020, most used public funds for private development.[56] Of the three Chinese companies in Stage 3 testing as of late August 2020, two were private and one was an SOE. Both Chinese private companies and SOEs are among the investors in major non-Chinese vaccine developers.[57] And there has yet to be a clear policy in the innovating countries concerning how the drugs are to be priced and the profits shared.

Patent enforcement, portfolios and frivolity. China has a bifurcated patent enforcement system: patent validity is established in litigation by the Patent Re-Examination Board (PRB) of CNIPA whereas patent infringement is established separately in the law courts. A patentee may file an infringement claim against an alleged infringing company. That company may then respond by filing a petition with the PRB alleging patent invalidity. The two actions would proceed independently and simultaneously in the two systems with the court judgement on infringement, if it is in the patentee's favor, enforced only if the validity of the patent is confirmed by the PRB. The bifurcated system follows the Japanese, Korean, and German models and is different from the U.S. and U.K. models, where validity and infringement are determined in the same court, in the same proceedings.

Most patents in the world are found to be invalid in litigation — administrative and/or judicial. Recent empirical studies showed that in China, 50.9% and 11.9% were determined to be completely and partly

---

[56]Ana Santos Rutschman, "The Covid-19 Vaccine Race: Intellectual Property, Collaboration(s), Nationalism and Misinformation", *Washington University Journal of Law and Policy* 64, 2020.

[57]Marc Greeven, "Inside the Chinese Companies Vying to Produce the World's First Coronavirus Vaccine", *The Conversation,* August 28, 2020. https://theconversation.com/inside-the-chinese-companies-vying-to-produce-the-worlds-first-coronavirus-vaccine-145146 (accessed September 20, 2020).

invalid respectively, leaving 37.2% of patents maintaining validity.[58] Because, in the judicial phase, 80% of cases, infringement was found in valid patents,[59] one can conclude that in China, where patents are litigated, the success rate of litigation defense ranges from about 30% (0.372 × 0.8 = 0.2976) to 40% (0.491 × 0.8 = 0.3928) of patents, with 60%–70% being ineffective. In the United States, which has a unitary system, about 80% of patents that go to court are found to be invalid or unenforceable.[60]

Asserting patent validity, regardless of jurisdiction, is expensive, time consuming, opaque, and somewhat random. For example, the famous case of Apple versus Samsung over cellphone technology in the United States was fought for seven years, racking up hundreds of millions of dollars of legal fees before being settled out of court for an undisclosed amount. No product was ever taken off the market.

China's patenting system, modeled on the U.S. system (and internationalized by WIPO), suffers from similar problems. In China, it normally takes from 6 to 18 months from petitioning a court to the ruling in the court of first instance. While this is slightly shorter than most other jurisdictions in the world and much shorter than in the United Kingdom and the United States (24–36 and 18–42 months, respectively), such a lapse of time can be critical in business. And it is expensive. Average costs in the first instance in China tend to be in the US$20,000 to US$150,000 range. Again, this is below the cost in other jurisdictions and far below the United Kingdom and the United States (US$1–2 million and US$1–6 million, respectively).[61] The high cost leads patentee companies to litigate only a very small fraction of patent violations — those where

---

[58] Bian Renjun, "Post-Grant Patent Review in China: An Empirical Analysis", *Queen Mary Journal of Intellectual Property* 10:3, 339–375.

[59] Bian Renjun, "Patent Litigation in China: Challenging Conventional Wisdom". *Berkeley Technology Law Journal*, 33:2 (2018), 413–486. Interestingly, Bian finds that foreign patent holders of Chinese patents had a higher (but not statistically higher) rates being upheld in courts against alleged infringement, eroding support for the belief that Chinese courts are biased against foreign litigants. This is contrary to the often expressed view that Chinese IP courts and arbitration panels are systematically prejudiced against foreign parties. See, for example Tang Zheng, "Judicial Enforcement of Intellectual Property Rights in China — From Technical Improvement to Institutional Reform", *Asia Pacific Law Review*, Hong Kong 27:2 (2019), 176–197.

[60] WIPO, "An Overview of Patent Litigation Systems across Jurisdictions", *WIPO World IP Indicators*, Geneva, 2018, pp. 12–22.

[61] *Ibid.*

patentee company is confident enough of victory to spend the money and time. So stronger patents tend to be litigated, suggesting that estimates of the percent of patents that are valid are over-statements.

Companies are under pressure to build ever-increasing patent portfolios, if for no other reasons than for defense: they need large portfolios to protect themselves in litigation. Both Huawei[62] and Google[63] have over 50,000 patents in force. And both are aggressively expanding their portfolio for the reasons expressed by Google senior patent council, Susanne Michele:

> if everybody else is running after every trivial patent and building a big portfolio, you have to too. What that does is put lots and lots of trivial patents out into the world, which you can't maintain, because the maintenance fees are too high, so you sell them off to trolls, who then go and litigate them forever, and that's happening more and more and more....[64]

The global patenting game, as joined by China, is increasingly expensive. Much of the expense involves what Baumol would call destructive entrepreneurship.[65]

Trademarks

Trademarks are the simplest form of IP. WIPO defines a trademark as "... a sign capable of distinguishing the goods or services of one enterprise

[62] Susan Decker, "Huawei Has 56,492 Patents and It's Not Afraid to Use Them", Bloomberg, June 15, 2019. https://www.bloomberg.com/news/articles/2019-06-14/huawei-has-56-492-patents-and-it-s-not-afraid-to-use-them (accessed September 20, 2020).

[63] Antonio Regalado, "Google's Growing Patent Stockpile: The Search Giant Says Patents Are Rubbish. Yet It's Accumulating More of Them than Ever", *MIT Technology Review*, November 2013 https://www.technologyreview.com/2013/11/29/175273/googles-growing-patent-stockpile/ (accessed September 20, 2020).

[64] Suzanne Michel, Senior Patent Counsel, Google, American University Washington College of Law Symposium, 2013. https://media.wcl.american.edu/Mediasite/Play/09bc7a3e-f0f2-4fd7-ad33-a650e705789e.

[65] William J. Baumol, "Entrepreneurship: Productive, Unproductive and Destructive", *Journal of Political Economy*, 98:5 (1990), 893.

from those of other enterprises".[66] A violation of trademark IP that successfully deceives the buyer of the good or service is the most incontrovertibly immoral act among IP violations: it is fraud. There is less moral or philosophical defense for trademark violations than for copyright or patent violations. Non-Chinese, looking at China's IP landscape, are most morally outraged when they see violation of trademark IP.

Trademarks have pervaded Chinese art, crafts, and manufacturing for two and a half millennia. Seals or "chops" have been used in China to certify documents and works of art since at least 544 BC.[67] Traditional pharmacy companies Guang Yu Yuan, Chen Li Ji, Tong Ren Tong, and Hu Qing Yu Tong, founded in 1541, 1600, 1669, and 1874, respectively are four of over 1,000 traditional Chinese brands with over a century of history that are still in use today.[68] China's most valuable brand, Kweichow Maotai,[69] is far more recent. It dates from the post-1949 collectivization of various distilleries in Guizhou Province into one SOE that became the preferred supplier of unique, distilled spirits to CPC banquets.[70] Today, the company, listed on the Shanghai Stock Exchange, is among the most valuable in China by market capitalization — over ¥2 Trillion as of mid 2020. The value flows from its iconic brand.[71]

A running joke in China is that the Maotai served even at well-respected restaurants is not likely to be *real* Maotai. With the cost of real Maotai running at over ten times the price of counterfeit Maotai, it's easy to understand the restaurateur's calculations even as authorities pursue criminal gangs breaking trademark regulations to supply the *mao pai*

---

[66] WIPO, "Trademarks: What Is a Trademark?" WIPO Website: https://www.wipo.int/trademarks/en/ (accessed September 21, 2020).

[67] "Chinese Seals", *China Online Museum*. http://www.chinaonlinemuseum.com/carving-seals.php (accessed September 21, 2020).

[68] Guangyuyuan 广誉远, Chen Li Ji 陈李济 Tong Ren Tong 同仁堂, and Hu Qing Yu Tong 胡庆余堂 were the four great medical houses of the Qing Dynasty. "China's Time Honoured Brands", *Baidu*. https://baike.baidu.com/item/中华老字号/9535297 (accessed September 21, 2020).

[69] "Kweichow Maotai" is the old Wade-Giles Romanization of Guizhou Maotai 贵州茅台, which continues to be used in its English trademark.

[70] Derek Sandhaus, "Unearthing China's Ancient Terroir in Maotai", *Punch,* August 19, 2014. https://punchdrink.com/articles/unearthing-chinas-ancient-terroir-in-maotai/ (accessed September 21, 2020).

[71] Tom Hancock, "Liquor Group Kweichow Moutai's Market Valuation Tops $200bn", *Financial Times,* August 23, 2019.

Maotai.[72] Ever since foreigners forced the Chinese market open in the 19th century, selling their branded products, they too have grappled with the difficulties — made greater by their foreignness — of enforcing trademark IP. The trademark law of 1904 was written more than a century ago by the British who ran the Chinese Maritime Customs office under the Qing Dynasty's Ministry of Foreign Affairs — a concession of sovereignty that was part of the settlement of the Boxer Rebellion.[73] In the 1920s, Republican China, though at war itself, passed laws essentially to provide foreign trademark IP holders with legal protection.

Notwithstanding its long trademark history and sporadic attempts in the early 20th century to implement western-style laws, trademarks in China prior to the 1990s were enforced by custom and extra-legal moral suasion, not law. It was only when China moved toward WTO entry that China implemented modern, western-inspired trademark IP laws. IP law in China today tracks TRIPS guidelines. Like copyright and patents, trademarks are the responsibility of the CNIPA, where they may be registered for terms of 10 years which can be renewed indefinitely. Trademarks are protected in law if they are registered. However, if an applicant attempts to register a trademark that has been in use by another entity and is widely recognized for belonging to that other entity, then CNIPA may deny the applicant. Even if it fails to do so, an entity with a prior, *un*registered claim, can still pursue remedy in the courts if it feels that its trademark has been misappropriated.

Yet today, trademark piracy — especially piracy of foreign trademarks — is rampant in China. Why?

Since the early 1980s, when China's special economic zones emerged as export processing zones, connected to global supply chains, Chinese entrepreneurs have been laser-focused on meticulously following the specifications of original equipment manufacturers (OEMs)[74] while

---

[72]"*Mao pai*" 冒牌 is Chinese for "fake brand". "The amount involved reaches 60 million! A gang selling counterfeit Moutai liquor in Shanghai was taken", Sina Web, October 8, 2019. https://finance.sina.com.cn/stock/relnews/cn/2019-10-18/doc-iicezuev3050613.shtml (accessed September 21, 2020).

[73]Robert Heuser, "The Chinese Trademark Law of 1904: A Preliminary Study in Exterritoriality, Competition, and Late Ch'ing Law Reform", *Oriens Extremus*, 22:2 (1975), 183–210. https://www.jstor.org/stable/43382411 (accessed September 21, 2020).

[74]The term "the OEM" may refer to the owner of the brand of the final product that outsources its production to parts suppliers and assemblers, or it may be the assembler of the

relentlessly forcing down their costs of production and searching for new profitable markets. The OEMs were typically off-shore foreign companies. The Chinese factories were manned by new arrivals from the countryside: peasants, with minimal secondary and no post-secondary education. Their wages were meager and their living conditions poor. The processes they learned were highly labor intensive and they learned them well. When the entrepreneurial souls among these migrant laborers spotted chances to better themselves, by taking their hard-earned knowledge into their own new companies, they did so. Manufacturing, distribution, and market knowledge rapidly spread into mushrooming new ventures.

If a Chinese supplier to an OEM could cut corners to increase margins, the supplier would do so. If a process could be subcontracted more cheaply than by keeping it in-house, it was subcontracted. If a domestic market or alternative foreign market could be penetrated with the products originally supplied to the OEM — without destroying a profitable relationship with the OEM — it was penetrated. And if it were not possible for the existing supplier to supply those new markets without destroying profitable OEM relationships, then the entrepreneurial souls in the existing supplier would typically start a new company to supply those new markets. For those suppliers — new and old — the design, the labels, the hang-tags, and the packaging, all of the items going to make up the trademark were just sets of specifications to be followed meticulously. And all the while the Chinese suppliers relentlessly forced down costs of production, while searching for new profitable opportunities.[75]

final product that outsources parts supplies but allows a value-added reseller to place brand the final product. In either case, however, the OEM is critical to determining the specifications of the product and communicates these specifications to parts suppliers and/or assemblers. See Julia Kagen, "Original Equipment Manufacturer (OEM)", *Investopedia*, July 28, 2020. https://www.investopedia.com/terms/o/oem.asp (accessed September 21, 2020).

[75]The Pirates of the Middle Kingdom series catalogues the decades-long struggle against counterfeiting of goods from the viewpoint of a highly informed, leading IP lawyer with a leading American law firm, Baker MacKenzie. See Tan Loke Khoon, *Pirates in the Middle Kingdom: The New Frontier*, Thomson Reuters, Hong Kong, 2017; Tan Loke Khoon, *Pirates in the Middle Kingdom: The Enusing Trademark Battle*, Sweet & Maxwell, 2007; Tan Loke Khoon, *Pirates in the Middle Kingdom: The Art of Trademark War*, Sweet & Maxwell, Hong Kong, 2004.

The copycat culture has a "Robin Hood" style ethos, known as "*shanzhai*". The term comes from Chinese and literally means "mountain village".[76] It harks back to the Ming Dynasty novel *The Water Margin* which tells the story of Song Dynasty bandits of the 14th century resisting the Mongol invaders who had taken over China. But in its modern concept, *shanzhai* is about nimble production with little concern for IP. The concept is one of copying from a mountain hideout, where the copying involves creativity, innovation, and Chinese national pride in the innovative copy. The copier surpasses rivals through mixture of imitation and innovation. Shanzhai is open and fun, operating with "Shenzhen speed". The rapid design, prototyping, and production processes are enabled by cooperation between suppliers, designers, and factory owners in an informal supply network.[77] The protagonists succeed because, as the old Chinese saying at the beginning of the chapter notes, "Heavens are high. The emperor is far away. People are few. Our friends are many".[78]

Law enforcement against trademark infringement requires catching manufacturers and distributors with the infringing product. But if they are disbursed, vigilant, informed, and on better terms with local authorities than the plaintiffs, the difficulty is increased. Chinese exporters are estimated to account for 72% of the US$461 billion trade in counterfeit goods,[79] implying that, if domestically sold counterfeit goods were added to the number it would even be higher. Production of counterfeit goods is an embarrassment to the CPC and the national government and a continuing source of friction with other countries in the world; hence, the CPC and the national government continue to tighten trademark IP education, legislation, and enforcement.

---

[76] *Shanzhai* 山寨.

[77] See in Chinese "What is Shanzhai", MBA Website: https://wiki.mbalib.com/zh-tw/山寨 (accessed September 21, 2020). For a highly accessible English language treatment of shanzhai concerning one of the leading DNA sequencing companies in the world, headquartered in Shenzhen, see Hallam Stevens, "Starting Up Biology in China: Performances of Life at BGI", *Osiris* University of Chicago Press, 33:1 (2018). https://www.journals.uchicago.edu/doi/10.1086/699235?mobileUi=0 (accessed September 21, 2020).

[78] See footnote 3.

[79] Global intellectual property center *Measuring the Magnitude of Global Counterfeiting* US Chamber of Commerce, 2016. https://www.uschamber.com/sites/default/files/documents/files/measuringthemagnitudeofglobalcounterfeiting.pdf (accessed September 21, 2020).

Figure 3.2: WIPO Trademark Filing Activity in 2019 (millions of trademarks field)

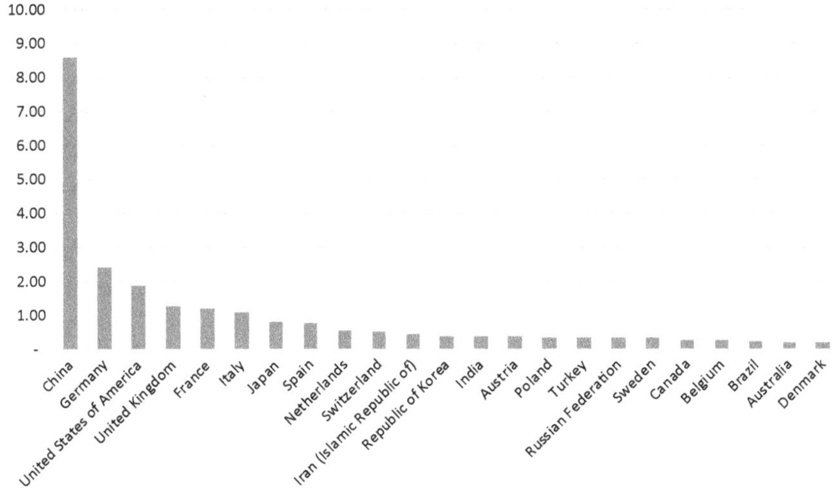

Source: WIPO World Intellectual Property Indicators 2020.

One of the initiatives of promoting IP laws on trademarks has been to encourage entrepreneurs to register their own trademarks by setting fees low and making registration of new trademarks easy.

In mid-2012, the Guangdong High People's Court recorded that the U.S. company Apple had ended its dispute with Proview, a Taiwanese-owned company registered in Shenzhen, concerning Proview's registration in China of the trademark "iPad" by paying a US$60-million out-of-court settlement to Proview. In return, Proview transferred the trademark "iPad" to Apple.[80]

The news rang out the shot of a starting gun in a gold rush! In a demonstration of the law of unintended consequences, hundreds of thousands of entrepreneurs staked claims over trademarks close to famous brands, that they hoped the brand owners might find useful enough to pay for. Companies with legitimate products or plans moved defensively to delineate the trademark territory they wished to own. The result has been to make China far and away the largest register of trademark IP in the world. By 2019, as Figure 3.2 shows, China was registering more than 8 million

[80]"Apple Settles iPadH Trademark Case with $60m", *ip4all Intellectual Property Portal, IP Network News*, Taiwan, October 10, 2012. http://ip4all.com/apple-settles-ipad-trademark-case-with-60m/ (accessed September 20, 2020).

new trademarks per year, more than 4 times the number of new trademarks per year registered in the United States.

Realizing the torrent of bad faith trademark filers they had unleashed, with some trademark squatter warehouses filing up to 5,000 marks in a day, the legislators quickly revised the trademark legislation. By the new trademark law of 2019, the trademark office has sweeping new powers to reject applications of bad faith filers lacking intent to use the trademarks and punish those knowing assisting pirates or maliciously launching trademark litigation. Increased statutory damages are ¥5 million per instance (up from ¥3 million) with punitive damages now five times the relevant base amount of loss. But the incentives to file — for legitimate defensive reasons even if not to squat — still persist.

Summary

IP rules of the game are key components of management of innovation in China. They form part of the legal framework for entrepreneurs and corporate executives forming their strategies. This fact is well understood by government, corporate, legal, and research professionals alike.

IP protection in China is work-in-progress. As this chapter emphasized, the IP ethos and standards that China is implementing are global. Chinese IP protection laws, regulations and procedures are being reformed at a pace never seen before in the world. But the world itself is changing. And IP protection throughout the world cannot but change.

Chapter 4

High Speed Rail — State Planning for Innovation

Make full use of the late-comer advantage. Learn from the railway technology of developed countries. Achieve a great leap forward in development of our country's trains. Accelerate the modernization of railways.[1]

— Liu Zhijun

With courtesy [gifts], one can travel the world; without courtesy [gifts], it's hard to take a single step.

— An old Chinese saying [with alternative translation for "礼" in brackets][2]

[1]"铁路实施跨越式发展战略　今后五年还将两次大提速", *Sina 新闻中心* [Railway Implements a Leap Forward Development Strategy *SinaWeb*], September 17, 2003. http://news.sina.com.cn/c/2003-09-17/0952765685s.shtml (accessed October 13, 2020).

[2]The Chinese word "li" "礼" can be translated as "courtesy". In Confucian texts it is often translated as "propriety" or "rites" encompassing everything from proper conventions of society to holy ritual. In modern Chinese the word can mean "courtesy" or "gifts" leading to a double *entende* of bribery. Yu Meiwen, "有'禮'走遍天下, 無'禮'寸步難行" *東方燕園商學院* [With Gifts, You Can Walk the World; without Gifts, It's Hard to Take a Single Step", *Dongfang Yanyuan School of Business*], November 28, 2019. https://kknews.cc/zh-hk/essay/q9rn44r.html (accessed October 3, 2020).

> The Ministry of Railways, the last "fortress of planned economy" is becoming history.
>
> — Wang Yejie[3]

This chapter introduces the largest single infrastructure project in world history, China's 36,000 km-and-counting HSR network, an investment costing over US$750 billion,[4] 20 times China's Three Gorges Dam and 50% greater than the cost of the US interstate highway system (adjusted for inflation) (Figure 4.1).[5]

---

[3]"铁道部最后一个计划经济的堡垒 将走入历史" *人民网* [The Ministry of Railways, the Last "Fortress of Planned Economy Is Becoming History", *The People's Web*], March 11, 2020. http://theory.people.com.cn/n/2013/0311/c49154-20746814.html (accessed October 10, 2020).

[4]There is no single accounting for HSR. One can roughly estimate the cost from Figure 4.1. The growth rate on annual fixed capital investments in rail from 1999 to 2003 was 7.3%. Grow 2003 ¥79 billion annual investments at 7.3% per year from 2003 to 2017, giving an estimate of what annual investments would be without HSR. The aggregate fixed capital investment from 2004 through 2017 would total about ¥2 trillion if HSR had not occurred. Subtract that from the ¥7 trillion aggregate fixed capital investment that actually occurred leaving ¥5 trillion (about US$750 billion) attributable to HSR through 2017. Similar estimates comes from taking the number of HSR kilometers built times the cost per km: US$20,000 per km. 20,000 × 36000 km = US$720 million. R. Sweet "Why China Can Build High-Speed Rail So Cheaply", *Global Construction Review*, July 14, 2014. https://www.globalconstructionreview.com/sectors/why-china-can-build-high-speed-rail-34socheaply7365/ (accessed October 22, 2020) and from adding investments reported in diverse sources.

[5]The US interstate highway system was launched in 1956 and completed in 35 years. It was, at the time, credibly called by US Commerce Secretary Sinclair Weeks "the greatest public-works program in the history of the world". Alex Planes "The Best $500 Billion the United States Has Ever Spent", *The Motley Fool*, June 29, 2013. https://www.fool.com/investing/general/2013/06/29/the-best-500-billion-the-united-states-has-ever-sp.aspx (accessed October 3, 2020). Leah Brooks and Zachary Liscow "Infrastructure Costs", *Brookings Institute Hutchins Center*, Working Paper #54, August 2019. https://www.brookings.edu/wp-content/uploads/2019/08/WP54_Brooks-Liscow_updated.pdf (accessed October 3, 2020). Jennifer Ericks "Top 10 U.S. Government Investments in 20th Century American Competitiveness: Why Federal Funding in the 21st Century is Equally Critical to U.S. Science and Economic Competitiveness", *Center for American Progress* January 6, 2012. https://www.americanprogress.org/issues/economy/reports/2012/01/06/10930/top-10-u-s-government-investments-in-20th-century-american-competitiveness/ (accessed October 3, 2020).

Figure 4.1: Fixed Capital Investment in Railroads in Billions or RMB Per Year

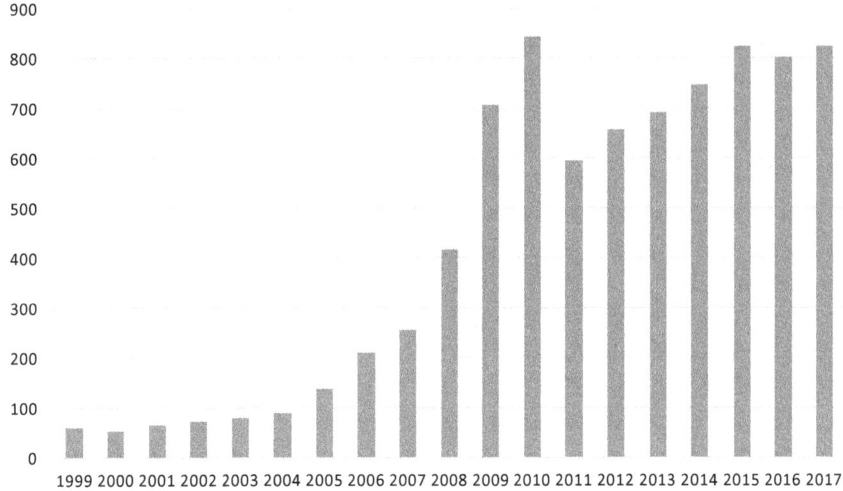

Source: Chinese Railway Yearbooks.

HSR in China involved substantial land acquisition, massive civil engineering investment and construction, and an unprecedented purchase of foreign rolling stock and technology for the benefit of domestic the Chinese HSR industry. In 15 years, China transformed from an also-ran in HSR construction, equipment manufacture, and rail system management into *the* world leader. The HSR project was conceived in the Ministry of Railways (MoR). It was implemented with central planning, reminiscent of the first 30 years of modern China's life. During implementation, operating parts of the MoR were devolved into quasi-market-oriented corporations, which have since been reorganized, and the administrative functions of the MoR have been folded into the Ministry of Transport. During HSR implementation, controversies surrounding corruption and violation of market norms circulated through the scores of government departments and domestic, domestic-domestic, and domestic-foreign joint ventures (JVs) and foreign commercial enterprises. And through the process China achieved substantial stimulation of innovation.

The State of the HSR Art at the Turn of the 21st Century

In October 1964, the world's first HSR, the electric traction, *Tokaido Shinkansen* bullet train travelled from Tokyo to Osaka at a speed of

210 km per hour ushering in the age of HSR. With rapid and smooth acceleration and breaking, stable operation, low internal and external noise, and comfortable ride, the bullet train established Japanese rolling stock companies Nippon Sharyo and Hitachi as global leaders in the technology. Europe followed Japan in HSR innovation: the UK produced its diesel Intercity 125 (named for its average speed in miles per hour) in 1976. In France the electric traction TGV (*trains a grande vitesse*) produced by Alstom started service in 1981 designed for speeds over 300 km per hour. Germany's HSR ICE (Inter-city Express) trains were delivered by Siemens starting in 1989. The Eurostar London Paris started operation in 1994. Italy's Fiat Ferroviaria (taken over by Alstom in 2000), developed the electrical multiple unit (EMU)[6] tilting train — designed to navigate, at high speeds, turns without special track by tilting the cars. North America's first HSR, Amtrak's Acela Express, started operations in 2000 with rolling stock supplied by the Canadian company Bombardier in a joint bid with Alstom. By the turn of the 21st century, more than 15,000 km of HSR lines existed in the world and the leaders in global HSR technology were well established.[7]

China entered the 21st century with a large and growing yet inadequate and antiquated rail system totalling 75,000 km. Mainly diesel but increasingly electric powered, China's railways also "boasted" the world's sole remaining steam engines in regular service. Steam train enthusiasts formed a small but loyal tourist cohort, making pilgrimages to China to witness the power that had driven the 19th century industrial revolution.[8]

Starting with the Eighth Five-Year Plan 1990 (1991–1995), the MoR researched the feasibility of a Beijing-Shanghai HSR line. Hundreds of technological research projects involving thousands of scientists and technologists were funded, resulting in major MoR reports to the State Council and the State Planning Commission. In 1998, the State Council came to the conclusion that the HSR line was both technically and

---

[6]EMUs dispense with a separate locomotive car, with traction units disbursed through various cars at different places in the train.

[7]Huang Jianran, "A Brief Introduction to the Development of High-speed Rail Transit in the 20th Century" [20世纪陆上高速有轨交通发展简况] *Chinese Railway Yearbook 2002*, pp. 627–631.

[8]Lloyd Lewis, "Last Stand for Chinese Steam", *Trains* 52:3, (1992), 44. Don Philipps, "China Is Much More than Steam Locomotives", *Trains* 64:5, (2004), 12–13.

economically feasible.[9] Using entirely domestic technology, the MoR commissioned from various SOEs the development of the China Star HSR System for a cost of ¥140 million. However, shortly after its unveiling in 2002, the system was declared "immature".[10] Something beyond domestic, organic growth was needed for the innovation to succeed at scale.

The HSR Great Leap Forward Decision

In March, 2003 Liu Zhijun was promoted to lead the MoR: the HSR great leap forward and begun. Officially announced by the State Council in the January 2004 "Medium to Long Term Railway Network Plan".[11] The plan recognized the shortcomings of the existing rail system: poor technology and low efficiency. The MoR concluded that the best way to solve its problems was to import on a nation-wide scale technology for a new modern rail system. Taking the late-comer advantage, the plan targeted catching up with the world's best by 2020. HSR was one part of a three-part strategy that included separating freight from passenger lines and building a heavy transport freight capacity. The initial plan was to build 27,000 km of HSR in a grid of four vertical (north–south) and four horizontal (east–west) lines, effectively knitting all cities with a population of more than 500,000 people in China closely together. Initial speed targets were to be over 200 km per hour. The importance of information technology was recognized as critical.[12] HSR technology would be obtained from overseas in a massive, state-led transfer program.

---

[9] Huang Jianran, "20世纪陆上高速有轨交通发展简况" *中国铁道年鉴* 2002 ["A Brief Introduction to the Development of High-speed Rail Transit in the 20th Century",] *Chinese Railway Yearbook*, 2002, pp. 627–631.

[10] Jamil Anderlini and Mure Dickie, "China: A Future on Track — A Look at China's High-Speed Rail Technology"], *Financial Times,* September 23, 2010.

[11] Chinese government portal "国家《中长期铁路网规划》内容简介" ["Medium to Long Term Railway Network Plan"], Department of Transportation, Development and Reform Commission September 16, 2005. http://www.gov.cn/ztzl/2005-09/16/content_64413.htm (accessed October 18, 2020).

[12] "铁路实施跨越式发展战略　今后五年还将两次大提速" ["Railway Implements a Leap Forward Development Strategy"] *SinaWeb*, September 17, 2003. http://news.sina.com.cn/c/2003-09-17/0952765685s.shtml (accessed October 13, 2020).

The initial estimated cost of the HSR project was ¥2 trillion[13] most of which would be domestic civil construction. At the time, China's government had little domestic debt and around $800 billion foreign exchange reserves. So China *had the money* to undertake the project. Yet the MoR needed a domestic business model to access the money. A key strategy was to enter JVs between the MoR and the 31 provinces, directly controlled cities and self-governing regions that make up the next level of authority after the central government. By 2008 , regional official investors were joined by domestic and foreign private and institutional capital.[14]

HSR itself was never likely to be profitable. But regional governments and other investors would join simply because it was the right thing to do. And related, profitable opportunities also beckoned. HSR brought not only the promise of access to construction, equipment, and management contracts. Its rail lines and stations would stimulate the largest and most rapidly growing asset class of the early 21st century in the entire world: Chinese real estate.

Real Estate and HSR

One of the major transformations of China from a planned economy to a market economy was the opening of the real-estate market. Prior to 1978, rural land was collectively owned under the communes and urban land was owned by the state under the control of industrial, commercial, and government units. Although the communes were dismantled in the late 1970s, rural land has continued to be collectively owned down to the present. Rural residents have effective personal claims to land but the claims cannot be sold in open markets. Urban land, however, is part of the market economy.

In the cities, starting in 1994, employees of companies and government departments who were previously supplied their accommodation as part of their employment package by the state or their collective

[13] 实现《中长期铁路网规划》目标将需2万亿元 [2 trillion yuan will be needed to achieve the goal of "Medium and Long-term Railway Network Planning"], September 21, 2005. http://www.chinanews.com/news/2005/2005-09-21/8/628835.shtml.

[14] Ouyang Bo, "铁路修建主体进一步多元化" *新浪财经* ["Further Diversification of Rail Project"], *Sina Finance*, August 13, 2008. http://finance.sina.com.cn/stock/t/20080813/05082372351.shtml (accessed October 12, 2020).

enterprises, were first allowed to purchase some restricted property rights to their apartments at greatly discounted prices. In 1998, the power to sell land use rights (but not the land itself) was granted to local governments; the discounted purchase system was abolished, and the People's Bank of China established procedures for mortgage funding. Each city designated land by its intended use (industrial, commercial, or residential) and the land use rights of different durations for different uses were allowed to be bought and sold in increasingly free markets. In the following years, local governments turned land conversion and sales into their largest sources of income; developers seized the opportunities; cities grew by taking over surrounding, formerly rural areas; urbanization more than doubled from 30% to 60% of the population; China became the largest mortgage market in Asia, and the Chinese property boomed for more than two decades.[15]

In every country of the world, property development is more susceptible to corruption than other industries. The visionary nature of building the future, the large number of steps from idea to completion, the plethora of opaque, changing and discretionary regulations, the high cost of land acquisition, preparation and construction, and the volatility of boom and bust cycles all offer opportunities for arbitrage and speculative activities. The activities often are judged as immoral, if not illegal.[16] This is true in the West. This is even more true in China.

In 2020, Chinese real estate had a market value of US$42.7 trillion, slightly larger than the US real estate market,[17] considerably larger than the US stock markets' capitalization and over four times the Chinese stock markets' capitalization. Real estate in China is by far the largest investible asset held by Chinese men and women of the rising middle class. And real estate is the by far the largest factor in the increasing inequality among Chinese under the new rules of the game.

Each of the hundreds of newly built HSR stations is itself a major real-estate development that exercises tremendous upward pressure on the value of surrounding lands, making their successful development

---

[15]Liu Chang and Xiong Wei, "China's Real Estate Market", NBER Working Paper 25297, November 2018. https://www.nber.org/papers/w25297.pdf (accessed October 20, 2020).

[16]Martin H. Krieger, "Corruption and the Culture of Real Estate Development", *Business & Professional Ethics Journal* 13:3 (Fall 1994), 19–32.

[17]Paul Tostevin, "The 10 Most Valuable Real Estate Markets in the World", *The Savills Blog*, 2017. https://www.savills.com/blog/article/219340/international-property/the-10-most-valuable-real-estate-markets-in-the-world.aspx (accessed October 21, 2020).

possible. To join this real-estate boom, as well as to be part of the vision for the future of China, local governments vied to join HSR. As of the end of 2008, the MoR (and its SOEs) had signed a total of 210 domestic JV agreements with provinces, cities and self-governing regions (and their SOEs) for a total investment of ¥5 trillion, of which ¥1.6 trillion would come from the local governments. SOEs contributed equity. HSR lines issued debt, and some equity was listed on domestic stock markets.[18]

The world-wide economy's plunge into the 2007–2008 Global Financial Crisis was, paradoxically, a stroke of good fortune for HSR. Determined not join the US and Europe in recession, the State Council of China embarked on a massive fiscal stimulus: infrastructure spending. HSR was the largest single recipient of the infrastructure spending, further accelerating the capital expenditures.[19]

Technology Transfer and *Quid Pro Quo*

Figure 4.2 shows that the vast majority of the cost of HSR was capital construction: land acquisition, roadbed construction, bridge-building, tunnel-boring, and the building of the hundreds of HSR stations. But without HSR's advanced technology, whose cost was imbedded largely in the rolling stock, HSR could never have existed. The technology was transferred from leading companies in the advanced countries of the world. It was transferred through outright purchase and through Chinese-foreign JVs.

One of the guiding principles of the WTO's TRIPS Accord was that developing countries accepting the global rules of the IP game should expect developed countries to facilitate the transfer of advanced technology in the interests of global prosperity.[20] Most major multinational companies (MNCs) doing business in China prior to and since HSR have understood

[18]"中国高铁之钱从何处来" *知乎* ["Where Did the Money for the HSR Come From?" *Zhihu Website*], 2019. https://zhuanlan.zhihu.com/p/101532959 (accessed October 22, 2020).

[19]Bill Powell, "China's Amazing New Bullet Train: This Year Beijing Will Spend $50 Billion on What Will Soon Be the World's Biggest High-Speed Train System", *Fortune*, August 6, 2009. https://archive.fortune.com/2009/08/03/news/international/china_high_speed_bullet_train.fortune/index.htm (accessed October 20, 2020).

[20]WTO, "Technology Transfer", *TRIPS Issues*. https://www.wto.org/english/tratop_e/trips_e/techtransfer_e.htm (accessed October 7, 2020).

Figure 4.2: Railway Fixed Capital Breakdown in Billions of RMB Per Year

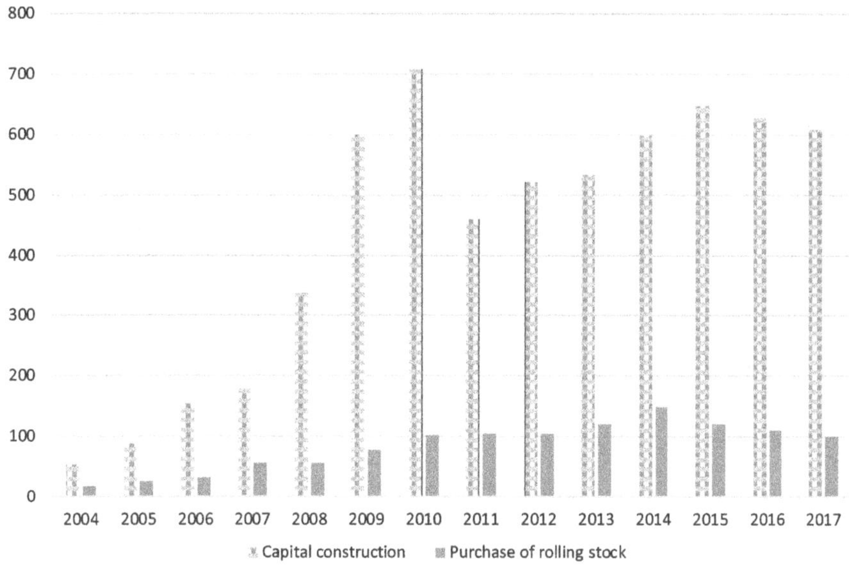

Source: Chinese Railway Yearbooks.

the Chinese *quid pro quo*: MNCs receive market access in return for technology. This bargain was China's explicit national policy throughout the 1980s and 1990s[21] and had been an implicit policy since then.

Initially MNCs could enter China *only* through JVs. The Chinese JV partner, typically an SOE, would often insist that the equity contribution of the MNC involve transferring technology. However, following the wholly foreign-owned enterprise (WFOE) law in mid 1980s, WFOEs became MNCs' preferred investment vehicle,[22] at least in the industries where they were allowed.[23] Although the WFOE structure mitigated for

[21] Julia Ya Qin, "Forced Technology Transfer and the US–China Trade War: Implications for International Economic Law", *Journal of International Economic Law* 22 (2019), 743–762.

[22] Luo Yadong and Neale O'Connor, "Structural Changes to Foreign Direct Investment in China: An Evolutionary Perspective", *Journal of Applied Management Studies* 7:1 (1998), 95–109.

[23] Starting from 2018 and 2019, WFOEs have been allowed in automobile manufacture and energy respectively. Prohibited industries still include secondary and post secondary education, antiques auctions, rare earths, GM crops, air traffic control, internet news, book publishing and tobacco and there are numerous restricted industries where restrictions

the MNC the risk of direct technology transfer to a Chinese JV partner and potential competitor, *quid pro quo,* broadly defined, continued. Even if a foreign MNC used a WFOE, government approval was required for the MNC's WFOE foreign direct investment (FDI) and subsequent regulatory benevolence was often explicitly conditioned on the MNC carrying out, *in China,* specific advanced activities, development and/or research. That requirement ensured that technology was transferred to the local Chinese workforce. And the fact that most technology lies in trade secrets, not patents, meant that it could move easily with employees when they, of their own volition, left their MNC employers, taking, in their minds (if not in "their" files), their former employer's secrets.

Explicit, government administered, *quid pro quo* ended, however, when China, as part of the deal for accession into the WTO in December 2001, covenanted:

> China shall ensure that … the right of importation or investment … is not conditioned on … performance requirements of any kind, such as local content, offsets, the transfer of technology, export performance or the conduct of research and development in China.[24]

Henceforth, official *quid pro quo* became implicit. The HSR project was a technology for market access *quid pro quo*. Twenty years after China's WTO accession, "forced technology transfer" still is, more than ever, among the complaints levelled against China by the West.[25]

---

would make a JV more desirable than a WFOE. Nathan Jansen "Encouraged, Restricted & Prohibited Industries in China", 1421 Consulting, November 27, 2018. https://www.1421.consulting/2018/11/foreign-investment-in-china/ (accessed October 22, 2020)

[24] Draft Protocol on the Accession of the People's Republic of China Section 7: Non-tariff barriers clause 3, WT/ACC/CHN/49 Page 76 page. https://docs.wto.org/dol2fe/Pages/SS/directdoc.aspx?filename=q:/WT/ACC/CHN49.pdf&Open=True (accessed October 7, 2020).

[25] Office of the United States Trade Representative, Executive Office of the President *Findings of the Investigation into China's Acts, Policies, and Practices Related to Technology Transfer, Intellectual Property and Innovation under Section 301 of the Trade Act of 1974*. March 22, 2018. https://ustr.gov/sites/default/files/Section%20301%20FINAL.PDF (accessed October 8, 2020). Nicholas R. Lardy, "Does China Force Foreign Firms to Surrender Their Sensitive Technology?" Peterson Institute for International Economics. December 10, 2018. https://www.piie.com/blogs/china-economic-watch/

China's WTO accession covenant disallowed *the Chinese government*, not Chinese companies, from requiring the transfer of technology as part of business transactions. All of the HSR technology acquisition transactions involved transfer to Chinese companies. The fact that these companies were SOEs did not change their corporate structure.

Most of the HSR technology transfer involved direct purchase. Any company in the world can purchase technology from any other company, subject to agreement on price and technology transfer terms and the satisfying of relevant import and export regulations.

Some technology transfer in HSR also involved Chinese — foreign JVs. The Chinese JV partners were SOEs, mainly the China Northern Railway (CNR) and the China Southern Railway (CSR). The MoR wanted technology transferred to China. CNR and CSR management wanted to increase their companies' technology level even without MoR direction: their long-term career prospects were conditioned on KPIs which went well beyond maximizing shareholder profits. In HSR, increasing the technological level of the SOEs they managed was important, but improving the general technology level of China rail was also important, irrespective of their companies' profitability. Moreover, with HSR negotiations for technology transfer, actual negotiations were carried on by the MoR not by CSR and CNR.

In Chinese SOE-foreign JVs, it is not really possible to tell if the demand for technology comes from the company or the government.[26] Chinese law courts and/or a dispute resolution panel at the WTO would be the venues to pursue complaints. If a company felt aggrieved by *quid pro quo* and filed a grievance with the WTO, the WTO would investigate. Yet no actions have ever been taken by HSR technology sellers or foreign JV partners or their governments with respect to *quid pro quo* of forced technology transfer.[27]

---

does-china-force-foreign-firms-surrender-their-sensitive-technology (accessed October 8, 2020).

[26] Julia Ya Qin, "Forced Technology Transfer and the US–China Trade War: Implications for International Economic Law", *Journal of International Economic Law* 22 (2019), 743–762.

[27] Georges Haour and Max Von Zedtwitz *Created in China,* Bloomsbury, London, 2016, pp. 76 and 163. It is noteworthy, however, that China stands accused in a pending WTO dispute for violating with its JV law the WTO principle of *national treatment.* Under WTO, domestic and foreign legal persons (i.e., the JV partners) should be treated equally

Does this absence of complaint mean that foreign partners in Chinese-foreign JVs feel that they are treated fairly? "Fair" in an international context means meeting WTO standards. If a complaint of unfairness would lead to losses of business in China, then one would not expect complaint from the MNC foreign JV partner, even in the face of unfairness. Currently, China stands accused in one pending WTO dispute concerning JVs. The plaintiff, not a specific company, but the US delegation to the WTO, credibly alleges that the letter of Chinese law treats the domestic JV partner more favorably than the foreign JV partner regarding ownership of IP developed at the JV: under Chinese law, it belongs to the Chinese JV partner. This suggests that China's JV laws violates the WTO principle of *national treatment.* Under WTO national treatment, domestic and foreign legal persons (i.e., the JV partners) should be treated equally before the law.[28] Although it is not directly related to HSR, and although it has nothing to do with *quid pro quo,* this dispute strongly suggests that China's IP acquisition policies through JV laws and, by implication, its IP acquisition policies in general have some way to go before meeting international norms of fairness.

Acquisition of HSR technologies occurred during the years following 2004 through the purchase by CNR and CSR of different train modes, with each mode coming from different consortia led by Alstom of France, Siemens of Germany, Kawasaki of Japan and Bombardier of Canada.[29] The MoR negotiated simultaneously but separately with each foreign technology supplier. The purchases involved importing of entire train sets, importing of critical components of train sets, and Chinese assembly with

---

before the law, but Chinese law treats the domestic JV partner more favorably than the foreign JV regarding ownership of IP developed at the JV. WTO, "WT/DS542/8 China — Certain Measures Concerning the Protection of Intellectual Property Rights: Request for the establishment of a Panel by the United States". https://docs.wto.org/dol2fe/Pages/SS/directdoc.aspx?filename=q:/WT/DS/542-8.pdf&Open=True (accessed October 14, 2020).

[28] WTO, "WT/DS542/8 China — Certain Measures Concerning the Protection of Intellectual Property Rights: Request for the establishment of a Panel by the United States". https://docs.wto.org/dol2fe/Pages/SS/directdoc.aspx?filename=q:/WT/DS/542-8.pdf&Open=True (accessed October 14, 2020).

[29] "China's High Speed Fleet Expands Steadily", *Railway Gazette*, August 1, 2007. https://www.railwaygazette.com/in-depth/chinas-high-speed-fleet-expands-steadily/32292.article (accessed October 23, 2020).

local production of non-critical components under foreign tutelage.[30] Chinese production of components and assembly occurred in about 30 separate factories owned by CSR and CNR. Technology transfer contracts generally contained designs, train blueprints, manufacturing procedure instructions and training of engineers. The technology suppliers showed the Chinese *how to* manufacture the four modes in the way they did. There was no general instruction by the foreign suppliers of *why:* the reasons for designing and manufacturing in the way that they did. The MoR was keen to develop local manufacturing of full train sets, so CNR and CSR receivers of technology had to figure out the "why" so that they could fully digest the technologies and build further innovations on what they had been taught. This "reverse engineering" was frequently conducted by CNR/CSR cooperation with researchers at neighboring universities and research institutes.[31] Technology exporters especially in Germany and Japan[32] were averse to loss of technology but they saw it as inevitable in pursuing the largest market in the world.[33]

Ambivalence was clear. When Siemens signed an order for 100 trains with CNR where 100% of the trains were to be assembled in China (Tangshan and Changchun) with some critical components — electrical equipment and chassis — purchased from Siemens, the company spokesperson commented that "under no circumstances will it sell its core technology".[34]

---

[30] "Siemens High Speed Train Sets Sail for China", *Railway Gazette*, December 20, 2007. https://www.railwaygazette.com/news/siemens-high-speed-train-sets-sail-for-china/32559.article (accessed October 23, 2020).

[31] Lin, Qin, Xie, "International Technology Transfer and Domestic Innovation: Evidence from the High-Speed Rail Sector in China", *Journal of Comparative Economics* 2020 (forthcoming).

[32] Michael Fitzpatrick, "Did China Steal Japan's High-Speed Train?", *Fortune*, April 15, 2013. https://fortune.com/2013/04/15/did-china-steal-japans-high-speed-train/ (accessed October 4, 2020).

[33] Mure Dickie, "China 'Digests' Japan's Bullet Train Technology", *Financial Times*, February 1, 2007.

[34] "Siemens Will Provide China with a Hundred High-Speed Trains without selling core technology", 西门子将向中方提供百列高速列车 不卖核心技术, Sina.com, April 2, 2009. http://news.sina.com.cn/c/2009-04-02/083617533481.shtml (accessed October 4, 2020).

Where domestic-foreign JV manufacture and assembly was pursued, technology transfer willingness of technology supplied varied. Pierre Beaudoin, President of Bombardier noted

> We are supplying the latest VHS [very high speed] technology for one of the most far-reaching high speed rail initiatives anywhere in the world. This is a landmark order for next-generation rail equipment and the result of a positive and productive, long-term relationship.[35]

Like Bombardier, Kawasaki also manufactured rolling stock through a Chinese-foreign JV. The Japanese apparently believed they had an agreement that CSR would not export the technology outside of China. By 2011 CSR had filed PCTs and subsequent national patent applications for HSR technologies in the United States, Brazil, Russia, Japan, and some European nations. Kawasaki complained but did not taken legal action.[36]

Innovation in Governance

HSR was designed and implemented with central planning by the MoR (and Yangqi SOEs) in coordination with provincial, regional, and direct city administrations (and their SOEs). This central planning model — whose "great leap forward" moniker recalled one of the *least* successful examples of Soviet-style governance — took place while the spirit of the times favored expanding the role of the market.

During the course of HSR implementation, the MoR, the "last fortress of the planned economy",[37] experienced substantial changes. Figure 4.3 shows that the Chinese rail system was large. At the turn of the century, it was entirely centralized within the MoR, the second most

---

[35] *Berlin Transportation*, "Bombardier Sifang Wins Contract to Build 80 Very High Speed Trains for China", *Bombardier Press Release*, September 28, 2009.

[36] "China denies Japan's rail patent-infringement claim", China.org.cn, July 8, 2011. http://www.china.org.cn/business/2011-07/08/content_22945196.htm (accessed October 23, 2020).

[37] "铁道部最后一个计划经济的堡垒 将走入历史" *人民网* ["The Ministry of Railways, the last fortress of planned economy is becoming history"], *The People's Web*, March 11, 2020. http://theory.people.com.cn/n/2013/0311/c49154-20746814.html (accessed October 10, 2020).

Figure 4.3: Employees in the Chinese Railway System in Millions

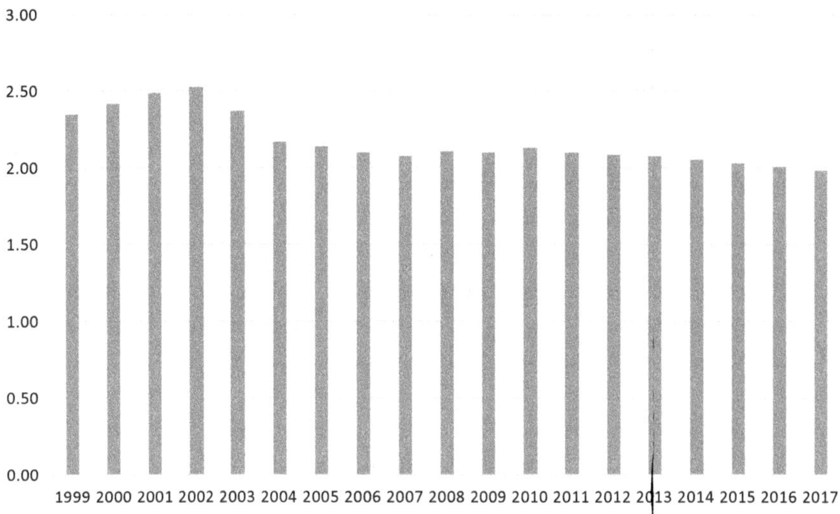

Source: Chinese Railway Yearbooks.

powerful ministry in China, second only to the Ministry of Defence. The MoR employed just over 2 million persons and controlled its own factories, research institutes, police force and health services in addition to the planning, construction, and management of the rail systems and the development manufacturing and sales of rolling stock. Today, the rail system of China is larger and far more advanced than 20 years ago, yet its employees are fewer and its organization has dramatically changed.

In the year 2000, in the lead up to Chinese WTO entry, the MoR split the operations of its wholly owned rolling stock company, the China National Railway Locomotive & Rolling Stock Industry Corporation — 33 factories, four research institutes, and ¥26 billion in assets — into two companies, CNR and CSR. Those two companies, along with four other large MoR SOEs — China Civil Engineering, China Railway Construction, China Railway Engineering, and China Railway Communications and Signal were divested from ministerial control but their ownership was held by the MoR. Two years later, in 2003, their shares were transferred to the newly formed SASAC, completing their separation from the MoR.

The objective of the CNR and CSR separation and spin-off was to end the monopolies and to introduce competition, not only into rolling stock production but into other parts of the railway supply chain. The split was engineered by using the Yangtze river as the dividing line. Assets to the north went to CNR. Assets to the south went to CSR. And the general principle was to distribute fairly good and bad assets. But the MoR remained basically the monopsony buyer for both. In the words of one CSR manager the result was

> One great positive and three great negatives. On the plus side, it promoted competition. On the minus side there was redundant construction (overcapacity), vicious competition and resulting corruption.[38]

Ten years later, CNR and CSR sales had increased more than 10 times and, like many SOEs, both had listed minority public floats in the Shanghai and Hong Kong stock exchanges.

The separation of CNR's and CSR's assets led the CNR and CSR to compete domestically: that was the point. As national priorities and competitive strengths shifted toward exporting HSR, rapid transit and other rail rolling stock, however, the two companies increasingly competed in global markets. This was a problem for the Chinese policy of encouraging national champions. CNR and CSR management had not supported separation in 2000 but, years later, the subsequent management of the separate companies did not support merging. The MoR resisted the merger, not wanting to face a near monopoly supplier of rolling stock. In the end, the international competition and national champion arguments won the day. In 2013, CNR and CSR fiercely competed for an Argentinian rolling stock contract in a way that undermined the confidence of the foreign buyer. The State Council decided: merge![39]

---

[38] Ma Yiwen, "业内称南北车整合只是时间问题　铁总极力反对" *财经* ["Industry Sources Say the integration of CNR and CSR is only a matter of time" *Caijing*], October 15, 2014. http://finance.china.com.cn/industry/company/20141015/2726754.shtml (accessed October 23, 2020).

[39] Huang Dongya, "Top-Level Design and Fragmented Decision-Making: A Case Study of an SOE Merger in China's High-Speed Rail Industry", *Journal of Contemporary China* 27:109 (2018). https://www.tandfonline.com/doi/full/10.1080/10670564.2017.1363027?casa_token=nquU1OZHuCcAAAAA%3AenijzPqJNrgd7dEm6cIBlqxC4jvWEJYXR2PpVXMueA7sjnbweXWKVxYNbibWJzT84KtDgOTIlDBhZg (accessed October 25, 2020).

As a CNR top manager put it

> … neither CNR nor CSR believed that the so-called vicious competition existed. Thus there's no need to merge. However, after several rounds of opinion-soliciting, the top managers finally got the point that the top-level government leaders were inclined towards a merger. The managers of SOEs should act like politicians in comprehending the intentions of their supervisors, so they took the initiative in applying for merging.[40]

The merger was launched in October 2014, and submitted to SASAC in December the same year. It was approved by relevant Chinese authorities in 2015 and in March 2016, the shareholders of the Hong Kong-listed H-shares and the Shanghai-listed A-shares voted to merge. Following anti-trust reviews the CNR and CSR merged into a single rolling stock corporation, the China Railway Rolling Stock Corporation (CRRC), in August 2016, ending more than a decade of fierce competition and creating the largest supplier of HSR rolling stock in the world.[41]

Management, Ministry, and Company. The unprecedented size, speed, and complexity of the HSR rollout strained governance at the MoR, the rail system and their suppliers. Throughout the process, the MoR Minister, Liu Zhijun, the person credited with masterminding and driving the HSR project, was never far from controversy. His seemingly limitless energy earned him the epithets of "Great Leap Liu", "The Engine driving HSR" and "Lunatic Liu".[42] In February 2011, he was placed under *shuang gui* (double appointment internal CPC investigation) for severe violations of discipline.

The Japanese have run their bullet trains for half a century without a single accident. The Germans had experienced one HSR accident. Seven years into China's HSR age, in June of 2011 lightning literally struck near

---

[40] *Ibid.*, taken from Wechat online, January 5, 2016.

[41] "中国中车整合效应初显:新签海外订单同比增126%" *财经* ["CRRC's Integration Yields Results: Show: New Overseas Orders Increased by 126% Year-on-Year", *Caijing*], November 21, 2016. http://money.163.com/16/1121/06/C6CJON7N002580S6.html (accessed October 23, 2020).

[42] Evan Osnos, "Boss Rail: The Disaster That Exposed the Underside of the Boom", *New Yorker* October 22, 2012. https://www.newyorker.com/magazine/2012/10/22/boss-rail (accessed October 25, 2020).

Wenzhou. An HSR train had to power down but the sensors failed to detect and relay the power-down properly. Minutes later the crippled train was rear-ended by another HSR train travelling in the same direction. Forty people died and 192 were injured.[43]

The investigations turned up the fact that corruption was rife in the MoR in general and HSR in particular. In the contracting and subcontracting webs that built HSR, middlemen expected cuts of between one and six percent.[44] An MoR internal report that investigated the accident found a long list of manufacturing quality and systems management problems.[45] Liu was stripped of his job and purged from the CPC.

If there had been any doubt that it was over for Liu Zhijun, the Wenzhou disaster ended that doubt. He was arrested and criminally charged. In August 2013, Liu was sentenced to death for corruption, that included money, cars and more than 350 flats, not to mention his 18 mistresses.[46] His death sentence was commuted to life imprisonment in 2016, but he remains in prison today. Liu, his relatives, and his friends have been implicated for a "paltry" few hundreds of millions of dollars of corruption. If one uses 1% as a lower bound, HSR has probably generated at least US$7.5 billion in bribery.

In March 2013, the MoR was dissolved. Planning, policy, and administrative governmental functions were folded into a new State Railways Administration under the Ministry of Communications and Commercial Activities — the ownership and running of China's freight and passenger railways — including HSR — were put into a new SOE owned by SASAC, the China Railways Corporation (CRC).[47] Since then the CRC has been reorganized several times, most recently in 2019 when its name was changed to the China State Railway Group (CR). The objective of the

---

[43] *Ibid.*

[44] *Ibid.*

[45] "China's Awkward Quest for Bullet Train Technology", Knowledge at Wharton, September 14, 2011. https://knowledge.wharton.upenn.edu/article/chinas-awkward-quest-for-bullet-train-technology/# (accessed October 24, 2020).

[46] Johathan Kaiman, "Liu Zhijun, China's Ex-Railway Minister, Sentenced To Death for corruption", *The Guardian* July 8, 2012. https://www.theguardian.com/world/2013/jul/08/liu-zhijun-sentenced-death-corruption (accessed October 23, 2020).

[47] Qi Zhongxi, "China Implements Radical Railway Reform", *International Railway Journal*, accessed October 23, 2020. https://www.railjournal.com/in_depth/china-implements-radical-railway-reform.

reorganization has been to reform its HSR's operations, establishing modern, market-oriented enterprises.[48]

Concluding Remarks

The HSR project broke records and lifted China into global infrastructure leadership. In pure cash flow terms, with total railway debt in 2020 of over ¥8 trillion, the operating revenues of CR would be insufficient to cover the debt service at market interest rates.[49] Yet the returns of HSR far exceed corporate revenues. It changed the face of travel, knitting the country together. And it highlighted the fact that central planning is very much a working model in Chinese management of innovation.

---

[48]Brenda Goh, "China Renames, Restructures State Railway Giant in Reform Push", *Reuters*, https://www.reuters.com/article/us-china-railway-idUSKCN1TJ09N (accessed October 25, 2020).

[49]Tom Mitchell and Xinning Liu, "China's High-Speed Rail and Fears of Fast Track to Debt", Financial Times, August 14, 2018. https://www.ft.com/content/ca28f58a-955d-11e8-b747-fb1e803ee64e (accessed October 17, 2020).

Chapter 5

Incubation and the Hong Kong Science and Technology Parks Corporation Introduction

This chapter presents the first teaching case of this book, *Incubation and the Hong Kong Science and Technology Parks Corporation*. The case describes Albert Wong, CEO of the Hong Kong Science and Technology Parks Corporation (HKSTP), assessing the marketing strategy for HKSTP's program to incubate high technology, start-up companies in Hong Kong. HKSTP provides services to incubatees — the start-ups admitted to the program — to increase their chances of success. HKSTP itself competes with other incubators to serve high quality incubatees. Marketing should engage its target. That's the issue to be discussed.

HKSTP resides in one of two special administrative regions (SARs) of China. The other is Macao. The SAR was a political innovation. Writing the rules of the political game is an important part of the management of innovation in China. This introduction to the HKSTP case will discuss the political innovation of the Hong Kong SAR.

Hong Kong is curious. It has been an integral part of China since the 3rd century BC. It became the final holdout of the last emperors of the Southern Song Dynasty retreating from the Mongol invaders in the 13th century.[1] It was the first prize for gunboat diplomacy awarded to the

[1]After the rout of the Southern Song army near Hangzhou by the Mongols in 1278, the Song emperor retreated to Kowloon City in today's Hong Kong, where he is

expanding British imperialists by a declining Qing Dynasty in the 19th century. And it was the final colony of the British Empire in East Asia, returned to China in 1997.

Non-Chinese refer to "the 1997 handover of Hong Kong". Chinese refer to "the 1997 return of Hong Kong".[2] Neither the People's Republic of China since 1949 nor its predecessor, the Republic of China, since 1911 had ever recognized the legitimacy of the unequal treaties[3] that had ceded control over Hong Kong to the British. And during the last half century of British occupation, the Chinese periodically made official statements such as Hong Kong "… is entirely within China's sovereign right and … should not be included in the list … granting of independence to colonial countries and people".[4]

Hong Kong Chinese culture differs somewhat from the rest of China's. As Figure 5.1 makes clear, the large population of Hong Kong is recent. It rose from just 160,000 in 1941, the first year of the Pacific Theatre of World War II, to over 7 million today. The vast majority of current Hong Kongers are not truly native. They are refugees and the descendants of refugees from south China who arrived immediately after the end of the civil war to avoid conflict, to escape the unification of China under the CPC and to flee from economic and political hardship during the first 30 years of the People's Republic of China. Wealthy individuals, business persons, intellectuals, and those with strong religious beliefs were over-represented among the refugees. The new Hong Kong

---

commemorated with a stone, a public garden and a recently completed MTR rapid transit station, the Sung Wong Toi Station. See Hon Tze-ki, "MTR's new Sha Tin to Central link will showcase important historical sites in our city", *YP Learn*, May 10, 2018. https://www.scmp.com/yp/learn/college-uni-life/university-programmes/article/3072023/mtrs-new-sha-tin-central-link-will (accessed January 21, 2021).

[2] A Google search for "the 1997 handover" elicits 90,000 results while "the 1997 return" elicits 16,000. The term in Chinese for "1997 return 1997 回归" elicits 16,200 results, but there are no competing terms in Chinese for "handover" that elicit more than 100 results.

[3] The term "unequal treaties" is a highly emotive term used by the Chinese to refer to treaties signed with foreign powers in the century of humiliation from the First Opium War to the end of the civil war in 1949 when Qing and Republican China, because of weakness, were unable to protect the integrity of the country. For a discussion of the term and its historical context, see Dong Wang, *China's Unequal Treaties: Narrating National History*, Lexington Books, Lanham, MD, 2005.

[4] *Ibid.*, p. 436.

Figure 5.1: Population of Hong Kong

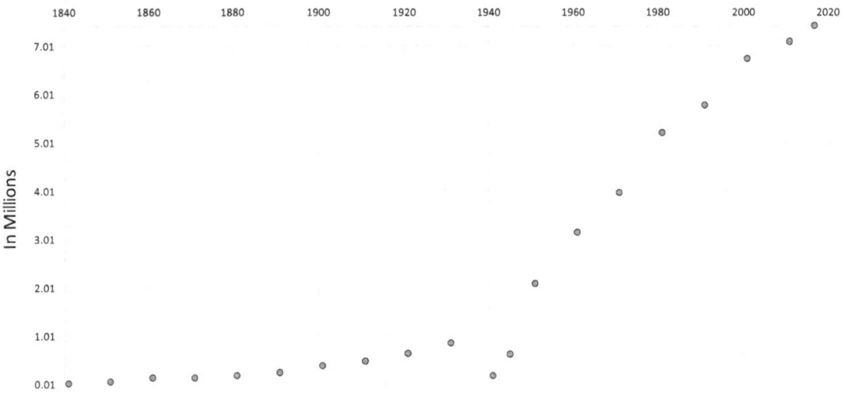

Source: Fan Shuh Ching, *The Population of Hong Kong* Department of Statistics University of Hong Kong, 1974; Hong Kong Government Census and Statistics Department.

residents were, variously, socially conservative, religiously traditional, intellectually educated, entrepreneurially inclined, Confucian, Daoist, Buddhist, Christian, pro-Western — in short, anti-communist. For them, Hong Kong was a waystation, "a borrowed place on borrowed time".[5]

In the chaotic years immediately following World War II, Hong Kong served as a haven for global and Chinese companies formerly based in Shanghai. When the CPC won the civil war in 1949, all remembered what the Japanese had demonstrated less than a decade earlier: Hong Kong was indefensible. The British would have been incapable of successfully resisting a takeover. Yet, China chose ***not*** to take over Hong Kong.

The Chinese refrained for half a century from recovering Hong Kong because the *status quo* was highly beneficial to them and to the British. It was

[5]The famous epithet has been attributed to Australian journalist Richard Hughes and by Mr. Hughes to the novelist Han Suyin and by Ms. Han to the Shanghai businessman and refugee to Hong Kong Tom Wu. Derek Davies, "Review: Precarious Balance: Hong Kong between China and Britain, 1942–1992 by Ming K. Chan and John D. Young", *China Review International* 2:2 (1995), 406–411. For a discussion of what the epithet means in modern, pre-2019 Hong Kong, see Evan Fowler, "A Borrowed Place on Borrowed Time: Can Hong Kong Ever Be Home?" *Hong Kong Free Press*, September 26, 2015. https://hongkongfp.com/2015/09/26/hong-kong-a-borrowed-place-on-borrowed-time/ (accessed January 20, 2021).

> an extraordinary symbiotic relationship between the capitalist and communist worlds [that] enabled the imaginative entrepreneurs and the hard-working population of Hong Kong to produce what some regard as an economic miracle. It is, or has been, widely assumed that both China and Great Britain, the principal partners in this joint venture, as well as the people of Hong Kong themselves, have derived sufficient benefit from it to outweigh any political cost.[6]

By keeping its Hong Kong colony, the British kept a full complement of administrators, business persons, major military bases, and substantial commercial assets. In return it presented a friendly face to the new rulers of China. Just four months after the declaration of the People's Republic of China, far earlier than other Western powers and a full 30 years before the US, the UK recognized the CPC government.

By leaving Hong Kong under the British, China immediately gained a window on the Western world. The Chinese banks that operated in the territory continued to serve as a conduit for foreign remittances from the Chinese diaspora. Chinese SOEs did good business in Hong Kong. And, notwithstanding the trade embargo imposed by the UK on China following its entry into the Korean War, Hong Kong served as China's most porous non-Soviet border — both legally and illegally. In return, China sold Hong Kong water, food, and other products, and provided business opportunities to her burgeoning population.[7]

The tacit understanding frayed in 1966 and, more seriously, in 1967. Radical leftists in Hong Kong, inspired by the Cultural Revolution raging at that time in the rest of China, hijacked demonstrations against inflation, British mismanagement, poor working conditions, and government corruption. They whipped the demonstrations into strikes, riots, bombings, and assassinations. The imminent threat that China would take over Hong Kong was diffused only when Premier Zhou Enlai ordered the radicals to stand down.[8]

---

[6]Anthony Dicks, "Treaty, Grant, Usage or Sufferance? Some Legal Aspects of the Status of Hong Kong", *The China Quarterly* 95 (1983), 428.

[7]See Chapters 1 and 2 in Catherine Schenk, *Hong Kong As an International Financial Centre: Emergence and Development, 1945–1965*, Routledge, London, 2001.

[8]Michael Sheridan, "China Plotted Hong Kong Invasion", *The Australian*, June 25, 2007. https://www.theaustralian.com.au/news/world/china-plotted-hong-kong-invasion/news-story/b2d84d0c4efc7d90ce5122a2df932052 (accessed January 25, 2021).

During the next 15 years, Hong Kong was an innovative socio-economic model, one of several in East Asia.[9] The Four Tigers, South Korea, Taiwan, Singapore, and Hong Kong, were re-writing the playbook of development. All four shared a traditional Confucian culture, but they took different paths, ranging from Hong Kong's *laissez faire* to the oligopolies of Korea. Yet, all four demonstrated the importance of stable macro-economic and legal structures, commercially based well-regulated banking systems, strong and open educational and agricultural policies, stable exchange rates, and the stimulation of exports. And even in Hong Kong, they demonstrated the usefulness of large-scale physical infrastructural development, massive public investment in housing, and the creation of industrial parks to house manufacturers.[10]

The 1978 and opening up reform of China came just in time for Hong Kong. After two decades of development, Hong Kong was suffering from wages and land price inflation, rendering Hong Kong less competitive. China's reform and opening involved creation of the Special Economic Zones (SEZs) where investors could set up export-oriented factories. Modeled on the export processing and industrial zones of the Four Tigers, they were located in Shantou and Xiamen, opposite Taiwan, in Zhuhai opposite Macao, and in Shenzhen, opposite Hong Kong. They attracted foreign capital and served as test-beds for new policies: crossing the river by feeling the stones. Once the innovations worked in the SEZs, they were replicated elsewhere. Of the four SEZs, Shenzhen proved to be by far the most successful. The manufacturers of Hong Kong moved their factories north. Often the distance from the old to the new factory was less than a hundred kilometers. And the cultural gap was minimal: Hong Kongers were investing in places they had left a generation before as refugees.

Hong Kong became far and away the largest single source of FDI into China. Hong Kong accounted for approximately 50% of total FDI into China from 1985 to 2017.[11] The Hong Kong investors brought more than

[9]The eight were Japan; the "four tigers": Hong Kong, the Republic of Korea, Singapore, and Taiwan, and the three newly industrializing economies of Indonesia, Malaysia, and Thailand. See John Page, "The East Asian Miracle: Four Lessons for Development Policy", *NBER Macroeconomics Annual 1994*, The World Bank, January 1994. http://www.nber.org/books/fisc94-1 (accessed January 25, 2021).

[10]John Page, *ibid.*

[11]See Michael J., Enright "Developing China: The Remarkable Impact of Foreign Direct Investment", The Hinrich Foundation, September 13, 2017. https://www.

just capital. They brought a way of life, modes of thinking, and new rules to the game. A generation of Hong Kong managers often found the road to success led through the mainland, where they found respect and prosperity. Shenzhen grew to a global city: by 2020 it exceeded Hong Kong in area, population, and GDP.

Meanwhile Hong Kong was returned to China.

The return was spurred by a British problem in Hong Kong with land titles. Although the most populous parts of Hong Kong had been ceded in perpetuity to the British by the Treaties of Nanjing (1842) and Tianjin (1856), the largest portion of Hong Kong in terms of area had been leased for 99 years by the Treaty of the Extension of Hong Kong Territory in 1898. Hence, the Hong Kong laws concerning landholding in the majority of the area of Hong Kong would legally (according to British/Hong Kong law) cease to be effective in 1997. When, in the early 1980s, the British raised the problem with the Chinese, the Chinese insisted that the whole of Hong Kong should be returned to China in 1997. The Joint Declaration, an international treaty to effect the transfer, was signed in 1984. It makes no mention of the legal status of Hong Kong before 1997 because the UK and the Chinese disagreed about it. The two parties simply agreed that …

> … a proper negotiated settlement of the question of Hong Kong, which is left over from the past, is conducive to the maintenance of the prosperity and stability of Hong Kong and to the further strengthening and development of the relations between the two countries on a new basis…[12]

The return was unconditional. In the Joint Declaration, however, China declared its basic policies with respect to Hong Kong, including…

---

hinrichfoundation.com/research/wp/fdi/hong-kong-pioneers-contribution-to-china-through-fdi/ (accessed January 26, 2021). Enright quotes a figure of 47% to from 1985 to 2014. FDI figures, exceeding 50% from 2015 to 2017 are taken from the China Data Online database.

[12]"Joint Declaration of the Government of the United Kingdom of Great Britain and Northern Ireland and the Government of the People's Republic of China on the Question of Hong Kong", December 19, 1984 listed by the Constitutional and Mainland Affairs Bureau, The Hong Kong Special Administrative Region (HKSAR). https://www.cmab.gov.hk/en/issues/jd2.htm (accessed January 25, 2021).

> The Hong Kong Special Administrative Region will enjoy a high degree of autonomy, except in foreign and defence affairs which are the responsibilities of the Central People's Government.[13]

Before the return, the governor was appointed by the UK. After the return, the Joint Declaration declared, …

> The chief executive will be appointed by the Central People's Government on the basis of the results of elections or consultations to be held locally. Principal officials will be nominated by the Chief Executive of the Hong Kong Special Administrative Region for appointment by the Central People's Government.[14]

The Joint Declaration stated that Hong Kong law would be subordinate to the National People's Congress and that the policies outlined in The Joint Declaration would be …

> … stipulated, in a Basic Law of the Hong Kong Special Administrative Region of the People's Republic of China, by the National People's Congress of the People's Republic of China, and they will remain unchanged for 50 years.[15]

The Basic Law, passed by the Chinese National People's Congress on April 4, 1990, technically an amendment to the Constitution of the People's Republic of China, became Hong Kong's mini-constitution.[16] But Article 45 of the Basic Law was somewhat problematic. Echoing the Joint Declaration it said,

> The Chief Executive of the Hong Kong Special Administrative Region shall be selected by election or through consultations held locally and be appointed by the Central People's Government. The method for selecting the Chief Executive shall be specified in the light of the actual

[13] *Ibid.*

[14] *Ibid.*

[15] *Ibid.*

[16] "Full Text of the Constitution and the Basic Law" listed by the Constitutional and Mainland Affairs Bureau, The Hong Kong Special Administrative Region (HKSAR). https://www.basiclaw.gov.hk/en/basiclaw/index.html (accessed December 14, 2021).

> situation in the Hong Kong Special Administrative Region and in accordance with the principle of gradual and orderly progress. The ultimate aim is the selection of the Chief Executive by universal suffrage upon nomination by a broadly representative nominating committee in accordance with democratic procedures.[17]

In theory the two principles of selection (1) "... appointed by the Central People's Government ..." and (2) "... universal suffrage ... in accordance with democratic procedures ..." could conflict. In fact, the Chief Executive of the Hong Kong SAR since 1997 has been selected by a small circle, electoral college from among candidates pre-vetted by the Central People's Government. This policy may be seen as a failure to deliver on the promise of the Basic Law. So even though Hong Kong, since 1997, has retained its legal and social system, and its economy has grown well, it has been plagued with recurring popular dissatisfaction with its chief executive.

As Table 5.1 demonstrates, although three out of four post-return chief executives of Hong Kong started their terms of office with approval ratings above that of the last British governor, three out of four scored average ratings below his and all four finished their terms of office with approval ratings well below his. The Hong Kong government disappoints.

Hong Kongers' disappointment has been combined with distrust of the Central People's Government, fear of being marginalized by an increasingly rich and strong China, and a personal identification with Hong Kong, rather than China.[18] This was the background for the political disturbances of 2014 and 2019.

Yet, following the demonstrations, violence, and reaction, Hong Kong remains a vibrant, cosmopolitan society with a highly educated populace, an open economy, a well-functioning independent judicial system, universal healthcare, and a high degree of social cohesion. It is true that Hong Kongers' levels of confidence in its universities, labor

---

[17] *Ibid.*

[18] 68.5% of Hong Kongers identify themselves as being "Hong Konger in a broad sense" (compared with 29.2% identifying as "Chinese, in a broad sense") up from 59.7% (down from 38.7%) in 1997. See Hong Kong Public Research Institute "People's Ethnic Identity". https://www.pori.hk/category/pop-poll/ethnic-identity-en?lang=en (accessed January 30, 2021).

Table 5.1: Approval Ratings of Chief Executives of Hong Kong Since 1992

	Chris Patten		Tung Chee-hwa		Donald Tsang		Leung Chun-ying		Carrie Lam	
Condition	Date	Rating	Date	Rating	Date	Rating	Date	Rating	Date	Rating
Initial	Apr-92	53.3	Jul-97	64.5	Jun-05	72.3	Jul-12	52.5	Jul-17	61.0
Maximum	Oct-92	64.1	Sep-97	67.7	Jun-05	72.3	Nov-12	52.6	Jul-17	61.0
Minimum	Oct-95	51.2	Jul-03	36.1	Jun-12	39.3	Dec-16	37.0	Feb-20	19.3
Last/latest	Jun-97	59.7	Jul-97	47.9	Jun-12	39.3	Jun-17	38.1	Jan-21	30.5
Average	na	57.0	na	52.1	na	57.4	na	43.5	na	41.5

Notes: (1) Chris Patten was the last British governor of Hong Kong. All others are Chief Executives of the Hong Kong SAR.

(2) The survey asked respondents to use scale of 0-100 to rate their extent of support to the Chief Executive, with 0 indicating absolutely not supportive, 100 indicating absolutely supportive, and 50 indicating half-half.

Source: Hong Kong Public Opinion Research Institute https://develo.pori.hk (accessed January 27, 2021).

unions, civil service, the justice system, the press, and government, are below those of Chinese in the rest of China. Yet, they are high by international standards exceeding, for example, those in the US.[19]

Albert Wong, the CEO of HKSPT and the protagonist in the following case, is an official in the service of Hong Kong. He reports to the Hong Kong government. To understand a little about the man and his philosophy, the reader should watch a video that we made when we interviewed him for this case.[20] Wong owes allegiance not only to the Hong Kong government, but also to the central Chinese government. In the organization he leads, HKSTP, incubation is but one program, but it is an important program.

Incubators, the policy instrument presented in the following case, are a US innovation. Since their birth more than 60 years ago in up-state New York, they have spread around the world. But as the case shows,

[19]See Table 2.2 in Chapter 2, page 49 and "Results in Percent by Country" World Values Survey Wave 7 (2017–2020), pp. 171–206. http://www.worldvaluessurvey.org/WVSDocumentationWV7.jsp (accessed January 29, 2021).

[20]Howard Lam and Hugh Thomas, "*Youtube Video* HKSTP". https://www.youtube.com/watch?v=RDQf2fu9PxE (accessed February 3, 2021).

there are more incubators now in China than in any other country of the world. HKSTP's incubator is located in Hong Kong, not in Mainland China.[21]

The case allows the reader to assess HKSTP's incubator competitors. Wong's goal is to foster a vibrant innovation and technology ecosystem. But his key performance indicators (KPIs) are far more specific, to attract entrepreneurs — from a global market — to join HKSTP's program and then to help them succeed. What services work and how those services are marketed are the questions that the reader is left to analyze in this first case.

[21]The term "Mainland China" is a somewhat confusing term, used by Hong Kongers to refer to the other parts of China not including the Hong Kong SAR, the Macao SAR, and Taiwan. The term is literally inaccurate because, while the *island* of Hong Kong was originally the only part of China ceded by the Treaty of Nanking in 1842, by far the greatest part of the Hong Kong SAR is located on the continent of Asia (i.e., on the mainland), not on islands. And the civic center of the Macao SAR, considered to be not part of "Mainland China" is actually on the mainland.

INCUBATION AND THE HONG KONG SCIENCE AND TECHNOLOGY PARKS CORPORATION

Hugh Thomas, Andrew Chi Fai Chan, Howard Pong Yuen Lam, and Icy Fong Ling Ngai wrote this case solely to provide material for class discussion. The authors do not intend to illustrate either effective or ineffective handling of a managerial situation.

How should the incubation programmes of the HKSTP be marketed to prospective incubatees? That was the problem facing HKSTP at the end of the fiscal year of March 31, 2018.

Albert Wong Chief Executive Officer of HKSTP firmly believed that start-up companies, especially the technology start-ups in HKSTP's incubation programmes, had to be passionate and self-reliant to survive and prosper. Yet HKSTP managed incubation programmes specifically to assist technology start-ups to survive the Valley of Death, where negative cash flow in its early stages might kill arbitrarily a highly innovative, potentially successful company (see Exhibit 1).

Hong Kong's government had given HKSTP unprecedented resources to support innovation and technology development in Hong Kong in its

2018–19 Budget announced in March 2018. Over HK$50 billion would be spent for innovation including development of the infrastructure, R&D, nurturing start-ups and promoting targeted industries. HK$10 billion of that HK$50 billion was for HKSTP. And in addition to the HK$10 billion, the government had allocated HK$20 billion for construction of the Hong Kong Shenzhen Innovation and Technology Park in Lok Ma Chau Loop, which would also be under the direction of the HKSTP's wholly-owned subsidiary, Hong Kong-Shenzhen Innovation and Technology Park Limited, for the promotion of innovation and technology.[1]

Incubation was an important part of the HKSTP's role in promoting technology development. Wong not only had to give HKSTP's incubatees the resources to help them survive and prosper; he also had to attract the best tech start-ups to join the programme.

INCUBATION PROGRAMMES

Business incubation programmes started in the late 1950s when a New York State real estate developer opted to sublet a large industrial facility to start-up companies, providing them with business services as well as space. In the 1970s, incubation was used by the United States National Science Foundation (NSF)'s Innovation Centers Program to facilitate commercialization of new technologies.[2] Incubators marshalled resources – office space, clerical, reception, accounting and legal support services, business knowledge, technology, access to customers and suppliers, a culture of entrepreneurship, etc. – for the benefit of newly established companies. By the second decade of the 21st century, numbers of US incubators swelled to over 1,200[3] and European Union incubators

---

[1]"Hong Kong Innovation and Technology Commission, "2018–19 Budget further speeds up Hong Kong's I&T development", *Newsletter* on 1 March 2018, accessed 21 August 2018, https://www.itc.gov.hk/enewsletter/180301/en/2018_19_budget_further_speeds_up_hk_it_development.html

[2]Hackett, S.M. and Dilts, D.M., 2004. "A Systematic Review Of Business Incubation Research". *Journal of Technology Transfer* 29 (1) 55–82.

[3]Ginger Lange in her PhD dissertation refers to 1,400 business incubators and accelerators in the USA of which approximately 1,200 are incubators. See Lange *The Value of Business Incubators and Accelerators from the Entrepreneurs Perspective* Georgia State University PhD dissertation, May 6, 2018.

to over 900.[4] In developing countries, cities around the globe, striving to become the next Silicon Valley, followed suit. And China became the country with the largest number of incubators (see Exhibit 2). Hong Kong, an autonomous, globally open, SAR of China, was among the first cities in China to use incubation to stimulate science, technology and entrepreneurship, with its leading incubator located in HKSTP.

HONG KONG SCIENCE AND TECHNOLOGY PARKS CORPORATION

HKSTP was established on 7 May 2001 by passage of the Hong Kong Science and Technology Parks Corporation Ordinance to

> facilitate the research and development and application of technologies in manufacturing and service industries in Hong Kong, … to support the development, transfer and use of new or advanced technologies in Hong Kong [and] … to engage in such activities or to perform such functions as the Chief Executive in Council may … permit or assign to it.[5]

The Ordinance merged three former organisations, the Hong Kong Industrial Estates Corporation, Hong Kong Industrial Technology Centre Corporation, and the Provisional Hong Kong Science Park Company Limited,[6] to create a larger, more vibrant innovation and technology ecosystem to deliver social and economic benefits to Hong Kong and the region. It was founded to connect stakeholders, facilitate knowledge transfer and nurture talents to accelerate technological innovation and commercialisation.[7]

The establishment of HKSTP was an important part of the Hong Kong government's plan. It was part of the Hong Kong government's

---

[4]Centre for Strategy & Evaluation Services Benchmarking of business incubators EU publications, 19 February 2014.

[5]"Cap. 56 Hong Kong Science and Technology Parks Corporation Ordinance" Hong Kong e-Legislation accessed May 22, 2019.

[6]Work of the Hong Kong Science and Technology Parks Corporation, meeting of LegCo Panel on Commerce and Industry, accessed on 25 August 2018. http://www.legco.gov.hk/yr06-07/english/panels/ci/papers/ci1219cb1-486-3-e.pdf

[7]HKSTP website "Our Commitment" accessed 7 August 2018.

tentative shift away from what Hong Kong entrepreneurship researchers[8] referred to as the traditional, *laissez faire* approach that was based on free trade, open finance, low taxes, small government, budget surpluses, and a staunch positive non-internationalist deference to market forces.[9] Hong Kong had grown from an *entrepôt* into a manufacturing center and then into a financial, logistics, and business services center benefitting from its role as the gateway to modern China. By the turn of the century, however, the Hong Kong government increasingly provided not only an open, level platform but also promotion of new technologies, innovation and entrepreneurship in specific clusters, drawing on local established industries and university research capabilities. HKSTP was formed at about the same time as Cyberport, a multi-building development on the western end of Hong Kong Island, to be an information and communications technologies (ICT) hub. HKSTP, in contrast, was substantially larger and strove to create five clusters: biomedical technology, electronics, green technology, ICT, and material and precision engineering. And it focused on three overarching application platforms: Healthy Ageing, Robotics and Smart City.

As of 31 March 2018, HKSTP had over 13,000 people working in 675 companies (of which 263 were incubatees) lodged in its over 3.5 million square feet of lab and office space at Hong Kong Science Park. Seven divisions of HKSTP reported to Wong, including but not limited to the Corporate Development Division that included the Incubation & Acceleration Programmes, Technology Clusters and Platforms, Investment/Corporate Venture Fund, etc. See Exhibit 3 for the corporate structure of HKSTP.

THE HKSTP INCUBATION PROGRAMMES

HKSTP provided work-space to technology start-up companies through three incubation programmes, the 18-month Incu-App Programme for web/mobile apps and games, the 3-year Incu-Tech Programme for

[8]Kevin Au, Erik Baark, Bee-leng Chua and Hugh Thomas, *Innovation Policy and High Growth Start-ups,* Center for Entrepreneurship, Chinese University of Hong Kong, Hong Kong, 2006 pages 7–12. accessed July 10, 2019.

[9]Haddon-Cave, Philip (1982). Public policy and economic success The Hong Kong Manager 18 15-19. (1982) p.17.

electronics, green technology, ICT as well as materials and precision engineering, and the 4-year Incu-Bio Programme for therapeutics, personal care, Chinese and herbal medicine, regenerative medicines, medical devices and diagnostics.[10] Incubatees paid HK$820 (US$105) per month for a desk in a co-working space that included access to conference rooms, telecoms and wifi, pantries, a gym and recreational facilities. For similar commercially available facilities in Hong Kong, a tenant would have to pay well in excess of HK$2000 (US$260)[11] per month. Incubatees also received mentorship, business partner matching, technical and professional consultation, marketing and promotion support, access to laboratory facilities, preparation for fund raising and matching with potential investors.

Each applicant had to be a Hong Kong registered company not older than two years from the date of application submission, with at least one (Incu-App) or two (Incu-Tech and Incu-Bio) full time staff, at least 50% of whom were technical personnel, working on project research and development. Particularly for Incu-App and Incu-Tech, the technical person or team had to own, individually or collectively, at least 10% of the applicant's equity.[12] In the fiscal year ending 31 March 2018, 234 companies applied and 97 were accepted into the incubation programs. Exhibit 4 summarizes the programme's key statistics while Exhibit 5 gives information about other major incubators in Hong Kong and the mainland city of Shenzhen, located on the northern border of Hong Kong.

MEASURING IMPACT

While stating the goals of incubators was easy, measuring their success was hard. In the US and China respectively, about 80% and 72% of start-ups survived their first year of business while about half and about one

---

[10] HKSTP website, accessed August 3, 2018. https://www.hkstp.org/en/how-we-serve/incubation-programmes

[11] Cocoon website, accessed 26 June 2017, https://www.hkcocoon.com

[12] For the admission criteria for the HKSTP Incubation Programmes, see HKSTP website, accessed August 7, 2018. https://www.hkstp.org/en/how-we-serve/incubation-programmes/incu-app (Incu-App) https://www.hkstp.org/en/how-we-serve/incubation-programmes/incu-tech (Incu-Tech)

quarter of companies survived for more than five years.[13] Exhibit 4's data from HKSTP showed that as of the end of each recent year, the ratio of cumulative graduates still in business to cumulative total graduates was stable at around 75%. HKSTP had carefully and competitively selected HKSTP's incubatees before they were admitted. Furthermore, during their residence, they enjoyed mentorship, access to professional advice, lower rents, access to financing, etc. In short, due to differences in samples and other factors, the above percentage of HKSTP's incubatees that were still in business could not directly be compared with the one and five year survival rates from the US and China.

The difficulty in measuring the impact of incubators was not unique to HKSTP. As Exhibit 6 shows, academic studies of the effectiveness of incubation came to diverse conclusions.

CHALLENGES FACING INCUBATEES

Incubatees viewed incubation programmes at HKSTP as a crucial support to enhance their prospects for survival and development. Incubatees' plans were formalized as milestones, specific actions or accomplishments to be completed by set dates. In fact, the vast majority of incubatees either successfully passed their milestones or appropriately re-set milestones with HKSTP's agreement. During the fiscal year ending on 31 March 2018, only 8.4% of incubatees withdrew from the programme.

The Head of Incubations Programmes, Peter Mok identified two main reasons for the withdrawals: team related issues and business opportunities (both good and bad). Team related issues included family matters, health reasons and irreconcilable arguments among founding team members over company direction. Business opportunities included, on the good side, a merger or an acquisition, leading to changes in ownership such that the founding team members held less than 50% of the company.

[13]For US estimates see US Department of Labour Bureau of Labor Statistics. Business Employment Dynamics Establishment Age and Survivor Data. Table 7 2017 https://www.bls.gov/bdm/ accessed 23 July 2017. For Chinese data see David Audretsch, Xiaodan Guo, Adrian Hepfer, Hugo Menendez, and Xingzhi Xiao "Ownership, productivity and firm survival in China" Economia e Politica Industriale; Heidelberg Vol. 43, Iss. 1, (Mar 2016), pp. 67–83.

Or the company could have changed its strategy so fundamentally that it no longer fit into the criteria for the programme. Finally, the business model could be proven unsustainable. Some companies simply developed products and/or services that failed to meet a market need.

Among the difficulties identified by incubatees, one was a lack of cash. Although Hong Kong was ranked as the third most powerful financial centre in the world, after New York and London but before Singapore (#4), Tokyo (#5), Shanghai (#6), Beijing (#10) and Shenzhen (#20),[14] local investors tended to be risk averse and preoccupied with real estate, not technology. Incubatees complained that, in the absence of local high-tech entrepreneurial business models and heroes, angel investors, talented engineers and managers were reluctant to bet their money and time.

The Hong Kong market had yet to build a critical mass to achieve economies of scale. Hong Kong was part of China, with national defence governed by Beijing and economically Hong Kong was an SAR, having its own legal system, and negotiating commercial treaties directly with other countries of the world. While companies starting in Hong Kong had to be born global,[15] those starting in China or the US could launch their globalization efforts after successfully establishing themselves domestically. Incubatees aimed to change customer habits with their new products and services, yet the change took time, especially when selling to conservative companies and government departments.

Shing Yuk Chow was the owner-manager of Lalamove, a logistics company specialized in on-demand short-haul deliveries in Asia using the sharing economy to match users and drivers in the same city, which had been in HKSTP incubation from June 2014, six months after its founding, until December 2015. Lalamove was affected by the pros and cons of its Hong Kong location, operating in Hong Kong, Bangkok, Manila, Singapore, Taipei and more than 90 cities in mainland China.[16] One of HKSTP's first unicorns, that is a privately funded, start-up

---

[14]Ben Moshinsky, "The 20 Most Powerful Financial Centres in the world" Business Insider 12 September 2017.

[15]Gary A Knight and S. Tamar Cavusgil "Innovation, Organizational Capabilities, and the Born-Global Firm" Journal of International Business Studies March 2004, Volume 35, Issue 2, pp 124–141.

[16]Lalamove website, accessed 18 June 2017.

technology company valued at over US$1 billion, Lalamove appreciated the convenience of Hong Kong, but as Chow commented, the size of the Hong Kong market was a disadvantage:

> Imagine: if my business model worked in San Francisco, it would also work in New York. But my Hong Kong model is unlikely to work in New York, and will not even work in Shenzhen. As a result, it narrows your target market. The biggest internet companies in the world come from the States and China, because their local market is large enough. But for Hong Kong, our local market is relatively small.

HKSTP strove to attract promising start-ups from around the world. Lumos Helmet was founded by Eu-wen Ding and Jeff Chen, who met at a weekend hackathon in Boston Mass, USA[17] while they were both students at Harvard in 2015. Their idea, a sculpted, smart bike helmet that integrated head- and brake lights and turn signals to improve bicycle safety and increase cyclists' confidence[18] was tested in Kickstarter and successfully attracted over 6000 backers who pledged over US$800,000 bringing the project to life.[19] Lumos joined the HKSTP incubation programme in November 2015. As of midyear 2017, Lumos was producing one helmet size in five colours selling at US$199 per piece in the North America and Europe markets. Ding was from Singapore and chose Hong Kong because of the ease of conducting business in the city. The company made a physical product, a helmet, and he felt that there was nowhere else in the world better to manufacture it than Shenzhen. Ideally, he would have chosen to live in Shenzhen, except that Lumos' marketing was all done online, using Google and Facebook, two services sporadically blocked by in China. Hong Kong presented a natural middle ground for Lumos' headquarters. Access to the internet was fast and reliable and travel to Shenzhen, where the Lumos engineering team was located, was convenient.

[17]A hackathon is an event in which teams compete to design specific software over a short period ranging from several hours to several days.

[18]Lumos Helmet website, accessed 18 June 2017.

[19]Kickstarter website, accessed 18 June 2017.

MEETING THE NEEDS OF START-UPS

Wong knew that Hong Kong was an innovator's paradox: according to the Global Innovation Index 2018 of 127 countries, Hong Kong's overall ranking was a credible 14th, ahead of China (17th), but behind Singapore (5th), Korea (12th) and Japan (13rd) in Asia. But this overall good ranking masked a dichotomy. While Hong Kong ranked 8th in the input sub-index, behind Singapore (1st) but above all other competitors in Asia, its innovation efficiency ratio was an unimpressive 64%. And in terms of overall entrepreneurial activity, Hong Kong ranked below its competitors (see Exhibit 7). To address these problems, Wong was determined to establish a new ecosystem at HKSTP. He wanted to do more than provide low rent to start-ups and helping them with the administrative details of running a business. He wanted to help incubatees connect with the rest of the world.

Wong saw Hong Kong as a well-positioned platform for marketing high potential technology start-up goods and services to the world. He felt Hong Kong was an ideal location to test products and services because Hong Kong was small, and the regulatory requirements set by the Hong Kong government were stringent. He also considered Hong Kong's location, next to the biggest market in the world, to be critical to any company with a strategy for China.

To help incubatees with their China strategies, HKSTP had developed partnerships so that incubatees in HKSTP could use facilities located in Beijing, Tianjin, Shanghai and Shenzhen on a reciprocal basis.[20]

One of the strongest elements of HKSTP's mainland China connection came from Hong Kong's universities. University researchers – professors and their post-graduate students – formed a significant source of HKSTP incubatees. And most post-graduate research students of those universities came from the Mainland.

Wong noted that HKSTP could help incubatees navigate through regulations. Start-up companies promoting new technologies – whether autonomous self-driving or shared cars or stem cell research – often confronted regulatory constraints. HKSTP helped incubatees to understand and deal with regulations. The recently implemented Public Sector Trial

---

[20]For HKSTP's Co-working Space Programme, see HKSTP website, accessed 7 August 2018. https://www.hkstp.org/innovate-with-us/passion-matters/infrastructure/labs-and-co-working-space/

Scheme for Incubatees and Graduate Tenants of HKSTP and Hong Kong Cyberport Management Company Limited (PSTS-SPC Projects) provided funding for prototypes and trials in the public sector to help incubatees commercialise their R&D.[21] HKSTP could facilitate those applications.

HKSTP could also help with financing. Given the technology focus of the companies and the speed with which they were growing, Wong felt that, in the long run, HKSTP would become a place-to-go for Asian or even global technology investors. One of his goals was to increase deal-flow for companies at Hong Kong Science Park. Doing so, however, involved educating investors. Hong Kong investors, many of whom had made their fortunes in traditional labor-intensive manufacturing, trading and real estate, tended to be averse to investing in new technologies. Part of this stemmed from their belief that Hong Kong had no competitive advantage in innovation and high technology. And part of it stemmed from a conservative strategy that set positive cash flow as a prerequisite for investment. Yet the global unicorns of new technologies typically had negative cash flows. To accomplish this education and matching of investors with investee companies, Wong created a new task force at HKSTP that he called the Investors' Team. The team sought to create opportunities for investors, introducing them to many HKSTP park companies in their areas of interest — AI, biotech, electronics, green-tech, ICT, new materials, etc.

Eric Z.X. Chen, Founder and Chief Commercial Officer of Vitargent (International) Biotechnology Ltd., appreciated the help extended by HKSTP in the company's start-up. He established Vitargent in 2010, and the company was in the incubation programme from 2011 to 2015. Vitargent applied its proprietary Transgenic Medaka and Zebrafish Fish Embryo Toxicity (FET) testing technology on food and skincare products. In 2013, Vitargent received the international standard ISO17025 Accreditation. As of 2017 it was the only test centre in Asia that could provide fish embryo toxicity testing with testing results officially recognized in more than 100 countries. Vitargent planned to use its consumer product safety information platform, Test-it™, to become the global

---

[21] Innovation and Technology Fund "Public Sector Trial Scheme". Accessed 11 August 2017.

The Innovation and Technology Fund (ITF) was administered by the Innovation and Technology Commission of the Hong Kong government "to increase the added value, productivity and competitiveness of economic activities in Hong Kong. See the Innovation and Technology website. Accessed 11 August 2017.

standard for consumer product safety. Chen felt that the key attraction of HKSTP incubation was its low rent, but HKSTP had also helped with fund-raising. As a university student, it was difficult for him to secure first-phase funding to launch his business. He secured initial funding from the government in 2010 and then reached out internationally for qualified employees. Chen commented that the HKSTP team was helpful in lining up additional funding and resources, as well as helping the new company with legal and accounting advice.

Unlike the CEO of a for-profit, private sector company, Wong did not restrict his mandate to HKSTP alone. He was responsible for promoting the Hong Kong technology start-up community. He believed that Hong Kong's economic and business environment was the best in the world, however, it was a city with only seven million people. HKSTP could help its incubatees to expand beyond Hong Kong. As Wong expressed it:

> If there are incubatees successful in Hong Kong and they move to Shenzhen, ... if their business or their products or services are good for the big market of China, we will support them to scale up and go global ... But ... Hong Kong is their anchor and they should keep an R&D arm in Science Park.

Wong defined his role as serving the Hong Kong start-up and innovation community. He viewed other incubators in Hong Kong, and indeed the whole Hong Kong innovative ecosystem as complementing, rather than competing with HKSTP. Within that evolving ecosystem, Shenzhen, a city with approximately the same GDP as and 50% greater population than Hong Kong, just 15 kilometres north of HKSTP was especially important. Moreover, the spirit of cooperation was being orchestrated not only by the Hong Kong government but also from the mainland China government through the promotion of the Greater Bay Area, a 70 million population innovation megalopolis, encompassing not only Hong Kong and Macao but also Shenzhen, the Guangdong Provincial capital of Guangzhou and seven other cities of the Pearl River Delta.[22]

---

[22]National Development and Reform Commission People's Government of Guangdong Province Government of the Hong Kong Special Administrative Region Government of the Macao Special Administrative Region Framework Agreement on Deepening Guangdong-Hong Kong-Macao Cooperation in the Development of the Greater Bay Area, July 1, 2017 accessed May 22, 2019.

In early 2017, the Chief Executive of the Hong Kong SAR announced that Hong Kong and Shenzhen would jointly construct the Hong Kong-Shenzhen Innovation and Technology Park at the 87-hectare formerly undeveloped loop of the river separating the two cities called the Lok Ma Chau Loop.[23] Physical infrastructure (i.e., roads, water, sewage, electricity, telecommunications, etc.) were in the early planning stage. A budget of HK$20 billion (US$2.56 billion) was allocated for construction.[24]

MARKETING TO PROSPECTIVE INCUBATEES

Setting a marketing plan for prospective incubatees generally required following steps, such as those outlined in Exhibit 8.

Although incubation programmes were a part of Wong's responsibilities at HKSTP, he saw them as critical to his mission to foster the development of the innovation, technology and entrepreneurship ecosystem. Inspiring and attracting young techno-savvy entrepreneurs was key. He envisioned the re-industrialisation of Hong Kong, not with labor-intensive traditional factories, but with high-end, R&D-intensive jobs.

HKSTP had been recognized by the International Business Innovation Association as the leading incubator in the world in 2016.[25] Wong was delighted with the accomplishment, and HKSTP had also made continued efforts to enhance its reputation as well as promote its vibrant innovation and technology system (see Exhibit 9). Notwithstanding HKSTP's accomplishments, however, Wong was aware that much work remained to be done. In that work, he saw marketing as a driving force. Why would a start-up choose to go to HKSTP? What did its brand convey? What

[23]Hong Kong and Shenzhen sign Memorandum of Understanding on Jointly Developing the Lok Ma Chau Loop, January 3, 2017, accessed 5 August 2017, http://www.info.gov.hk/gia/general/201701/03/P2017010300609.htm

[24]"Hong Kong Innovation and Technology Commission "2018-19 Budget further speeds up Hong Kong's I&T development" Newsletter on 1 March 2018, accessed 21 August 2018, https://www.itc.gov.hk/enewsletter/180301/en/2018_19_budget_further_speeds_up_hk_it_development.html

[25]CISION PR Newswire "HKSTP wins Technology/IT Incubator of the Year at International Business Innovation Association Awards". http://www.prnewswire.com/news-releases/hkstp-wins-technologyit-incubator-of-the-year-at-international-business-innovation-association-awards-300243315.html (accessed July 2017).

services did it deliver to improve a start-ups' chances of success? How should HKSTP market itself and identify potential incubatees to enhance its position in the global market for incubator services?

EXHIBIT 1: THE VALLEY OF DEATH

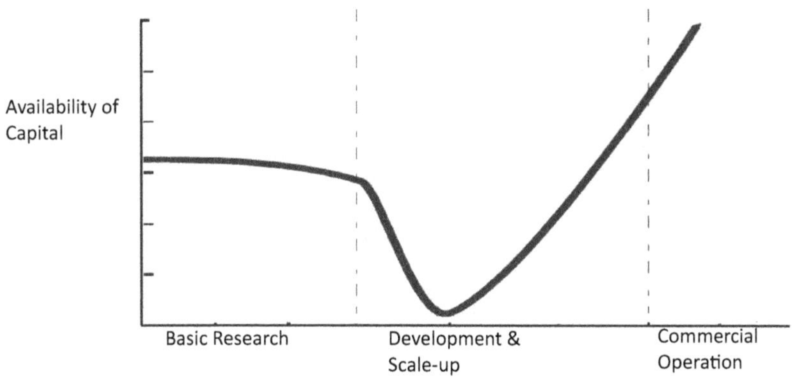

Source: Adapted from WonKoo Park, KwangSook Lee, SeoYoung Doo and Sung-Soo Yoon, *The Advanced Technology Program: Reform with a Purpose* Office of the Secretary, US Department of Commerce, Washington, February 2002.

The introduction to Evans (2002) states "…the so-called "Valley of Death" refers to the time period prior to the demonstration of technical and economic feasibility of a new technological concept, when the risks are very high due to uncertainty or complexity. It is believed that transcending the "valley" in the shortest time is crucial for success in exploiting the new technology in the market place…." For recent measurement of the shape of the "valley" see Won Koo Park, Kwang Sook Lee, Seo Young Doo and Sung-Soo Yoon, "Investments for New Product Development: A Break-Even Time Analysis", *Engineering Management Journal* 28:3 (September 2016) 154–167.

EXHIBIT 2: TECHNOLOGY INCUBATORS IN CHINA

A. Growth of Technology Incubators in China

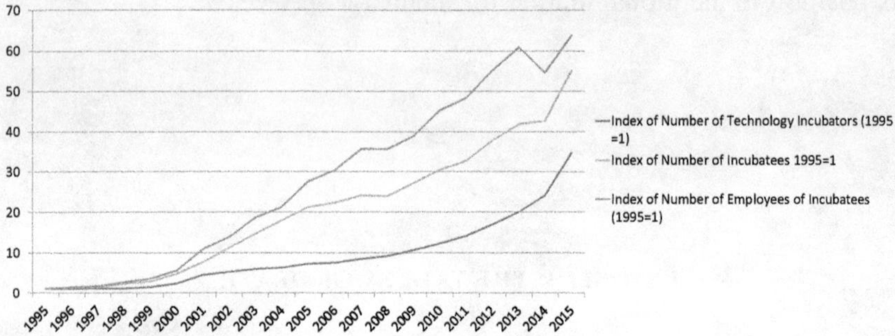

Note: Graph shows the number of technology incubators, the number of incubatees and the number of incubatee employees as multiple of their numbers in 1995. In 1995 there were 73 incubators, 1,854 incubatees and 26,000 employees of incubates. In 2015 there were 2,536 incubators, 102,170 incubatees and 1.662 million employees of incubatees. The figures include national-, provincial-, municipal- and district-sponsored technology incubators.
Source: "Main Indicators of Technology Based Incubators" Torch High Technology Industry Development Center, Ministry of Science and Technology, PRC.

B. Average Characteristics of Nationally Sponsored Technology Incubators in China

Item	Average Amount	Note
Resident incubatees	130	number
Age of incubator	12	years
Management staff of incubator	22	number
Floor space of incubator	53,741	square meters
Proportion of incubatee workers with tertiary education	78	percent
Business service fees paid by incubatees to incubator	0.822	USD million per year
Trademarks and patents registered	77.5	number per year
Incubatees graduating	12.4	number per year
Venture capital funding	17.3	million USD per year
GDP per capita of host city	9,894	USD per year
Inward FDI of the host city	4.0	billion USD per year

Note: The above data are averages of 120 technology incubators from a 2012 survey of the National Productivity Promotion Center of China.
Source: Jin Hong and Jinfeng Lu, "Assessing the effectiveness of business incubators in fostering SMEs: evidence from China", *International Journal of Entrepreneurship and Innovation Management*, Vol. 20, Nos. 1/2, 2016.

EXHIBIT 3: HKSTP ORGANIZATION CHART

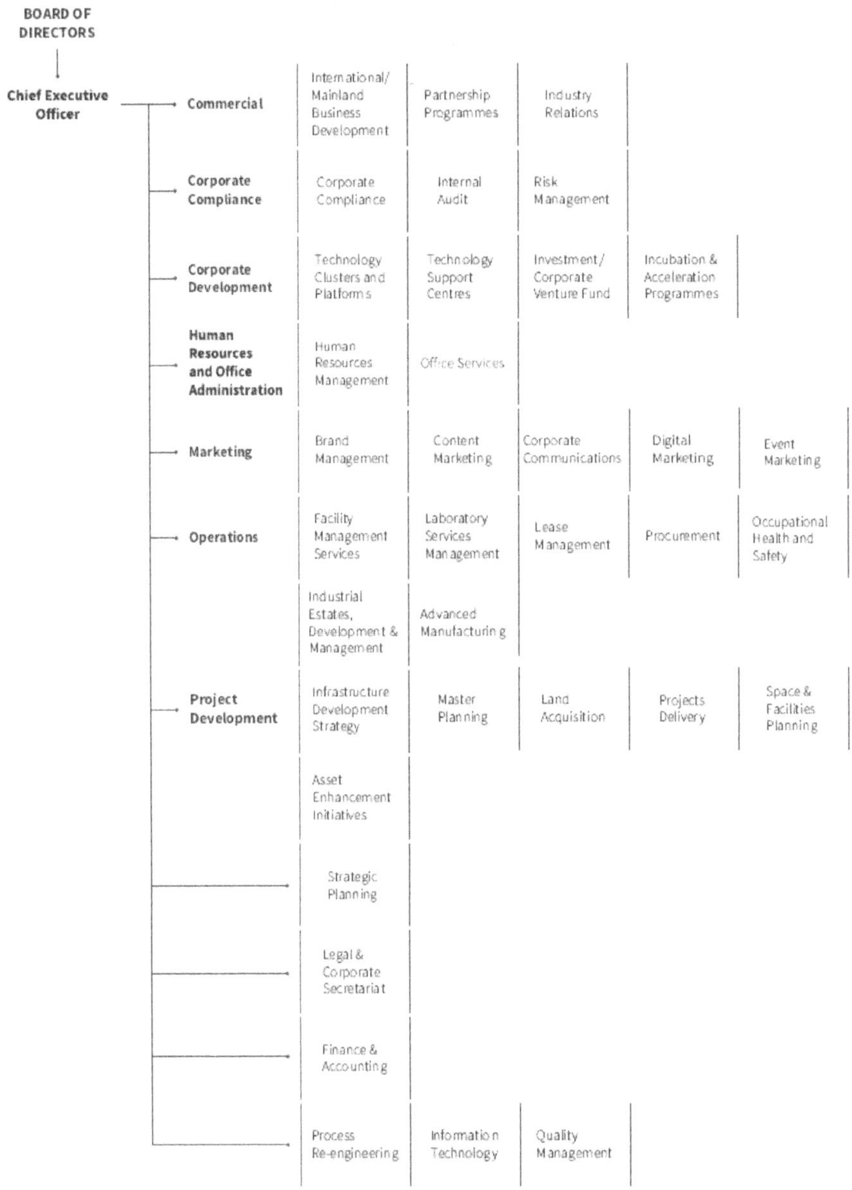

Source: HKSTP's Annual Report 2017–18.

EXHIBIT 4: HKSTP INCUBATEES AND THEIR ACCOMPLISHMENTS

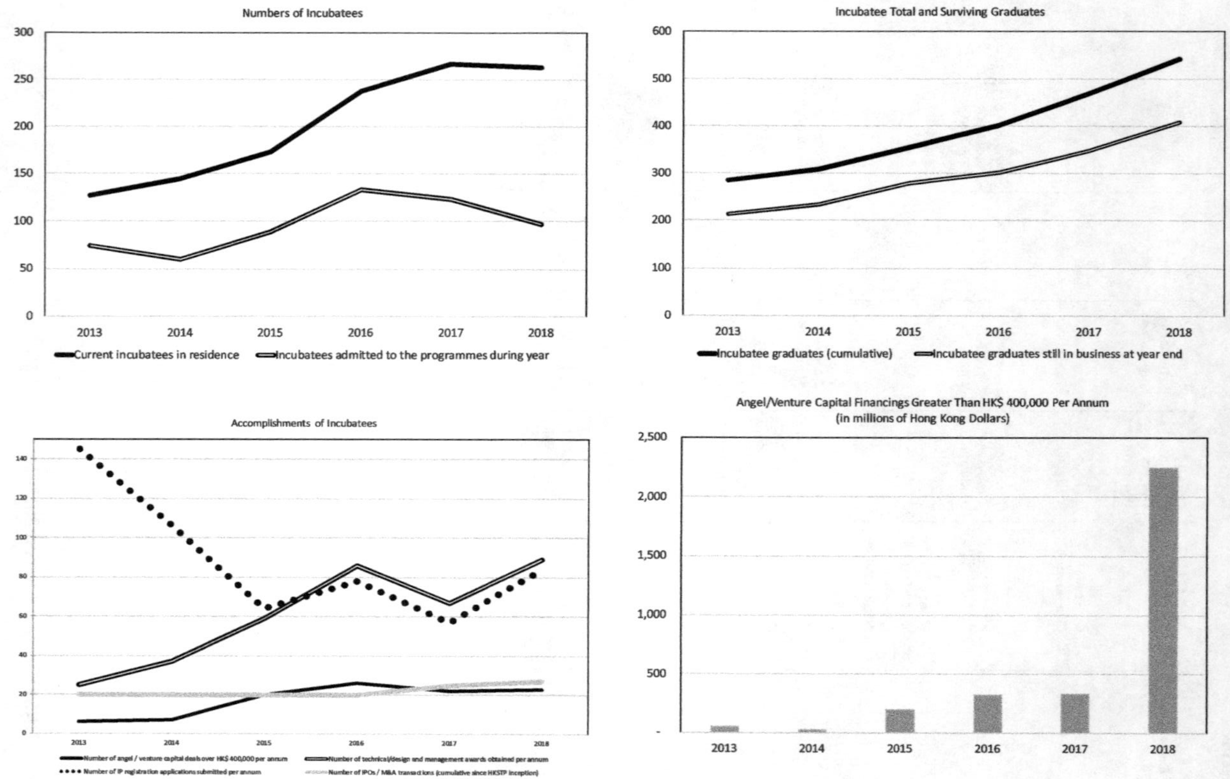

Source: HKSTP.

EXHIBIT 5: MAJOR INCUBATORS IN THE HONG KONG AND SHENZHEN REGION

	HKSTP	Cyberport	Cocoon Hong Kong	Shenzhen E-Hub	Shenzhen Bay Inno Park
Date Established	May 2001	April 2002; Incubation program opens October 2005	May 2012	Dec 2014	June 2015
Funding by	Public Funding	Hong Kong Government	Private	Shenzhen Government	Shenzhen Government
Total Facilities Size	22-hectare with R&D offices (330,000 m^2)	92,000-square-metre office complex with a 28,000-square-metre shopping mall and a 173-room hotel	836 square meters situated in a commercial office building	27,000 square meters in the planned area sized of about 40,000 square meters	500,000 square meters, 400 meters long street along with 18 buildings as the community
Number of Incubatees	267 as of March 2017	289 of which 51 were on-site and 238 off-site as of March 2017	approximately 70* based on 9-month residency over 5-year period	Up to 200	45 professional incubators and start up services companies and 200+ start-up companies as of Oct 2016
Vision	Create a vibrant innovation and technology ecosystem to deliver social and economic benefits to Hong Kong and the region.	Establish Cyberport as a leading ICT hub in Asia-Pacific region.	Reignite the entrepreneurial spirit in Hong Kong and be a world class entrepreneurship hub at the cutting edge internationally in community building, entrepreneurship education and early stage investments.	Create an entrepreneur hub for innovative youth start-ups from around the world	Implement the Shenzhen government's innovation-driven development strategy and develop an international entrepreneurial venture capital center
Area(s) of Focus	Biomedical Technology, Green Technology, Electronics, Materials & Precision Engineering and Information & Communications Technology	FinTech, eCommerce, IoT/ Wearables and Big Data/AI	Community building, entrepreneurship education and early stage investments.	Modern logistics, financial services, information services, technology, cultural and creative industries and related professional services.	Professional incubation, start-up/venture investment and seed fund trading market

(Continued)

EXHIBIT 5: (*Continued*)

	HKSTP	Cyberport	Cocoon Hong Kong	Shenzhen E-Hub	Shenzhen Bay Inno Park
Programmes & Services	Incu-App, Incu-Tech and Incu-Bio Programmes: subsidised office space and shared facilities, matching potential investors, financial aid package, business matching, legal consultation, market promotion and development assistance, strategic partners building, business plan consultation, technical and management support and laboratory. Leading Enterprises Acceleration Programme (LEAP) provides in-depth services to nurture high potential candidates into regional/global companies	Subsidized office space, networking opportunities, business development and financing consulting, financial assistance up to HK$330,000 (US$42,300); Access to accelerator programmes	Subsidized office space, lightning fast Wi-fi, a 3D printer, and access to a community of partners and investors	Subsidized office space, seed money, training, consulting, networking; access to angel investors and venture capital and tax incentives.	Entrepreneurship training, Entrepreneurship show, public acceleration, creative apartment, business media, business exchange

Note: * Based on 450 incubatees cumulative since start-up in May 2012 with each resident staying approximately 9 months.

Source: See Report of the Advisory Committee on Innovation and Technology by Advisory Committee on Innovation and Technology March 2017, p40, http://www.itc.gov.hk/en/doc/ACIT_Report_Eng.pdf and https://www.hkstp.org/hkstp_web/en/what-we-do/nurture-technology-talents/incubation-programme accessed on 20 June 2017. Report of the Advisory Committee on Innovation and Technology by Advisory Committee on Innovation and Technology March 2017, p41, accessed on 20 June 2017, https://www.cyberport.hk/en/about_cyberport/cyberport_entrepreneurs/cyberport_incubation_programme; CoCoon Hong Kong website accessed on 20 June 2017, Shenzhen Youth Federation and the Hong Kong Federation of Youth Groups, accessed on 20 June 2017, http://ehub.hkfyg.org.hk/aboutus.php Introduction of Shenzhen Bay Inno Park, accessed on 20 June 2017, http://www.szbay.com/gc_91.html# (Chinese Only).

EXHIBIT 6: ACADEMIC STUDIES OF INCUBATORS

				Sample						
Authors	Title	Publication Venue	Publication/ release Date	Country	Dates of Sample	Number of incubators	Types of incubator	Number of incubatees/ companies	Study Design	Conclusions
Jin Hong and Jinfeng Lu*	Assessing the effectiveness of business incubators in fostering SMEs: evidence from China	International Journal of Entrepreneurship and Innovation Management	2016	China	2008-2012	120	state level technology incubators	600	Regression of incubatee performance as a function of incubator characteristics	Infrastructure support does not contribute to intellectual property generation or venture capital acquisition. Business assistance helps access to venture capital. Technical assistance increases growth. Larger and older incubators perform better than younger smaller incubators.
Alejandro S. Amezcua	Boon or Boondoggle? Business Incubation as Entrepreneurship Policy	Working Paper Whitman School of Management, Syracuse University	2010	USA	1990-2008	994	all types	35,000	Incubatee and non-incubatee similar company matched-paired businesses performance evaluation	Incubation reduces the lifespan of new ventures. Incubation increases the rates of growth of employment and sales
EU Center for Strategy and Evaluation Services	Benchmarking of Business Incubators	European Commission Enterprise General	2002	European Union	prior to 2002 publication date	78	all types, but 75 % technology oriented	71	Questionnaires to incubators and incubatees followed by sub-sample interviews	Incubators make a significant contribution to job and wealth creation and substantially increase chance of incubatee survival. The cost per job creation is low and they are effective in very effective promoting knowledge intensive, new technology-based activities

Source: Jin Hong and Jinfeng Lu "Assessing the effectiveness of business incubators in fostering SMEs: evidence from China" International Journal of Entrepreneurship and Innovation Management, Vol. 20, Nos. 1/2, 2016.

Alejandro S. Amezcua "Boon or Boondoggle? Business Incubation as Entrepreneurship Policy" Working Paper Whitman School of Management, Syracuse University" 2010. Accessed April 30, 2019 https://search.proquest.com/openview/48c3c0f7864b7e8000660d54527efcd7/1?pq-origsite=gscholar&cbl=18750&diss=y

EU Center for Strategy and Evaluation Services "Benchmarking of Business Incubators" European Commission Enterprise General, 2002 accessed April 30, 2019.

EXHIBIT 7: INNOVATIVE AND ENTREPRENEURIAL ENVIRONMENT OF HONG KONG AND COMPETITORS

A. Global Innovation Index 2018 (Top 20)

Country/Region	GII Score	Rank of GII	Input Subindex Score	Input Subindex Rank	Output Subindex Score	Output Subindex Rank	Efficiency Ratio
Switzerland	68.40	1	69.67	2	67.13	1	0.96
Netherlands	63.32	2	66.45	9	60.19	2	0.91
Sweden	63.08	3	69.21	3	56.94	3	0.82
United Kingdom	60.13	4	67.89	4	52.37	6	0.77
Singapore	59.83	5	74.23	1	45.43	15	0.61
United States of America	59.81	6	67.81	6	51.81	7	0.76
Finland	59.63	7	67.88	5	51.38	8	0.76
Denmark	58.39	8	67.43	7	49.34	13	0.73
Germany	58.03	9	63.27	17	52.79	5	0.83
Ireland	57.19	10	63.14	18	51.25	9	0.81
Israel	56.79	11	62.76	19	50.83	11	0.81
Korea, Republic of	56.63	12	63.42	14	49.84	12	0.79
Japan	54.95	13	65.41	12	44.49	18	0.68
Hong Kong (China)	54.62	14	66.71	8	42.53	21	0.64
Luxembourg	54.53	15	56.19	25	52.87	4	0.94
France	54.36	16	63.31	16	45.40	16	0.72
China	53.06	17	55.13	27	50.98	10	0.92
Canada	52.98	18	65.67	10	40.28	26	0.61
Norway	52.63	19	64.18	13	41.08	24	0.64
Australia	51.98	20	65.66	11	38.30	31	0.58

Note: The Global Innovation Index GII score is the simple average of the Input and Output Sub-Index scores. The Innovation Efficiency Ratio is the ratio of the Output Sub-Index score over the Input Sub-Index score. It shows how much innovation output a given country is getting for its inputs. The Innovation Input Sub-Index is comprised of five input pillars that capture elements of the national economy that enable innovative activities: (1) Institutions, (2) Human capital and research, (3) Infrastructure, (4) Market sophistication, and (5) Business sophistication.

The Innovation Output Sub-Index provides information about outputs that are the results of innovative activities within the economy. There are two output pillars: (6) Knowledge and technology outputs and (7) Creative outputs. The GII does not separately calculate indices for Mainland China cities.

Source: Cornell INSEAD WIPO The Global Innovation Index 2018 (accessed 3 September, 2018) https://www.globalinnovationindex.org/.

B. Global Entrepreneurship Monitor

	Entrepreneurial Activity (percent of adult population)					GDP Per Capita (US dollars)
	Nascent	New	Total Early Activity (TEA)	Established	Overall	
Hong Kong (China)	4.99	4.66	9.44	6.12	15.30	56,719
Shenzhen (China)	6.26	9.98	16.04	7.82	23.38	25,038
China	4.45	6.09	10.29	7.49	17.51	14,239
USA	8.88	4.00	12.63	9.22	20.99	55,837

Note: Table shows the percent of the population from 18 to 64 years of age engaged in entrepreneurial activities Nascent=those who have taken steps to start a new business, but have not yet paid for more than 3 months salaries or wages; New=those running new businesses that have been in operation for between 3 months and 42 months; TEA=New and Nascent; Established Business Owners=those running a mature business in operation for more than 42 months New + Nascent > TEA and TEA + Established > Overall because some entrepreneurs have multiple businesses.
Source: M. Dowejko and K. Au, Global Entrepreneurship Monitor: Hong Kong and Shenzhen Report 2016.

EXHIBIT 8: STEPS IN DEVELOPING A SERVICE MARKETING STRATEGY

1. **Define the Team**
   - What people/divisions in the organization will implement the strategy?
   - What external strategic partners will help implementation?
2. **Describe the target market**
   - List characteristics of customers (location, size, demographics, psychographics, etc)
   - Specify task(s) that the organization helps the customers do
   - List the alternatives to the organization's service and the process by which customers decide among those alternatives
3. **Specify current and potential contact points and communication channels with customers**
   - Describe contact and communications now used
   - List the owned, earned and paid media available
4. **Set the SMART goals of marketing strategy. Each goal is:**
   - *Specific* enough for the team to understand it exactly
   - *Measurable* and quantified so the team understand when the goal is reached
   - *Achievable* so the team and planners agree that, in theory, the goals can be met
   - *Realistic*, taking into consideration the macro-economy, resources, competitors, budget and the ability and commitment of the team.
   - *Timely* and subject to specific deadlines
5. **Set the message(s) to be at the heart of communications with the target customer**
   - Give each goal a single message, (for example, care, quality, price, convenience, impact, etc.). Different goals can share the same message.
   - Each message should differentiate the service of the organization from the competition in helping the customer accomplish the task
6. **Decide on the brand. This can involve maintaining or re-setting the brand**
   - The brand elicits the emotion that the organization wishes the target market to associate with its service
   - The brand should be consistent with organization history, target customer perceptions and the message(s) to be conveyed
7. **Set the marketing channels for delivering the message(s), promoting the brand and maintaining contact with the target market during and following the communication**
   - The channels should effectively and efficiently reach the target market
8. **Summarize the strategy in a plan with a budget**

Note: These steps should be followed iteratively. For example, a new goal may necessitate redefining the team, or an excessive budget may require redefining realistic goals.
Source: The Authors.

EXHIBIT 9: RECENT EXAMPLES OF HKSTP'S MARKETING INITIATIVES

A. HKSTP Corporate Advertisement (2018)

Source: HKSTP.

B. HKSTP's Community Engagement Campaign (2018) – Makeithongkong

Source: HKSTP.

C. HKSTP's Education Programme (2018) – Robo Workshop@Science Park

Brief translation of the Chinese content in the above poster:

Robo Workshop @SciencePark

Robots carry human's creativity and imagination of the future. Remember the Gundam invincible fighters that grew up with you, or the cute Xiaoyun 小雲 (Arale Norimaki), Xiaoji 小吉 (Gatchan) (Don't forget! Doraemon is also a robotic cat!) Robots have been pushing the advancement of modern technology. Today's applications cover industrial, entertainment, medical, and disaster relief. In education, the use of robots for learning subjects of STEM (Science, Technology, Engineering, Mathematics) has become a global trend.

Robo Workshops are the best tool for learning about STEM subjects.

Building a robot is an educational tool that integrates multiple STEM areas. It involves considerable basic knowledge, mechanical principles and computer coursework. Through the Robo Workshop @ Science Park, students can flexibly apply scientific theoretical knowledge learned in textbooks and workshops to control and operate robots to complete tasks. In the process of learning, students can develop a sense of space, logical thinking, creativity, and also nurture their interest in STEM learning.

Robo Workshop @ Science Park has a diverse range of learning kits on robotics which are suitable for students of various ages. Our workshops are designed with different levels of difficulty for both teachers and students of different age groups. Students can master the application of technology in daily life, and put their knowledge into practice. We also host specific workshops from time to time for the general public.

Source: HKSTP.

Chapter 6

Cisco and Cloud-Based Education in China

Introduction

"Cisco and Cloud-based Education in China" is a marketing case about entry of a large non-Chinese MNC into the China market. The protagonist in the case is Aglaia Kong, vice president and chief technology officer at Cisco Greater China. She is considering how Cisco can develop and market equipment for the Chinese education information technology revolution.

Sea Turtles

Aglaia Kong is a sea turtle. The term "sea turtle" in Chinese is a homonym for "returnee from overseas"[1] and refers to those Chinese who, after receiving a higher education and starting a career in the West, return to China.

International travel was extremely restricted for Chinese following the revolution of 1949 and became virtually impossible during the 1960s and early 1970s. Yet many Chinese were (and continue to be) intensely curious about the world outside China. In the late 1970s, a trickle of students left the country for the West. The trickle gradually grew to a

[1]The term in Chinese is "*hai gui*" 海龟 (sea turtle) but "*hai gui*" can also be written 海归 (returnee from overseas).

flood. Most who left in the early years became permanent emigrants. But in the 1990s, as ever more young Chinese went abroad, increasing numbers also returned. From 2000 to 2019, 6.2 million Chinese left to study overseas. Over four million of them have since returned.[2] They have brought deep, first-hand knowledge of the West — technology, products, business models, companies, philosophies, and lifestyles. They have profoundly changed China. Kong is one of them.

Kong was born in Guangdong Province. After studying in Macao, Canada, and the United States, she built an impressive career in the United States as an entrepreneur and executive before returning to China to lead Cisco's technology initiatives.[3] In the case, she is proposing a new product, the Sunbird, a rugged, small, classroom, point-of-interface between the cloud, the student backpack, and the teacher. Kong proposed to develop, build, and distribute the Sunbird. However, she faces the problem of how to sell it to Chinese schools. It's a market entry problem.

Cisco's "Entry into China"

MNCs can enter China through direct sales, contract manufacturing, JVs or WFOEs. As of 2010, the cut-off date of the case,[4] Cisco has been in China for more than 20 years. And during that time it has been involved in all four methods of market entry into China. Yet in the case, Cisco is entering a market that it has never entered in China — education information technology (IT) equipment.

Cisco is an electronics equipment company but does not make electronics equipment. Players in the global electronics industry can be classified into four main groups: (1) brand-name designers and systems suppliers with substantial integrated in-house production; (2) brand-name

[2]"A bale of sea turtles" *The Economist* 438: 9229, London, January 23, 2021.

[3]For a video of Kong's story (with early pictures of her youth) and the background to the Cisco case, see Hugh Thomas, "Cisco Cloud-Based Education in China", Youtube Video, posted September 11, 2014. https://www.youtube.com/watch?v=Fa9uTc1JKDI&t=80s (accessed December 14, 2021).

[4]Every teaching case that involves making a decision for a protagonist has a cut-off date. The cut-off date is the date at which the protagonist is making the decision. The instructor should remind students that they can only use information available prior to the cut-off date in their analysis of which course of action the protagonist should take.

designers and systems suppliers with little or no in-house production; (3) large contract manufacturers with no end-product brand name, and (4) specialized component suppliers.[5] Cisco is in category 2. It does not manufacture products to supply its largely corporate and government buyers. It relies on category 3 members of the global electronics industry like the Taiwan-based company, Foxconn[6] to manufacture/assemble the branded final product. And it relies on many category 4 members to supply specific components (assembled into its products by category 3 companies). The most famous category 4 company is Taiwan Semiconductor,[7] the leading integrated circuit producer in the world. In designing specific chips for its products, Cisco is a fabless designer (i.e., it does not fabricate the chips it uses). In terms of its final product, Cisco is an OEM.[8]

Firms, Specialization, and Electronics Industry Supply Chains

Over the last half century, the electronics industry has moved away from large, integrated companies (category 1 companies like IBM and General Electric in the 1960s) toward greater specialization, knit together by complex, global supply chains. Many independent firms participate in the manufacturing clusters of China, serving the OEMs. They started in the Shenzhen SEZ and expanded throughout the Pearl River Delta. Today, there are several electronics contracting clusters around China: Shanghai — Hangzhou, the Bohai basin of Beijing and Tianjin and into

[5]Although I have altered somewhat the terminology, the categorization comes from Boy Luthje and Florian Buto, "Why the Foxconn Model Does Not Die: Production Networks and Labour Relations in the IT Industry in South China", *Globalizations* 14:2(2017), 216–231.

[6]Foxconn, also known as Hon Hai Technology and by its Chinese name 富士康 is the largest electronics manufacturer in the world. See the Foxconn corporate website: https://www.foxconn.com/en-us/ (accessed February 2, 2021).

[7]Taiwan Semiconductor, also known as TSMC and in Chinese 台积公司 is the largest semiconductor foundry company in the world. See TSMC's website: https://www.tsmc.com/english (accessed February 2, 2021).

[8]For an alternative discussion about the global electronics contract manufacturing system and how it affects innovation, see Hau L. Lee and Glen Schmidt, "Using Value Chains to Enhance Innovation", *Production and Operations Management Special Issue on Management of Technology* 26:4(2017), 617–632.

the western provinces of Sichuan and Chongqing.[9] They are interwoven internationally through Taiwan, Korea, and Japan into the developed western markets of Europe and the United States.

Is business more efficient when carried out in large integrated companies or in many small companies connected by markets?

Classical free market economics has very little to say about this. To the founders of economics, free markets solved the problems of efficient allocation of factors of production and outputs of goods and services by free economic agents. Yet firms dominate commerce. Within firms, factors of production are allocated by the entrepreneur or corporate executive. Firms are able to exist because they reduce the informational and transactions costs of production by internalizing them.

The tension between internalizing production in the firm and outsourcing begs the question, asked by the British economist, Ronald Coase: "Why is not all production carried on by one big firm?"[10] Coase was writing when central planning in the USSR prior to its collapse in the late 1980s, and China prior to 1978 carried out production in one big "firm": the state. That was inefficient. The deadweight costs bureaucratic inertia — what Coase called the "diminishing returns to management" — yield to the efficiencies of the open market if and when the players in the market are sufficiently well informed, educated and sophisticated to contract, de-contract and re-contract efficiently. The digital revolution increases information, education and sophistication. So, increasingly, decentralization should optimally occur. The electronics contracting industry, centred in China, and servicing global supply chains, should benefit from this trend.

Yet tides ebb and flow.

For three quarters of a century, the United States was the unswerving promoter of globalization. The OEMs in electronics epitomized the efficiencies of decentralized supply chains. Today the United States, still the pre-eminent world power, faces its own inequities and loss of sole power status, while it addresses security fears concerning reliance on

---

[9]Ian Colotla, Yvonne Zhou, John Wong, Jeff Walters, Justin Rose, and Lars Maecker, "China's Next Leap in Manufacturing", Boston Consulting Group, December 2018. https://www.bcg.com/publications/2018/china-next-leap-in-manufacturing (accessed February 2, 2021).

[10]R. H. Coase, "The Nature of the Firm", *Economica*, November 1937. https://onlinelibrary.wiley.com/doi/full/10.1111/j.1468-0335.1937.tb00002.x (accessed February 2021).

global sourcing. The United States is no longer the standard bearer of globalization. Yet the very size of Chinese market and the scope of its electronics contracting industry argues for decentralization of production to continue to flow, expanding Chinese global sphere of interest even if it ebbs between China and the United States.[11]

The Decision

In the case, Aglaia Kong is deciding how to enter the Chinese market for cloud-based education equipment. She is using a new philosophy, a vertical, customer centric, rather than a horizontal, product-centric approach.

The cut-off date is May 10, 2010. The Cisco of 2010 was a friend of China. As a 20-year veteran in the country, it had a well-established system of 28 Chinese contract manufacturers. These were not Cisco-owned companies. They were partners with whom Cisco had worked for many years as part of its global supply chain. Any new electronics product for the China market could be manufactured within that supply chain.

Cisco had recently shown itself to be a friend in need. When the Sichuan earthquake disaster struck in 2008, two years before the case's cut-off date, Cisco had given generously. The friendship was warmly felt at Cisco's head office in Silicon Valley and in the halls of power in Beijing. The reader is invited to analyze the possibilities for distribution of Aglaia's new product. Clearly distribution through Cisco's existing channel partners is not ideal. Readers should consider the advantages and disadvantages of alternative entry modes. Cisco also had to address the difficulty of getting the Sunbird authorized for IT use in schools. And as a foreign company, even though it was a friend of China, Cisco was unlikely to be on a preferred list of school IT equipment distributors. There are challenges and opportunities for Sunbird, Aglaia, and Cisco. The reader must suspend anti-globalist cynicism built up over the last decade to put him- or herself into a simpler, perhaps more naive, certainly more hopeful time to analyze the case.

[11] Heiwai Tang, "Globalization in Crisis: Lessons from the Past Two Centuries with Some Thoughts on the Current Events", HKU Business School and Johns Hopkins SAIS, September 7, 2020. http://faculty.wwu.edu/~patrick/envs342-geo312/AA%20new%20readings/tang-2020_Globalization%20in%20Crisis_agi_paper_short.pdf (accessed February 2, 2020).

CISCO AND CLOUD-BASED EDUCATION IN CHINA

Hugh Thomas and Robert P. Lee wrote this case solely to provide material for class discussion. The authors do not intend to illustrate either effective or ineffective handling of a managerial situation.

It was May 12, 2010. Aglaia Kong, vice president and chief technology officer of Enterprise Networking Group, Cisco Greater China, had just returned to her hotel room in Chengdu, the provincial capital of Sichuan, China, from a ceremony celebrating the opening of digital classrooms donated by Cisco to help rebuild communities devastated two years before by the 2008 Sichuan earthquake.

At 2:28 p.m. on May 12, 2008, an earthquake registering eight on the Richter scale struck the poor, rural area of Wenchuan, about 80 kilometres north of Chengdu. Over 87,000 people were killed, including thousands of students who died when their schools collapsed. The tragedy focused the nation and the world's attention on massive human suffering and led to an outpouring of disaster relief aid. Cisco committed ¥300 million (about US$45 million) to help reconstruct schools and medical facilities (see Exhibit 1). A major part of Cisco's aid converted the IT in schools of the earthquake-stricken area from among the most backward in China into state-of-the-art, 21st-century IT models.

Kong had spent much of the day of the ceremony with Liu Yandong, Politburo member of the CPC and State Councilor with responsibilities including China's science, technology and education policies. Kong had introduced Cisco's global operations to Liu and they had discussed partnering, technology transfer, cross branding, joint product and service development, cooperation with Chinese companies, and the IT revolution and its effect on Chinese education. The discussion had inspired Kong even as it forced her to confront the question: "How could Cisco profitably join in the Chinese education IT revolution?"

CISCO

Cisco Systems, Inc., based in San Jose, California, was the dominant global supplier of the routers and switches that formed the backbone of the Internet. Founded in 1984 by Leonard Bosack and Sandy Lerner of Stanford University, and named after the city of San Francisco, Cisco received early financing from Sequoia Capital, and grew with the Internet to become, in 2000, the largest company in the world by market capitalization. When the dot-com bubble burst in 2001, Cisco's shares lost over 80 per cent of their value, but in recent years the share price had performed well relative to the market. Cisco maintained its dominance in the IT network infrastructure. It designed its products but outsourced manufacturing on renewable, short-term contracts. In 2010, Cisco had 65,000 employees, gross margins of 60 per cent and after-tax profits of $6.1 billion on sales of $36.1 billion. Routers and switches accounted for over 50 per cent of sales, yet the firm was under pressure from the Great Recession and competitors, the most aggressive of which was Huawei Technologies Co. Ltd., a privately held telecommunications equipment company based in Shenzhen, China. In contrast, sales of both Cisco New Products and Cisco Services recorded double-digit annual sales growth. Exhibit 2 summarizes Cisco's recent financial performance.

Most of Cisco's sales were made through over 13,000 channel partners. The channel partners worked with Internet service providers, telecommunications companies and other companies with intranet needs and assessed the match between Cisco's products and customer requirements. If necessary, channel partners would liaise with Cisco to develop customized products. Cisco certified each channel partner based on sales volume, technical competence and strategic importance, into one of four categories (from the least to the most important): Select, Premier, Silver and Gold. Exhibit 3 summarizes the channel partners by certification category and location.

Since Cisco entered China in 1994, it had expanded to include contract manufacturing sourcing of Cisco equipment for global distribution, an R&D facility in Shanghai, and a substantial sales force. Exhibit 4 summarizes Cisco's operations in China as of 2010. As in the rest of the world, routers and switches accounted for most of Cisco's Chinese sales and most were sold through channel partners. China offered unique challenges to Cisco. Its major competitor, Huawei, was Chinese and the Chinese telecommunications industry remained largely government-controlled. Yet top management at Cisco was keen to pursue the Chinese market. To help this pursuit, Cisco had hired Kong in 2009.

AGLAIA KONG

Kong, a focused, infectiously optimistic woman in her mid-40s, had spent her early years in Huaxian, a small town just north of Guangzhou in the Pearl River Delta of China. She emigrated from Huaxian with her father, an engineer, and mother, a chemistry professor, to Macau when she was 10 and went to Canada for high school. After graduating with an electronics engineering degree from the University of Minnesota in 1988, she worked as a software engineer, patented several devices, started and successfully sold her own company before joining Symantec Corporation, where she became Symantec's first female Symantec Fellow and chief architect for storage foundation products. Before she left Symantec in 2009 to join Cisco to spearhead its Chinese enterprise networking operations, she gave the following advice: "Help others to grow so that they can eventually take over your job. Then you can move up to something else that is even more fun!"[1]

EDUCATION AND CONNECTIVITY

After 30 years of rapid economic growth, China's economy rivaled America's and Europe's. Chinese cities led the world in size and physical infrastructure, if not in quality of life. A small wealthy class and a large middle class were increasingly important to global consumption. However, the gap between the rich and the poor in China was widening. To improve

[1] "Aglaia Kong is Symantec's first woman Fellow", Diversity/Careers in Engineering & Information Technology, February/March 2008.

the equality of opportunity, the Chinese government focused on education. In 2004, the Ministry of Education (MoE) launched a policy to assist schools in upgrading their multimedia capabilities. Schools in advanced coastal cities quickly set up electronic classrooms (usually one or two per school) with whiteboards interacting with audiovisual systems and a server. But frequently, after installation, the electronic classrooms encountered difficulties; software and content lagged behind hardware, and the digital classrooms tended to be underutilized. Notwithstanding such difficulties, however, Kong believed that China was well on its way to achieving digital connectivity, that Cisco had a role to play, and that education presented tremendous opportunities:

> About 50 per cent of the area in China has Internet coverage. About 30–40 per cent of the people actually have Internet access at home and [there is] … 3G coverage in the whole of China. Over the next five years, China will invest heavily to achieve 100 per cent Internet access. When fiber-to-home is completed you will get 100 per cent Internet coverage…. Wenchuan was totally destroyed. Cisco and others built out the network in Wenchuan. Now, those quake areas have one of the best coverage areas for Internet in all of China. All of the companies were trying to help them. That's why Cisco spent RMB300 million.

Both Kong and Liu believed that digital connectivity would host a Chinese education cloud.

SUNBIRD

Kong envisioned a single "black box" device — which she liked to call the Sunbird[2] — to be designed and manufactured under the direction of Cisco that could control access from each digitally enabled classroom. The device would include the provision of local Wi-Fi and would take the place of a controlling computer for interfacing with an electronic whiteboard, camera, projector and sound system and the devices used by the teacher, students and parents. Those devices could be desktop computers for the teacher and parents and any mobile device of the students in a bring-your-own-device (BYOD) mode — i.e., a smartphone, laptop or tablet. Student

---

[2] She chose the name Sunbird after the emblem of Chengdu city, a 3000-year-old gold foil cut-out of a mythical bird discovered at the Jinshadui archeological site near the city.

virtual backpacks would reside in the cloud, accessed by students, teachers and parents. As long as Internet connectivity was achieved — through local Wi-Fi, broadband or 3G access — each teacher could receive up-to-date curriculum materials from the appropriate authorities and could communicate with students' virtual backpacks. And if the lack of qualified teachers in rural areas was a problem, the Sunbird would allow remote teaching. As long as digitally enabled classrooms controlled by Sunbirds were in a particular remote location, a single qualified teacher could teach multiple remote classes there. Kong enthused:

> One teacher teaches both classes.... All students share an electronic backpack. All content in the computer is shared in the whiteboard and is available to the backpacks.... [Sunbird] creates an environment of interaction. The student can enter the same class through the cloud from home. The parent can log into a class. Any number of people can enter as remote participants.... Cisco is a networking company so we can naturally provide state-of-the-art networking gear. I can make it cheaper and faster and with more features.

Sunbird might help address the lack of IT expertise in local schools:

> How many schools have really top-notch IT experts? Not that many. A lot of the time, you just overload a computer science teacher and expect that guy to manage.... Why don't we combine all of these random electronics devices into one? Put the applications on this box. Make it very simple. For the teacher, all they have to do is plug the Internet cable in and magic will happen. We come up with a converge box: this has the compute power, the switch capability, the wire and the wireless capability all in one. We focus on plug and play. The moment you plug in the network it will configure.

Schools that Kong had visited had problems with their digital classrooms. She believed that the Sunbird could solve them.

> What is the current challenge of education? One is the complexity of IT.... We combine three or four formally separate devices into one. In management of schools' current computers, they give the schools computers. It's a computer. The moment you install it, there will be a virus. The moment you start to install software, it will be out of configuration.

> The PC [personal computer] becomes unusable so the schools stop using it because of viruses. IT in schools should be a semi-closed platform. So when the computer is loading, only the administrator can log in and put software on.... The computer has our configuration. If somehow the teacher messes it up, the teacher presses a button and it goes back to the manufacturer's configuration. Whatever software is needed for that box gets streamed down from the cloud.

Cloud-based education offered additional benefits that suited China's particular needs:

> Content gets out of date soon. In China there are 510,000 schools from K [kindergarten] through [grade] 12 and there are about 300 million students in this environment. We want to make sure that all of the schools have the same content.... Basic education should be fair and consistent [so] even an inexperienced teacher in a village has a chance. If that teacher has to make the content up, it becomes impossible.

Kong considered that money was not an issue. China had decided to spend four per cent of its gross domestic product on education — about ¥2 trillion (US $300 billion) per year. If the MoE decided to mandate virtual student backpacks connected through a Sunbird-style in-classroom device to a centrally coordinated education cloud, Kong concluded, the MoE had the resources and political power to make it happen.

PRODUCT DEVELOPMENT CHALLENGES

Cisco's development processes consistently delivered very predictable, high-quality and well-managed products. New product development took seven distinct steps: market research and requirements gathering; product definition; engineering feedback; business commitment; concept commitment; execution commitment; and product release.

At each step, the product-sponsoring unit would recalculate and seek approval for the development budget. If the product failed to meet technical or financial requirements, development could be terminated. The product development process was designed for and best suited to Cisco's core products — routers and switches — for which Cisco owned the complete end-to-end technology, including architecture, application-specific integrated circuits, hardware components, operation systems, etc. Given this ownership, Cisco could anticipate what problems and issues a new product would face.

The Sunbird, however, would face challenges if it went through the seven-step process. It would have to source many components from third-party vendors. It would not be based on Cisco's operating system. It would be a single platform combining applications, computing, switching and wireless in a single device. It would target a market that was not mainstream IT. It would require quick time to market and low cost. It would need tight integration with applications. The Sunbird matched neither Cisco's process engineering skill sets nor its development steps.

Kong considered that developing the Sunbird in China might be easier than in San Jose. Using university interns and entry-level engineers, with high motivation and new ideas, would be cheaper and possibly better than using experienced, senior engineers. Yet Cisco had never designed and developed a product outside of the United States, let alone in China.

MARKETING SUNBIRD

If the Sunbird were developed, how could Cisco persuade China's schools to adopt it? Although Cisco had been in China for 16 years, its entry into education would be new. A new market could be entered using one or several strategies outlined in Exhibit 5.

The Sunbird's buyers would be government-controlled public schools. Governments typically preferred domestic suppliers, choosing foreigners only if they met the required standards. As Kong said, one needed to "get the buy-in of the person who wishes to standardize the education." Ultimately, that person was the very woman that she had spent the day with, Liu, and the daunting Chinese bureaucracy she led (see Exhibit 6). The Sunbird would be a classroom node in the future cloud education service meeting the standards of the MoE. As Kong expressed it:

> In China, they don't believe slides. They want to see actual deployment of the product.... They need proof points....We have the right architecture and the right products to help China transform its education using the end-to-end cloud concept.... I need to understand this architecture and to influence everybody. You must try to influence the policymakers, otherwise you do not make it.... I spend a lot of time with government officials. I want to learn from them. That is what I really like about new Chinese officials. They call themselves technocrats. You can't bullshit

> them. They are all well-educated and understand technology.... I spend a lot of time not selling Cisco products or any products but just trying to understand. And it's really nice that once they respect you they go out of their way to help you. So government officials took me to 30 to 40 schools. Some are really shitty and some are really fancy. To really explain to me — don't try to solve for the rich. Don't try to solve for the poor. Solve for them all.

Only equipment providers vetted by the MoE could supply the IT equipment to schools, each of which would make the purchase decision locally. Unfortunately, Cisco was a foreign company. So even if the concept of end-to-end cloud education of a high standard was something that the Sunbird, and only the Sunbird, could provide, Cisco would need to become, acquire or distribute through a company that was an authorized IT equipment provider. In Kong's words:

> They do this exercise twice a year.... They qualify all of the electronic equipment suppliers.... Cisco says, "I want to be an IT provider". But the MoE says, "You are a foreign company". So we don't make it into the preferred list. But then we say, "We build most of our equipment in China". And they say, "Well, maybe".

THE DILEMMA

Kong faced several questions. Should she request that Cisco develop the Sunbird? Cisco had never entered the educational IT equipment space in any part of the world with its own dedicated product. Should the Enterprise Network Group's China Theater take the R&D lead? Cisco had always developed in the United States for the U.S. market and then sold to the world. If Sunbird were to go ahead, should Cisco sell it alone, relying on its own connections with the Ministry of Education? Should it distribute through regular channel partners? Or should it pursue a different style of relationship with a different type of partner? Kong had much to consider on the flight back to San Jose.

The authors are grateful for the financing provided by the Victor and William Fung Foundation to the Fung Service Leadership Initiative that made production of this case possible. Case development benefitted considerably from in-depth discussions with Professor Didier Guillot.

EXHIBIT 1: CISCO TO PROVIDE US$45M (RMB300M) TO SUPPORT REBUILDING EFFORTS IN CHINA'S EARTHQUAKE-AFFECTED SICHUAN PROVINCE

Contribution focused on helping to rebuild education and healthcare through 21st century technology infrastructure and public-private partnerships.

Cisco Encourages Global Public and Private Sector to Join in Rebuilding Efforts.

CHENGDU, China, July 1, 2008 — Cisco today announced a US$45 million (¥300 million) three-year commitment to support reconstruction efforts in China's Sichuan Province, which was hit on May 12th by one of the most devastating earthquakes in China's history. Cisco made this commitment today during the signing of a memorandum of understanding (MOU) overseen by Sichuan Governor Jiang Jufeng and Cisco Chairman and CEO John Chambers.

In addition to employee engagement in relief efforts during the earthquake's immediate aftermath, a Cisco team has been in China for several weeks meeting with national, provincial and local officials to better understand the situation and learn how Cisco can best offer long-term rebuilding assistance. This week, Chambers and other U.S. private and public sector leaders are in China as members of a U.S. Business Roundtable fact-finding delegation under the auspices of the United States Agency for International Development (USAID) and the Chinese Government.

Resulting from these discussions, Cisco and Chinese business, government and NGO leaders have identified areas where Cisco will commit its collaborative networking solutions, human expertise and resources towards reconstruction and redevelopment in Sichuan. The initiatives outlined in today's MOU focus on working with public-private partnerships to help develop 21st century education and healthcare models, enabled by collaborative networked IT and communications. These initiatives have been developed to help bridge the gap between urban and rural areas, using 21st century connectivity to help more broadly share the best possible education and healthcare resources. These 21st century healthcare and education models will be designed with the potential for replication and scaling in countries around the world.

EXHIBIT 1: (*Continued*)

"As we witnessed firsthand the unimaginable destruction and spoke with those who have lost so much, it was impossible not to feel an urgency to help in the rebuilding and sustainability efforts", said John Chambers. "Even in the face of such terrible devastation, this clearly is a resilient citizenry and a country that is committed to both rapidly rebuilding as well as looking to the future. It would be an honor to play even a small supporting role in these efforts".

"We have been deeply moved by the unwavering courage and resilience of the Sichuan people, as well as the leadership demonstrated by national, provincial and local government in the face of this tragic natural disaster", continued Chambers. "Cisco has always had a strong culture of social responsibility; and we believe it is our duty to assist in the redevelopment efforts. Since our initial resource and financial donations in the days immediately following the earthquake, we have been working closely with China's citizens, businesses, national, provincial and local leaders to assess how Cisco can best contribute to the rebuilding and sustainability efforts now underway. Cisco's commitment is to make a long-term and lasting public-private partnership contribution to a 21st century education and health care system".

Healthcare efforts outlined in today's MOU will build on the foundation of Sichuan's Health 2020 initiative. Cisco will work in collaboration with healthcare officials to develop a network of connected hospitals and healthcare solutions. Healthcare providers will be able to collaborate across the province, with access to online patient health records and other key innovative solutions that will help deliver higher quality care.

Cisco's education initiatives will be designed to support students and teachers to increase their competitiveness in a global marketplace, with a focus on the collaborative development of 21st century schools and education models. In addition to academic skills, this education model will focus on teacher training and the development of 21st century skills — including collaboration, problem solving, teamwork and communication — and will be enabled by leading-edge collaborative technologies.

The company previously announced it has donated in excess of US $2.5 million raised from Cisco, the Cisco Foundation, and Cisco employees. Today's commitment builds on Cisco's past corporate social responsibility responses to humanitarian disasters, including Hurricane Katrina in the United States in 2005 and the Indian Ocean Tsunami in 2004.

Cisco first established operations in China in 1994 and now employs more than 3,000 staff in sales, customer support and service, research and development, business process outsourcing, IT outsourcing, Cisco Capital TM programs, and manufacturing. The company has 12 offices in China, a major R&D facility in Shanghai, Scientific Atlanta R&D and manufacturing facilities, and several WebEx development centers. In April 2008, Cisco announced the next phase of its corporate strategy for China, marked by new public-private collaborative programs within the country that deliver upon its US $16 billion multi-year innovation and sustainability initiative announced in late 2007.

Source: Cisco press release.

EXHIBIT 2: CISCO SYSTEMS, INC. SUMMARY FINANCIAL INFORMATION

a. Sales and Gross Margins by Region (in millions of US$)

Years Ended	25 July 2009	26 July 2008	28 July 2007
Sales			
United States and Canada	19,345	21,242	19,315
European Markets	7,683	8,123	7,389
Emerging Markets	3,999	4,530	3,239
Asia Pacific Markets	5,090	5,645	4,979
Total Sales	36,117	39,540	34,922
Gross Margin			
United States and Canada	12,660	13,882	12,437
European Markets	5,116	5,321	4,817
Emerging Markets	2,438	2,790	2,030
Asia Pacific Markets	3,272	3,734	3,274
Segment Total	23,486	25,727	22,558
Unallocated Corporate Items	(392)	(381)	(299)
Total Gross Margin	23,094	25,346	22,259
Cisco Net Income After Tax	6,134	8,052	7,333

The Emerging Markets segment consists of Eastern Europe, Latin America, the Middle East and Africa, and Russia and the Commonwealth of Independent States.

Exhibit 2: (*Continued*)

b. Sales by Product and Service Group (in millions of US$)

Years Ended	25 July 2009	26 July 2008	28 July 2007
Net Sales:			
Routers	6,521	7,940	7,064
Switches	11,923	13,538	12,432
New Products	9,859	9,446	7,926
Other Products	828	2,175	2,040
Products	29,131	33,099	29,462
Services	6,986	6,441	5,460
Total Sales	36,117	39,540	34,922

New Products relate to collaboration (i.e. integrating voice, video, data and mobile applications on fixed and mobile networks), data center, security, wireless and video-connected home.
Other Products consist of optical networking products, emerging technologies such as physical security and video surveillance, and digital media systems. The Other Products include optical networking and emerging technology items.
Services include technical support services and advanced services. Technical support services directly facilitate the efficiently, availability and compatibility with new software of Cisco's products. Advanced services support networking devices, applications, solutions, and complete infrastructures.

c. Consolidated Balance Sheets (in millions of US$)

Years Ended	25 July 2009	26 July 2008	28 July 2007
Assets			
Cash and Cash Equivalents	5,718	5,191	3,728
Investments	29,283	21,044	18,538
Inventories	1,074	1,235	1,322
Accounts Receivable	3,177	3,821	3,989
Other	4,925	4,408	3,997
Total Current Assets	44,177	35,699	31,574
Property and Equipment, Net	4,043	4,151	3,893
Goodwill	12,925	12,392	12,121
Purchased Intangible Assets, Net	1,702	2,089	2,540
Other Assets	5,281	4,403	3,212
Net Fixed Assets	23,951	23,035	21,766
Total Assets	68,128	58,734	53,340

Exhibit 2: (*Continued*)

c. Consolidated Balance Sheets (in millions of US$)

Years Ended	25 July 2009	26 July 2008	28 July 2007
Liabilities and Owner's Equity			
Short-term Debt	—	500	—
Other Current Liabilities	13,655	13,358	13,358
Total Current Liabilities	13,655	13,858	13,358
Long-term Debt	10,295	6,393	6,408
Other Liabilities	5,501	4,081	2,084
Total Liabilities	29,451	24,332	21,850
Total Equity	38,677	34,402	31,490
Total Liabilities and Stockholders' Equity	68,128	58,734	53,340

Investments are over 90 percent in US government and US government agency securities. Goodwill represents a residual value as of the acquisition date, primarily the excess of the purchase price over the book value of net assets acquired.

Source: Annual Reports 2007–2009 of Cisco Systems, Inc.

d. Cisco Monthly Stock Price Versus the S&P: January 2005 to May 2010 and January 2000 to May 2010

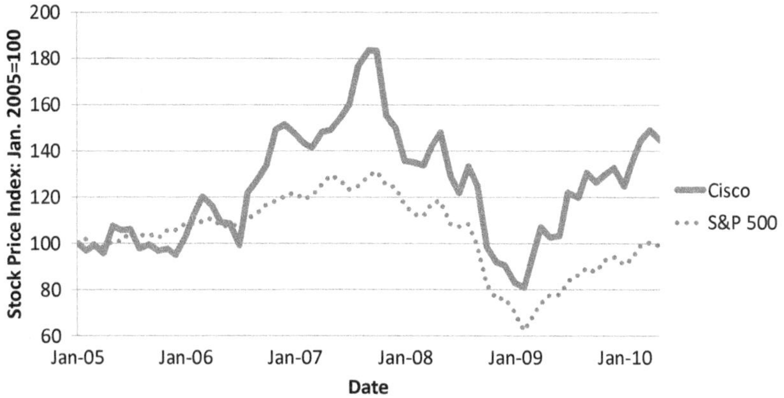

Source: Yahoo! Finance.

EXHIBIT 3: CISCO'S CHANNEL PARTNERS

Certification	USA	%	China	%	Worldwide	%
Gold	150	6%	84	9%	739	5%
Silver	37	1%	34	4%	314	2%
Premier	725	27%	301	34%	2,815	20%
Select	1,750	66%	478	53%	9,882	72%
Total	**2,662**	**100%**	**897**	**100%**	**13,750**	**100%**

Gold Certification: The partner has the broadest range of expertise in advanced technologies, has integrated Cisco Lifecycle Services into its offerings, and has demonstrated a measurably high level of customer satisfaction.
Silver Certification: The partner has critical expertise in Cisco advanced technologies, has integrated Cisco Lifecycle Services into its offerings, and has proven levels of customer satisfaction.
Premier Certification: The partner has achieved technical competency in the integration of basic routing and switching, wireless LAN and security technologies.
Select Certification: The partner has technology and business expertise specific to small and medium-sized businesses (SMBs) with fewer than 250 employees.
Note: LAN stands for "local area network".
Source: Result of the Search Engine on Cisco's "Locate a Cisco Partner".

EXHIBIT 4: THE CISCO CHINA THEATER

Location (Province, City, or Autonomous Region under National Government)	City	Manufacturing Partners	Cisco Research Facilities	Cisco Sales Offices	Cisco Customer Service Centers	Cisco Finance and Leasing	CCIE Labs*
Beijing	Beijing	2		1	1	1	
Shanghai	Shanghai		1	1			1
Fujian	Fuzhou	2		1			
Guangdong	Guangzhou	2		1			
Guangdong	Shenzhen	3		1	1		1
Hubei	Wuhan	6		1			
Hunan	Changsha			1			
Jiangsu	Nanjing			1			
Jiangsu	Suzhou	3		1			
Shaanxi	Xian			1			
Sichuan	Chengdu			1	1		

EXHIBIT 4: (*Continued*)

Location (Province, City, or Autonomous Region under National Government)	City	Manufacturing Partners	Cisco Research Facilities	Cisco Sales Offices	Cisco Customer Service Centers	Cisco Finance and Leasing	CCIE Labs*
Shandong	Jinan	9					1
Xinjiang	Ürümqi			1			
Zhejiang	Hangzhou	1		1			
Total	-	**28**	**1**	**13**	**3**	**1**	**3**

*Cisco Certified Internetwork Expert (CCIE) certification is accepted worldwide as the most prestigious networking certification in the industry, recognizing expert network engineering skills and mastery of Cisco products and solutions.

Source: *Sike ZaiZhongGuo Cisco* China marketing powerpoint slides; Aglaia Kong, March 2013.

EXHIBIT 5: ADVANTAGES AND DISADVANTAGES OF DIFFERENT MODES OF MARKET ENTRY

Advantages and Disadvantages of Different Modes of Entry

Entry Mode	Advantages	Disadvantages
Indirect exporting	Low commitment (in terms of resources)	Lack of control
	Low risk	Lack of contact with foreign market
		No learning experience
		Potential opportunity cost
Direct exporting	More control (compared to indirect exporting)	Need to build up export organization
	More sales push	More demanding on resources
Licensing	Little or no investment	Lack of control
	Rapid way to gain entry	Potential opportunity cost
	Means to bridge import barriers	Need for quality control
	Low risk	Risk of creating competitor
		Limits market development
Franchising	Little or no investment	Need for quality control
	Rapid way to gain entry	Lack of control
	Managerial motivation	Risk of creating competitor

(*Continued*)

EXHIBIT 5: (*Continued*)

Advantages and Disadvantages of Different Modes of Entry

Entry Mode	Advantages	Disadvantages
Contract manufacturing	Little or no investment	Need for quality control
	Overcomes import barriers	Risk of bad press (e.g. child labor)
	Cost savings	Diversion to gray and/or black markets
Joint venture	Risk sharing	Risk of conflicts with partner(s)
	Less demanding on resources (compared to wholly owned)	Lack of control
	Potential of synergies (e.g. access to local distribution network)	Risk of creating competitor
Acquisition	Full control	Costly
	Access to local assets (e.g. plants, distribution network, brand assets)	High risk
	Less competition	Need to integrate differing national/ corporate cultures
		Cultural clashes
Greenfield	Full control	Costly
	Latest technologies	Time consuming
	No risk of cultural conflicts	High potential; high financial risks

Source: M. Kotabe and K. Helsen, "Global Market Entry Strategies" (Chapter 9), Global Marketing Management, 5th Ed., Wiley, Hoboken, New Jersey, 2010, p. 323.

EXHIBIT 6: UNITS OF THE CENTRAL GOVERNMENT OF THE PEOPLE'S REPUBLIC OF CHINA RELEVANT TO THE MARKETING OF CLOUD COMPUTING

A private enterprise selling goods or services to the Chinese government or seeking to influence the implementation of government policy dealt with civil servants in the appropriate government offices, departments, bureaus, ministries or other organizations. China had about 10 million government workers (not including teachers, administrators of public schools and universities, doctors, administrators of public hospitals, etc.). Most civil servants entered through civil service examinations and held their jobs for life. Approximately 95% of civil servants were members of the CPC. Party regulations took precedence over laws governing conduct of party-member civil servants.

The State Council

The top organ of the National Government of China, headed by the Premier, Wen Jiabao, was made up of 10 members and one secretary. Liu Yandong was the State Council member responsible for education, science and technology.

The MoE was one of 27 ministries directly under the State Council

Yuan Guiren was the Minister of Education. Among the 17 responsibilities of the Chinese MoE included "*promoting all-round development of compulsory, equitable education…., providing guidance for the supervision over education nationwide … and … taking charge of the overall management of the educational funds under the jurisdiction of this Ministry, taking part in formulating policies for the raising and allocation of educational funds, and capital investment in construction for educational purposes, and preparing statistics of the funds for education across the country*".

The MoE was made up of 22 departments with specific responsibilities. Of these, two departments were relevant to cloud education:

The Department of Basic Education I, which was responsible, among other things, for "*undertaking compulsory education macro management … and setting policies and measures to assure equal access of all students to compulsory education; development of compulsory education school standards in conjunction with relevant parties…*".

The Department of Basic Education II, which was responsible, among other things, for "*promoting curriculum reform; guide the work of developing IT, libraries and laboratory equipment in primary and secondary schools*".

The MoE had 34 specialized units under its direction including five units whose ambit overlapped, to some degree, with cloud education:

The Central Electronic Teaching Unit (MoE Basic Education Materials Center)

The Research Center for Pedagogical Equipment
The Chinese Educational Television Station
Education Management Information Center of the Ministry of Education
MOE Basic Education Curriculum and Textbook Development Center

Source: Ministry of Education of the People's Republic of China, Website accessed 5 January 2013; K.E. Brødsgaard and G. Chen, "China's Civil Service Reform: An Update", EAI Background Brief No. 493, December 16, 2009.

Chapter 7

Two Chinese Entrepreneurs: Zhang Ruimin and Ren Zhengfei

This chapter discusses how Daoism and Confucianism affect management of innovation by two modern Chinese entrepreneurs.

Traditional Chinese culture extols *dao — the way*, the method, the philosophy by which one *should* live. Each person can have his or her own *dao*. The Chinese character for *dao* 道 is made up of two parts, one representing the head and the other the foot. *Dao* involves thinking and acting. Also Romanized in English as "tao" the character is used for the religion of Daoism[1] (Taoism). Daoism was first described by the philosopher Laozi in the early Eastern Zhou Dynasty, coincident with the 6th century BC Axial Age when the innovation of self-conscious religion sprang up simultaneously in several different parts of the Eurasian Continent (see Chapter 1). Yet, like all "new" religions at that time, Daoism had far older roots. Daoism drew on traditions of divination and nature worship predating Laozi by over a thousand years. And Daoism continues as an active religion today.

The reader should note that both Confucianism and Daoism are far less rigorously defined and organized than other religions, for example Christianity, Islam or Buddhism. Today, the term *Daoist* is usually narrowly applied only to masters, priests and monks of diverse Daoist

[1]Daoism expressed by Daoist in opposition to other schools of thought arose several generations after Laozi. See Alicia Hennig, "Daoism in Management", *Philosophy of Management* 16(2017), 161–182. https://link.springer.com/article/10.1007/s40926-015-0024-4 (accessed February 25, 2021).

schools whose full time work is their religion. Among Chinese, those who simply draw on the philosophy of the Laozi and Zhuangzi, the ancient founders of Daoism, would not generally call themselves Daoists. Nor would those who visit Daoist temples, who have Daoist shrines at home, who pray to Daoist saints and/or who seek Daoist guidance about the future. Confucianism is not even considered a religion in China today, not being among the five officially recognized religions: Buddhism, Taoism, Catholicism, Protestantism, and Islam.[2] Although this chapter refers to Daoist and Confucian influences on two entrepreneurs, probably neither of the two entrepreneurs would refer to himself as an adherent of either *religion* although they would probably acknowledge being influenced by their *philosophies.*

A confusion surrounds the term *dao*. The *dao* goes far beyond Daoism. It was and is applied to philosophies and modes of action, separate from any Daoist religion. Confucianism was and is concerned to practice correctly *the dao.* But Confucianism's *dao* differs from Daoism's *dao*.[3] Leading correctly a country, a business, a family or simply one's own life, involves following a *way,* following a *dao*.

This chapter discusses the *dao* of two of the most famous entrepreneurs in modern Chinese manufacturing: Zhang Ruimin of Haier and Ren Zhengfei of Huawei. Both entrepreneurs started humbly. Both are highly innovative. Both are laser-focused on the market. Both are highly respected members of the CPC.[4] The enterprises that each built now rank as number one in world in their respective industries — home appliances

---

[2] The five recognized religions of China each has a formal organization set up under the United Front Work Department of the CPC to handles liaison between religious organizations and the government, share information on conferences, grant recognition and protection, and opine on doctrine. See for example the Chinese Taoist Association http://www.taoist.org.cn/loadData.do.

[3] In Axial Age Confucian cannon, the word *dao* comes up over 2,200 times, not in opposition to a formal religious Daoism, but meaning the right *way* to think and act. The number was arrived at by doing a word search on pre-qin Confucian cannon in *The China Text Project* and then confirming that the references to *dao* were not references to the philosophy of Laozi, Zhuangzi, etc., but to the *way* the superior man should think and act.

[4] Zhang Ruimin served in the 16th, 17th and 18th Central Committees of the CPC. See "Members of the 18th Central Committee of the CPC". https://zh.wikipedia.org/wiki/中国共产党第十八届中央委员会候补委员列表 (accessed February 26, 2021). Ren Zhengfei attended the 12th National Congress of the CPC in 1982. (https://www.huxiu.com/article/282202.html) but otherwise has held no formal position in the CPC.

and telecommunications equipment. Both men studied and are heavily influenced by western ways: technology and management philosophy. Yet the *ways* of both men, each rooted in Chinese tradition, are very different from each other.

The vast majority of Chinese entrepreneurs and managers are, like Zhang and Ren, home grown. Zhang and Ren are role models for many Chinese. This book presented innovation models in the previous three chapters that mainly borrowed from the rest of the world: importing massive technologies for the HSR project, attracting and fostering entrepreneurs through HKSTP incubator and developing products by a US MNC, Cisco, in and for the China market. This chapter will look at the syncretic philosophies of two famous Chinese entrepreneurs who meld Western thought with Chinese *dao*. They are part of a rising trend.[5]

Zhang Ruimin and Haier

Founding Haier. Born in 1949, the year of the founding of new China, into a working-class family in Qingdao, Shandong Province, Zhang Ruimin was 17 when the Cultural Revolution swept across China, cutting short Zhang's formal education at the Shangdong Qingdao #1 Middle School.[6] He joined the Red Guards, the teenage, ideological, shock troops of the Cultural Revolution, travelling the country in support of Chairman Mao, sworn to complete the revolution, to teach Marxism–Leninism, Mao Zedong Thought, and to eradicate the four olds: old customs, old culture, old habits, and old ideas. Those were heady times to be a Red Guard!

Two years later, the most tumultuous years of the Cultural Revolution were over. The Red Guards were disbanded. Zhang went to work as clerk

---

[5]Recent organizations promote and formalize drawing inspiration from classical Chinese Confucian and Daoist philosophy and melding it with western management philosophy. Bai Lixin's Yangming Philosophy Academy [阳明教育研究院] and the Zhiliangzhi Siheyuan [致良知四合院] holds management philosophy conferences, webinars and sharing groups in China and the United States. See "Philosophy Internet (Xiong An) Conference Successfully Ends" [互联网哲学 (雄安) 学习会圆满落幕] *China Daily Web*, October 24, 2019. https://cn.chinadaily.com.cn/a/201910/24/WS5db11c91a31099ab995e77fc.html (accessed March 5, 2021).

[6]Shandong, Qingdao #1 Middle School Website, "Glorious Alumni", 2017. http://www.qdyz.com/contents/44/21426.html (accessed February 5, 2021).

in the Qingdao Municipal Government Construction Company.[7] Denied a higher university education by the times and disillusioned by how China was being run, Zhang — on his own — studied western management. In 1984, after rising through the Qingdao municipal government ranks to vice-general manager of the Household Appliance Division, he took the position as the leader of the loss-making, debt-ridden, 600 person, collectively owned, municipally controlled, Qingdao Electric Refrigerator General Company.

He quickly established, with style, two principles: (1) use the factory's own talent and (2) provide customer satisfaction.

First he borrowed money from a local rural production brigade (banks would not lend to his struggling, collectively owned, indebted factory). The factory's workers had not been paid for months. He paid them their overdue salaries, gave each employee fish for Chinese New Year festivities, and bought a new company bus.[8] With his new-found credibility among his employees and with appropriate incentives, he implemented discipline.

He turned to customers. Reacting to their complaints, he examined the refrigerators in inventory. Seventy-six had serious quality problems. Refrigerators in the mid-1980s in China were in very short supply. The market was fragmented. Although quality was generally poor, virtually any box that provided refrigeration *could* be sold. Zhang's managers suggested selling off the faulty fridges by cutting their prices. But Zhang insisted, "if we let them go, tomorrow there will be even more". He lined up the 76 faulty fridges and, with an iron sledgehammer, smashed one. He ordered his managers and workers personally to smash the remaining 75. With tears in their eyes, they obeyed. They learned that quality matters.[9]

---

[7] Yi, Jeannie Jinsheng, *The Haier Way: The Making of a Chinese Business Leader and a Global Brand*, Homa & Sekey, Dumont NJ, 2003; Landler, Mark, "In China, a Management Maverick Builds a Brand", *New York Times*, July 23, 2000. https://www.nytimes.com/2000/07/23/business/business-in-china-a-management-maverick-builds-a-brand.html?pagewanted=1 (retrieved February 5, 2021).

[8] Zhang Ruimin, "Raising Haier", *Harvard Business Review Raising Haier*, February 2007. https://hbr.org/2007/02/raising-haier (accessed February 22, 2021).

[9] Original camera footage of the smashing of the 76 refrigerators can be seen in the video at minute 0:40 and following "中國第一CEO, 張瑞敏：要不斷打倒自己" *Tianxia* December 4, 2009, Youtube Video. https://www.youtube.com/watch?v=46JQgn8a3fw (accessed February 4, 2021). For a dramatized, docu-drama re-enactment of the iconic

The factory's technology was old. Zhang negotiated a JV with Liebherr-Haushaltsgerate of Germany to learn how to make modern refrigerators. Having learned how others made refrigerators, Haier would henceforth develop its own innovations. And from the JV, the factory acquired the name which it would market to the world, Haier from the "herr" of "Leibherr".[10]

The story of the rise of Haier has been told by leading western management thinkers for over a quarter of a century. Harvard's first Chinese management case, Lynn Payne's "The Haier Group (A)"[11] describes, from a corporate governance perspective, Haier's rapid turnaround in the mid-1980s, how the company evolved as the Chinese economy reformed, Haier's path to national leadership, and the western and Chinese management philosophies that influenced Zhang. Since Payne's first case, Haier has been a recurring star on Harvard Business Publishing's website appearing in 26 more cases, 14 articles, three books two videos, and an industry backgrounder.[12]

Zhang and Daoism. Zhang has welcomed and indeed sought international exposure. Writing in the *Harvard Business Review (HBR)* in 2007, Zhang summarized the reasons for Haier's success. He cited his dedication and humility as well as the seminal work of Daoism, Laozi's 6th century BC *Daodejing*:

> People respect the leadership of an organization for different reasons in different periods. When you start a business, your employees are willing to follow you if you set a good example and bear more hardships than they do. In my early days at Haier, when I went on a business trip, I often had to set out right away. If there was no seat available on the train,

---

moment, see minute 2:58 in 《财经人物周刊》 海尔集团首席执行官—张瑞敏：企业重塑之求索 20190225 | CCTV财经. https://www.youtube.com/watch?v=OYCOcrBiHR4.

[10]The JV name 琴岛-利勃海尔, Romanized "*Qindao Libohai'er*" was commonly referred to by the last two characters 海尔 or "Haier".

[11]Lynn Sharp Paine and Robert J. Crawford, "The Haier Group (A)" Harvard Business School, case #9-398-101, revised July 27, 2001. https://store.hbr.org/product/haier-group-a/398101 (accessed February 22, 2021).

[12]See Harvard Business Publishing Website: https://hbsp.harvard.edu/educator/ (accessed February 22, 2021).

> I would spend two yuan to rent a small camp stool and sit in the aisle. That was seen and heeded by employees.
>
> Later, it's conviction that appeals to people. When we started building Haier Industrial Park in the 1990s, people held back, expecting problems to arise. But as it became clear to them that I'd spare no effort to make it a reality, everyone got on board.
>
> Today, I believe, what Haier's employees need is to be allowed to make decisions for themselves and not to feel that they are following me in their work. The philosopher Laozi said, "In the highest antiquity, the people did not know that there were rulers".[13] I take his meaning to be that a leader whose existence is unknown to his subordinates is really the most brilliant one.[14]

Zhang is inspired by Laozi. Verse 17 of the *Daodejing,* the first line of which he quotes, explains, how the successful Daoist leader emulates the styles of the legendary sage kings of the Chinese golden age. Both Confucius and Laozi believed that the Chinese golden age occurred during the early years of the Zhou Dynasty of 11th century BC, half a millennium before Laozi and Confucius were writing (during what I referred to in Chapter 1 as the Axial Age). According to Laozi, those sage kings gave their subjects as much freedom as possible, even at the risk of appearing irresolute and reticent. By doing so, the kings gave their subjects the satisfaction of freedom: doing and taking pride in their own work. In the last line of Verse 17, the subjects happily say, "We do it naturally, ourselves!"[15]

A key tenet of Daoism, which Zhang's management style exemplifies, is *wu wei* (无为), often translated as *non-action*. In the *Daodejing* verse 37, Laozi epigrammatically says "The Dao does nothing so nothing doesn't get done".[16] Also translated as "nothing", "no bodily form" and "doing nothing fruitlessly", *wu wei* involves having the intention to

---

[13] Zhang refers to the first phrase in Laozi *Daodejing* Verse 17 (Subtitled in the Legge Translation as "The unadulterated influence" see *China Text Project*. https://ctext.org/dictionary.pl?if=en&id=11608 (accessed February 22, 2021).

[14] Zhang Ruimin "Raising Haier" *Harvard Business Review Raising Haier*, February 2007. https://hbr.org/2007/02/raising-haier (accessed February 22, 2021).

[15] Legge's 19th century translation of the last line says "We are as we are, of ourselves!" See "Daodejing", China Text Project, *op. cit.*

[16] The Chinese "道常無為而無不為" is translated more loquaciously by Legge as "The Dao in its regular course does nothing (for the sake of doing it), and so there is nothing

accomplish something but accomplishing it, successfully, without any outward sign of effort.[17]

As well as being a student of Laozi, Zhang is also a student of the most influential management philosopher of 20th century, the Viennese-born American, Peter Drucker. Zhang's admiration for Drucker is well known: he was selected by Alan Kantrow in the HBR cover story article on the centennial of Drucker's birth[18] as one of only five global management practitioners to comment on Drucker's influence. Quoting Drucker, Zhang notes "… there is only one valid definition of business purpose — to create a customer".[19] In that article, Zhang further notes

> There is one picture on my desk: the sinking *Titanic.* I wrote on it these words from Drucker about why companies find themselves in crisis: "The assumptions on which the organization has been built and is being run no longer fit reality".[20]

Zhang believes that one must confront change, every day, by asking the question

> … how on earth are we different from the competition? If a company has no points of differentiation, it rapidly devolves into a commodity player with no chance for long-term success.[21]

---

which it does not do". Laozi *Daodejing*: 37 China Test Project. https://ctext.org/dictionary.pl?if=en&id=11628#s10101498 (accessed February 26, 2021).

[17] See, for example, Zhuangzi, "The Normal Course of Rulers and Kings", [應帝王] *The China Text Project.* https://ctext.org/dictionary.pl?if=en&id=2768#s10026083 (accessed February 26, 2021). Zhangzi or Zhuang Zhou was a major Daoist philosopher of the 4th century BC.

[18] Alan Kantrow, "Why Read Peter Drucker", *Harvard Business Review*, November 2009, pp. 72–82.

[19] Peter Drucker, *Management: Tasks, Responsibilities, Practices*, Harper & Row, 1974, p. 61.

[20] Zhang Ruimin, "Distance has been Eliminated", in Alan Kantrow "Why Read Peter Drucker", *Harvard Business Review*, November 2009, pp. 72–82. The quote from Drucker comes from Peter Drucker, "The Theory of the Business", *Harvard Business Review* September–October 1994, p. 95.

[21] Zhang Ruimin, "Raising Haier", *Harvard Business Review Raising Haier*. February 2007. https://hbr.org/2007/02/raising-haier (accessed February 22, 2021).

Rendanheyi. Today, Zhang runs a 100,000 person, ¥200 billion sales, global MNC, located in 160 countries and regions throughout the world.[22] Haier is by far the world's leading white goods manufacturer, holding the top world slot in refrigerators, freezers, washing machines and interconnected air conditioners, owning, in addition to its own brands, General Electric Appliances (GE) of Louisville, Kentucky USA, Candy of Brugherio, Italy, Fisher and Paykel of New Zealand and the Asian white-goods business of Sanyo of Japan.[23]

Zhang says that the biggest problem facing established companies, including Haier, is

> … the sick big company problem: bureaucracy gets worse and worse; the distance from the customer is greater and greater; the company becomes slower and slower.[24]

To address the sick big company problem, Zhang developed and implemented, over the last 20 years, his management philosophy of *zero distance to the customer*.[25] Today, the philosophy is formally known as *Rendanheyi*.[26] *Ren* (人 meaning people) are the employees. *Dan* (单 meaning customer orders) refers to user value. *Heyi* (合一 meaning united) joins employees with the customer.

Rendanheyi has Daoist hues. It involves subverting the traditional corporate pyramid structure with a network of independent, fluid, freely contracting work units. Zhang believes that the internet has allowed

---

[22]Haier website: https://www.haier.com/global/about-haier/?spm=net.32043_pc.header_141693_20200720.1 (accessed February 4).

[23]"Hai'er completes Sanyo Acquisition in Southeast Asia". https://www.haier.com/my/about-haier/news/20190604_74016.shtml.

[24]CCTV Finance "Haier Group CEO — Zhang Ruimin: Quest for Enterprise Remodeling", *Finance and Economics Weekly* 《财经人物周刊》 海尔集团首席执行官--张瑞敏：企业重塑之求索 20190225 | CCTV财经, February 25, 2019. https://www.youtube.com/watch?v=OYCOcrBiHR4. YouTube Video minute 5:55–6:05.

[25]The concept in, its early form, was first explained in western terminology by Bill Fischer, Umbrerto Lage and Fang Liu *Reinventing Giants* Jossey Bass, San Francisco, 2013 and the Harvard case by Campbell, Meyer, Li, Stack, "Haier: Zero Distance to the Customer", Harvard, 9-115-006 2015.

[26]For a lighthearted cartoon version of the *Rendanheyi* Model, see "A General Understanding of Rendanheyi Model", Youtube video, September 11, 2018. https://www.youtube.com/watch?v=zsfKfWshtiE (accessed February 25, 2021).

Rendanheyi to function. Corporate leaders, prior to the information age, had far better access to information than their employees. Now, however, all motivated members of an organization, thanks to the internet, can be as well informed as top management and, on issues such as production process and customer service, are likely to be better informed. *Rendanheyi* gets rid of centralization by distributing decision-making to take advantage of employee knowledge and stimulate their enthusiasm[27] so they, too, can say "We do it naturally ourselves!"[28]

Rendanheyi replaces the pyramid-shaped company that traditionally provided jobs to employees with a network of platforms providing employees with opportunities to start businesses. These start-ups are micro-enterprises.[29] The new system has three kinds of people: platform owners, micro-enterprise owners and customer creators. *Platform owners* host micro-enterprises. Haier tasks each platform owner to act as a servant the micro-enterprises the platform hosts, cultivating the ecosystem, and not act as a senior line officials or a top managers in a position of power. *Micro-enterprise owners* are leaders of teams of entrepreneurs who populate the platforms. And the former employees become *customer creators*, the staff members, working in each micro-enterprise to put the customers first. Coincident with implementing *Rendanheyi*, Haier re-positioned itself away from goods production and into customer service, where improving the user experience is the paramount objective.

Anyone in Haier can start a micro-enterprise. Three things are required. The micro-enterprise owner must entice at least two colleagues to join him or her. He or she must convince one of the owners of one of the platforms (of which there are less than a dozen, including "internet of food, internet of clothing, biomedical, moving air through spaces, etc.) to accept the new micro-enterprise as a member. And the micro-enterprise owner must bring in the resources to start the micro-enterprise. Initial funding for a new micro-enterprise does not come from Haier. Typically, it comes from the micro-enterprise owner(s) and sources external to Haier. Haier itself, however, may play the role of investor in later stages of the

---

[27]"Haier CEO Zhang Ruimin discusses Rendanheyi with Professor Felipe Monteiro of INSEAD", YouTube Video, January 21, 2019. https://www.youtube.com/watch?v=5pI3IN6VDA8 (accessed February 25, 2021).

[28]Legge's 19th century translation of the last line says "We are as we are, of ourselves!" See "Daodejing", *China Text Project*, *op. cit.*

[29]These are known as Xiaowei companies (小微公司).

micro-enterprise's life — like a VC — after it has demonstrated its viability.

The size of a micro-enterprise can vary widely, from three employees to several hundred. Micro-enterprises may source inputs from within or without Haier and may sell their goods and services internally or externally. Haier usually supplies information technology internally. But supply chain and legal services are often supplied by the micro-enterprise contracting with external companies. Compensation within each micro-enterprise is tied directly to the value created by the micro-enterprise — hence compensation varies widely between employees within Haier.

Micro-enterprises can live within Haier, can fail and die, or can be spun off as independent enterprises. Most micro-enterprises actually fail fairly rapidly. Employees of failed micro-enterprises (and employees dismissed or resigning from micro-enterprises) go into Haier corporate labor pool, earning the provincial minimum wage. To remain in Haier, they must apply to other micro-enterprises for employment. When *Rendanheyi* first started, there were about 2,000 micro-enterprises. Since then, many have died; many have been born; some have enjoyed tremendous success, and a few have graduated into fully independent and separately registered companies.

The micro-enterprise owner's position is not secure even if the micro-enterprise is successful. Any Haier employee can, at any time, challenge, for any reason, the leadership of any existing micro-enterprise. The employees of the micro-enterprises whose leader is challenged then vote to determine whether they support the existing micro-enterprise owner(s) or accept the challenger(s).

Rendanheyi has reversed the flow of decision-making in Haier. Zhang says that the challenge facing each micro-enterprise is to transform its customers from the goods economy to the services economies and, with mass customization, the uniting of production and consumption, and the rise of the sharing economy, to the experience economy.[30] But now corporate strategy is no longer a pre-planned blueprint from Zhang or other top managers. It is an *ex-post* rationalization of what the micro-enterprises are doing.[31]

---

[30] However Frynas *et al.*, conclude that the innovation and its effectiveness is highly context-oriented and not subject to global application. See Jedrzej George Frynas, Michael J. Mol and Kamel Mellahi, "Management Innovation Made in China: Haier's Rendanheyi", *California Management Review* 61:1(2018), 71–93.

[31] The micro-enterprises, how they innovate to meet customer demands, how the models are developing and how applicable they are to foreign environments are the subject of

Since *Rendanheyi's* implementation, Haier has continued to grow and prosper, demonstrating that the managerial innovation is practical and that the Haier competitive advantages lie in much more than cheap disciplined labor.

Zhang has caught the attention of the management science world, yet *Rendanheyi* remains work in progress. His *dao* is evolving.[32] His objective, however, is constant:

> ... to create a platform so that everyone can give full play to his value. An egg breaking from the outside must be human food, but breaking from the inside must be the birth of new life. Our task is to enable every employee to be able to "hatched" out and break out of the shell.[33]

Ren Zhengfei: Huawei

The *dao* of Ren Zhengfei is far more Confucian than Daoist and it is tinged with Maoism.

In Chinese one does not refer to "Confucianism" as "the religion of Confucius". Instead, Chinese uses the term *Ru-ism* "儒教" where *ru*

---

many cases and articles. See Dennis Campbell, Marshall Meyer, Xin Li, Kristin Stack, "Haier: Zero Distance to the Customer", Harvard, 9-115-006, 2015 case refers to the micro-enterprises as *zizhujingyingti (ZZJYT)* 自主经营体 which translates as self-managed operational units. The evolution of ZZJYT into micro-enterprises more independent micro-enterprises is covered in Rosabeth Moss Kanter and Nancy Hua Dai, "Haier: Incubating Entrepreneurs in a Chinese Giant", Harvard Business Review Store Product #: 318104-PDF-ENG 2018. https://store.hbr.org/product/haier-incubating-entrepreneurs-in-a-chinese-giant/318104. The application of *rendanheyi* at the GE plant in Louisville Kentucky USA is the subject of Dennis Campbell, Marshall Meyer, Bonnie Yining Cao and Dawn H. Lau, "GE Appliances: Implementing Haier's Made-In-China Management System", Harvard Business School Product # 9-119-099, 2019.

[32] One should classify Zhang's *dao* as neither exclusively Daoist nor static. Fan *et al.* place Zhang Ruimin's *Rendanheyi* management model firmly in a Daoist tradition. But they also place trace his philanthropic roots to Confucianism. See Fan Zheng, Tong Xiner, Fan Peihua, and Fan Qingli, "A glacier model of Chinese management: perspectives from new institutionalism", *Chinese Management Studies* 13:4(2019), 742–759.

[33] *Rendanheyi* is work in progress. The description in this paragraph dates from early 2020 and paraphrases Zhang Ruimin's "Speech delivered to the Second Haier Business Model Innovation Global Forum" Haier Group and Xinhua News Agency Beijing. February 2, 2020. https://zhuanlan.zhihu.com/p/94809667 (accessed February 25, 2021).

means "scholarship". Confucianism is the religion of scholarship: nothing is more important for the betterment of human society than learning. The reader will remember from Chapter 1 that Confucianism involves the striving of the scholar, the gentleman, the superior man, the man of culture, towards a morally righteous life. Morality stems from understanding. Understanding is achieved from the study of society and nature. But historically, from the time of Confucius, the scholar has been a voice of morality and reason acting as the conscience to the realpolitik of power. He seeks practical management, but tempers it with morality to achieve a better society.

Confucianism is paternalistic: it involves living in a highly stratified society with empathy, restraint and humility. The superior man is conservative, deferring with propriety and custom to those above and treating with benevolence and courtesy those below. The superior man, however, never defers but always speaks truth to immoral authority, which must be confronted, even at the risk of personal sacrifice.[34]

Family Background

Ren, a Han Chinese whose family hailed from the traditionally prosperous provinces of Zhejiang and Jiangsu, was born in a poor, rural, minority county (i.e., an area where the majority of people were non-Han) in Guizhou in the last year of World War II. His parents were school teachers who accepted the CPC directives to bring education to the peasants.

Ren speaks of his parents with the devotion of Confucianism. His parents themselves were neither peasants nor workers, the social classes favored by the CPC. They were intellectuals. His father, as a young man, had been a leftist activist and an early supporter of the CPC. But he had also worked for a time as an accountant in a factory owned by the Nationalist Guomindang Party, the party that lost the Chinese civil war in 1949.

His father was a dedicated scholar and, after liberation, rose to a position of local authority: the town's middle school principal. His intellectual leanings and pre-liberation association with the Guomindang, however,

---

[34] See Mencius "Liang Hui Wang Xia" [梁惠王下] 梁惠王下 Verse 15, *China Text Project*. https://ctext.org/dictionary.pl?if=en&id=12989 (accessed March 9, 2021) and for a discussion of the mission of Confucius see Tu Wei-ming, *Way, Learning, and Politics: Essays on the Confucian Intellectual*, State University of New York, New York, 1993.

meant that his wish to become a CPC member was fulfilled only in 1958, the year when the CPC invited large numbers of intellectuals to join.

CPC membership did not bring the Ren family material comfort. Ren recalls the sacrifices his parents made to bring up and educate him and his six siblings, especially during the years of famine: 1959 to 1961:

> The biggest difficulty at the time was hunger. I was hungry every day and I didn't want to study.... I had no lofty ideals. My ideal for three years in high school was to be able to eat a bun.[35]

With parental pressure and guidance, Ren persevered and, in 1963, obtained sufficiently high middle school-leaving examination results to be admitted to the Institute of Civil Engineering and Architecture in China's largest city, Chongqing.

Two years after Ren entered university, the Cultural Revolution broke out bringing disaster to his family. Poverty, authority, and CPC party membership were to no avail: his father, an intellectual, was lumped together with eight other undesirable segments of society: landlords, rich peasants, counter-revolutionaries, rascals, rightists, traitors, spies, and capitalist roaders. Known as the stinking ninth, intellectuals were soon subject to public criticism, humiliation, incarceration, physical mistreatment, and sometimes murder. Desperate to help his parents, Ren secretly left his university and, without the money for a ticket, hopped trains home — suffering a beating *en route* at the hands of a band of Shanghai Red Guards.[36] Greeting Ren on his arrival, his father, fearful that the son would share the father's fate, begged Ren to return to university immediately. Ren obeyed. At their parting the next morning, the father took off his only pair of leather shoes which he gave to his son with the words

> Remember: knowledge is power. Others don't study. You must study. Don't follow the crowd.[37]

---

[35]Ren Zhengfei, "My Father, Mother" [我的父親、母親] *Zhihu* 2001. https://zhuanlan.zhihu.com/p/52263631 (accessed March 1, 2021).

[36]Zhuang Heqing, "Ren Zhengfei: 5 Suggestions for Young People Who Have Dreams" [任正非：我给有梦想的年轻人总结的5点建议] *Direct Finance*. April 28, 2018 https://www.zhitongcaijing.com/content/detail/122228.html (accessed February 26, 2021).

[37]Chi Tianjin, "Ren Zhengfei is known as a Generous Petty Man" [任正非被称大方的小气鬼], *Sina Finance Web*, February 6, 2013. http://finance.sina.com.cn/leadership/crz/20130206/092814518281.shtml (accessed February 26, 2021).

Ren's parents survived. His father's colleague broke under the pressure and committed suicide but, through their incarceration, his parents faithfully followed their leaders' directions.

Ren deeply regrets his parents' suffering and mourns their loss. After his parents died, Ren obtained their personal files from the CPC authorities and read their many painful self-criticisms, written under duress, during their incarceration. Ren laments the anguish they endured to achieve a level of ideological purity demanded by the CPC during the Cultural Revolution which was neither achievable nor desirable:

> Actually, their only crime was to want a good education system for China. That's the same as we say today: *rejuvenating the country through science and education.* Now we can shout the slogan: *rejuvenate the country through science and education.* In the last hundred years, how many people have been martyred for that![38]

His parents' distress was counter-productive. Their waste is one guide to Ren's management style. He hires only those with dedication, professionalism and a sense of mission, and he treats his junior employees leniently, with compassion. He reserves stricter standards only for senior cadres.[39]

His sadness about his parents' devotion, notwithstanding their suffering and loss, is deepened by Ren's knowledge that he could have been closer to them in their declining years, had it not been for his devotion to work. Yet even here, Ren had followed his father's example. When released from prison, his father, with no regrets, had completely submerged himself in his educational work so that he could make up for lost decade, once again contributing to building the country. Ren reflects:

> They took no pleasure in possessions. They felt no sorrow in loss. They kept no score of glory or disgrace. Their spirit — love China; love the CPC; be true to your career — is worthy for us, for the next generation and for the generation after that to emulate. It is impossible to have no setbacks in life, but a person who is struggling for the people can't be shaken.[40]

[38]Ren Zhengfei, "My Father, My Mother" [我的父親、母親], *Zhihu*, 2001. https://zhuanlan.zhihu.com/p/52263631 (accessed March 1, 2021).

[39]*Ibid.*

[40]*Ibid.*

Ren's father has inspired Ren's own life. One recalls the words Mengzi, concerning the legendary Emperor Yu, tamer of the floods and founder of the Xia Dynasty. Consumed with the urgency of serving the state, he hurriedly passed by the doors of his own home three times, failing to enter.[41]

Ren comments on his debt to his parents:

> I do not think it's shameful to be poor. What's shameful is poor thought and poor knowledge. Being born rich and noble is ***not*** glorious. My childhood was spent in poverty and hunger. My parents forced me to study to overcome it. Without them, seeing the light in that time of hardship, guiding us and forcing us to work hard, today could never have come.[42]

From the Army to Founding Huawei

On graduation, delayed for a year because of the Cultural Revolution,[43] Ren was assigned to work as a construction engineer, but continued studying on his own, learning computer engineering, programming, control systems, philosophy, English and Japanese. In 1974, he was recruited by the PLA, not as a military officer, but as a non-military, non-ranked, expert to participate in the construction of the Liaoyang Chemical Fiber Plant, a facility that used technology imported from France to address the national shortage of synthetic fibers. There, he served as technician, engineer, and deputy director. Although he wished to join the CPC, he, like his father before him, was unable to do so. After all, Ren's father was still in prison: a member of "the stinking ninth" and accused of being a capitalist roader. Yet due to Ren's diligence and successful work in the Liaoyang Chemical Fiber Plant technology transfer program, he was chosen as a delegate to attend the National Science Conference in 1978 in Beijing, even though he was ***not*** CPC.

[41] Mengzi, "Lilou II: 57", *The China Text Project*. https://ctext.org/dictionary.pl?if=en&id=1728#s10034217 (accessed February 26, 2021).

[42] Ren Zhengfei, "My Father, My Mother" [我的父親、母親], *Zhihu*, 2001. https://zhuanlan.zhihu.com/p/52263631 (accessed March 1, 2021).

[43] The Institute is now a part of Chongqing University. "A Discussion about School-Mate Ren Zhengfei" [有关任正非校友的讨论], Chongqing University. https://www.cquaa.ca/you-guan-ren-zheng-fei-xiao-you-de-tao-lun/ (accessed February 26, 2021).

Ren remarked:

> Back then, you couldn't even become a head chef in a kitchen if you were not a CPC member. I was a delegate to the National Science Conference. The leaders thought it was pretty strange, so with the help of the organization, they let me become a CPC member.[44]

In the mid-1980s more than a million soldiers were demobilized from the PLA as part of an effort to save money, reduce the non-military role of the army in the economy and professionalize and modernize the armed forces.[45] Ren was honorably discharged. In 1987 he moved to the booming city of Shenzhen. With several ex-comrades-in-arms and ¥21,000 in cash, they founded Huawei, whose name in Chinese (华为) means "Chinese Action".[46]

Ren reflects back on those years:

> I had no experience when I started Huawei at the age of 44, and I took the plunge blindly. After leaving the military, retired soldiers like us had quite a hard time adapting to the market economy, much harder than Western soldiers did. Though Western militaries at that time were not market-oriented, their countries were. So their soldiers knew what the market economy was, and were more adaptive to working in companies after retiring from the military. But we were not adaptive at all. We had got so used to a planned economy, under which we couldn't even think of making a penny.[47]

---

[44]"Ren Zhengfei says that under some circumstances he would rather close the company" [任正非说他在某种情况下，宁可关闭公司], Transcript of Ren Zhengfei News Conference, January 21, 2019 *Hu Xiu*. https://www.huxiu.com/article/282202.html (accessed February 26, 2021).

[45]Reuters, "Troop Cuts to Save Money, Deng Says", *Los Angeles Times*, May 6, 1985. https://www.latimes.com/archives/la-xpm-1985-05-06-mn-4457-story.html (accessed February 26, 2021).

[46]The name 华为 (or 華為 in traditional script) uses the same "wei" as the wu wei "无为" of non-action in Daoism referred to above. In Huawei, however, the character for China (华) is substituted for the negative (无). The title means Chinese action, pure and simple. No non-action here!

[47]"Ren Zhengfei's Interview with UK Documentary Producer", *Voices of Huawei*, Huawei website July 23, 2019. https://www.huawei.com/en/facts/voices-of-huawei/ren-zhengfeis-interview-with-uk-documentary-producer (accessed February 26, 2021).

Huawei's Culture

The company initially imported and then manufactured simple private branch exchanges (PBX) to route phone calls within a company. Ren remembers:

> I had only one idea: to survive. At that time, Huawei was not only a production workshop and a warehouse, but also a kitchen and a bedroom. More than a dozen beds were lined up next to the wall. Because there were not enough beds we used foam boards and mattresses instead. Everyone ate and slept there, whether they were leaders or employees. We slept for a while when tired, and then resumed work when we woke up.[48]

Huawei succeeded through military-style comradery and discipline and through hard work directed by clear reward and punishment systems. The structure is a centralized matrix hierarchy. The company has addressed one crisis after another. Huawei perceives success as the fruit of unswerving loyalty to the company and absolute dedication to customers, through endless research and through ceaseless striving to improve products.[49]

Ren is fiercely patriotic. He experienced the privations of the 50s. He came of age in the radical years of the sixties. He served in the PLA in the 70s. He is loyalty to the CPC and inspired by the words and achievements of Mao. When asked about the early culture of Huawei, Ren replied:

> During the start-up stage at Huawei, there was no recognizable corporate culture. Mao Zedong's thought was the company's thought! … Foreigners come to China to make money. They don't teach core

---

[48] Zhuang Heqing, "Ren Zhengfei: 5 Suggestions for Young People Who Have Dreams" [任正非：我给有梦想的年轻人总结的5点建议], *Direct Finance*. https://www.zhitongcaijing.com/content/detail/122228.html (accessed February 26, 2021).

[49] For a recent teaching case (with full teaching note) focussed on Huawei's management system and human resource management, and especially Ren's authoritarian, benevolent and moral leadership philosophy, see Jiing-Lih Larry Farh, Xin Pi "Huawei the Ren Zhengfei Wei: The 'Tough Guy' and His Corporate Philosophy" CEIBS/Harvard Business Publishing, 2020. The case ends with the question of succession to the "godfather-like influence" of Ren and the steering of Huawei through its current crises.

> technologies to Chinese. They expect us to import it, import it and import it again, so our company could never be independent. If you buy technology in the market, you lose the market and in truth you master no technology.[50]

Huawei prized Maoist virtues: self-reliance and hard work[51] were particularly important. Huawei's top priority was to get sales.[52] To get the sales, Ren implemented the culture of "Wolf Management". In the pursuit of sales, Huawei's teams were like wolves. They had keen senses of smell, were unyielding and fearless, hunted in packs, obeyed completely their leader, were alert to danger and were fiercely loyal to each other.[53]

The loyalty of the subordinate to the leader is reciprocated within paternalism of the leader towards the subordinate who gives the leader its trust. Effective paternalism — authority, benevolence and integrity — involves leading by example. Effective paternalism is reciprocated by compliance, gratitude and identification.[54] These Confucian virtues were sharpened in imperial Chinese society by Legalism — which Mao praised and persist in Chinese management style today.[55]

---

[50]Little Flower of the post 90 generation, "Learning from the Mao Model: Huawei President Ren Zhengfei — Mao Zedong Thought is the company's thinking!" [学毛标兵" 华为总裁任正非：毛泽东思想就是公司的思想!], *Kunlunce*, March 20, 2019. https://www.kunlunce.com/ssjj/guojipinglun/2019-03-20/132058.html (accessed March 10, 2021).

[51]Mao Zedong, "Chapter 21: Self Reliance and Arduous Struggle", *Quotations of Chairman Mao* English second edition, Peking, 1967. Reposted by Terebess Asia Online. https://terebess.hu/english/maotse2.html#21 (accessed March 10, 2021).

[52]Chi Tianjin, "Ren Zhengfei is known as a Generous Petty Man" [任正非被称大方的小气鬼], Sina Finance Web, February 6, 2013. http://finance.sina.com.cn/leadership/crz/20130206/092814518281.shtml (accessed February 26, 2021).

[53]Wang Yongde, *Wolf Management: Huawei* [狼性管理：华为], Wuhan University Press, Wuhan, 2010.

[54]Farh J. L and Cheng B. S., "A Cultural Analysis of Paternalistic Leadership in Chinese Organizations", in J.T. Li A.S. Tsui and E. Weldon (eds.), *Management and Organization in the Chinese Context*. MacMillan, London, 2000.

[55]Farh J. L. and Cheng B. S. "A Cultural Analysis of Paternalistic Leadership in Chinese Organizations", in J.T. Li, A.S. Tsui and E. Weldon (eds.), *Management and Organization in the Chinese Context*. MacMillan, London, 2000. https://link.springer.com/content/pdf/10.1057/9780230511590_5.pdf (accessed March 15, 2021).

Competing with the MNCs

As the company expanded in the mid-1990s into routers and switches for the nascent internet in China, Huawei had to compete with MNC telecommunications companies already established in China. Yet initially its products were inferior. Huawei made up for its shortcomings by meeting needs of users in remote locations — going to post and telecommunications bureaus in rural areas, rather than trying to compete head-on in the tier one cities. It reflected Mao's military strategy, successful in the Chinese civil war prior to 1949, of "surrounding the cities from the countryside" or perhaps a Clayton Christensen strategy of disruptive innovation.[56] Either way, it worked.

In Heilongjiang Province, Huawei battled Ericsson by sending ten times more technical personnel than Ericsson to each county's telecommunication bureau. Ren commented:

> Where there was a problem, the people from Huawei rushed to the scene immediately. In order to win a project, Huawei would spend seven or eight months and an investment that does not match the return.... It seems stupid, but it snatched customers from the hands of multinational giants.[57]

From the outset, Ren emphasized relentless study: basic technology, existing states of art, customers' objectives and problems, competitors' innovations. In-house product R&D — whether it was reverse engineering foreign products for domestic buyers or customizing products to meet individual customer needs — was critical. At Huawei, R&D personnel have always exceeded those in manufacturing or sales. And

---

[56]Regarding surrounding the cities with the countryside, see Mao Zedong, "The Chinese Revolution: 2. The targets of the Chinese Revolution", *The Chinese Revolution and Chinese Armed Struggle* 1939 Selected Works of Mao Tse-tung Marxist Internet Archive. https://www.marxists.org/reference/archive/mao/selected-works/volume-2/mswv2_23.htm (accessed March 11, 2021). For a detailed analysis using Christensen disruptive innovation, see Zhen Wei Using, *Christensen's models to make sense of changes in the Chinese telecommunications equipment supplier industry*, Carleton University, PhD Thesis, ProQuest Dissertation Publishing, 2005.

[57]Zhuang Heqing, "Ren Zhengfei: 5 Suggestions for Young People Who Have Dreams" [任正非：我给有梦想的年轻人总结的5点建议], *Direct Finance*. https://www.zhitongcaijing.com/content/detail/122228.html (accessed February 26, 2021).

they are well rewarded. Ren set his R&D personnel salaries to exceed market rates.

In Ren's words, "Huawei is a technology-centric company that possesses nothing except knowledge and customer recognition".[58] Since the mid-1990s, over 40% of its employees have been involved in R&D and it has consistently spent 10 to 15% of sales revenue on R&D. At the same time its profit margins have varied between 5% and 15%.

Huawei's output-input cost ratio for R&D swamped those of its foreign competitors. In 2005, one researcher calculated that Huawei engineers worked 2750 hours per year, twice those of European engineers. Yet Huawei's salary expense per annum for an engineer was only US$25,000, only one fifth of the expense of an engineer of a European competitor (in the early 2000s). So an engineering hour of output at Huawei was just a tenth of the cost of a European competitor. Even assuming erosion of 5% per annum of that advantage, the Huawei advantage is still a factor of five.[59]

Ren emphasizes focus in Huawei's R&D:

> we can possibly surpass US companies only when our area of focus is as big as the tip of a needle. If we enlarge the focus area … surpassing US companies will be out of the question.… We must avoid innovating blindly. If there is cry for innovation everywhere, that will be a death song for us.… We survive because we embrace self-criticism.[60]

Huawei's "surrounding the cities from the countryside" strategy was again used when it approached international markets. It started in less

[58] Ren Zhengfei, "Letter from the CEO", *Huawei 2011 Annual Report*. https://www.huawei.com/ucmf/groups/public/documents/attachments/hw_126991.pdf (accessed March 3, 2021).

[59] Sun, Sunny Li, "Internationalization Strategy of MNEs from Emerging Economies: The Case of Huawei", *Multinational Business Review* 17:2(2009), 129–155. Sun's calculation uses date 15 years out of date, but even if one calculates that engineering wages have increased at 5% per year faster in China than elsewhere, the 10X IO ratio has only been reduced ton 5X, still a tremendous advantage.

[60] Ren Zhengfei, "Letter from the CEO", Huawei 2013 Annual Report. https://www.huawei.com/ucmf/groups/public/documents/attachments/hw_u_323372.pdf (accessed March 3, 2021).

developed markets first. In 1997, it moved into Hong Kong, and, in the following years, Algeria, Brazil, Columbia, Ecuador, Egypt, India, Iran, Laos, Russia, Uzbekistan, Yemen, etc.[61]

At the beginning of the 1990s, Chinese firms held about 1% of the domestic market share of office exchanges. By 1997, they held over 50%.[62] By the turn of the century Huawei was had the telecommunications equipment leader in China. Huawei's rise had been helped by Chinese protectionism — forcing MNCs into cumbersome JVs to compete in domestic markets.

No such help existed in international markets. And the global marketplace offered additional challenges. Without strong domestic competitors, without a national Chinese research base, without disruptive start-ups challenging the industry and without well informed, highly trained and educated people in domestic competitors, universities, and research institutes with cutting-edge technologies, Huawei faced a dilemma. Its location — China — was not conducive to telecommunications innovation. If Huawei relied only on the domestic Chinese environment, it was unlikely to challenge international competitors in top-of-the line products. Huawei addressed this problem by internationalizing its R&D through FDI.

Although several possible FDI routes — foreign acquisitions, JVs and greenfield investments — are available to develop a globally leading culture, Huawei increasingly favored greenfield investment. Huawei was an early proponent of setting up Chinese research centers, institutes and joint innovation centers with operators and carriers to develop new products for customers. In moving the concept offshore, Huawei followed the example set by Japanese, Korean and Taiwanese companies in previous decades.[63] It set up R&D labs in leading telecommunications research hubs around the world to develop products for foreign buyers. Huawei directly hired

---

[61] G. V. Muralidhara and Hadiya Faheem, "Huawei's Quest for Global Markets", *China-Focused Cases*, China Europe International Business School, Springer, Shanghai, 2020 pp. 65–80.

[62] Zhen Wei, *Using Christensen's models to make sense of changes in the Chinese telecommunications equipment supplier industry*, Carleton University, PhD Thesis, ProQuest Dissertation Publishing, 2005.

[63] Kerstin J. Schaefer, "Catching Up by Hiring: The Case of Huawei", *Journal of International Business Studies* 51:9(2020).

leading researchers abroad. In 2002, Huawei founded a subsidiary company in Texas. The next year Huawei established a JV with 3Com in the United States to develop routers,[64] and Siemens in Germany to develop the 3G standards.[65] Other FDI followed in San Jose and San Diego and elsewhere. The bankruptcy of Nortel in 2009 presented a great opportunity to open a facility in Ottawa, staffed with the former pioneers of mobile telephony.

Huawei located its offshore R&D centers close to competitors. If a rival downsized, laying off staff without non-compete agreements, Huawei hired them.

In the new research facilities, Huawei hired both recent promising PhDs with cutting edge technology and those with industry legitimacy — professionals, recent retirees, those who could embed themselves in Huawei and could embed Huawei into western markets helping with increasing credibility, honing strategy, and facilitating government contracts, while mentor Huawei's domestic employees in global telecommunications industry practices and improve English fluency of the whole company.

One barrier in hiring was Huawei's initial lack of legitimacy in the eyes of prospective employees. Non-Chinese industry top professionals often perceived the company as a dark force, controlled by the Chinese government and the CPC. This perception was the same prejudice that Huawei encountered when trying to enter foreign markets to make sales. Overcoming of that perception that was key to Huawei succeeding in foreign sales at the same time catching up with the state of the art.[66]

The foreign hires were incentivized to patent and contribute to academic and professional periodicals. Those who joined and stayed welcomed the job option provided by Huawei, the higher salaries and the professional freedom and the power to hire their own teams. Outward FDI in R&D allowed Huawei to combine its outstanding domestic Chinese customer service with its R&D output-input ratio advantage to reach and

[64] Zhen Wei, *op. cit.*, p. 38.

[65] Jeff Shepard, "Siemens and Huawei Form TD-SCDMA Joint Venture", *EE Power*, August 28, 2003. https://eepower.com/news/siemens-and-huawei-form-td-scdma-joint-venture/# (accessed March 15, 2021).

[66] Kerstin J. Schaefer, "Catching Up by Hiring: The Case of Huawei", *Journal of International Business Studies* 51:7(2020).

substantially advance the global state of the art. Its global patent applications surged.

The U.S. Market, Global Dominance, and Politics

Huawei challenged Cisco in the United States with mixed success. It advertised its internet routers with the slogan, "the only difference between us and them is the price" and a picture of the Golden Gate Bridge, a veiled reference to Cisco's logo. Cisco responded first by offering Huawei its market for low-end routers and switches in the United States on an OEM basis. In return, Cisco wanted Huawei to abandon its R&D into high end products. Huawei refused. So Cisco sued Huawei for IP theft.[67]

Cisco alleged that Huawei had copied Cisco source code and manuals — even including errors in those manuals on some of its routers.[68] Huawei counter-sued Cisco. In September 2003, Huawei and Cisco came to a settlement. Huawei stopped selling routers at issue in the United States, undertook to sell only new and modified routers and agreed to submit new products for review by a neutral expert. Both sides dropped their suits with each paying their own legal costs.[69] Huawei had been forced to dial back its U.S. market entry — at that time the largest market in the world for routers and switches — but it persisted.[70] Based on price, quality, service and credibility, Huawei's products were increasingly seen as too good to resist.

---

[67] Lanhua Li, Bin Guo, Johann Peter Murmann, and Dong Wu, "Huawei's R&D Management Transformation", in Xiaobo Wu, *The Management Transformation of Huawei: From Humble Beginnings to Global Leadership*, Cambridge University Press, London, 2020. https://www.alexandria.unisg.ch/262033/1/huaweis_rd_management_transformation.pdf (accessed March 5, 2021).

[68] Jen Lin-liu, "Huawei-Cisco Tests China's Respect for Property Rights" *IEEE Spectrum* (August 2003).

[69] Barbera Jorgensen, "Cisco and Huawei Settle IP Infringement Case", *Electronic Business Highlands Ranch* 30:9(2004). For a business strategy case on Huawei's early U.S. expansion, see Ali Farhoomand and Phoebe Ho, "Huawei: Cisco's Chinese Challenger", Asia Case Research Centre #HKU599, Hong Kong, 2006.

[70] Sun, Sunny Li, "Internationalization Strategy of MNEs from Emerging Economies: The Case of Huawei", *Multinational Business Review* 17:2(2009), 129–155.

Concerning the frequently repeated complaint that Huawei has prospered by stealing U.S. technology, it should be pointed out that little evidence for it exists. In 2013, the wireless carrier T-Mobile sued Huawei concerning alleged theft of a phone-testing robot called “Tappy”. A jury awarded T-Mobile the relatively small settlement of $4.8 million with no punitive fines finding that there was neither damage nor unjust enrichment nor willful and malicious conduct by Huawei.[71] The most damaging allegation of a culture of IP disrespect in Huawei is the un-litigated allegation that Huawei offered employees bonuses for obtaining confidential information from competitors.[72]

Yet notwithstanding Huawei’s relatively clean bill of health, politics has entered. Huawei, like any equipment supplier, is trying to dominate global markets. As Ren describes it, Huawei is “... providing future-oriented information pipes to build a better connected world”.[73] Yet those “pipes” of interconnection for the new digital age — the routers, switches, base stations, etc., — are the critical infrastructure for increasing volumes of data, the driving force in the fourth industrial revolution. For non-Chinese, especially Americans viewing China as a challenge, Huawei’s control of “the pipes” is problematic — if not actually malign.

Huawei has supplied telecommunications equipment to Iran (which the United States had embargoed). Huawei sold product to the PLA. Huawei, is, after all, Chinese at a time when China has been identified increasingly by Americans either as unfriendly (33%) or “an enemy” (32%).[74]

---

[71] Mark Dano, “T-Mobile Wins $4.8M Ruling against Huawei over Alleged Theft of Smartphone-Testing Robot ‘Tappy’”, *Fierce Wireless*, May 22, 2017. https://www.fiercewireless.com/wireless/t-mobile-wins-4-8m-ruling-against-huawei-over-alleged-theft-smartphone-testing-robot-tappy (accessed March 16, 2021).

[72] “Huawei Accused of Offering Bonuses to Staff to Steal Secrets”, *Financial Times*, January 29, 2019.

[73] Ren Zhengfei, “Letter from the CEO”, Huawei 2015 Annual Report. https://www.huawei.com/-/media/corporate/pdf/annual-report/annualreport2015_en.pdf (accessed March 3, 2021).

[74] Graeme Bruce, “American’s Opinion of China Continues to Slide”, *Yougov*, July 8, 2020. https://today.yougov.com/topics/politics/articles-reports/2020/07/07/china-americas-enemy (accessed March 20, 2021).

Starting under the Bush administration and continuing through the Obama administration members of congress and American executive administrations increasingly intervened to block Huawei's market growth in the United States.[75] Huawei became see as a security threat.

The leaks in 2013 by Edward Snowden, the American counter-intelligence to the U.S. government's National Security Agency (NSA) that the NSA and the Central Intelligence Agency (CIA) carried out massive data collection activities on the internet with the aid of U.S. telecommunications hardware and software companies from was a watershed. The United States was ostensibly one of countries of the world most concerned about individual liberties, at least of Americans, if not about foreigners. Yet here was proof that the United States' data collection posture regarding citizens and non-citizens, residents and non-residents was

> …"Collect it All", "Process it All", "Exploit it All", "Partner it All", "Sniff it All" and, ultimately, "Know it All".[76]

The United States had entered the realm of big data domestic and international surveillance. Surely, then, so had China. The United States and China signed an agreement to prohibit economic espionage. Yet no such agreement exists that prohibits nation-state spying.[77] Spying is part of the accepted rules of the global game.

Does Huawei defer to the Chinese government? Of course! Would Huawei place the interests of the CPC over the interests of U.S. consumers in a crisis? Certainly! Has it already built backdoors into its pipes — the telecommunications equipment that enable the digital revolution?

---

[75] Wolf Frank, "Threat from Huawei", *Congressional Record, House* H1376, March 19, 2012. https://www.congress.gov/112/crec/2012/03/19/CREC-2012-03-19-pt1-PgH1376-4.pdf (accessed March 12, 2021). Permanent Select Committee on Intelligence, "Investigative Report on the U.S. National Security Issues Posed by Chinese Telecommunications Companies Huawei and ZTE", October 8, 2012. https://intelligence.house.gov/news/documentsingle.aspx?DocumentID=96 (accessed December 16, 2021).

[76] Margaret Hu, "Taxonomy of the Snowden Disclosures", *Washington and Lee Law Review* Lexington 72:4(2015). 1687.

[77] Kim Zetter, "US and China Reach Historic Agreement on Economic Espionage", *Wired* September 25, 2015. https://perma.cc/VUH7-VU25 (accessed March 15, 2021).

Probably not?[78] Could it hack its own systems if the need arose in the event of a national request? Probably.

Huawei's Foray into Mobile Phones

Apple's launch of the iPhone in 2007 introduced a market opened for Huawei a market with larger potential than telecommunications equipment. It had been among the top producers of cell phones, but they were low end and OEM. In 2010 Huawei focused its impressive R&D talent onto moving into the smart phone market. It was aided by the fact that its headquarters, in Shenzhen, was the location of assembly for most of the Apple and Samsung smart phones, so it was able to tap into the global supply chains relying American operating systems and chip designs, Taiwanese and Korean chip fabrication and Chinese assembly. It used Android operating system. It had to cultivate channel partners. By the end of 2017, Huawei was on the cusp of becoming the top smart phone brand in the world by unit sales.[79]

Huawei in the Crosshairs

By 2018, the popular attitude to China in the United States had turned decisively negative. The foreign policy community had come to a consensus that the United States should be "doing away with the hopeful thinking that has long characterized the United States' approach to China".[80]

In July 2018, Trump started his trade war with China. In December, on his instructions, Ren's daughter, Meng Wanzhou was arrested in the Vancouver airport under a U.S.–Canada extradition treaty. The crime? Alleged bank fraud, misleading HSBC bank in Hong Kong concerning the

---

[78] Ren Zhengfei has credibly argued on numerous occasions that no such backdoors were built into any 5G equipment or its software, see for example, Dan Strumpf and Josh Chin, "Huawei's Mysterious Founder Denies Spying for China, Praises Trump", *Wall Street Journal*, New York, New York, January 15, 2019.

[79] For a comprehensive marketing strategy case comparing Huawei, Samsung and Apple in late 2017, see Elie Ofek, Tian Tao, Eden Yin, Nancy Hua Dai, "Huawei: How Can We Lead The Way?", Harvard Business School #9-218-071, 2018.

[80] Kurt Campbell and Ely Ratner, "The China Reckoning", *Foreign Affairs* 97:2 (2018).

business dealings of Huawei in Iran. Underpinning these actions was the American assessment that China had become a strategic threat to the West. And China's 5-G star, Huawei, therefore should be excluded from any and all the United States and U.S. allied countries' markets.[81]

In May 2019, the U.S. government placed Huawei on the "Entity List" restricting any U.S. companies from doing any business with it. For network equipment, this represented the final nail in the coffin of Huawei business in the United States. The United States with no domestic company capable of challenging Huawei on 5-G is meeting its needs from other foreign competitors: Korean (Samsung), Finnish (Nokia) or Swedish (Ericsson). To meet what it sees as a national telecommunications emergency, it is actively considering implementing government-led industrial policies to build or buy a national champion.[82]

The attack on Huawei has extended to its smart phone business. No new Huawei smartphones can be installed with Google apps.[83] As these are a key component of the Android-powered smart phone experience, Huawei no longer can claim to produce a first rate world class smart phone.[84] Huawei has become the face of Chinese techno-politics that the United States has decided must be humbled to preserve its own technical hegemony, through a new grand alliance.

Today, Huawei presents a paradox. It is the global leader in 5G technology, realizing an ambition declared in 2009. It is an IP powerhouse: of its approximately 200,000 workers, about 100,000 are in R&D with 15,000 in basic R&D. Its products are in 170 countries and its "pipes" for information serve more than 3 billion people. It has ongoing cooperation with the Chinese Research Institute of Telecommunications Transmission,

---

[81] For a very well-written, balanced treatment of China's entry into the global trading system and subsequent disillusionment with its role in the current international community, including the not-insignificant role of Huawei, see Paul Blustein, *Schism: China, America, and the Fracturing of the Global Trading System*, Center for International Governance Innovation, Waterloo, Canada, 2019.

[82] Drew FitzGerald and Sarah Krouse, "White House Considers Broad Federal Intervention to Secure 5G Future; The Trump Administration Has Discussed a Range of Strategies to Build Competition against Huawei", Wall Street Journal, New York, New York, June 25, 2020.

[83] "The new grand bargain" *The Economist*, London, 437: 9221, November 21, 2020, pp. 23–26.

[84] C. Scott Brown, "The Huawei Ban Explained: A Complete Timeline and Everything You Need to Know", *The Android Authority*, February 2, 2021. https://www.androidauthority.com/huawei-google-android-ban-988382/ (accessed March 15, 2021).

the China Academy of Telecommunications Research, the Xi'an Electronics Engineering Institute, and the Beijing Design Institute. Over the last decade, it has spent about ¥600 billion in R&D. It holds over 85,000 active patents. It has over 20 research institutes and over 30 joint innovation centers run with global carriers, its main customers. As we noted in Chapter 3, Huawei is a global force in IP, filing over the last decade, more PCT applications than any other company in the world. It is active in more than 80 international standards-setting organizations. In the recent past, it has enjoyed close technical cooperation with 3Con, Agere Systems, Ericson, Google, IBM, Infineon, Intel, Microsoft, Motorola, Qualcomm, Sun Microsystems, Symantec, Telefoncia, Texas Instruments, Vodaphone, and many others. But those with U.S. companies have now been cancelled while others have been dialed back.

Huawei retains its iconic status in China but has become, in a few short years, a pariah in much of the West. William Kirby's recent Harvard case presents the reader with Huawei's development, culture, and dilemma — "... in a world at once interconnected and unstable, how would Huawei prepare for the future?"[85]

Confronted with the Western attack on Huawei, Ren personally counter-attacked. Although the dominant figure in Huawei for 30 years, Ren had never sought media attention beyond the company. In the CPC, he had never taken leadership positions, which had certainly been available to him, and could arguably have benefited himself and Huawei. And prior to 2018, he had not conducted more than a dozen interviews with members of the press. But since the attack, he has mounted a personal public relations campaign to defend his reputation.

He has demonstrated he is straight-shooting and morally-founded. He is a tireless worker. He is a humanist. He is an exacting parent and he has deep respect for his own parents. He is loyal and highly values loyalty in others. He believes in the redemptive power of knowledge. He respects and has contributed much to IP. He is autocratic. He is patriotic. But he is not now and has never been a pawn of the government. He is an internationalist. His vision for the future is a unified world where consumers' lives are made better by integrated digital technologies.

---

[85] William C. Kirby, Billy Chan, John P. McHugh, "Huawei: A Global Tech Giant in the Crossfire of a Digital Cold War", Harvard Business Publishing, p320089-PDF-ENG, 2020.

One can trace his *way* from Confucian philosophers. He is inspired by those who took China to its rightful position in the world today — Mao Zedong and the leaders of the CPC since the reform and opening up. He has developed an organization equipped to grapple with the personnel, technical, commercial and political issues of global telecommunications.

Conclusion

One can look with nostalgia back on the world of pre-WTO China in the first 20 years of the reform and opening up period. China was viewed by a confident West as a new member of the triumphant liberal world, soon to be fully integrated. In that world, Haier and Huawei were founded, copied western models, grew, and prospered.

The world has moved on. Today, those striving to banish management bureaucracy — like Zhang — are not necessarily Western libertarians. Those in favor of free trade and competition and against government restrictions — like Ren — are not necessary classical liberals. Those pushing for state subsidies, restrictions of foreign corporations and planned national technological developments are not necessarily the socialists.

Today the Zhangs and the Rens of China are globalists. They are the proponents of customer as king, of the power of the market and of IP development and protection. Any international marketing specialist, economist or technically competent engineer graduating today in China can handle English in his or her specialty. They are plugged into a borderless academic space. They, and the hundreds of millions of other English speakers in China are part of humanity on a path of innovation.

Within the global community, however, China *is* a very separate nation. Its people's patriotism runs deep. The support that the government enjoys in China from its people is not a grand bargain where the CPC achieves creditability if and only if it delivers economic growth. The CPC is the leader of a moral society. China has legitimate traditions of how society should be organized, how leaders should lead, how followers should contribute. These traditions — which themselves are developing — affect the strategies of leading companies.

In this chapter we considered two *ways* of leaders of two global companies. The philosophies of Zhang and Ren, while not opposite, include elements which are orthogonal to each other. If Zhang had run Huawei and Ren had run Haier, the results would certainly have been different: one can no more imagine Zhang implementing a fiercely loyal, wolf management style than one can imagine Ren implementing the hierarchy-destroying *rendanheyi* model. Yet both models are firmly rooted in a Chinese humanist tradition going back 2,500 years and both present viable models for those studying management of innovation in China.

Chapter 8

Fuyao Glass: Global Strategy for U.S. Country Risk

Introduction

This chapter presents a case about a practicing Buddhist, Cao Dewang, and the company he started, Fuyao Glass, the largest and most profitable auto glass producer in the world. Cao like Zhang Ruimin and Ren Zhengfei discussed in Chapter 7, is from the first generation of private entrepreneurs who started their own companies in the early years of the reform and opening up of China. Cao, like Zhang and Ren, was born before liberation. Cao's father, a rich Shanghai-based businessmen, relocated the family back to their ancestral home in Fuqing County, Fujian Province immediately following liberation. There Cao's father's business foundered and the family was reduced to abject poverty.

Cao grew up during the years of strict CPC control, centralized planning and ideological volatility. He came of age during the Cultural Revolution. And he heartily welcomed the reform and opening up of the late 1970s. Cao, like Zhang and Ren, is heavily influenced by traditional Chinese culture. In the last chapter, I described the *way* of Zhang and Ren as Daoist and Confucian respectively. And I said that those descriptions may be debatable.

Cao on the other hand, is undoubtedly Buddhist.[1]

---

[1]Buddhist Chinese use "*dao*" (道) when referring to *the way* to achieve enlightenment. See "The Way of the Buddha", [菩萨道] Wikipedia [Chinese]. https://zh.wikipedia.org/

Buddhism in China

Imperial China from third to the 19th century, had three main teachings: Daoism, Buddhism and Confucianism.[2] All three originated in the Axial Age of the 6th century BC but, unlike Daoism and Confucianism, Buddhism did not start in China. The Gautama Siddhartha Shakyamuni[3] — i.e., the Buddha — was born in what is now southern Nepal. His disciples developed his teachings orally and through a plethora of sacred texts. Buddhism briefly became the state religion of the Maurya Dynasty in present-day northern India in the 3rd century BC under the emperor Ashoka. It blossomed into many diverse schools before yielding its dominance in India to resurgent Hindu beliefs. Buddhism made its way northwest to the Greco-Bactrian Kingdom, the Indo-Greek Kingdom and Kushan Empire, centered on modern Afghanistan. There Buddhism acquired the unmistakable Greek influence in its statuary,[4] and then Buddhism went east along the silk road reaching China at about the same time that Christ was teaching his Gospel in the Province of Judea of the Roman Empire.

Buddhist ideas that reached the Eastern Han and the dynasties of China's dark ages were many, enigmatic, fragmentary, and popularly absorbed into schools of Daoism. Buddhism received state patronage in the Northern Wei (a nomadic central Asian dynasty that ruled northern China from 386 to 534). Those years saw the construction of the massive

---

wiki/菩薩道 (accessed March 25, 2021). "*Dao*" is also used by Christians. The Bible translation of "the word" is also *dao*. "The Gospel According to John" 1:1 *Bible Gateway*. https://www.biblegateway.com/passage/?search=john+1&version=CNVS (accessed March 25, 2021).

[2] In Chinese, the three teachings are 道释儒 (*Dao*, *Shi*, *Ru*). Buddhism as a religion in Chinese is 佛教 (*Fojiao*) but is also called 释教 (*Shi Jiao*). The "*Fo*" in *Fojiao* is a short form of "*Fotuo*" (佛陀) which is a transliteration of the Pali language name meaning "enlightened". That same Pali language word is transliterated into English as "Buddha".

[3] Shakyamuni means "the sage of the Shakyas", (Siddhartha came from the Shakya clan) and is the Buddha's most often used name in Chinese, written as 释迦牟尼 (pronounced "*Shijiamoni*"). The usual name for Buddhist teaching in China 释教 (*Shijiao*) comes from the first character of his name, 释 (*Shi*).

[4] See John Boardman, "The East after Alexander the Great", in *The Diffusion of Classical Art in Antiquity*, Princeton University Press, Princeton, 1994.

Yungang[5] and Longmen[6] Caves and the founding of the legendary Shaolin Monastery. Buddhism was promoted by the Sui (581–618), who re-united China, and by early Tang emperors.

630 AD was the year that Mohammed's Islamic forces took control of the Kaaba in Mecca, Arabia. It was also the year that in China, the Buddhist monk Xuan Zang, arrived in Turpan (in modern Xinjiang) the first stop on his Journey to the West[7] — i.e., his journey to India. There he spent 15 years earnestly studying Buddhism, returning with details of Buddhist history, schools, practices and beliefs and voluminous sets of Buddhist texts.

The peak of Chinese state patronage of Buddhism was under China's only female emperor, Wu Zetian (who ruled from 690 to 705).[8] About a century and a half later, Buddhism was persecuted and its monasteries were nationalized, in a wave of anti-foreign sentiment that saw the suppression of Nestorian Christianity, Judaism and Manicheanism. Thereafter, Buddhism never received substantial Chinese imperial patronage or persecution. And until the 20th century, Buddhism's role as one of China's three great teachings was indisputable.

The three teachings — Confucianism, Daoism and Buddhism — form three interweaving strains of the traditional social, philosophical and religious *rules of the game*. The three teachings were not mutually exclusive. In the West, religions frequently conflict. Each of the West's great religions — Islam (both Shia and Sunni), pre-reformation Christianity (The Church of the East, The Oriental Orthodox Church, The Eastern Orthodox Church and The Holy Catholic Church) and the many strains of Protestantism following the 16th century — claims to hold exclusive truth. The truth is "good"; the alternative is "evil". Conflict between "good" and

---

[5] "Yungang Grottos", *World Heritage Site Weibo*. https://weibo.com/yungangwangzhan?is_all=1 (accessed March 25, 2021).

[6] "Longmen Municipal Government Webpage". http://www.lmsk.gov.cn (accessed Mary 25, 2021).

[7] The tale of Xuanzang's epic journey forms the historic core of the fantastic 16th century Ming Dynasty novel, one of the four great novels of imperial China *Journey to the West*. See Wu Cheng En, *Journey to the West* [*西游记*] also known in English as *Monkey King*. Journey to the West [in Chinese] China Text Project https://ctext.org/xiyouji/zhs (accessed December 16, 2021).

[8] "Connecting Women to the Silk Roads: Empress Wu Zetian and the Spread of Buddhism", *Women in World History Curriculum*. http://www.womeninworldhistory.com/silk-road-04.html.

"evil" ensues. One might blame the Greeks and their philosophical debate. One might blame the Persian Zoroastrians with their dualistic cosmology. One might blame the Imperial Romans, who prescribed polytheist religion prior to 325 AD and then, under Constantine codified official Christianity at Nicaea. One might blame the Bishops of Rome and the Ecumenical Patriarchates of Constantinople who detailed the nature of God and his Word and excommunicated those who disagreed. One might blame the Prophet Mohammed who, fed up with Christian bickering, declared that there was only one god, God, and he, Mohammed, as the last prophet of God, had the last word on the truth. One might blame the Caliphates, the Christian kingdoms, and the many religions countries who continued the rich tradition of intolerance down to the present day. China, in comparison, has been blessed with more syncretizing, intertwining and melding of different *ways*.

That non-confrontational Chinese tradition, however, was largely abandoned in 1949. During the next 30 years, the state suppressed religion and, during the Cultural Revolution, the suppression was often violent. After the reform and opening up, freedom of religious belief and "normal religions activities" have been protected by the Constitution of the PRC. However, the question as to what constitutes "normal activities" is relevant. Religious practice is protected if carried out in religions organizations registered with the government and/or if it does not cross an important line — threatening the legitimacy of the CPC. The CPC has determined that the line would be crossed, for example, if the Vatican named bishops in the Chinese Catholic Church, if American Protestant churches funded congregations in China, if Muslims promoted Sharia law in Xinjiang or if the Falun Gong was recognized as a religion.[9]

The Falun Gong (法轮功) which can be translated as "Buddhist Law" or "Dharma Wheel Practice"[10] was founded in 1992 by a Buddhist adherent, Li Hongzhi and was officially registered with the Chinese government as an organization to teach breathing techniques (*qigong* 气功). In just seven years, thanks to the charisma of Master Li, the popularity of

[9]See the website of the United Front Work Department of the CPC Central Committee. http://www.zytzb.gov.cn/html/index.html (accessed March 26, 2021) and US Commission on International Religions Freedom. https://www.uscirf.gov/countries/china (accessed March 26, 2021).

[10]Dharma is a Pali word that means the right way of doing things, here meaning the teachings (laws) of Buddha.

qigong and the evident desire for moral dimensions to life, Falun Gong swelled to over 70 million adherents. Falun Gong's leaders petitioned to have the movement registered as a religion but the CPC denied its petition. In protest, Falun Gong adherents organized a mass demonstration in Beijing in 1999. The CPC determined that Falun Gong, by that demonstration and other activities, had challenged its authority. So the government banned and suppressed the movement.[11]

In China today, self-declared Buddhists represent 16.6% of the Chinese population, the third most numerous group after agnostics (31.8%) and practitioners of folk religion[12] (30.8%). Self-declared Buddhists are more numerous than Christians (7.4%), atheists[13] (6.8%), ethnic religion adherents (4.2%), Muslims (1.8%) and Daoists (0.4%).[14] Given that folk religion in China is largely a mixture of Buddhist and Daoist beliefs and practices, and that ethnic religions include some Buddhist groups, I conclude that Chinese who are in some measure Buddhist make up about a third of Chinese.

Buddhist Rules of the Game

Because Buddhism is unambiguously classified as the most popular religion in China today, I feel compelled to suggest how Buddhist ideas may affect management of innovation in China. The reader should remember

[11] Seth Faison, "In Beijing: A Roar of Silent Protesters", *New York Times*, April 27, 1999. https://www.nytimes.com/1999/04/27/world/in-beijing-a-roar-of-silent-protesters.html (accessed December 16, 2021).

[12] These have been collectively described as *Shen Jiao* (神教) and are typically practiced in prayers to the spirits at local temples or shrines known as *bai shen* (拜神) that may combine Buddhist and Taoist traditions. See Kuah-Pearce Khun Eng, "Diversities and Unities: toward a reformist Buddhism in Singapore", Lei Ah Eng [ed], *Religious Diversity in Singapore*, Institute of South Asian Studies, Singapore, 2008 for a discussion of this syncretic tradition transplanted to the overseas Chinese community of Singapore.

[13] As Marxism-Leninism is doctrinally atheist, this low percentage of atheists in China is noteworthy. It reflects the reality that many, including CPC members, are not atheists. I have frequently been informed by CPC members that "religion is good" and that they, themselves are agnostic, highly respectful of Confucian traditions, or interested in Buddhist, Daoist or Christian beliefs.

[14] "Religion in China", *US Council on Foreign Relations*. https://www.cfr.org/backgrounder/religion-china (accessed March 24, 2021).

that Buddhism itself has hundreds of millions of adherents, actively developing their ideas today. The reader should also remember that Buddhism is a living, formally practiced religion that boasts a two and a half millennia tradition, in thousands of schools, in hundreds of regions, through dozens of major languages. Buddhists may find my ideas on their religion infantile, incomplete and incorrect. For that I sincerely apologize.

The Buddha — Shijiamoni — is not an idol.[15] Buddha was not God. He was a person (and not the only person) who attained enlightenment. Having attained enlightenment, he started a movement of those who also seek enlightenment.

Enlightenment comes from understanding. All sentient beings suffer. Sufferers include humans, animals, probably plants, and possibly inanimate entities whose sentience we do not understand. Suffering comes from craving: desires for food, for fun, for stuff, for sex, for prestige, for power, etc. Craving is ignorant. The enlightened understand that the objects of craving, that craving itself, and that life in general, are empty.

What is emptiness? One modern Buddhist astronomer comments that "… phenomena are devoid of an existence that is permanent and independent of the observer…." In Buddhist cosmology, all things, because they are observer-dependent, interdependent and ceaselessly changing, are "empty".[16]

The *way* (the *dao*) to understanding in Buddhism involves *dharma-chakra* (or *falun*, in Chinese): holding right views, aspirations, speech, actions, livelihood, exertion, mindfulness and concentration.[17] The *way* involves achieving pure thought to end craving and to achieve emptiness. Buddhist practices include meditation as part of the *way*. Practices typically involve traditional breathing techniques like *qigong*, traditional medicine, various philosophies and/or schools of mental and/or martial

---

[15] I use the term "idol" in the Christian sense of a physical representation of a non-Christian god who is worshipped.

[16] Trinh Xuan Thuan, "Cosmic Design from a Buddhist Perspective", *Annals of the New York Academy of Sciences*, 206, January 2006, 215–224.

[17] *Dharma-chakra* is a Sanskrit word. One of the challenges for an English speaker approaching Chinese Mahayana Buddhism is that the original texts on which the religion is based are in ancient Pali or Sanskrit languages, and their greatest developments are written in classical Chinese. The term for *dharma-chakra* in Chinese is *falun* 法轮, the same name as the name of the outlawed modern Buddhist sect, *Falun Gong*, referred to above.

arts. Popularly, different sects have involved divination, spiritualism, astral travel, miracles, commuting with the dead, etc.

The only way to escape the karmic cycle of craving and suffering is through enlightenment. Buddhist karmic cycles are both intra- and inter-generational. Those on the *way* of enlightenment are to be compassionate to *all* sentient beings because all sentient beings are entrapped in suffering. Suffering repeats in continuous cycles of reincarnation, throughout the eons. The age of the world in traditional Buddhist reckoning is long, longer than the time it would take one monk, one day each year, to polish one cubic mile of rock away to nothing with a silk cloth.[18] Yet the old, vast universe is empty.

Buddhism and Innovation

Does Buddhism in China impact management? Yes.

Empirical evidence shows that companies registered in regions with a higher concentrations of Buddhist monasteries suffer less from tunnelling — accounting schemes to channel resources through inter-corporate transfers away from publicly listed companies into the hands of controlling shareholders. Studies also show that earnings management — accounting techniques to obfuscate volatility of corporate earnings — is reduced by the proximity Buddhist and Daoist sites to the location of company listing.[19] One can conclude that Buddhism (and Daoism) promote transparency.

But what about innovation?

Joseph Needham, the great chronicler of *Science and Civilization in China* was scathing. He refers to Buddhism's "… vulgar magic …" and comments that, historically,

> … Buddhism was not interested in coordinating and interpreting experience or finding reality in the fullest and most harmonious statement of facts of experience, but in seeking some kind of "reality" behind

[18] Pali Canon, "Kappa". http://www.palikanon.com/english/wtb/g_m/kappa.htm (accessed March 26, 2021).

[19] Du Xingqiang, "Does Religion Mitigate Tunnelling? Evidence from Chinese Buddhism", *Journal of Business Ethics*, 125 (2014), 299–327 and Du Xingqiang, Wei Jian, Lai Shaojuan, Du Yingjie, and Pei Hongmei, "Does Religion Mitigate Earnings Management? Evidence from China", *Journal of Business Ethics* 131:3 (2015), 699–749.

the phenomenal world and then brushing the latter away as a useless curtain....[20]

Although he grants that Buddhism's "... attention to relief of pain ..." gave Buddhists in China's imperial past impetus to study medicine, in general he sees Buddhism as inhibiting innovation much more than Confucianism or Daoism.

Thriving (and registered) Buddhist charitable organizations today in China offer care and education, especially for poor, aged and weak members of society as they did in traditional China.[21] The more famous Buddhist sites are tourist attractions. Yet, returning to innovation, in general Buddhist organizations look to tradition, not to the future. They are certainly not at the forefront of innovation in China.[22]

Going forward, however, the Buddhist perspective may provide a useful approach to cope with the rapid changes of automation, digitalization, AI, and the biotechnological transformation that are discussed in the final four chapters of this book. Buddhism prescribes globalism. For Buddhists, China is not the center, the "middle kingdom" but is part of a wider world that, in fact, extends far beyond our planet. The Buddhist truth originates from outside of China and its protagonists — the Buddha and the arhats (those early disciples of the Buddha who attained enlightenment) are (often cartoonishly) clearly identified as non-Chinese.[23]

Buddhism embraces a definition of sentient beings where the human is but one of many. Suffering is gender-, class-, nation- and species-neutral. In a rapidly changing world, where traditional roles are being relegated to history by the digital revolution, a Buddhist frame of

---

[20] Joseph Needham and Wang Ling, *Science and Civilization in China Volume 2 History of Scientific Thought*, Cambridge University Press, London, 1956, p. 417.

[21] Daniela Campo, "Chinese Buddhism in the Post-Mao Era: Preserving and Reinventing the Received Tradition", Chapter 12 in Stephan Feuchtwang [ed], *Handbook on Religion in China*, Edward Elgar, Northampton, 2020.

[22] "The Profession of Renunciation", *The Economist*, 437: 9225, London, December 19, 2020, pp. 115–116.

[23] Called *a-luohan* (阿罗汉) or simply *luohan* in Chinese, the arhats in Chinese art have often grotesque, non-Chinese appearance. See "What Does Luohan Mean? The 18 Luohan's Names and Origins" [羅漢是什麼意思？十八羅漢的名稱及由來], *Daily Headline*, September 12, 2015. https://kknews.cc/foI/qe3jrab.html (accessed March 30, 2021).

mind may help one to cope with waves of change likely to cascade over our future.

Buddhism and Cao

Cao Dewang, unlike Zhang Ruimin and Ren Zhengfei, is first and foremost a Buddhist. He is not now and never has been a member of the CPC. Yet he has always worked very closely with the government. The factory that eventually became the core of Fuyao Glass, like Zhang Ruimin's Haier, was originally a collectively owned enterprise under the local government. All policies of Fuyao are made "… within the context of what is good for society and the country".[24] Cao is a delegate to the National People's Consultative Conference and he became in 2013 China's greatest philanthropist, donating about US$1.3 billion (in Fuyao shares) to the Heren Charitable Foundation (河仁基金会),[25] which is dedicated to improving children's education. The Heren Foundation is the first and, so far, the only charity to be directly approved by the State Council, the highest executive authority in China. And the Heren Foundation is the second largest shareholder of Fuyao Glass after Cao himself.[26]

Cao's autobiography is entitled *Enlightenment* (心如菩提)[27] or, literally, "The Heart of a Bodhisattva". A bodhisattva is one who, having been enlightened, helps other sufferers. Cao speech is forthright, even blunt. He has an unassuming, simple, transparent, lifestyle. He is paternalistic but demanding of his workers. He sees his company as building long-term

---

[24] "Dividend Policy at Fuyao Glass", *Youtube Video*, April 13, 2016. https://www.youtube.com/watch?v=vKlpK3pNu8A (accessed March 26, 2021).

[25] See the Heren Foundation website. http://www.hcf.org.cn/#/ (accessed March 26, 2021) and Demetri Sevastopulo and Julie Zhu, "The Tycoon Who Opened the Window of Opportunity: Monday Interview", *Financial Times*, London, May 26, 2014.

[26] Heren Foundation owns 11.5% versus 19.6% for Cao. See 2019 Fuyao Annual Report.

[27] The autobiography's title also alludes to lines of the twin, competing, poems by Shen Xiu and Hui Neng, two famous Tang Dynasty Zen (*Chan* 禅) Buddhist Shao Lin Temple monks. Hui Neng left to found the southern Shaolin in Cao's home county of Fuqing, Fujian. See Yuming Yao, "Huining and Shenxiu", *Vajra Buddha Sea*. http://www.drbachinese.org/vbs/publish/311/vbs311p036.htm (accessed March 25, 2021).

win-win relationships among suppliers and buyers.[28] He has a global perspective. The most striking decoration in Cao's office in Fuyao's headquarters is a white porcelain statue of Guan Yin — the bodhisattva who hears the cries of suffering.[29] He has often said that "… the more I give to charity, the less need I have for money …" And he believes that "… nothing is permanent, yet we find meaning and value in following our ancestors' pursuit of development and helping the world…."[30]

The case, "Fuyao Glass: Global Strategy for U.S. Country Risk" involves Cao assessing Fuyao's foreign direct investment (FDI) into the United States.

Cao sees two prerequisites to success for a Chinese company going into global markets: a strong brand and its own IP. Like Haier and Huawei, Fuyao initially relied on importing technology. And like Zhang and Ren, Cao became a world IP leader by learning the world state of the art and then developing his company's own technology.

Unlike Haier and Huawei however, Fuyao is not a globally recognized household name. The reason is that Fuyao produces an intermediate good, not a final product. Fuyao's customers are the leading global automobile OEMs (i.e., the giants of the auto industry like Chrysler, Ford, GM, Toyota, etc.).

In making its investment into the United States, Fuyao brought its own, state-of-the art technology. Yet even though Fuyao did not invest in the United States to get U.S. auto glass technology, Fuyao *did* plan to obtain an R&D advantage by investing in the United States.

OEMs develop new models of cars in the United States and assemble them in locations all over the world, including China and the US. The time it takes from making the fashion sketches of a new concept car to the completion of the sales-ready end product car on an assembly line is usually over a year. During that time OEMs liaise with parts suppliers to realize the concept. Being in the United States, close to the largest concentration of automobile R&D in the world, is important for Fuyao to

---

[28] Hugh Thomas, Joyce L. Wang, Yuhui Wu, "Fuyao Glass Dividend Policy", *YouTube*, April 13, 2016. www.youtube.com/watch?v=vKlpK3pNu8A (accessed April 12, 2019).

[29] Guan Shi Yin 觀世音, often called, somewhat inaccurately in the west, the Goddess of Mercy. See "Guan Yin, Guan Yim, Kuan Yim, Kuan Yin", *One World*. https://www.nationsonline.org/oneworld/Chinese_Customs/Guan_Yin.htm (accessed March 25, 2021)

[30] "Dividend Policy at Fuyao Glass", *Youtube Video*, April 13, 2016. https://www.youtube.com/watch?v=vKlpK3pNu8A (accessed March 26, 2021).

understand and meet OEM needs. Although auto glass is a small component of the overall cost of the automobile and although the production technology of that auto glass is more advanced in China than in the United States, Fuyao gains from working with the OEMs from concept cars through mass manufacture. While Fuyao integrates more intimately into the OEMs' supply chains, it improves both mutual trust with the OEMs and its own technology relative to auto glass competitors.

In the case that follows, Fuyao has recently completed setting up the largest auto glass manufacturing facility in the world and the most sophisticated float glass facility the United States. The case provides sufficient information for the reader to analyse issues of global supply chain management (SCM) in the auto glass industry and the trade-offs of shifting sourcing from a home to an offshore location. Country risk looms large among potential risks.[31] After Fuyao made its FDI investment, those risks have become more serious as U.S.–China relations have deteriorated. One factor within those risk is cultural conflict.

American Factory

Cao Dewang, like Ren Zhengfei of Huawei, is understated. He did not seek the global limelight. Were it not for the ex-U.S. president Barack Obama's financing of the Netflix winner of the Sundance Award and the Academy Award for best full-length documentary picture, *American Factory*, Cao would not have achieved his current global fame.

No movie portrays more clearly the cultural contrast between traditional American and modern Chinese factory production than *American Factory*. The documentary describes the personal impact of globalization and automation. One gets the flavor from the movie trailer,[32] but the whole movie gives much deeper portrayals of the leading characters: Cao; American management, workers, politicians, and union campaigners; and

[31]Another Harvard Business School case also addresses global SCM (without going into country risk) through Fuyao's decision to source auto glass for a Canadian manufacturer from the United States or from China based on costing and transportation. Willy Shih, "Fuyao Glass America: Sourcing Decision", *Harvard Business Publishing*, product no. 9-618-007, August 15, 2018.

[32]"American Factory Official Trailer", *Youtube*, August 14, 2019. https://www.youtube.com/watch?v=m36QeKOJ2Fc (accessed March 29, 2021).

the Chinese shop-floor bosses brought to the United States to make Fuyao's investment in Moraine Ohio a success.

The footage is honest and detailed. Director Steven Bognar marveled that Fuyao "... really gave us access, real access". That access far exceeded what an American MNC would grant to an American production team, let alone a Chinese team. And it allowed the creation of a work of art celebrating shared humanity.[33]

Cao is the face of modern SCM innovation. In giving uninterrupted access to the movie crew, he shows his life's work: Fuyao Glass. He desires to dominate a global, efficient auto glass market and to share the benefits with equity holders, workers, OEMs, and auto buyers. And he desires transparency.

[33] Izabella Kaminska, "American Factory, Netflix — Harsh Truths about the New World of Work", *Financial Times,* London, August 25, 2019.

Fuyao Glass: Global Strategy for U.S. Country Risk

Vernon Hsu, Hugh Thomas, Joyce Wang and Yuhui Wu wrote this case solely to provide material for class discussion. The authors do not intend to illustrate either effective or ineffective handling of a managerial situation.

Reviewing the first half year results of 2018, Mr. Cao Dewang, Chairman of Fuyao Glass Industry Group Co. Ltd. (Fuyao) confidently asserted:

> *I'm really satisfied with our performance under the conditions we face this year. Because this year a lot of businesses are suffering. We basically relied on our technology and we worked together with our customers to achieve our goals. This year's first half results are better than last year's. The main reason is our foreign investments: this year they are profitable; last year they lost money.... They call me a hick. I don't care. They tell me to go onto the internet and do P2P, build a financial platform. I'm sure I could make money. But I tell them I'm not in it for the money.*

Fuyao's subsidiary, Fuyao Glass America Inc. (FGA) had, two years before, completed construction of the largest auto glass (AG) manufacturing facility in the world, located in Moraine, near Dayton, Ohio USA. Its revenues in the first half of 2018 had surged 27 percent compared with the previous year while group wide revenues of Fuyao had grown 16 percent. FGA had changed a ¥65 million[34] loss into a ¥48 million profit (See Exhibit 1). While deteriorating relations between China and the US promised an uncertain future and some social pundits had criticized Cao for deserting China by investing overseas,[35] Cao remained defiant, retorting to critical reporters

> *It is extremely glorious to be able to go out from our country and establish factories. There are only a few entrepreneurs in our country with the technology and the strategy to do this.*

Although Cao was confidence in his strategy, he and Fuyao's top management had to review how the company's US expansion and global strategy was affected by recent developments in the relations between China and the US.

FUYAO'S DEVELOPMENT

Fuyao had just celebrated its 30th birthday. Established as Chinese-foreign joint venture in Fuqing County, Fujian Province, China in 1987 and initially named the Fujian Yaohua Glass Industry Company Limited, Fuyao had been founded by Cao to supply inexpensive AG to the local auto repair glass (ARG) market. In 1989, Fuyao expanded into the OEM market, providing AG for installation in new manufactured vehicles in China, where its first OEM purchaser was Peugeot located in Guangzhou. At the same time it entered global AG markets by exporting ARG to Hong Kong.

In 1993 it listed its common shares on the Shanghai Stock Exchange and established its first foreign subsidiary (in Hong Kong) and in 1994 it set up an ARG sales subsidiary in the US. In 2000, to establish its domestic dominance, Fuyao set up a subsidiary in Changchun, Jilin province, the

[34]The Chinese Yuan (CNY)) was valued, as of the end of August 2018, at approximately US$0.15 per ¥1.00.

[35]Toutiao Chinaso.com, "曹德旺在美国建厂: 10亿美元换来控诉和罚单", ["Cao Dewang builds in the United States: $1 billion for complaints and fines"], June 18, 2017.

traditional Chinese automobile capital. Fuyao concentrated on brand-building. Cao commented:

> At the time, we had an equity partnership with Saint-Gobain. They told me to use their brand, their famous brand. I said I couldn't because we had to use the Fuyao brand. We had to build our own brand.

Shortly after China entered the WTO, in the first ruling concerning China, the WTO in 2001 found Fuyao not guilty of dumping[36] AG in the Canadian market. The next year, Fuyao contracted with Hyundai Motor Company to provide OEM AG to its auto assembly operations in Korea: it was Fuyao's first overseas OEM. From 2013 to 2017 sales revenues of Fuyao grew at a compound annual rate of 13 percent based on a growing global automobile market and Fuyao's growing share of that market. And OEM sales grew to 59 percent of Fuyao's sales revenues.

THE MARKET FOR AG

By 2018 Fuyao was the largest supplier of AG in the world with OEMs including Audi, BMW, Chrysler, FAW,[37] Ford, GM, Hyundai, Mercedes Benz, Toyota and Volkswagen. Fuyao had a mature corporate structure with shares listed in Shanghai and Hong Kong,[38] major operations in many locations across China and substantial presences in USA, Germany,

[36]Dumping is an act that occurs "… when goods are exported at a price less than their normal value, generally meaning they are exported for less than they are sold in the domestic market or third-country markets, or at less than production cost". WTO "Glossary: a guide to 'WTO speak'" accessed June 6, 2019. https://www.wto.org/english/thewto_e/glossary_e/glossary_e.htm.

[37]FAW Group, based in Changchun China and originally known as First Auto Works was the first automobile manufacturer in China. In 2018 it was the 14th largest auto manufacturer in the world (Carlogos.org, "The Largest Car Companies in the World" May 15, 2019, accessed June 6, 2015. https://www.carlogos.org/reviews/Largest-Car-Companies-in-the-World.html.

[38]A-Shares were valued in RMB, traded on the Shanghai Stock Exchange and available for purchase by all domestic Chinese investors but only a limited set of authorized international investors while H-Shares were traded on the Hong Kong Stock Exchange and purchased by Hong Kong and international investors without restriction. As of 2017 Fuyao had approximately 2.5 billion shares outstanding of which about 80% were A-Shares and 20% H-Shares. A-Shares and H-Shares enjoyed identical cashflow and voting rights.

Japan, Russia and South Korea. And it was still controlled by its founder, Cao, from its corporate headquarters in Fuqing, Fujian, China.

Although Fuyao's sales accounted for just over 20% of the global AG market, its three largest competitors, Asahi Glass Co., Ltd. (AGC), Nippon Sheet Glass Co., Ltd. (NSG) and Saint-Gobain were not much smaller: each had just under 20% of the market and the four competed to be AG suppliers for each model that the OEM's launched. A forth competitor, Vitro Glass of Mexico, had recently acquired the US AG manufacturing facilities of Pittsburgh Glass Works.[39] Among the five global AG industry leaders, Fuyao was the youngest and was the only company that specialized exclusively in AG production. The others had interests in building materials (Saint-Gobain), electronics, chemicals and ceramics (AGC), construction glass (NSG and Vitro) and glass containers (Vitro) that outweighed their AG businesses. But as Cao proudly pointed out, "our profits are greater than our four largest competitors combined profits."

Global annual sales of all automobiles was about 97 million in 2017, with the largest markets being China (30 percent), the US, Mexico and Canada comprising the North American Free Trade Association (NAFTA) (22 percent) and the European Union plus the European Free Trade Association (19 percent) as shown in Exhibit 2. Fuyao management, citing internal data, said that automobile ownership in 2015 had reached 12, 18 and 80 units percent of total population in China, the world and the US respectively. Given the low but rising Chinese ownership level, expected increases in Chinese consumer spending power, continuing improvement of China's road and highway infrastructure, the technological advances anticipated in the automobile industry, especially in new energy and intelligent automobiles, Fuyao management considered that the Chinese market offered strong, long term growth opportunities. In contrast, the growth opportunities in the US were modest: the 3.8 percent per year projected growth in auto sales in NAFTA was largely attributable to Mexico.[40]

---

[39]G. Roberts, "Vitro acquires PGW's automotive OEM glass business", *Bromsgrove just — auto global news,* Mar 2, 2017. The purchase included US AG manufacturing plants, two US float glass facilities, and AG plant in Poland, and Mexican and Chinese joint ventures. See Vitro *Annual Report 2018* pp. 44 and 98, accessed January 12, 2019. PGW was formerly the AG operations of PPG.

[40]"Going Global: Fuyao Glass Goes Where Chinese Carmakers Fear To Tread", Forbes Asia https://www.forbes.com/sites/shuchingjeanchen/2016/04/06/going-global-fuyao-glass-goes-where-chinese-carmakers-fear-to-tread/#4f52928335dc (accessed 9 October 2017).

VERTICAL INTEGRATION

Cao had avoided diversification in favor of vertical integration. Starting in 2005, Fuyao produced flat glass through the float (or "Pilkington") glass manufacturing technique. Molten glass was mixed in a furnace at over 1,500 degrees Celsius and was poured into a ribbon of glass drawn continuously over a molten tin bath in a protective atmosphere of nitrogen and hydrogen, creating, through the force of gravity, plate glass with perfectly flat parallel surfaces on both the top and bottom of the sheet. The consistent thickness was determined by the speed of pulling. Float glass production was highly capital- and energy-intensive. And once the furnace was fired up, it could not be cooled down without destroying the kiln brick lining, so float glass production at Fuyao continued 24 hours a day.

Fuyao's float glass production in China, Russia and the US was almost exclusively for its own use (see Exhibit 3a). Its float glass had to be of sufficiently high quality to meet the AG requirements of the top OEMs in the industry, so it was considerably more expensive than the flat glass (also produced by the float glass method) for use in the construction industry. Higher quality and price made float glass produced for AG unsuitable for non-AG markets.

In 2014 Fuyao announced its purchase from PPG (formerly called Pittsburgh Plate Glass) of the Mt. Zion, Illinois, USA float glass facility that produced glass for the construction industry. Subsequently, FGA rebuilt and retrofitted the facility, using Fuyao technology from China, to meet the higher requirements of AG. As Cao commented, "we gutted the old lines and put in new equipment. Now the best float glass lines in the US are ours."

The new facility started producing float glass prior to the scaling up of FGA's Moraine AG plant. Hence, FGA exported the AG output of the Mt Zion facility back to China for use of Fuyao in China. Thereafter Mt Zion became the in-house, captive supplier of AG to FGA.

LOCAL MANUFACTURING VERSUS IMPORTING FROM CHINA

In deciding the location of its AG manufacturing facilities, Fuyao considered raw materials, manufacturing, transportation, and inventory costs, and the benefits versus costs of proximity to OEMs for joint product development and supply chain flexibility. The aggregate manufacturing costs of AG reflected in the annual financial statements were approximately 53 percent raw materials, 17 percent labor, 13 percent energy and 17 percent other costs but, as Exhibit 3b shows, those proportions were not stable. Changes came from raw material, energy and labor costs, but also from Fuyao's globalization strategy.

Costs differed between the US and China. In 2017 the cost per hour of white and blue collar workers in the US were about three and eight times the cost in China respectively. However Chinese labor costs were increasing at over 10 percent per year while US labor costs were flat. The cost of energy in the US was approximately two thirds of the Chinese cost. While energy prices had dropped from 2015 to 2017, they were rising again in early 2018. The cost of shipping AG half way around the world was considerable. Including the cost of financing the inventory, the transportation costs of AG to be shipped from China to New York, and then on to Detroit Michigan, the largest center of US automobile manufacturing, would add about 30 percent to ex-factory China costs relative to the transport cost of trucking AG from Moraine to Detroit.

Those transportation costs did not include import duties. Free trade areas were important to auto parts suppliers' supply chain management not only because they allowed passage of parts and finished goods, without tariffs and quotas, but also because they saved time. Goods crossing borders in a free trade zone did not need to clear customs, a process that could take anywhere from a few hours to a week or more, depending on the efficiency of customs and forwarder agents on one hand and the queues of cargos for customs clearance on the other. The US automotive industry had been integrated into the North American market since NAFTA came into force in 1994. However, AG shipped from China to the US enjoyed no reduced tariffs. Tariffs applied to such imports were at "most favored nation" rates that were applied to products from any member of the WTO. Those tariffs are found in Exhibit 4.

Fuyao kept about a month of finished goods inventory for its China sales (see Exhibit 5). It needed this buffer for the OEM buyers "just in time" policies. Each OEM buyer reduced its inventory costs by storing minimal parts, requiring its suppliers to deliver precisely when the OEM needed the parts. And if a suppliers failed to deliver on time, causing the OEM's lines to stop, the offending supplier would be fined by the OEM according to schedules agreed in the supply contact.

Comparative costs discussed above did not include the implied costs of time lost to react to changing OEM specifications. Typically, from 12 to 18 months elapsed between model concept and model launch for a newly designed model. The additional approximately one month of shipping between China and the US reduced the ability of Fuyao to work effectively with the OEM. Proximity facilitated joint development (during the 12 to 18 month development period) and production trouble-shooting (if the AG modules were found to have issues during OEM assembly). OEMs could source AG from more than one supplier for each model, but for each model each OEM had a preferred supplier. And on some models, location for the preferred supplier was a deal breaker: the OEM would choose a local supplier regardless of a competitive bid from a non-local supplier.

INVESTING IN RUSSIA AND THE USA

Fuyao invested in Russia and the US in 2011 and 2014 respectively, acting on direct requests of its OEMs.

Volkswagen had been importing complete knocked down kits (CKD) of cars from Germany to their assembly line in the Kaluga Oblast of Russia. The oblast authorities, looking for higher domestic value-added, insisted that Volkswagen use Russian-made AG, rather than importing it from Germany. But Volkswagen had been importing AG from Fuyao in Changchun, China. As Cao explained:

> *The Russians said, "The glass has to be made in Russia because it's such a simple thing." Volkswagen told them, "if you really want to bring in an AG factory, You should go to China. They build factories quickly." So the provincial governor came here in person.*

After Cao visited Kaluga and obtained from the oblast government its guarantee to purchase the output of Fuyao's proposed green field integrated AG facility, Fuqing made the investment.

Fuyao's US investment was made at GM's request in a strategic partnership dating back to 2010. As Cao noted, "the problem they faced was the safety of their supply chain." In return for a large order, Fuyao undertook that, by the end of 2016, it would produce the OEM's AG in the US.

RISKS IN FOREIGN DIRECT INVESTMENT AND TRADE

Fuyao noted in the *Potential Risks* of its 2017 annual report two major potential risks, "risks on economic, political and social conditions, and government policies" commonly known as country risk and "risks of the industry development." Regarding the former, it said:

> Most assets of the Company are located in the PRC and approximately 65% of the income is from the business in the PRC. Therefore, the operating results, financial status and prospects of the Company are influenced by the changes in economy, politics, policies and laws.[41]

Fuyao's globalization strategy, however, had exposed the company to other country risks, especially Russian and American.

During the second half of the 20th century, US and European multinationals dominated global FDI, giving them together an aggregate stock of over 75 percent of outward FDI and over 62 percent of inward FDI in 2005. But from 2005 to 2016, those percentages dropped to 55 percent and 50 percent respectively. One reason for that drop was China's emergence. Chinese outward FDI grew from under 1 percent to over 5 percent of global outward FDI while inward FDI (i.e., foreign FDI into China) rose from 4 percent to 10 percent of global inward FDI. At the same time China became a major player in inward foreign direct investment into the US. (see Exhibit 6).

Yet FDI was difficult and controversial. Not only did the investing company face foreign laws, language and culture. It was frequently subject to political discrimination. Outward FDI brought complaints that the company was undermining the value of the domestic currency by selling it to make the investment, was foregoing domestic investment (and the employment and taxation it brought), hollowing out domestic industry and benefitting foreign countries, or was serving as a conduit to transfer ill-gotten gains away from the control of the home government. Inward FDI could also be subject to criticism with locals fearing exploitation by foreigners, loss of control of their industry and resources, theft of their technologies and dilution of their local cultures.

---

[41] Fuyao, *2017 Annual Report,* Section V Report of the Board of Directors, page 20.

Fuyao had faced difficulties in the US, but Cao considered that the most serious was labor and management supply:

> *Of course there were challenges. But it wasn't a problem of this culture or that culture. The critical problem was there were no people. We couldn't find people.... The bright ones went to Wall Street and Silicon Valley. The young people don't want to work in manufacturing.*

FGA addressed the problem, the same problem Fuyao faced in China, through training and automation. Cao commented:

> *Now we use automation to replace workers. So there are more robots. In China we also use robots. In China if you don't use robots, you can't succeed. The government encourages it. Foreigners don't understand China.*

Each of Fuyao's factories in China, like the Chinese factories of all large enterprises, had labor unions. But those unions, under the supervision of the local CPC committee, were conciliatory, not confrontational. Labor unrest, when it occurred in China, was not union-led. Cao was proud that Fuyao had never had *any* labor unrest. He felt a responsibility to take care of his workers as a parent would take care of his children. FGA's Moraine factory from the outset was non-union. Soon after it opened, however, the International Union, United Automobile, Aerospace and Agricultural Implement Workers of America (UAW), one of the largest, most powerful and diverse unions in North America, started recruiting FGA's workers at its Moraine plant to join the UAW. FGA lobbied its employees against the UAW bid and, in late 2017, the employees of Fuyao's Moraine plant voted to reject UAW union membership. During that campaign, the UAW brought action against FGA for breaches of US Occupational Safety and Health Administration (OSHA) standards. FGA addressed the OSHA issues and paid a fine of US$100,000 in early 2017. But 2018 saw continued worker complaints and conflict with the UAW over OSHA issues.[42] Management at FGA felt that such worker complaints and OSHA actions were unfair. Moreover, FGA management felt responsible for raising the efficiency of its workforce, because they observed

[42] Noam Scheiber and Keith Bradsher "Culture Clash at a Chinese-Owned Plant in Ohio" The New York Times June 10, 2017; UAW "Fuyao Workers Forward" petition targeted at Jeff Daochuan Liu, President, Fuyao Glass America.

that their workers in the US were only about half as productive as Fuyao workers in China.

LOOKING TO THE FUTURE

Shortly after FGA's Moraine facility started production, the China-US trade dispute erupted. On September 17, 2018, the Trump administration announced 10 percent tariffs on a list of $200 billion worth of Chinese imports and with threatened increases to 25 percent in 2019. At the same time, the re-negotiation of NAFTA into the United States-Mexico-Canada Agreement increased the percent of value of automobiles (eligible for zero tariffs) to be made within North America from 62.5 percent to 75 percent to be phased in over a five-year transition period. The rules of international trade and investment were shifting. If for no other reason than to analyze the changes brought by the dramatic shift in American country risk, Fuyao needed to reassess its global strategy.

EXHIBIT 1: FINANCIAL SUMMARY

Figures in thousands of RMB							
	Half Year Ending June 30		Year Ending December 31				
Item	2018	2017	2017	2016	2015	2014	2013
Revenue	1,00,85,175	87,13,963	1,87,15,609	1,66,21,336	1,35,73,495	1,29,28,182	1,15,01,210
Cost of Sales	59,51,399	50,66,724	1,09,17,999	96,48,615	79,38,515	75,65,501	68,30,550
Gross profit	41,33,776	36,47,239	77,97,610	69,72,721	56,34,980	53,62,681	46,70,660
Distribution costs and Selling Expenses	6,72,245	6,11,652	12,74,309	11,84,740	10,20,585	9,82,165	8,76,776
Administrative Expenses	9,34,275	8,42,216	18,03,411	16,73,626	12,87,869	10,31,342	9,07,576
R&D Expenses	4,21,543	3,89,069	8,03,441	7,27,586	5,92,889	5,17,924	3,88,758
Other income	53,227	60,889	1,88,117	89,542	97,836	46,017	54,297
Other loss/gain net	80,425	−1,94,394	-3,93,640	4,93,785	3,75,797	-43,091	177
Operating profit	22,39,365	16,70,797	37,10,926	39,70,096	32,07,270	28,34,176	25,52,024
Finance income	1,03,883	81,063	1,56,659	1,06,576	19,725	14,362	3,116
Finance costs	−1,66,904	−65,402	1,82,373	1,57,713	1,90,512	2,41,223	2,02,297
Finance costs (net)	−63,021	15,661	25,714	51,137	1,70,787	2,26,861	1,99,181
Share of results of JVs and associates	1,164	−245	−6,017	−112	5,559	31,029	25,748
Profit before income tax	21,77,508	16,86,213	36,79,195	39,18,847	30,42,042	26,38,344	23,78,591
Income tax expenses	3,08,680	3,01,697	5,31,479	7,76,909	4,35,226	4,21,567	4,61,924
Profit	18,68,828	13,84,516	31,47,716	31,41,938	26,06,816	22,16,777	19,16,667
Earnings per share	0.74	0.55	1.25	1.25	1.1	1.11	0.96

(*Continued*)

EXHIBIT 1: (*Continued*)

Figures in thousands of RMB							
	Half Year Ending June 30			Year Ending December 31			
Item	2018	2017	2017	2016	2015	2014	2013
CONSOLIDATED BALANCE SHEET							
Total assets	3,54,20,077	3,17,17,365	3,17,17,365	2,98,79,729	2,48,41,632	1,68,90,937	1,46,83,141
Total liabilities	1,63,80,795	1,26,98,751	1,26,98,751	1,18,27,301	84,11,905	80,72,971	68,21,546
Total equity	1,90,39,282	1,90,18,614	1,90,18,614	1,80,52,428	1,64,29,727	88,17,966	78,61,595
Fuyao Glass America Operating Revenue	9,06,950	7,13,998	19,77,775	6,47,522	na	na	na
Fuyao Glass America Net Profit	47,946	−64,734	4,675	−2,57,926	na	na	na

Source: Fuyao annual reports.

EXHIBIT 2: GLOBAL AUTOMOBILE SALES

	millions of automobiles												
Country / Region	2005	2006	2007	2008	2009	2010	2011	2012	2013	2014	2015	2016	2017
Europe EU + EFTA	18.2	18.5	18.9	17.4	16.2	15.7	15.7	14.4	14.1	15.0	16.5	17.6	18.1
Russia	1.8	2.2	2.9	3.2	1.6	2.1	2.9	3.1	3.0	2.6	1.4	1.4	1.6
Other Europe (including Turkey)	1.1	1.1	1.2	1.3	0.8	1.0	1.2	1.2	1.2	1.0	1.1	1.2	1.2
United States	17.4	17.0	16.5	13.5	10.6	11.8	13.0	14.8	15.9	16.8	17.8	17.9	17.6
Other NAFTA (Canada and Mexico)	2.8	2.9	2.8	2.7	2.3	2.4	2.6	2.7	2.9	3.1	3.3	3.6	3.6
Other Americas	3.1	3.5	4.3	4.7	4.6	5.5	6.0	6.1	6.3	5.6	4.5	4.1	4.6
China	5.8	7.2	8.8	9.4	13.6	18.1	18.5	19.3	22.0	23.5	24.7	28.0	29.1
India	1.4	1.8	2.0	2.0	2.3	3.0	3.3	3.6	3.2	3.2	3.4	3.7	4.0
Japan	5.9	5.7	5.3	5.1	4.6	5.0	4.2	5.4	5.4	5.6	5.0	5.0	5.2
Australia and New Zealand	1.1	1.1	1.2	1.1	1.0	1.1	1.1	1.2	1.2	1.2	1.3	1.3	1.3
Other Asia Oceana and ME	6.3	6.0	6.4	6.7	6.7	8.0	8.3	8.7	8.7	9.1	9.0	8.9	9.2
Africa	1.1	1.3	1.3	1.3	1.2	1.3	1.4	1.6	1.7	1.7	1.5	1.3	1.2
Global Total	65.9	68.4	71.6	68.3	65.6	75.0	78.2	82.1	85.6	88.3	89.7	93.9	96.8
	percent of global sales												
Europe EU + EFTA	27.6	27.1	26.4	25.4	24.7	20.9	20.0	17.5	16.5	17.0	18.3	18.7	18.7
Russia	2.7	3.3	4.0	4.7	2.4	2.8	3.7	3.8	3.5	2.9	1.6	1.5	1.7
Other Europe (including Turkey)	1.6	1.6	1.7	1.9	1.3	1.4	1.5	1.4	1.4	1.1	1.3	1.2	1.2

(Continued)

EXHIBIT 2: (*Continued*)

	percent of global sales												
Country / Region	2005	2006	2007	2008	2009	2010	2011	2012	2013	2014	2015	2016	2017
United States	26.5	24.9	23.0	19.8	16.2	15.7	16.7	18.0	18.6	19.1	19.9	19.0	18.2
Other NAFTA (Canada and Mexico)	4.2	4.2	4.0	4.0	3.4	3.2	3.3	3.3	3.4	3.5	3.7	3.9	3.8
Other Americas	4.7	5.1	6.0	6.8	7.1	7.4	7.7	7.5	7.3	6.3	5.0	4.3	4.7
China	8.7	10.6	12.3	13.7	20.8	24.1	23.7	23.5	25.7	26.6	27.5	29.9	30.1
India	2.2	2.6	2.8	2.9	3.5	4.1	4.2	4.4	3.8	3.6	3.8	3.9	4.2
Japan	8.9	8.4	7.4	7.4	7.0	6.6	5.4	6.5	6.3	6.3	5.6	5.3	5.4
Australia and New Zealand	1.7	1.6	1.6	1.6	1.5	1.5	1.4	1.5	1.5	1.4	1.4	1.4	1.4
Other Asia Oceana and ME	9.5	8.8	8.9	9.8	10.3	10.7	10.6	10.6	10.2	10.3	10.0	9.4	9.5
Africa	1.7	1.9	1.8	1.8	1.8	1.7	1.9	1.9	1.9	1.9	1.7	1.4	1.2
Global Total	100.0	100.0	100.0	100.0	100.0	100.0	100.0	100.0	100.0	100.0	100.0	100.0	100.0

Source: Organisation Internationale des Constructeurs d'Automobiles (OICA).

World Motor Vehicle Sales by country by type 2005-2017: all vehicles accessed September 14, 2018. http://www.oica.net/category/sales-statistics/

EXHIBIT 3: FUYAO'S BUSINESS LINES

a: Fuyao Sales by Business Lines

	2017		2016		2015	
Business Line	millions of RMB	Percent	millions of RMB	Percent	millions of RMB	Percent
Automotive Glass	17,868	95.47	16,145	97.14	13,138	96.79
Float Glass	2,899	15.49	2,729	16.42	2,485	18.31
Others	621	3.32	404	2.43	462	3.4
Less Intergroup Purchases	–2,672	–14.28	–2,657	–15.99	–2,511	–18.5
Total	18,716	100	16,621	100	13,573	100

Source: Fuyao Annual Reports.

b: Cost Breakdowns by Business Lines and Major Categories

		2017		2016		2016–17	2015		2015–16
		Millions of RMB	Percent	Millions of RMB	Percent	Percent Change	Millions of RMB	Percent	Percent Change
Auto Glass	Materials	7356	64.4	6586	64.5	11.7	5,406	65	21.8
	Energy	856	7.5	838	8.2	2.2	797	10	5.1
	Labor	1719	15.0	1452	14.2	18.4	1,010	12	43.8
	Other	1498	13.1	1330	13.0	12.6	1,111	13	19.8
	Total	11,430	100.0	10,206	100.0		8,324	100	
Float Glass									
	Materials	617	32.8	571	29.6	8.0	512	27	11.5
	Energy	602	32.1	686	35.5	−12.1	871	46	−21.3
	Labor	180	9.6	163	8.4	10.5	73	4	122.9
	Other	480	25.5	511	26.5	−6.0	452	24	13.0
	Total	1,879	100.0	1,930	100.0		1,908	100	
Aggregate costs assuming all float glass used by Fuyao	Materials	6,094	53.3	5,227	51.2	16.6	4,010	48.2	30.4
	Energy	1,459	12.8	1,523	14.9	−4.2	1,669	20.0	−8.7
	Labor	1,899	16.6	1,615	15.8	17.6	1,083	13.0	49.1
	Other	1,977	17.3	1,841	18.0	7.4	1,563	18.8	17.8
	Total	11,430	100.0	10,206	100.0		8,324	100.0	

Note: Figures may not add up exactly because of rounding.
Source: Fuyao Annual Reports; authors analysis.

EXHIBIT 4: US TARIFFS ON AUTO GLASS

Item	Harmonized System Code	Number of Tariff Lines	Number of Duties	Average of Duties (percent)	Minimum Duty (percent)	Maximum Duty (percent)	Percent of tariff lines that are duty Free
Motor cars and other motor vehicles principally designed for the transport of persons (other than those of heading 87.02), including station wagons and racing cars.	8703	15.0	15.0	2.5	2.5	2.5	0.0
Float glass and surface ground or polished glass, in sheets, whether or not having an absorbent, reflecting or non-reflecting layer, but not otherwise worked.	7005	10.0	6.0	3.1	0.0	5.6	22.5
Float glass and surface ground or polished glass, in sheets, having an absorbent, reflecting or non-reflecting layer, but not otherwise worked (excl. wired glass)	700510	2.0	2.0	2.2	0.0	4.4	50.0
Toughened "tempered" safety glass, of size and shape suitable for incorporation in motor vehicles, aircraft, spacecraft, vessels and other vehicles	700711	1.0	1.0	5.5	5.5	5.5	0.0
Laminated safety glass, of size and shape suitable for incorporation in motor vehicles, aircraft, spacecraft, vessels and other vehicles (excl. multiple-walled insulating units of glass)	700721	3.0	3.0	3.3	0.0	4.9	33.3

Note: The above table gives the tariffs applied on products from countries that are signatories to the World Trade Organization and enjoying "most favored nation" status. They do not reflect lower tariffs available to countries in free trade areas such as NAFTA.

Source: World Trade Organization Integrated Database (IDB) notifications. Accessed September 14, 2018 http://tariffdata.wto.org/TariffList.aspx.

EXHIBIT 5: FUYAO'S INVENTORIES

Item	As of December 31 ¥ millions 2017	2016	2015
Raw materials	1,226	1,185	1,039
Work in process	116	119	84
Finished goods	1,631	1,481	1,366
Low value consumables	10	11	16
Less: writedown to net realizable value	–8	–9	–10
Net Inventories	2,975	2,786	2,495

Source: Fuyao Annual Reports.

EXHIBIT 6: FOREIGN DIRECT INVESTMENT:

a. Global Stocks of FDI

Country or Region		in trillions of USD		in percent of GDP		in percent of World	
		2005	2016	2005	2016	2005	2016
US	outward	3.64	6.36	27.8	34.3	32.1	22.8
	inward	2.82	6.56	21.5	35.3	24.9	23.5
European Union	outward	4.92	9.03	34.6	60.0	43.4	32.3
	inward	4.23	7.58	29.7	50.3	37.4	27.1
Russia	outward	0.14	0.34	17.1	26.5	1.2	1.2
	inward	0.18	0.38	21.9	29.9	1.6	1.4
China	outward	0.06	1.32	2.8	11.6	0.6	4.7
	inward	0.47	2.87	20.6	25.2	4.2	10.3
Japan	outward	0.39	1.23	8.5	27.8	3.4	4.4
	inward	0.10	0.19	2.2	4.0	0.9	0.7
World	*	11.33	27.94	23.9	36.9	100.0	100.0

* as inward does one equal outward, we set the level at "inward".

**Note*: There exists a minor discrepancy between the sum of inward FDI and the sum of outward FDI. We set the denominator for the World as the total of inward FDI.

Source: OECD FDI Flows, accessed September 15, 2018. https://data.oecd.org/fdi/fdi-flows.htm

b. Annual and quarterly net flows of direct investment from other countries into the US in millions of USD

					2016				2017				2018
Country / Region	2014	2015	2016	2017	1	2	3	4	1	2	3	4	1
All Countries	**2,01,733**	**4,67,625**	**4,71,792**	**2,77,258**	**1,46,528**	**1,61,730**	**1,09,388**	**54,146**	**89,690**	**85,617**	**64,590**	**37,361**	**51,306**
NAFTA	25,221	60,003	69,425	72,606	9,478	21,965	21,826	16,155	34,076	19,689	9,983	8,857	4,269
China	**2,201**	**5,127**	**25,445**	**–504**	**4,488**	**4,979**	**5,712**	**10,266**	**–97**	**4**	**135**	**–547**	**–294**
Japan	44,891	32,997	31,610	43,868	**11,700**	**10,122**	**6,813**	**2,976**	**11,255**	**13,390**	**10,697**	**8,525**	**5,720**
Rest of Asia Pacific	**24,490**	**33,458**	**8,904**	**8,627**	**7,212**	**5,143**	**1,101**	**–7,290**	**9,707**	**-683**	**393**	**–788**	**-6,014**
Rest of the World	1,04,930	3,36,040	3,36,408	1,52,661	1,13,650	1,19,521	73,936	32,039	34,749	53,217	43,382	21,314	47,625

Note: a negative number occurs when disposal of FDI assets exceeds acquisition of FDI assets.

Source: Foreign Direct Investment in the U.S.: Balance of Payments and Direct Investment Position Data US Bureau of Economic Analysis Accessed September 15, 2058 https://www.bea.gov/international/di1fdibal

Chapter 9

ofo: Innovation and the Little Yellow Bicycle

Introduction

Innovation flourishes in youth. Optimistic, vigorous and enthusiastic, quick in thought and action, unburdened by history, the young creates the new.

This chapter describes the meteoric rise of a start-up in dockless bikes: ofo. Entrepreneurs are the diving force of China's development. Socialism with Chinese characteristics gives the market the leading role, letting profit-seeking individuals work their magic, while the CPC through government policy channels entrepreneurship to achieve social ends. China's economic miracle is the product of not one, but three successive, successful generations of entrepreneurs. The entrepreneurs who started ofo are members of the third generation.

The First Generation

The three entrepreneurs of the last two chapters — Zhang Ruimin, Ren Zhengfei, and Cao Dewang — hail from the first generation.

They are now in their 70s. They were born before the revolution. They came of age in a time when the country was poor; wealth was equally distributed; revolutionary fervour and patriotism were high; the planned economy was paramount; information from outside China was sparce and unreliable; politics was mercurial; ideological purity was essential, and

Chairman Mao was synonymous with the new China. The best years of their working lives spanned the end of the Cultural Revolution and the early years of reform and opening up when commercial laws were new and often honored in the breech; regulations were in flux and possibilities seemed endless. The countryside led the reforms with the household responsibility system. Enterprises were morphing from collective to private ownership. Corrupt officials were the flies that flew in when the windows were opened to welcome the fresh air.[1] Giddy growth defined the 80s, the first decade of opportunity. Zhang, Ren and Cao were part of a moral, stable, steadfast *minority* of entrepreneurs who not only made money, but in subsequent decades created innovative, lasting enterprises that now dominate the world in their industries.[2]

The Second Generation

The second generation of entrepreneurs was born in the first three decades of New China (1950–1980). They were from the last great baby boom of the most populous nation on earth. Born before planned parenthood — a movement conceived in the West but embraced by China[3] — they were the generation of demographic dividend.[4] They never personally

---

[1] Jiang Xiusheng describes the first case in post reform and opening up China involving the death sentence for corruption, the case of Wang Zong, Assistant CPC secretary, Hai Feng County in Shantou, Guangdong. He refers to the comment that Deng Xiaoping famously made at the time, "You open the window to get some fresh air and flies also come in". See Jiang Xiusheng, "Since Reform and Opening Up, on One Hand We Grasp Reform and Opening While on the Other We Punish Corruption" [改革开放以来 一手抓改革开放，一手抓惩治腐败], *China Discipline Inspection and Supervision* 19, 2019. https://www.cnki.com.cn/Article/CJFDTOTAL-JANC201919027.htm (accessed April 10, 2021).

[2] For an excellent discussion of four decades of entrepreneurs, see Edward Tse, *China's Disruptors*, Penguin, New York, 2015.

[3] It is easy to forget that Mao did not promote planned parenthood. The one child policy was implemented after his death and was fully in accord at the time with leading Western developmental thinking. See for example the 1983 speech of Tom Clausen, president of Bank of America and later president of the World Bank. A. W. Clausen, "Population Growth and Economic and Social Development", *Journal of Economic Education: Content Articles in Economics* 16:3 (1985).

[4] The labor force in China peaked in 2016 at 776 million [see "Number of Employed Persons in China", *Statista*, November 20, 2020. https://www.statista.com/statistics/251380/number-of-employed-persons-in-china/ (accessed April 10, 2021)] and the total population

experienced pre-revolutionary China. Yes, poverty and the planned economy were indelibly imprinted in their childhood memories, but they came of age as the nation was clearly getting richer. Yes, the CPC continued its monopoly of power but China had forever broken the strictures of Maoism, embracing the world in all its exciting, variegated realities, philosophies, possibilities, fantasies, and foolishness. Bright and ambitious scholars went abroad in droves and came back to the fatherland, sea turtles,[5] first as a trickle and then in a growing flood.

Whether one was in China or abroad one could study anything. To get ahead, one ***had*** to study: the exam system returned with a vengeance. And study brought rewards: the demand for good tertiary education far exceeded supply. Yes, China in the 1980s and 1990s was second rate in almost every product it produced. But produce it did! China's momentum was irresistible. The direction was clear. Grasping the large and releasing the small, flipping foreign business models into China and then tweaking the models with innovation.

The second generation defines China's current corporate environment. China's over 1,000 billionaires, a number greater than those in the United States, hail largely from the second generation.[6] Perhaps to its discredit, this casebook has only two cases featuring entrepreneurs the second generation — Aglaia Kong of Cisco[7] and Tang Xiao'ou of Sensetime.[8] And I have included no cases featuring the two men from the second generation who tower above all others entrepreneurs[9]: Jack Ma Yun, founder

---

will peak before 2025 below 1.3 billion with the country severely aging through the first half of the 21st century. Li Handong, Zhou Tianmin and Jia Can, "The Influence of the Universal Two-Child Policy on China's Future Population and Ageing", *Journal of Population Research* 36:3 (2019), 183–203.

[5]Like Aglaia Kong in Chapter 5.

[6]https://www.globaltimes.cn/page/202103/1217047.shtml.

[7]After her time at Cisco, Aglaia Kong left to found a new start-up, Exaleap, a company using RISC-V architecture to build internet of things (IoT) system-on-chips for smart use case solutions. Exaleap is based in Santa Clara California with its main research facility in Foshan, Guangdong and its principal investor is Henderson Land of Hong Kong. See Exaleap website: https://www.exaleap.ai/leadership/ (accessed May 4, 2021).

[8]See Chapter 10: Sensetime Group Limited: Business Model and Expansion.

[9]"The others" in the second generation are very numerous, have made innovations each of which can be fruitfully studied and included (among the billionaires): Cheng Wei, founder of Didi Chuxing, Ding Lei, founder of NetEase, Guo Guangchang, founder of Fosun, Colin Huang Zheng, founder of Pinduoduo, Lei Jun, founder of Xiaomi, Robin Li Yanhong, and

of Alibaba/Ant, and Pony Ma Huateng, founder of Tencent. Both pursue one vision: creating digital ecosystems.[10] Alibaba/Ant and Tencent each have over 50 cases or academic articles listed on the Harvard Business Publishing Education Website.[11] Those numbers will only swell in the future because the two Mas' digital ecosystems — which dominate China — are models used and copied across the world. Jack and Pony Ma are 17th and 20th richest persons in the world respectively.[12]

As the chairman of the academic council of the Alibaba Group, Ming Zeng notes:

> Alibaba today is not just an online commerce company. It is what you get if you take all the functions associated with retail and coordinate them online into a sprawling, data-driven network of sellers, marketers, service providers, logistics companies, and manufacturers. In other words, Alibaba does what Amazon, eBay, PayPal, Google, FedEx, wholesalers and a good portion of manufacturers do in the United States, with a healthy helping of financial services for garnish.[13]

Alibaba does it with smart business — datafying, ubiquitous use of software, interoperability, standardization and AI algorithms. The two Mas are digital evangelists — leaders who inspire their (highly educated) staff to innovation rather than directing them to accomplish set tasks.[14]

Eric Xu Yong, founders of Baidu, Li Shufu, founder of Geely, Liu Qiangdong, founder of JD.com, Liu Yonghao, founder of New Hope Agricultural Feed, Wang Xing, founder of Meituan Dianping, Wang Wei, founder of SF Express, Wu Yajun, founder of Longfor Properties, Xu Shihui, founder of Dali Foods, Yao Zhenhua, founder of Baoneng Insurance, and Zhang Jindong, founder of Suning.

[10] The reader will note that one vision of the digital ecosystem was described in Chapter 7. Zhang Ruimin of Haier's *Rendanheyi* has many elements of what Alibaba/Ant and Tencent have realized. As with most innovations, the digital ecosystem far less a linear progression, than a braided stream evolution or a progressing network of ideas.

[11] Harvard Business Publishing Education https://hbsp.harvard.edu/ (accessed April 4, 2021).

[12] "World's Billionaires List: The Richest in 2020", *Forbes*. https://www.forbes.com/billionaires/ (accessed April 10, 2021). Ranking varies from minute to minute based on exchange rates and value of stock holdings.

[13] Ming Zeng, "Alibaba and the Future of Business: Lessons from China's Innovative Digital Giant", *Harvard Business Review*, September–October 2018.

[14] *Ibid.*

Jack Ma is a performer. He was trained as an English teacher, but when he discovered the internet in the late 1990s, he saw its potential for solving the problem of small businesses in China selling their products. He loves expressing his views on innovation, as he eloquently did to Israel's Benjamin Netanyahu extolling the entrepreneurship of his host country at the Israeli Innovation Summit.[15]

Pony Ma personally is more understated. He was trained as an engineer and has a deep understanding of technology. Starting from video games and instant messaging, Tencent culture is centered on fun energising business. Its ecosystem is based on the micro-messaging service WeChat (or Weixin 微信)[16] that provides suites of programs to enterprises letting them tap into China's digitally empowered consumers.[17] He describes how Tencent stimulates innovation how digital ecosystem will develop in his video interview with Fortune Magazine.[18]

The Third Generation

The third generation of entrepreneurs was born starting in 1981. They have no experience of the famine of the 50s, the political madness of the 60s and the stagnation of the 70s. They are children of the one child

[15] Zhang Hongpei, "Alibaba's Jack Ma Steals Stage with Speech at Israel Forum", *Global Times*, October 27, 2018. https://www.globaltimes.cn/content/1124686.shtml (accessed May 4, 2021). For the full video of the speech that goes into vivid detail about Jack Ma's philosophy of management of innovation, see Jack Ma, "The Best Tips for Innovation", YouTube Video, October 26, 2018. https://youtu.be/z5vTFRqwpXE (accessed May 4, 2021).

[16] For a recent, good case on management of innovation in the WeChat business of Tencent, see Julian Birkinshaw, Dickie Liang-Hong Ke, and Enrique de Diego, "Innovation and agility at Tencent's WeChat", London Business School Case Collection, Harvard Business Publishing Reference LBS220, August 2019.

[17] See for example, "Weixin's Expanding Ecosystem Creates Exciting New Opportunities For Brands", *Tencent Website*, January 19, 2021. https://www.tencent.com/en-us/articles/2201109.html (accessed April 10, 2021).

[18] Pony Ma with interviewer Adam Lashinsky, "Innovation and Ecosystem", *Fortune,* Youtube Video, December 7, 2017, https://www.youtube.com/watch?v=gGnby27ypRo (accessed May 4, 2021).

policy, chided as "little emperors".[19] They came of age in a world of tertiary education massification — with enrolment rates going from 2% (1981) to 8% (1994) to 42% (2016) and to over 50% (2019). And they observed those rapidly growing institutions becoming, like the rest of society, increasingly stratified in terms of quality, resources, and reputation.[20] For the third generation, a tertiary education, while seen as necessary for employment and status, no longer guarantees a good job.[21]

In eyes of the members of the third generation, China has always been central to the world trading system. The third generation no longer sees the West — suffering from political, social and economic troubles — as an inexhaustible font of models to be flipped into the Chinese market. They look back on the two previous generations who have shown that entrepreneurs drive the economy and that extreme ambition can pay off handsomely.[22] The members of the third generation are only now entering their most productive years, but already they have demonstrated their potential to disrupt.

Disruption

The case in this chapter takes the viewpoint of Austin Zhang, a co-founder of ofo, the world's first dockless-bicycle-sharing company. Their business model was made possible by the digital platforms of Alibaba and Tencent. The cut-off date for the case is mid-year, 2017. Zhang is part of a management team running a 2-year old company valued at over US$1 billion

---

[19] Steve Connor, "One-Child Policy: China's Army of Little Emperors", *The Independent*, January 10, 2013. https://www.independent.co.uk/news/world/asia/one-child-policy-china-s-army-little-emperors-8446713.html (accessed April 10, 2021).

[20] Terry Bodenhorn, "Change, Contradiction and the State: Higher Education in Greater China", *China Quarterly* 244, 2020, pp. 920–941. "Overview of Educational Achievements", Ministry of Education Website, October 7, 2020. http://en.moe.gov.cn/documents/reports/202102/t20210209_513095.html (accessed April 10, 2021).

[21] Vivian Wang, "China's College Graduates Can't Find Jobs. The Solution: Grad School", *The New York Times*, New York, January 19, 2021.

[22] The profitability of extreme ambition is one of Edward Tse's observations. Edward Tse, *China's Disruptors*, Penguin, New York, 2015. Also see his commentary on entrepreneurs in China — in both the SOE and the privately owned enterprises on his consulting firm website. Gao Feng Advisory. http://www.gaofengadv.com/ (accessed April 1, 2021).

Figure 9.1: Disruptive Innovation

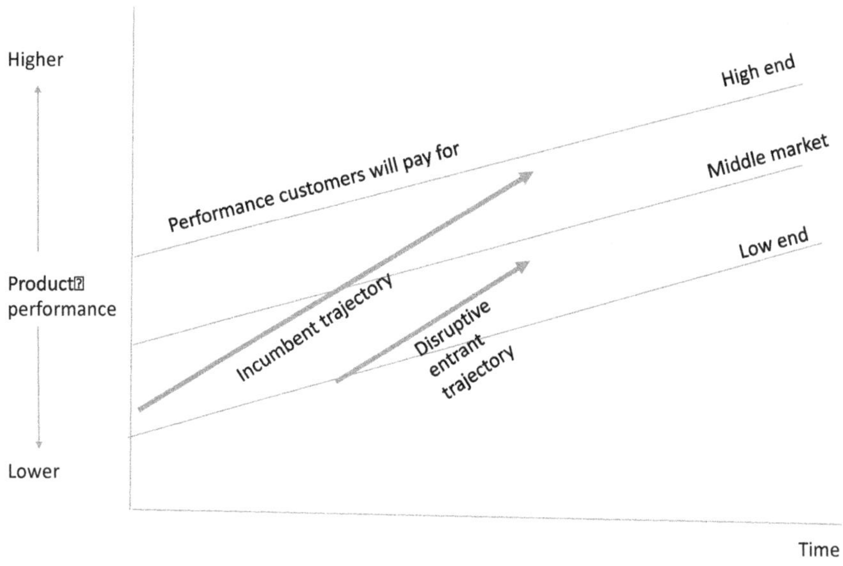

Source: Adapted by the author from Clayton M. Christensen, Michael E. Raynor, and Rory McDonald, "What Is Disruptive Innovation?", *Harvard Business Review*, December 2015.

thanks, not only to its innovation, but also to readily available VC financing — some of which has come from Alibaba and Tencent. The case asks students to assess ofo's position in a rapidly changing environment, competing viciously with fellow unicorn, Mobike.[23] Readers can see some of the effects of this extreme competition in video footage.[24] Clearly the flood of millions of dockless bicycles has disrupted urban transportation.

One theme of this case is innovation. Another theme is disruption. Putting together the two terms, it is hard not to think of the late, great,

---

[23] Instructors can consider using a related case on ofo's major competitor, Mobike. See Guijie Qi, Jiali Chen, and John Zhang, *Mobike: A Smart Bike-Sharing Service Platform* (London, ON: Ivey Publishing, 2018).

[24] "China's Bike Sharing Disaster", YouTube video, 7:24, posted by "China Uncensored", November 16, 2018. https://www.youtube.com/watch?v=OXX423ErY1U (accessed April 1, 2021).

Harvard Business School management guru, Clayton Christensen, and his "disruptive innovation"[25] illustrated by the famous Figure 9.1.

Clayton Christensen's Disruptive Innovation

Describing his concept of disruptive innovation, Christiensen notes:

> As incumbents focus on improving their products and services for their most demanding (and usually most profitable) customers, they exceed the needs of some segments and ignore the needs of others. Entrants that prove disruptive begin by successfully targeting those overlooked segments, gaining a foothold by delivering more-suitable functionality — frequently at a lower price. Incumbents, chasing higher profitability in more-demanding segments, tend not to respond vigorously. Entrants then move upmarket, delivering the performance that incumbents' mainstream customers require, while preserving the advantages that drove their early success. When mainstream customers start adopting the entrants' offerings in volume, disruption has occurred.[26]

Both Cao Dewang, introduced in Chapter 8 and Zhang Ruimin, introduced in Chapter 7 engaged in Christensen-style disruptive innovation. Cao's Fuyao Glass entered the auto glass market at the low end — the replacement glass market. Then it improved its product performance to displace incumbents providing new auto glass to OEMs. Zhang's Huawei similarly entered a overlooked segment of the telecommunications equipment market: rural markets in China and less developed countries in the rest of the world. Both can be characterized as Christensen disruptive innovators: smaller companies with fewer resources undercut the market of larger incumbents by producing innovative products that satisfy the needs of lower-quality niches in the main market at lower prices and with less demanding specifications. The incumbents responded by moving upmarket, satisfying the needs of customers prepared to pay higher margins for more expensive products. Incumbents thereby ceded increasing segments of their old markets to the disrupters.

---

[25] Clayton M. Christensen, Michael E. Raynor, and Rory McDonald, "What Is Disruptive Innovation?", *Harvard Business Review*, December 2015, 44–53.

[26] *Ibid.*

The reader of the case should consider whether ofo's dockless bikes constitute Christensen style disruptive innovation.

The Role of the Government

Another theme of the ofo case is the role of the government in promoting innovation. Chinese policies have demonstrated viable alternatives to the Washington consensus, that 1980s and 1990s ideology of the World Bank, the International Monetary Fund and the U.S. Treasury of

> privatization, liberalization, and macro-stability (meaning mostly price stability); a set of policies predicated upon a strong faith — stronger than warranted — in unfettered markets and aimed at reducing, or even minimizing, the role of government … [including] policies to deregulate national and international financial markets, push for free trade, make labour markets more flexible, privatise state-owned banks and enterprises, change corporate governance towards a shareholder value system, allow for stronger and increasingly dominant multinational companies, [leading to] financialisation, including a more important role of financial markets in the economy and a stronger position of agents in financial markets[27]

Governments have tremendous influence over the final structure of the market for dockless bicycles especially if they evolve into utilities. This is as true in Beijing as it is in Boston or Birmingham. The political dynamic between companies, pedestrians, cyclists, drivers, public transit authorities, regulators, etc. would have similar issues the world over, although the persistence of the CPC's leadership in China differs from that in the United States or the Untied Kingdom. And the presence in China of CPC party committees in every large government organization and enterprise — even in private enterprises like ofo and Mobike — offers potential for coordination not available outside of China. Every city in the world controls the roads, sidewalks and public spaces on which bicycles are peddled, pushed, and parked. Their regulations determine the competitive space of dockless bikes. The direction and degree to which various

[27] Joseph Stiglitz, "The Post Washington Consensus Consensus", *The Initiative for Policy Dialogue*. http://policydialogue.org/files/events/Stiglitz_Post_Washington_Consensus_Paper.pdf (accessed April 9, 2021).

Chinese government agencies assert themselves in dockless bikes will be of interest to the rest of the world because China leads the world in this innovation.

But as Austin Zhang in the case notes,

> Compared to governments in foreign countries, Chinese governments are very supportive. When we deal with foreign governments, they usually say, "Wait. We want to see what happens in China! And then maybe you can enter".

This "can do" attitude of the government regarding innovation is, at least in the dockless bicycle market, a distinct advantage for companies like ofo.

OFO: INNOVATION AND THE LITTLE YELLOW BICYCLE

Professors Mingkang Liu and Hugh Thomas wrote this case solely to provide material for class discussion. The authors do not intend to illustrate either effective or ineffective handling of a managerial situation.

Austin Zhang, co-founder of ofo, a Beijing-based bicycle-sharing company, looked north from his 10th-floor window in the Ideal International Plaza, over the 4th Ring Road and towards the sprawling Peking University campus. It was July 2017. Less than two years ago, he and four other bicycle enthusiasts — Dai Wei, chief executive officer (CEO) of ofo; Xue Ding; Yang Pinjie; and Yu Xin — had founded the global bicycle-sharing industry. Since then, Chinese bicycle sharing had grown from nothing into a dockless smart phone application (app) service industry with revenues of ¥3.9 billion[1] per quarter[2] and over 120 million monthly active app users sharing over 30 million bicycles in cities across China and around the world (see Exhibit 1). Over 90 per cent of the bicycles were either ofo's little yellow bicycles or the bright orange bicycles

[1] iResearch 共享单车 Q2 市场规模突破 30 亿 较 Q1 月度活跃用户成倍增长, "Shared Bike Market Exceeds 3 billion Yuan in Q2.accessed November 17, 2017 http://www.iresearch.com.cn ¥ = CNY = Chinese yuan renminbi; US$1 = ¥6.94 on July 1, 2017.

[2] iResearch estimated total industry sales as ¥33 million, ¥296 million, ¥937 million, and ¥3.878 billion in the four quarters from 2016 quarter 3 to 2017 quarter 2.

owned by ofo's main competitor Mobike. Zhang was not focused on the competition: "Actually the war has already ended.... We should always get more market share, but what is more important is what next? What is the future of sharing bicycles?"

INDUSTRY BACKGROUND

Summer 2017 was not only ofo's second year of bicycle sharing but also the 200th anniversary of the bicycle, invented by the German Karl Freiherr von Drais.[3] Drais patented his spoked, two-wheeled, steerable wood-and-iron-framed velocipede (known in German as the *Laufmaschine* and in French as the *draisine*) in 1818, unleashing two centuries of innovation. Large-scale production of various designs took off in the 1860s after entrepreneurs, especially in France, developed fully iron frames, cranked peddle drives, wire-spoked wheels, and solid rubber tires. By the 1890s, a diamond-shaped frame, tube steel construction, pneumatic tires, peddle-chain rear-wheel drive, and mass production were transforming the bicycle into a society-changing mode of transportation. In the first third of the twentieth century, the centre of bicycle production and innovation shifted to the United Kingdom, with Raleigh Bicycle Company of Nottingham becoming the leading manufacturer in the world; but by then, motorcycles and motor cars were displacing the bicycle.

In the two intervening centuries between 1817 and 2017, the world produced a billion bicycles, half of which were made by the Chinese bicycle company Flying Pigeon. The original Flying Pigeon bicycle was reverse-engineered by Huo Baoji, an employee of the Changho Works bicycle factory in Tianjin, from his 1932 English Raleigh Roadster.[4] By the 1970s, the bicycle, together with the watch and the sewing machine, was one of three items Chinese brides required of their grooms before marriage.

Then, in 1978, China embarked on its economic reform and opening up policy, unleashing four decades of rising incomes, urbanization, highway and mass transit construction, and the growth of a domestic

---

[3] Tony Hadland and Hans-Erhard Lessing, *Bicycle Design: An Illustrated History* (Boston, MIT Press: 2016).

[4] "History: Flying Pigeon Bicycle Co. Ltd.," Flying Pigeon, accessed November 7, 2017, www.flying-pigeon.eu/historia.htm.

automobile industry. By the time Zhang and his fellow founders of ofo enrolled in Peking University, China had become the world's top manufacturer and consumer of cars, gaining global notoriety for its traffic congestion and air pollution.[5] At the same time, after a long period of relative decline in bicycle use, China was experiencing a minor bicycle revival based on the pursuit of healthier lifestyles and environmental sustainability.

OFO'S HISTORY

As Zhang, a graduate in archaeology and museology from Peking University, explained, "I am not a business person and did not set out to be an entrepreneur. I just simply love cycling." In fall 2014, he and four friends started ofo (whose three-letter logo represented the two wheels and rider of a bicycle) to organize bicycle tours. They peddled around Taiwan, crossed Hainan, cycled through Luoping in Yunnan, and toured the sparsely populated and breathtaking natural scenery of Qinghai Lake in western China. But a year after they founded their company, they had made no money. Zhuang reflected:

> It was a total disaster. We had to save the company to save our dream.… We told our parents and friends that we were short of money, but they just tried to persuade me to give up and find a new job in a museum. 2015 at Peking University was "the capital spring." All of our friends had started businesses — in AI, in education — and they could get a lot of money, but we could get nothing. We were very frustrated.… Finally we decided to insist on the bicycles but change direction. We looked at sharing bikes.

Sharing bicycles was not new. It had a forty-year history in Europe before the Chinese government introduced it on a large scale in 2007 for the Beijing 2008 Olympic Games.[6] Beijing's bicycle-sharing service was

---

[5] Colum Murphy, "China's Urban Nightmare: Gridlock," *Wall Street Journal*, January 2, 2014, www.wsj.com/articles/no-headline-available-1388702641.

[6] Susan Shaheen, Stacey Guzman, and Hua Zhang, "Bikesharing in Europe, the Americas, and Asia: Past, Present, and Future" (Davis, California: Institute of Transportation Studies, University of California, Davis, 2010), 159–167, https://escholarship.org/uc/item/79v822k5.

replicated in other Chinese cities, becoming successful in Wuhan and Guangzhou, but, as Zhang explained, it had weaknesses: users needed stored-value cards, sold at inconvenient locations, and bicycles had to be taken from, and returned to, limited docking spaces.

ofo was dockless. Initially, it restricted sharing to students and faculty within Peking University. It allowed those users to pick up and leave the bicycles anywhere they wished on the campus. ofo launched its bicycle-sharing service in June 2015 with bicycles from faculty and students. It was an immediate success. In September 2015 they introduced 2,000 specially manufactured little bright-yellow ofo-branded bicycles. Again successful, ofo expanded its fleet to 4,000 little yellow bicycles and six other campuses in northwestern Beijing. By the end of 2015, ofo's daily order volume had reached 20,000. The company secured its first external financing two months later and expanded to 20 campuses. Series B financing in May 2016 allowed ofo to expand to campuses throughout China, boosting daily orders to 400,000 at the start of September 2016.

ofo's success was noticed. In April 2016, Mobike in Shanghai rolled out its city-wide, dockless, orange app-based sharing bicycles with GPS, a driveshaft (rather than a chain), and an electronic QR code–activated lock. Mobike's founders, Hu Weiwei, a journalist with 10 years' experience covering cycling, and Davis Wang, a business administration graduate with experience at Tencent Holdings Limited (Tencent) and Uber, stated that Mobike's mission was "to solve the urban last kilometre problem."[7] When Mobike successfully received external financing and rapidly expanded to other cities in China, more competitors piled in.

As more bicycle-sharing companies raced into city markets, ofo's management questioned its focus on campuses. Staying in its protected environment gave ofo a very high frequency of bicycle use. The cities were unfamiliar environments: how could ofo forecast bicycle demand and required distribution over large areas? Bicycles might be sabotaged by the underground drivers whose businesses would be affected by bicycle sharing. The partners worried about inclement weather, the complexity of city roads, and safety.

---

[7] Jincheng Technology Internet "Mobai VS OFO: Where will the battle between the walls go?" 景辰 科技互联网摩拜 VS OFO: 一墙之隔的争斗将何去何从, January 10, 2016 accessed November 2, 2017 https://www.zhihu.com/question/50166272.

Just when the window of opportunity was about to close, ofo obtained series C financing of US$130 million[8] to finance its entry into cities. As CEO Dai Wei said, "as long as our minds are on track, there will be more solutions than problems, so we should go into the cities immediately." On the first day in the cities, ofo's server was hacked multiple times and crashed. Rumours forecasting ofo's failure flooded online chat rooms. In retrospect, however, Zhang concluded, "Going back two years, we should have gone straight into the cities and not wasted our time.... Time and speed are very important. During the time we were developing our service on the campuses, we [had] already lost some of our speed."

ofo rented its bicycles for ¥1 per hour, which was comparable with the competition, but required a deposit of only ¥99, versus the ¥299 required by Mobike. To accelerate its entry into the cities, ofo embraced partnership with Flying Pigeon and the traditional top-of-the-line Chinese bicycle manufacturer Phoenix Company Ltd. Yellow OEM[9] bicycles poured into the cities, bought with cash from ofo's third round of external financing. By early 2017, over 70 bicycle-sharing companies[10] were contending with Mobike and ofo for the market (see Exhibit 2).

GROWING PAINS AND GAINS

The flood of millions of dockless bicycles into China's cities was disruptive. Difficulties included local oversupply and under-supply, mechanical failure, the random piling of bicycles blocking pedestrian and road traffic, theft, and vandalism. As one academic commented, "From about 20 years ago, China has turned its automobile industry into a pillar industry.... Therefore, you see Chinese cities today are built for the convenience of cars. Cities are very unfriendly for bicycles."[11]

---

[8]All dollar amounts are in USD unless otherwise stated.

[9]An OEM was a company that produced items sold by another company that was often itself a manufacturer. In ofo's case, Flying Pigeon and Phoenix were OEMs for ofo-designed bikes.

[10]Xinhua, "New Guidelines to Keep China's Bike Sharing on Track," The State Council, The People's Republic of China, August 3, 2017, http://english.gov.cn/state_council/ministries/2017/08/03/content_281475769343734.htm.

[11]"China's bike sharing boom has put millions of new bicycles on city streets now mainly designed for cars, and that's causing problems in a country previously known as the

Although it was each city's responsibility to enact and enforce municipal traffic regulations, on May 22, 2017, the central government's Ministry of Transportation issued a draft set of national guidelines to facilitate solutions to the dockless-bicycle problem (see Exhibit 3).

Zhang considered short-term urban disruption a small price for social gains — including a reduction in traffic and pollution and increased employment:

> In 20 cities that suffer from traffic jams that are using ofo, 19 of the 20 cities reported traffic jam decreases. Taking Beijing as an example, morning and evening rush hour traffic jams in the city centre declined by 5%. Secondly, there is a very obvious environmental issue: the reduction of carbon emissions. Domestic gasoline consumption in April in 2017 [in China] is in negative growth for the first time, dropping by 6%, compared with the same period last year. The expansion of bicycle sharing helps solving unemployment ... the bicycle sharing economy has expanded 100,000 employment opportunities.

These gains led Zhang to have an upbeat stance concerning ofo's relationship with the government:

> We really solve problems. We are creating jobs for people. And we are lowering $PM_{2.5}$.[12] And traffic congestion is declining. So we think we can provide value for society.... The Chinese government is very interested in us ... Compared to governments in foreign countries, Chinese governments are very supportive. When we deal with foreign governments, they usually say, "Wait. We want to see what happens in China! And then maybe you can enter."

'kingdom of bicycles.'" Yang Fengchun, associate professor, Peking University, quoted in Josh Ye, "Why China's Bike-Sharing Boom Is Causing Headaches," *South China Morning Post*, April 9, 2017, accessed November 1, 2017, www.scmp.com/news/china/society/article/2085751/chinas-bike-sharing-boom-puts-pressure-planners.

[12] $PM_{2.5}$ refers to an index reporting the density in ambient air particles with a diameter of 2.5 microns or less. Inhaling substantial quantities of such particles could cause chronic health problems. See "Particulate Matter (PM) Pollution," United States Environmental Protection Agency, accessed November 8, 2017, www.epa.gov/pm-pollution.

CONTINUOUS IMPROVEMENT AND QUALITY MANAGEMENT

The little yellow bicycle that ofo took to the cities in October 2016 was chain driven and mechanically locked. Its OEM-manufactured cost of ¥400 was less than Mobike's smart orange bicycle manufactured in-house at a cost of ¥1,000. Although ofo's was substantially lighter, owing to Mobike's heavy driveshaft, the little yellow bicycle proved harder to locate than its orange rival, and its mechanical locks were more likely to fail or be hacked than Mobike's digital locks.[13] Zhang commented:

> We used a massive number of mechanical locks and I think that you have heard the stories. During fierce competition, you should make choices with what you have. At that time, we were still in the campuses and we wanted to make sure that we could be faster: always be faster than the competitors. So we made the choice to use mechanical locks. But now we have changed our locks to digital locks.

Through its 2017 partnerships with China Mobile Communications Corporation, Huawei Technologies Co. Ltd. (Huawei), and 700Bike, ofo redesigned and rolled out its improved little yellow bicycle in early 2017 (see Exhibit 4).

Zhang believed that three key features in the new model would improve the all-important user riding experience: the tires, the hub, and the lock. Normal bicycle tires were pneumatic, which made them comfortable and light but increased the risk of a blowout. The increased maintenance required for pneumatic tires rendered them unfeasible for shared bicycles, but the solid tires used for the first little yellow bicycles were hard and uncomfortable. To solve the problem, ofo partnered with BASF, the company that provided soles for Nike Inc.'s athletic shoes. The density of the external part of the tire, like that of the sole of high-quality running shoes, was then far harder than the interior, increasing riding comfort without sacrificing durability. ofo was also improving the hub to achieve the goal of "peddling for five seconds and gliding for two minutes." But the most important innovation was the lock. The NarrowBand Internet of

[13]李成东, "摩拜单车和 ofo 共享单车有什么不同?" Li Chengdong, [What's the difference between bike sharing Mobike and ofo?], November 23, 2016, Sohu, accessed November 8, 2017, www.zhihu.com/question/50166272.

Things (NB-IoT) smart lock co-developed with Huawei and China Telecommunications Corporation could be quickly unlocked because scanning the QR code both recorded the actual renting and unlocked the bicycle at the same time. NB-IoT had strong enough signal penetration to allow a smart phone user to detect a bicycle parked in a basement parking lot. The battery of the NB-IoT lock would last for three years between replacements.

An equally important part of the user experience was locating a bicycle that was in good working order. As of mid-2017, about 5 per cent of ofo bicycles became faulty per day. The NB-IoT provided GPS location, tracking each bicycle as it was ridden and recording its location when the ride was over. Sudden decreases of speed during a ride or unauthorized shifts in the location of a locked bicycle could signal that a bicycle had become defective — perhaps because it had been vandalized or stolen. A bicycle left unrented for an unusual period of time could also indicate that the bicycle was no longer in good working order — either because it had been damaged or because a user had illegally "reserved" the bicycle for his or her exclusive use by double locking or hiding it.

Although ofo had only 3,500 full-time employees, it had 10,000 contract employees whose jobs included repairing faulty bicycles, re-parking badly parked bicycles, and moving poorly located bicycles from areas of low demand to areas of high demand. Contract employees could quickly do simple repairs such as cutting double locks and removing fake QR codes. By mid-2017, only about 1.5 per cent of bicycles per month were completely written off as irreparably damaged or stolen, and the number was continuing to fall. Contract employees were directed by an app called ofo-work. Input from the ofo department that handled faulty bicycles showed which bicycles had not been used for long periods of time, the affected bicycle's approximate location on a map, and the work to be performed. ofo-work also monitored contract employees' work volume, checked for unusual spikes in dysfunctional bicycles (which might indicate a contract employee sabotaging bicycles), and calculated contract employee incentive pay.

USER CREDIT AND DATA

ofo collected large amounts of user data, including the user's identity, the time of use, and the routes travelled.

> We have 200 million registered users, but we want to increase that.... When you use our bicycles, you scan the QR code and wherever you go is recorded on our system. So the most valuable thing is the location. We know whether you went to the bookstore or the grocery store or somewhere else. I think that data is very precious.

ofo protected its customer data, not sharing it with outsiders. ofo had a 40-person department dedicated to big data analysis, headed by a former manager of Baidu Inc. (a leading Internet and AI company that provided China's dominant search engine). The department's main task was designing and monitoring the user credit system to determine the quality of the user, reward those who were good users, and penalize those who damaged bicycles. The department also analyzed dysfunctional bicycles and contract worker performance. Zhang indicated that the department would ultimately predict locational bicycle demand, so that when users exited a bus, railway, or metro station, their need to locate a bicycle would be anticipated and met.

THE E ROUND

On July 6, 2017, ofo announced its fifth (or "E") round of raising external capital, which resulted in a $700 million injection that confirmed ofo's status as a "unicorn."[14] The money would be provided by Alibaba Group Holding Limited (the world's leading retailer and a major business-to-business product platform), Hony Capital, and CITIC Capital Holdings Limited (two leading Chinese private equity (PE) firms). Additional participation came from investors who participated in the $450 million D round of February 2017 (including Didi Chuxing Technology Co. [China's leading digital ride-sharing company] and DST Global (a PE company focused on the global internet]) (see Exhibit 5). ofo's E round followed a similar E round for Mobike led by Tencent (the world's leading electronic games company, the leading mobile messaging group, and [with Alibaba] one of China's two leading mobile payment companies) (see Exhibit 6).

ofo's new funds would be used to buy bicycles for international expansion and hire more talent. ofo's management did not see any good opportunities to purchase companies: Mobike was not for sale, and

[14] A "unicorn" refers to a recently started company valued at more than US$ 1 billion.

smaller competitors were being forced out of the market by ofo and Mobike. ofo had no wish to vertically integrate, but it wanted to predict the future shape of the bicycle-sharing industry in order to formulate its strategies. As Zhang opined, "If you buy a manufacturer, it will cost you a lot of time. And time is very important.... We are not like Mobike. They chose to make their own bicycle (and we think it's too heavy). And it cost them a lot of time."

ofo had yet to turn a profit. External financing had allowed it to forgo profitability in pursuit of market share, but ofo had conducted tests of steady-state operations in two second-tier Chinese cities,[15] and the tests had indicated that its bicycle-sharing model could break even.

FUTURE DIRECTIONS

ofo was young and international. Its employees' average age was 26, and it was in 180 cities (the vast majority of which were in China) and 17 countries. Zhang considered ofo's comparative advantage its DNA, its culture of openness, and its ability to design and connect bicycles. As he said, "We really love bicycles and know bicycles. And we really want to do something with bicycles. But for other companies, maybe they are just doing something to show off or make money."

Zhang believed that ofo's creativity flowed from its users. If its users had not provided the start-up bicycles in Peking University, he said, ofo's bicycle-sharing platform would never have been created. Zhang was confident that ofo's passion for cycling could help make the world more sustainable, equal, flat,[16] and convenient. ofo had the resources and the platform to build and roll out more transport tools—not just one design of a little yellow bicycle but many bicycle designs—as well as vehicles beyond bicycles. He had only to identify and grasp the opportunities.

---

[15]A second-tier city in China indicated a city such as Changchun, Changsha, Chengdu, Dalian, Fuzhou, Guangzhou, Guiyang, Hangzhou, Harbin, Hefei, Jinan, Nanjing, Ningbo, Qingdao, Quanzhou, Shantou, Shenyang, Shijiazhuang, Suzhou, Taiyuan, Wuhan, Wuxi, Xi'an, and Zhengzhou — in other words, substantial cities with populations of several millions but much smaller than Beijing, Chongqing, Shanghai, Shenzhen, or Tianjin.

[16]In describing the world as "flat" Zhang was referring to the book by Thomas Friedman, *The World is Flat: A Brief History of the Twenty-first Century*, Farrar, Straus and Giroux, New York, 2005, which uses the idea of "flattening" to mean leveling, or making competitively fair, the global playing field.

EXHIBIT 1: INDUSTRY TRENDS

1A: Monthly Use of All Bicycle-Sharing Apps and Average Frequency of Use

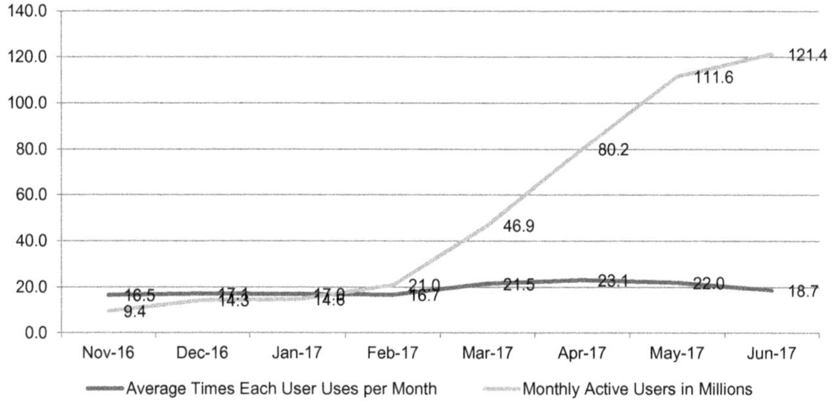

Note: Apps = applications.
Source: iResearch Consulting Group, "共享单车Q2 市场规模捅破30亿较Q1 月度活跃用户成倍额增" [Share cycling Q2 market size exceeded 3 billion more activity than the Q1 sales growth], September 2017, accessed December 10, 2018, www.iresearchchina.com.

1B: ofo and Mobike Active Daily App Users

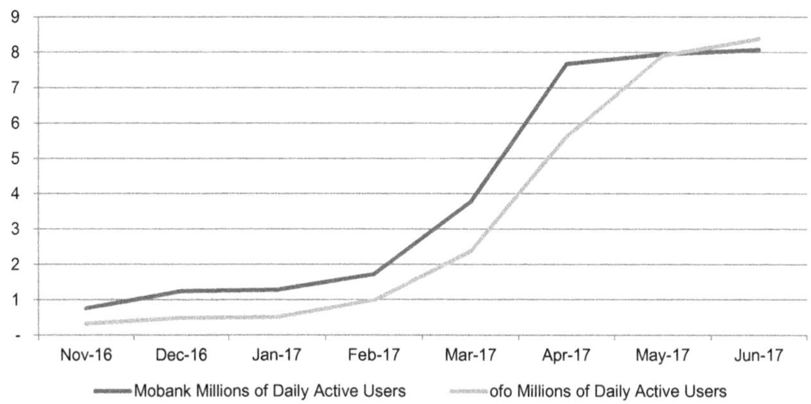

Note: Apps = applications.
Source: iResearch Consulting Group, "共享单车 Q2 市场规模捅破 30 亿较 Q1 月度活跃用户成倍额增" [Share cycling Q2 market size exceeded 3 billion more activity than the Q1 sales growth], September 2017, accessed December 10, 2018, www.iresearchchina.com.

EXHIBIT 1: (*Continued*)

1C: ofo and Mobike Users (Orders per Day) and Percent of Orders That Are Repeat Users

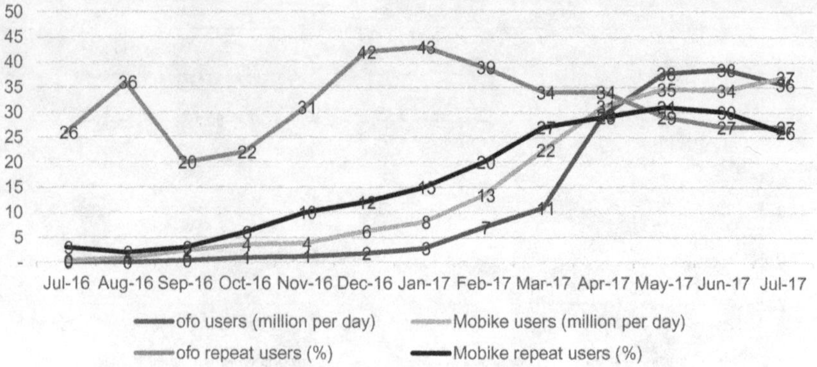

Source: QuestMobile, "摩拜单车和 ofo 共享单车有什么不同?" [What is the difference between a Mobike and an ofo shared bicycle?], Sohu, January 10, 2017, accessed 6 November 2017, www.zhihu.com/question/50166272.

EXHIBIT 2: THE COMPETITIVE SPACE

Tier	MAUs	Companies	Name in Chinese	Headquarters	Partners	Focus
1	> 30 million	ofo	ofo	Beijing	Financed by Alibaba Group, Ant Financial Services Group, Hony Capital, CITIC Group, Didi Chuxing Technology	China, International
		Mobike	摩拜	Shanghai	Financed by Tencent, Sequoia Capital, TPG Capital, Hillhouse Capital Group, ICBC International, Farallon Capital	China, International

(*Continued*)

EXHIBIT 2: (*Continued*)

Tier	MAUs	Companies	Name in Chinese	Headquarters	Partners	Focus
2	> 1 million	Hellobike	哈罗单车	Shanghai	Financed by Ant Financial Services Group, Fosun International, GGV Capital	China. third-tier cities
		Youon Bike	永安	Changzhou	Financed by Ant Financial Services	Profitable docking bicycles, expands to dockless bicycles; planned IPO Aug. 2017
		Xiaoming Bike	小鸣单车	Guangzhou	Financed with angel capital	Better location and lock technology
		Ubike	优拜单车	Shanghai	Financed by Black Hole Capital	Design/China
		Bluegogo	小蓝车	Tianjin	SpeedX bicycle manufacturer	Six Chinese cities and San Francisco
3	< 1 million	Qibei Technology	骑呗单车	Hangzhou	Ant Financial Services Group (credit system to reduce deposits)	Design/Technology
		Green Bike-Transit	拜客出行	Guangzhou	"Ride of Silence": International bicycle ride to commemorate cyclists killed in accidents	Social enterprise devoted to making cities bicycle friendly through regulatory change

Note: Listing of first-tier competitors is exhaustive; second- and third-tier companies are illustrative only. MAU = monthly active users; IPO = initial public offering.

Source: iResearch Consulting Group, "共享单车 Q2 市场规模捅破 30 亿较 Q1 月度活跃用户成倍额增" [Share cycling Q2 market size exceeded 3 billion more activity than the Q1 sales growth], September 2017, accessed December 10, 2018, www.iresearchchina.com; iResearch Consulting Group, "中国共享单车行业研究报告" [china's shared bicycle market research report 2017], accessed December 10, 2018, www.iresearchchina.com; Websites of Mobike, Hellobike, Youon Bike, Xiaoming Bike, Ubike, Bluegogo, Qibike and Greenbike-Transit accessed December 10, 2019.

EXHIBIT 3: EXCERPTS FROM THE MINISTRY OF TRANSPORT'S GUIDANCE CONCERNING ENCOURAGING AND REGULATING INTERNET RENTAL BICYCLES, MAY 22, 2017

The following is a translation by the authors of excerpts from the document issued by the Ministry of Transport requesting comments from interested parties concerning developing national regulations for the shared-bicycle industry.

Internet rental bicycles (commonly known as "shared bicycles") are a new service model developed by merging the mobile Internet and bicycle rentals. In recent years, China's Internet rental bicycle industry has developed rapidly and has played an active role in better meeting the needs of public travel, effectively solving the "last mile" problem of urban transportation, alleviating urban traffic congestion, and building a green travel system. However, it also has problems such as chaotic parking, inappropriate business operations and maintenance, irresponsible management, security risks regarding user deposits and private information, etc. In order to encourage and standardize the development of the Internet rental bicycle industry, the Ministry proposes the following guidance.

Overall requirements

- Guiding ideology. Fully implement the spirit of the 18th [National] Party Congress [of the CPC]'s Third, Fourth, Fifth, and Six Plenary Sessions, thoroughly implementing the spirit of the important speeches of General Secretary Xi Jinping … promoting the "Internet +" action plan, encouraging and standardizing the development of Internet rental bicycles, improving the level of Internet rental bicycle services, optimizing the transportation structure, and building a green, low-carbon travel system to better meet the travel needs of the people.
- Basic principles.
- Be service-based
  - Reform and innovate
  - Standardize and be orderly
  - Localize. The people's government of each municipality is the main body responsible for the management of Internet rental bicycles[,] … adapting to local conditions[,] … [and] exploring development models that conform to local realities

EXHIBIT 3: (*Continued*)

- Consider the interests of all stakeholders, tapping their enthusiasm and increasing industry self-regulation and public participation ...

Policy implementation

- Scientifically determined development. Do a good job in planning for slow traffic in light of the characteristics of the city.... The development of electric-powered Internet rental bicycles is discouraged.
- Guide the orderly bringing of bicycles into circulation.... [E]ach city should ... establish a mechanism for bringing bicycles into circulation that is compatible with the urban space carrying capacity, parking facilities' resources, and public travel demand.
- Improve the bicycle road network....
- Promote the planning and construction of bicycle parking spots.... Important urban commercial areas, public transportation stations, transportation hubs, residential areas, and tourist attractions should have ... designated bicycle parking.

Standardize bicycle business operation and maintenance

- Strengthen standardization by encouraging relevant social organizations and industrial technology alliances.
- Standardize business services.... Strengthen vehicle dispatching, parking, and maintenance management to ensure safe and convenient use of bicycles ... Ensure that users give their real names. Clarify the rights and obligations of companies and users.... Renting to children under the age of 12 is prohibited.... Provide innovative insurance for personal accident and third party liability.... Strengthen information reporting and timely sharing with local authorities ....
- Strengthen parking management, supervision, and enforcement ... using electronic fences and other technologies ... comprehensively adopting economic penalties to effectively regulate user parking behaviour.... Punctually clean up illegal parking.
- Encourage users to cycle safely and politely.... preventing double riding and installing child seats.... complying with traffic laws and regulations, and abiding by social morality.

EXHIBIT 3: (*Continued*)

- Strengthen credit scoring.... Establish a database of corporate and user credits, and regularly... integrating it with ... the national credit-information sharing platform ... to strengthen corporate service quality and user credit evaluation....

Safeguard user deposits and personal information

- Strengthen the management of user deposits.... Internet rental bicycle operators should provide rental services in a deposit-free manner. Companies that collect deposits and prepaid funds from users shall strictly segregate deposits from the company's own funds ... placing the deposits ... in special accounts.... Companies should establish and improve user deposit refund systems.... provided by banks and non-bank payment institutions....
- Strengthen network and information security protection.... Information taken shall not infringe on the legitimate rights and interests of the users and the public interest, and shall not exceed the scope necessary for the provision of Internet rental bicycle services. The information and related data generated shall be stored and used in the country.

Create a good environment for industry development

- Divide government department responsibilities clearly....
- Strengthen public governance ... Give full play to the role of industry associations and alliances ... supporting the formulation and release of industry conventions, and implementing relevant standards.... Increase the protection of consumer rights and interests, and prevent the transfer of business risks to consumers.
- Establish a fair, competitive market. Internet rental bicycle companies ... shall not hinder fair competition in the market, and shall not infringe upon the legitimate rights and interests of users and the public interest....

Source: "关于鼓励和规范互联网租赁自行车发展的指导意见(征求意见稿" [Ministry of Transport guidance concerning encouraging and regulating Internet rental bicycles, Guidance for development (Draft for comments)], accessed December 10, 2018, http://xxgk.mot.gov.cn.

EXHIBIT 4: OFO, LITTLE YELLOW BICYCLE SPECIFICATIONS: MID-YEAR 2017

Procedures for Using ofo:

1. Download the ofo app.
2. Open the app to look for the bicycle.
3. Find a bicycle on the map.
4. Look for the bicycle in a public space.
5. Unlock it by scanning the QR code.
6. At destination, put bicycle in the suggested area.
7. Lock it.

Note: App = application.

Source: Company files.

EXHIBIT 5: PRESS RELEASE

ofo Raises over US$700 Million in Series E Financing Round

BEIJING, July 6, 2017—ofo, the world's first station-free bicycle sharing platform and industry leader, announced that the company has raised over US$700 million in its latest round of financing, the largest in the bicycle sharing industry to date. The funding round is being led by Alibaba Group, Hony Capital and CITIC Private Equity, with additional participation from current investors Didi Chuxing and DST Global.

Since its launch in June of 2015, ofo has become the world's largest bicycle sharing platform in regard to both size and market share. So far, ofo has connected over 6.5 million bicycles to riders in 150 cities across

EXHIBIT 5: (*Continued*)

five countries, generating more than 25 million transactions daily. In total, more than 2 billion rides have been provided to over 100 million users globally.

"ofo is committed to providing global users with a convenient, efficient, green and healthy way of travel," said Dai Wei, founder and CEO of ofo. "We will further upgrade our service for better user experiences, accelerate our global expansion strategy, and continue to lead the bicycle sharing industry. Our vision is to unlock every corner of the world, and make ofo the universal language."

As one of the leading investors in this landmark financing, Alibaba is confident in ofo's growth potential. "ofo has redefined short-distance commuting, enabling a low-carbon footprint experience and delivering value to users and society," said Joe Tsai, Executive Vice Chairman of Alibaba Group. "ofo is the industry leader and we support its open platform strategy. We look forward to working closely with the ofo team to unlock the full potential of the bicycle sharing industry."

John Zhao, Chairman and CEO of Hony Capital said, "Hony Capital thinks highly of ofo's business strategy, innovation capacity and team execution. We believe that we will establish another flagship enterprise in the sharing economy."

Didi Chuxing stated that Didi and ofo are both practitioners under China's "Mass Entrepreneurship and Innovation" policy, benefit from the sharing economy and hold common values. Didi has full confidence in the strategy and execution of ofo's management team.

By the end of 2017, ofo plans to deploy 20 million bicycles to the bicycle sharing ecosystem, growing its service to reach 200 cities in 20 countries across the globe. Additionally, ofo has become one of the first enterprises to adopt the global NB-IOT (Narrow Band Internet of Things) technology for extensive commercial use. China Telecom will provide nationwide wireless Internet coverage for ofo, while Huawei has equipped ofo bicycles with NB-IOT chips and other useful telecommunication technologies. In the near future, ofo's bicycles will serve as central hubs connecting riders to net-based resources via the Internet of Things and creating an AI-based eco closed loop.

Source: Company files.

EXHIBIT 6: MOBIKE AND OFO FINANCING

Item	Mobike	ofo
Website	www.mobike.com	www.ofo.so
Legal Name	Mobike Singapore Pte. Ltd.	Beijing Bicyclelock Technology Co. Ltd
Primary Business	Application Software; Transportation; Social Platform	Application Software; Transportation; Social Platform
Year Founded	2014	2013
Co-founder and CEO	Davis Wang	David Wei
Business	The company raised US$600 million* of series E venture funding in a deal led by Tencent, Sequoia, TPG, and Hillhouse Capital on June 15, 2017, putting the company's post-money valuation at an estimated $3 billion. BOCOM International, ICBC International, and Farallon Capital also participated in the round. The company, which had raised more than $900 million in total funding to date, intended to use the funds to accelerate the pace of global expansion, as well as for investment in IoT and AI technology to support the brand.	The company was in talks to raise $1 billion in a deal led by SoftBank Group on July 26, 2017, putting the company's valuation at about $3 billion. Didi Chuxing also participated in the round. The company also raised $700 million of series E venture funding in a deal led by Alibaba Capital Partners, Hony Capital, and CITIC Private Equity Funds Management on July 6, 2017. Didi Chuxing and DST Global also participated in the round. The funds would be used to upgrade its services for a better user experience and to accelerate its global expansion. Previously, the company raised $450 million of series D and D+ venture funding in a deal led by DST Global and Ant Financial on April 24, 2017, putting the company's pre-money valuation at $550 million. The company was being actively tracked by PitchBook.
Series A	—	01-Jan-2016 $36.34 million
Series B	22-Aug-2016 $10 million	02-Sep-2016 $100 million
Series C	30-Sep-2016 $100 million	10-Oct-2016 $130 million
Series D	20-Feb-2017 $300 million	24-Apr-2017 $450 million
Series E	15-Jun-2017 $600 million	07-Aug-2017 $700 million

Note: * All dollar amounts are in USD; CEO = chief executive officer.

Source: Mobike Company Profile PitchBook, August 1, 2017; ofo Company Profile PitchBook, October 24, 2017.

Chapter 10

SenseTime Group Limited: Business Model and Expansion

Introduction

SenseTime, the company in this chapter's case, is one of the world's leading start-ups in AI, a science based on artificial neural networks (ANN).

The neuron is stupid. If its input stimulus is less than a threshold level the neuron does nothing. If its stimulus is more than the threshold, the neuron fires an output. But neurons can be interlinked and trained. A million neurons — linked to sensory stimuli, interconnected, with weighted inputs and firing into motor neurons that control muscles and glands — guide a well-functioning cockroach. A hundred billion neurons form the self-conscious mind of a human.[1] Put tens of thousands of humans together for thousands of years and you get civilization. Increase their numbers to billions and electronically network their activities and you get modern society. All from stupid neurons.

Management involves picking winners: people, products, services, companies, ideas and, yes, technologies. AI is currently the CPC's top technology pick.[2] This pick gives those using and developing AI

[1]Douglas Fox, "Consciousness in a Cockroach: The Insect Nervous System Provides Clues to Attention, Consciousness, and the Origin of the Brain", *Discovery*, January 10, 2007. https://www.discovermagazine.com/mind/consciousness-in-a-cockroach (accessed April 15, 2021).

[2]AI is the first technology mentioned in the 14th Five-Year Plan. Proposals of the Central Committee of the Communist Party of China on the formulation of the 14th Five-Year Plan

preferential access to projects getting research funding at universities and laboratories, to start-ups gaining entry into incubators, to growing companies receiving financing and to those seeking favourable development and interpretation of regulations.

AI offers tremendous promise to increase value. Like steam or electric power, it is an enabling technology. As *Wired* Magazine observed at the dawn of the AI age, a scant seven years ago, "like all utilities, AI will be supremely boring, even as it transforms the Internet, the global economy, and civilization".[3] Virtually any repetitive analytical activity can be improved through AI. Efficiency will rise in extraction, agriculture, manufacturing, logistics, medicine, law, finance, pedagogy, retail, and many more industries.

China is uniquely positioned to take advantage of AI. It has digital platforms with the largest membership base in the world. It is integrated by highly competitive, rapid, wide bandwidth telecommunications flowing with large volumes of clean, real-time data. It has a highly educated, consumer-based society committed to digitally enhancing its lifestyle. It is relatively unconstrained by legacy systems. It boasts highly competitive, profit-driven companies competing in a fast-paced, market-oriented environment. Its scientists and engineers are fully, bilingually, engaged in cutting-edge global AI development. It has an active and well-funded VC industry, with many VCs focused on AI. And, as we noted above, the CPC — which permeates government, business and society — has picked AI.[4]

---

and the 2035-year long-term goals", [中共中央關於制定十四五規劃和二〇三五年遠景目標的建議], The People's Net, November 4, 2020. Section 3 Clause 7.

[3]Kevin Kelley, "The Three Breakthroughs That Have Finally Unleashed AI on the World", *Wired*, October 27, 2014. https://www.wired.com/2014/10/future-of-artificial-intelligence/ (Accessed April 17, 2021).

[4]For a highly informed view of Chinese and global AI's potential, see Lee, Kai-fu, *AI Superpowers: China, Silicon Valley, and the New World Order*, Houghton, Boston, MA, 2018. Li is a Taiwan born, American, who did his PhD at Carnegie Mellon on AI speech recognition before becoming a researcher at Apple and then moving to Beijing to found Microsoft Research Asia. He became President of Google China before starting his own AI-focused, venture capitalist firm, Sinovation, which currently manages over US$2.5 billion. See "Dr. Kai-Fu Lee", Sinovation Website: https://sinovationventures.com/index.php/home/aboutus/teams.html (accessed April 19, 2021).

AI and Open R&D

AI R&D thrives in an open environment. The un-patentability of algorithms works against strong IP protection. AI's culture is open. AI knowledge, while complex, is widely available and of high quality. So connections external to the firm can be more important for stimulating the generation of knowledge than jealous retention of IP within the firm.[5] Ideas, technologies, models, and data are often optimally sourced and used externally from scientists, researchers, academics, and practitioners outside of any given company's teams. This R&D architecture differs from the traditional vertically organized research lab of large the US MNC — the classic example being Bell Labs.[6] And it also differs from the Chinese bureaucratic, top down research initiatives of ministries,[7] the one-professor-many-students model of Chinese universities and national key laboratories[8] and the anti-entrepreneurial culture in Chinese SOEs.[9]

SenseTime reflects this open environment of R&D. At the top of SenseTime, its founder Sean Tang Xiao Ou discloses through scientific papers and conferences his research. Comparative advantage is

---

[5]The open innovation approach is described by Henry Chesbrough, "Open Innovation: A New Paradigm for Understanding Industrial Innovation", in Henry Chesbrough *et al.* (ed.) *Open Innovation: Researching a New Paradigm*, Oxford University Press, New York, 2006.

[6]Bell Labs, dating from Alexander Graham Bell, the inventor of the telephone, was as a subsidiary of AT&T, the premier telecommunications R&D institute of the 20th century developing for, among other inventions, information theory, the transistor, lasers, the radio telescope, the language C+ and early AI. Bell Labs is now owned by Nokia and is called Nokia Bell Labs. See "About Us: History", Nokia Bell Labs Website: https://www.bell-labs.com/about/history/#gref (accessed May 3, 2021).

[7]Richard P. Suttmeier, "Inventing the Future in Chinese Labs: How Does China Do Science Today?" *The Conversation*, June 28, 2018. https://theconversation.com/inventing-the-future-in-chinese-labs-how-does-china-do-science-today-93830 (accessed April 19, 2021).

[8]Joy Yueyue Zhang, "The Organization of Scientists and Its Relation to Scientific Productivity: Perceptions of Chinese Stem Cell Researchers", *Biosocieties*. 5:2 (June 2010), 219–235. https://www.ncbi.nlm.nih.gov/pmc/articles/PMC3797515/ (accessed April 19, 2021).

[9]M. Hemmert, A. Cross, Yin Cheng, Jae-Jin Kim and K. Kohlbacher, "The Distinctiveness and Diversity of Entrepreneurial Ecosystems in China, Japan, and South Korea: An Exploratory Analysis", *Asian Business & Management* 18:3 (July 2019), 211–247.

maintained more by openly demonstrating that the company is at the cutting edge of the field than through patenting, non-compete employment contracts and keeping the results of research exclusively for in-house use. SenseTime's strategy of partnering globally with leading academic institutions and companies recalls the strategy of Ren Zhengfei's Huawei. The company's membership in government-sponsored initiatives and leadership in developing industry standards also speaks to its openness.

AI value is increased by minimizing the distance to the customer, recalling the platform solutions applied by Zhang Ruimin in Haier's *rendanheyi.* Whether the company is co-developing applications on the edge of the cloud or supplying a metered AI solution, SenseTime seeks to develop its role in the evolving ecosystem. Contributing to and working within that transcendent ecosystem is more important than creating independent, self-sustaining, silos.[10]

The AI industry in China is highly competitive. SenseTime is just one of several start-ups in AI. More muscular than the start-ups are the established ICT competitors. These include global bemouths like Amazon, Apple, Facebook, Google and Microsoft and leading established Chinese ICT companies such as Alibaba, Baidu, Bytedance, Didi, JD, Meituan, NetEase, Tencent and Xiaomi whose R&D budgets are many times the size of SenseTime's.

The large Chinese ITCs are also pursuing open development. Just prior to this book's publication, Alibaba, for example, completed its M6 project with Tsinghua University which used 50 million product titles and images from its ecommerce platform, Taobao, combining them with crawled web pages and web encyclopaedia to produce a 100 billion parameter multimodal pre-trainer that can generate text from images and images from text. In addition to being the largest Chinese language pre-trainer, M6 can write passable Chinese poetry.[11]

It is important to note that, even though AI is the top CPC pick of technologies, Alibaba, SenseTime, and the competitors in AI in China are ***not*** the product of CPC planning. SenseTime's founder, Professor Tang, is from the second generation entrepreneurs, born in the late 1960s. He is

---

[10]Farok Contractor, "Can a Firm Find the Balance between Openness and Secrecy? Towards a Theory of an Optimum Level of Disclosure", *Journal of International Business Studies* 50 (2019), 261–274.

[11]Lin Junyang, Rui Men *et al.*, "M6: A Chinese Multimodal Pretrainer", *arXiv* Cornell University, March 2, 2021. https://arxiv.org/abs/2103.00823 (accessed April 16, 2021).

first and foremost an academic, rather than an entrepreneur. He is a "sea turtle" having travelled and studied abroad before returning to take advantage of the opportunities in China. He received his bachelor of science degree from the University of Science and Technology in Hefei (1990) before completing his masters in University of Rochester (1991) and PhD in Massachusetts Institute of Technology (1996). Then he became a professor at CUHK for over a decade, rising to Associate Dean of the Faculty of Engineering.[12]

Although SenseTime's main markets are in Mainland China, the company was founded and is headquartered in Hong Kong, one of the freest economies in the world.[13] Hong Kong has never been part of the national planning system of the rest of China, although it benefits from the opportunities that planning affords. SenseTime became a unicorn thanks its technology, its people, its market, its global outlook and its business model which was financed by the global venture capital community. It has not received state funding.

SenseTime's Model Analysis through the Business Model Canvas

The case places the reader in the role of Dr. Xu Li, the co-founder and CEO of SenseTime. Xu Li was born in 1980, the cusp between the second generation and the third generation of China's entrepreneurs. The case features him reviewing SenseTime's business model.

SenseTime is the only case in this book that was researched without primary information from the protagonists. Cases based on primary

---

[12] "Professor Tang Xiaoou, Sean", *Department of Information Engineering, The Chinese University of Hong Kong.* https://www.ie.cuhk.edu.hk/people/xotang.shtml (accessed April 19, 2021).

[13] The conservative American think tank, The Heritage Foundation, rated Hong Kong as the freest economy in the world using its Economic Freedom Index from its inaugural year of 1995 until 2019. In 2020, it ranked Hong Kong as the second freest economy, second to Singapore. In 2021, the Heritage Foundation dropped Hong Kong from the rankings not because it lacked economic freedom but because Hong Kong's "... policies are ultimately controlled from Beijing". Dean Napolitano, "Heritage Foundation Drops Hong Kong from 'Economic Freedom' Index", *Nikkei Asia* March 4, 2021. https://asia.nikkei.com/Economy/Heritage-Foundation-drops-Hong-Kong-from-economic-freedom-index (accessed April 16, 2021).

research are generally preferred compared to those based solely on secondary sources because they can give more insight into the frames of mind of the decision makers. Typically, the case writers in a primary research case meet with the protagonists, interview them, obtain information from them, and finally seek their explicit written permission to publish the case.

We met the protagonists in the SenseTime case and we sent drafts of case to them. But they ignored our request for formal interviews and the case drafts we gave them. Whether they did so on the advice of their financial backers in anticipation of potential information disclosure issues around their Hong Kong initial public offering (successfully launched on December 30, 2021)[14] or simply because they were too busy and saw no advantage having a case about them available to educators around the world, we do not know.

Notwithstanding this drawback of the case, we wrote it because we are convinced that AI is a critical technology for China and the world. We also wrote it to present a local unicorn to be analyzed using the business model canvas (BMC). The BMC was developed by the Swiss business theorist, Alexander Osterwalder, and is marketed by his company, Strategizer.[15] Instructors of students in entrepreneurship courses frequently use the BMC, and we wanted the tool presented in the context of a recent, successful, local, startup. The BMC can be considered part of the lean start-up model in entrepreneurship where, rather than aiming for a full business plan, an entrepreneur sketches out the key factors of a business model on a single page.[16] The case uses the BMC to summarize SenseTime's nearest start-up competitor, CloudWalk. BMC's use for CloudWalk invites the reader to apply the same tool to SenseTime. The exercise clarifies SenseTime's value propositions for customer segments,

---

[14] Jill Disis, "SenseTime rallies in Hong Kong trading debut after delay forced by US sanctions", *CNN Business*, December 30, 2021, accessed December 31, 2021 https://edition.cnn.com/2021/12/29/investing/sensetime-ipo-stock-hong-kong-intl-hnk/index.html.

[15] Alexander Osterwalder, "Business Model Canvas", Strategizer, 2019. https://strategyzer.com/app (accessed September 25, 2019, accessed July 20, 2018).

[16] The lean start-up is most associated with the work of Stanford's Steve Blank. He presents the BMC in Steve Blank, "Why the Lean Startup Changes Everything", *Harvard Business Review* (May 2013), 65–72.

the relationships and marketing channels of SenseTime, the key partners, the corporate activities and the in-house resources needed.

Utopian and Dystopian Visions of AI

The opening quote in the SenseTime case asserts that "... we will be captured on film...." Society is becoming transparent. By one estimate, as of 2021, there are one billion closed circuit camera in use — one for every seven persons on earth. These closed circuit cameras, in addition to ubiquitous mobile phones, addictive apps, grid-integrated smart vehicles, other devices in the IoT etc. provide data. All are digitally recorded. Unprocessed, these "films" (i.e., the digital signals) are meaningless. However, AI is making that data meaningful and irresistibly attractive to the market. Trading privacy for service, all members of society are complicit in building the new panopticon.[17] This is true in the West.[18] This is more true in China.[19]

China's attitudes toward privacy and legitimacy of government access to personal data are substantially more relaxed than the West's, reinforcing the advantages that Chinese AI firms enjoy over their Western

[17]The panopticon is a prison whose architecture allows small numbers of jailers to observe large numbers of prisoners who do not know when they are being observed and so act as if they are always being observed. The panopticon metaphor is applied to the phenomenon of self-censorship in China or in any transparent society. See Simon K. Zhen, "An Explanation of Self-Censorship in China: The Enforcement of Social Control through a Panoptic Infrastructure", *Inquiries* 7:9 (2015). http://www.inquiriesjournal.com/articles/1093/an-explanation-of-self-censorship-in-china-the-enforcement-of-social-control-through-a-panoptic-infrastructure (accessed April 20, 2021).

[18]There has been a steady erosion in the West of privacy, even as laws to secure privacy have been "strengthened". This failure has occurred because (1) the state has ultimate access to information and (2) all owners of private information have the right to buy and sell that information. Perry Keller, "The Reconstruction of Privacy through Law: A Strategy of Diminishing Expectations", *International Data Privacy Law*, 9:3 (2019). https://papers.ssrn.com/sol3/papers.cfm?abstract_id=3246876 (accessed April 20, 2021).

[19]Only London makes it into the top ten surveilled cities of the world in terms of cameras on streets per capita. The other nine are all Chinese. Matthew Keegan, "The Most Surveilled Cities in the World", *US News*, August 14, 2020. https://www.usnews.com/news/cities/articles/2020-08-14/the-top-10-most-surveilled-cities-in-the-world (accessed April 19, 2021).

competitors.[20] This advantage is just one of the ways China is seen by the West as not playing by the rules. Western critics often view the widespread use of AI in China as evidence that the CPC does not sufficiently value the civil liberties of its citizens.[21] And some critics see China's embrace of AI monitoring as a malign threat not only to Chinese but to people everywhere. Privacy has become a global political issue.

Political issues are increasing the likelihood of military conflict. AI is a dual use technology. In the United States, both AI and the internet were initially funded by the Defence Advanced Research Projects Agency (DARPA) a research agency of the U.S. Department of Defense. Although neither SenseTime's key partners nor its service offerings nor its customer segments include the military, SenseTime's competitors do. Other Chinese AI companies use image recognition technology for battlefield deployment. China is increasingly perceived in the West as a threat. AI, a dual-use technology is consequently viewed as requiring restrictions to prevent leakage from the West to China.

Although only two years have passed since we wrote SenseTime, the company's paradigm of cooperation for a globally shared AI-enhanced future now looks slightly naive. East-West divergence has increased. Many technology-focused, global research initiatives have withered. In October 2019, SenseTime was put on the U.S. Entity List.[22] The company now faces very restricted access to U.S.-advanced technologies. This severely limits cooperative R&D programs between SenseTime and Western companies and universities.

I am optimistic that this short-term trend toward global disengagement will be reversed. I hope that the reversal will occur peacefully. The world is increasingly interconnected. The pressure for globalization will

[20] Lee Kai-fu, *AI Superpowers: China, Silicon Valley, and the New World Order*, Houghton, Boston, MA, 2018.

[21] Allegations that a minority-owned subsidiary of SenseTime has supplied face recognition technology to for surveillance systems to re-education facilities in Xinjiang. L. Gorman and M. Schrader, "U.S. Firms Are Helping Build China's Orwellian State", *FP* March 19, 2019. https://foreignpolicy.com/2019/03/19/962492-orwell-china-socialcredit-surveillance/ (accessed April 19, 2021).

[22] "Addition of Certain Entities to the Entity List", *The Daily Journal of the United States Government*, October 9, 2019. https://www.federalregister.gov/documents/2019/10/09/2019-22210/addition-of-certain-entities-to-the-entity-list (accessed April 20, 2021).

ultimately prevail. Similarly, society's accelerating rush to transparency will continue both in China and in the West. These trends are neither good nor bad. They are just facts, framing government policy, corporate strategy, and personal lifestyle decisions.

SENSETIME GROUP LIMITED: BUSINESS MODEL AND EXPANSION[1]

Professors Howard Pong Yuen Lam, Hugh Thomas, and Mr. Keith Chi Ho Wong wrote this case solely to provide material for class discussion. The authors do not intend to illustrate either effective or ineffective handling of a managerial situation.

The question is not whether we will be captured on film over the course of our daily lives....

We need to figure out the best way to responsibly enhance what is already a reality with a technology that will create greater levels of safety and service.[2]

Michael Xie, Forbes Technology Council

[1]This case has been written on the basis of published sources only. Consequently, the interpretation and perspectives presented in this case are not necessarily those of SenseTime Group Limited or any of its employees.

[2]Michael Xie, "The Future of Biometric Facial Recognition," *Forbes*, September 19, 2018, accessed September 13, 2019, www.forbes.com/sites/forbestechcouncil/2018/09/19/the-future-of-biometric-facial-recognition/#6e739bf43c74.

> AI will unlock another era of China-led global development, and the R&D and deployment of computer vision and deep learning technologies will redefine human life as we know it and establish a new connection between us and the world at large. Not only will this transform society as a whole, but it will push mankind forward as well.[3]
>
> Xu Li, co-founder and chief executive officer of SenseTime Group Limited

SenseTime Group Limited (SenseTime)[4] was founded in Hong Kong in 2014 by Tang Xiao'ou, to commercialize AI for digital recognition of images, particularly human faces. After only three years in business, the company was profitable,[5] with annual sales revenue of about US$100 million.[6] In 2018, SenseTime employed over 2,000 workers and was referred to as "the world's most valuable AI startup,"[7] with a valuation of $7.6 billion.[8] China had become the largest market in the world for facial recognition technologies, with its share of global sales expected to grow from 29 per cent in 2017 to 45 per cent in 2023. And the global facial recognition market was forecast to be worth $6.5 billion by 2021.[9] SenseTime aimed to empower more industries

---

[3] B.A. Woo, "Facial Recognition Firm SenseTime Raises $620 mn.," Mint Asia ST, June 8, 2018, accessed September 29, 2019.

[4] The name of the company in Chinese was 商汤 (*ShangTang*), meaning "Commercial Broth" and incorporating Tang's surname into the company name.

[5] Jumpstart, "SenseTime Raises US$620 Million in Series C+ Funding," May 31, 2018, accessed September 29, 2019, https://jumpstartmag.com/sensetime-raises-us620-million-in-series-c-funding-cementing-its-global-ai-industry-leadership-with-a-us4-5-billion-valuation/.

[6] All currency amounts are in US dollars unless otherwise specified; Jianqing Su, "After 60 Billion in Financing, How Is SenseTime Bleeding [in Chinese]," TMT Base, May 29, 2018 accessed January 12, 2019, www.tmtpost.com/3262876.html.

[7] Eamon Barrett, "In China, Facial Recognition Tech Is Watching You," *Fortune*, October 28, 2018, accessed September 13, 2019, https://finance.yahoo.com/news/china-facial-recognition-tech-watching-140042239.html.

[8] "SenseTime Private Company Profile," Pitchbook Database, accessed January 22, 2020.

[9] Sarah Dai, "China's Latest AI Champion Says Technical Standards Needed for Healthy Development of Facial Recognition Industry," *South China Morning Post*, October 2, 2018, www.scmp.com/tech/start-ups/article/2166472/chinas-latest-ai-champion-says-technical-standards-needed-healthy.

throughout the world with its AI platform.[10] In early 2019, how could Xu Li, the co-founder and chief executive officer of SenseTime, adapt the company's strategy to achieve that mission in an increasingly fraught global environment?

ARTIFICIAL INTELLIGENCE

MIT mathematicians Marvin Minsky and John McCarthy started the discipline of AI in the early 1950s to electronically mimic human psychological processes, which resulted in the MIT Artificial Intelligence Project (later the Artificial Intelligence Laboratory).[11] The 1960s was a decade of optimistic AI research centred at MIT and Stanford University and fuelled by funding from DARPA. That decade, however, was followed by the AI winter of the mid to late 1970s, as initial hype gave way to disappointment and to funding cuts. A second wave of AI enthusiasm in the early 1980s, this time funded largely by commercial sources, took a similar path of technology boom and bust. But a third wave of AI emerged as a feasible technology in the early twenty-first century from the development of improved ANN algorithms, powered by increased computing speed and trained with vast amounts of data.[12] In 2019, with global AI investment predicted to increase by 44 per cent, the third AI wave had yet to crest.[13]

Relative to other quantitative methods of analysis, AI required tremendous numbers of computations. Early ANN research was limited by

---

[10]"About Us [in Chinese]," SenseTime Group Limited, accessed September 29, 2019, www.sensetime.com/en/about.html.

[11]Glenn Rifkin, "Marvin Minsky, Pioneer in Artificial Intelligence, Dies at 88," *The New York Times*, January 25, 2016, accessed September 16, 2019, www.nytimes.com/2016/01/26/business/marvin-minsky-pioneer-in-artificial-intelligence-dies-at-88.html; Martin Childs, "John McCarthy: Computer Scientist Known as the Father of AI," *The Independent*, November 1, 2011, accessed September 16, 2019, www.independent.co.uk/news/obituaries/john-mccarthy-computer-scientist-known-as-the-father-of-ai-6255307.html.

[12]This is a narrow definition of AI, restricting it to the use of one set of computing algorithms, namely neural networks. For the original broad definition, see A. M. Turing, "Computing, Machinery and Intelligence," *Mind* 49 (1950): 433–460.

[13]A. Amoroso, "In Focus: How AI Is Reshaping the Future—and Our Investments," J.P. Morgan Private Bank, 2019.

computing cost to relatively shallow ANNs (i.e., ANNs with few hidden layers). Shallow ANNs were inappropriate for analyzing vast amounts of input data used for image processing and other complex problems because they did not allow for appropriate interactions among the input data. However, the acceleration of computing speeds and the use of graphics processing units (GPUs) allowed ANNs with dozens of hidden layers, ushering in the development of deep learning, where "deep" referred to the depth of the ANN or number of hidden layers (see Exhibit 1).[14]

By 2018, AI had become a core technology of major capitalization growth stocks in the United States, such as Amazon Inc., Apple Inc., Facebook Inc., Google LLC (Google), and Microsoft Corporation. Deep learning was increasingly viewed as holding promise to automate, accelerate, and improve many activities formerly relegated to human intelligence.[15] During its forecast of AI's economic potential, a report by PricewaterhouseCoopers examined the potential global impact of AI by industry sector and reached the following conclusions (see Exhibit 2):

> Global GDP could be up to 14% higher in 2030 as a result of AI—the equivalent of an additional $15.7 trillion—making it the biggest commercial opportunity in today's fast changing economy. The greatest gains … are likely to be in China ($7.0 trillion), North America ($3.7 trillion), Northern Europe ($1.8 trillion), Africa, Oceania and other Asian markets ($1.2 trillion), Southern Europe ($0.7 trillion), Developed Asia ($0.9 trillion) and Latin America ($0.5 trillion).… The biggest sector gains will be in retail, financial services and healthcare as AI increases productivity, product quality and consumption.[16]

---

[14] Francois Chollet, *Deep Learning with Python*, Grand Forks, ND: Manning Publications, 2017, 4–11.

[15] John Devine, "FANG Stocks: Which One Is Leading in AI?," US News, May 19, 2017, accessed January 8, 2019, https://money.usnews.com/investing/articles/2017-05-19/fang-stocks-which-one-is-leading-in-ai.

[16] PricewaterhouseCoopers, *Sizing the Prize: What's the Real Value of AI for Your Business and How Can You Capitalise?*, accessed December 28, 2018, www.pwc.com/gx/en/issues/data-and-analytics/publications/artificial-intelligence-study.html.

COMPANY ORIGINS AND GROWTH

SenseTime originated among faculty and students at CUHK, where Tang was chair of the department of information engineering and led the research in computer vision and imaging during the early 2000s.[17] Tang was one of the most influential scientists in the fields of computer vision, pattern recognition, and video processing in the world, as confirmed by numerous research awards.[18] He was a PhD graduate from MIT and a fellow of the Institute of Electrical and Electronic Engineers[19], the world's largest technical professional organization[20]. Tang kept his professorship at CUHK and his associate directorship of the Shenzhen Institute of Advanced Technology in China even after he founded SenseTime. [21]

Xu was Tang's protégé at CUHK, where he gained wide R&D experience in computer vision with technology leaders such as Lenovo Group Limited, Motorola Mobility LLC, OMRON Keihanna Innovation Centre, and Microsoft Research, before joining SenseTime.[22] His doctoral research in computer vision and imaging at CUHK also led to the publication of more than 40 papers in top academic conference and journals, with over 1,000 citations identified by Google Scholar.[23]

---

[17]Shu-Ching Jean Chan, "The Faces Behind China's Artificial Intelligence Unicorn," *Forbes Asia*, March 7, 2018, accessed December 24, 2018, www.forbes.com/sites/shuchingjeanchen/2018/03/07/the-faces-behind-chinas-omniscient-video-surveillance-technology/#3e0ea5df4afc.

[18]"Prof. Tang Xiaoou, Sean," Department of Information Engineering, The Chinese University of Hong Kong, accessed January 8, 2019, www.ie.cuhk.edu.hk/people/xotang.shtml.

[19]*Ibid.*

[20]IEEE "Communities" accessed June 6, 2020, https://www.ieee.org/communities/index.html

[21]Shenzhen Institutes of Advanced Technology "TANG Xiaoou" *The Administration,* accessed June 13, 2020, http://english.siat.cas.cn/AU2017/Administration2017/PP2017/201707/t20170719_179908.html.

[22]Li Xu, "Making Sense of SenseTime: There's More to This Unicorn than Meets the Eye," *Jumpstart Magazine*, April 6, 2018.

[23]"Dr. Xu Li, SenseTime Co-founder CEO," Hong Kong X-Tech, accessed December 24, 2018, www.hkxtech.com/dr-li-xu/?lang=en.

In its inaugural year, SenseTime gained global recognition by showing how its algorithms could outperform the human eye in detecting human faces.[24] Tang and his colleagues demonstrated that deep learning was extremely successful in enabling computer vision, modelling face variations, and using facial expressions to predict interpersonal relations such as dominant, competitive, and friendly.[25] In 2015, the company won two awards at ImageNet, a global industry contest for visual recognition, beating Google and other industry leaders.[26] That year also saw the establishment of the company's proprietary deep learning supercomputing platform, named Parrots. The development of Parrots distinguished SenseTime from many other AI companies that relied on open-source platforms, such as TensorFlow and Keras from Google,[27] Microsoft Cognitive Toolkit (CNTK),[28] and PyTorch from Facebook Inc.[29] Xu explained the reasons behind developing the Parrots platform:

> From PC (such as Linux) to mobile phones (such as Android) to AI, the source code for operating systems has long been controlled by companies like Google and Microsoft, which are building their own ecosystems. It's true that using their trained and proven systems can save you investment in hardware and infrastructure, but there will be little you can

[24] Shu-Ching Jean Chan, *op. cit*.

[25] Yi Sun, Xiaogang Wang, and Xiaoou Tang, "Hybrid Deep Learning for Face Verification," Pattern Analysis and Machine Intelligence, *IEEE Transactions* 38, no. 10 (2016): 1997–2009; Zhanpeng Zhang, Ping Luo, Chen Change Loy, and Xiaoou Tang, "From Facial Expression Recognition to Interpersonal Relation Prediction," *International Journal of Computer Vision* 126, no. 5 (2018): 550–569.

[26] Josh Horwitz, "The Billion-Dollar, Alibaba-Backed AI Company that's Quietly Watching People in China," Quartz, April 16, 2018, accessed December 21, 2018, https://qz.com/1248493/sensetime-the-billion-dollar-alibaba-backed-ai-company-thats-quietly-watching-everyone-in-china.

[27] Francois Chollet, *op. cit*., 62.

[28] "The Microsoft Cognitive Toolkit," Microsoft Azure, January 22, 2017, accessed December 28, 2018, www.microsoft.com/en-us/cognitive-toolkit.

[29] Serdar Yegulalp, "Facebook Brings GPU-Powered Machine Learning to Python," InfoWorld Tech Watch, January 19, 2017, accessed December 28, 2018, www.infoworld.com/article/3159120/artificial-intelligence/facebook-brings-gpu-powered-machine-learning-to-python.html.

> do if their algorithms turn out to be not good enough or deviate from where you are going. This is the problem with everyone using the same system.[30]

Xu believed that by owning its operating system and training platforms, SenseTime enjoyed a competitive advantage over companies that were using open-source platforms.[31]

Leveraging its hardware, proprietary software, and competence in developing algorithms, SenseTime launched AI facial recognition, image recognition, text recognition, video image analysis, image and video editing, remote sensing, autonomous driving, medical image recognition, and specialty computer microchips.[32] At the same time, SenseTime continued basic academic research in AI, publishing over 400 academic papers at international conferences and in leading journals.[33] By the end of 2018, SenseTime had five patents approved in the United States and 35 in China.[34]

SenseTime raised $30 million in series A investment from the US VC company IDG Capital and the Chinese VC company StarVC in 2014, before Tang even finished registering the business. Justin Niu, a VC at IDG Beijing, recalled being stunned by Tang's demo that identified blurry faces in a picture of Tiananmen Square on a smoggy day.[35] Series A+ investments followed in November 2015,[36] with $410 million in series B funding led by Chinese venture capital companies CDH Investment and

---

[30]"$600 Million on Two Things: Interview with SenseTime CEO XU Li, Part (1/2)," KrASIA, May 3, 2018, accessed December 25, 2018, https://kr-asia.com/make-sure-your-pace-of-innovation-is-faster-than-others-interview-with-sensetime-ceo-xu-li-part-1-2.

[31]*Ibid.*

[32]Li Xu, *op. cit.*

[33]"What Has the US$3 Billion Valued SenseTime over All These Years [in Chinese]," Tencent Technology, April 9, 2018.

[34]"Search for Patents," United States Patent and Trademark Office, accessed January 15, 2019, www.uspto.gov/patents-application-process/search-patents; "Public Inquiry," China and Global Patent Examination Information Inquiry, accessed January 21, 2019.

[35]Shu-Ching Jean Chan, *op. cit.*

[36]"Milestones," SenseTime Group Limited, accessed December 24, 2018, www.sensetime.com/en/about.html#progress.

Sailing Capital in July 2017.[37] This funding, which was the largest amount ever raised in the world for AI, cemented the company's unicorn status with a pre-money valuation of $1.1 billion.[38]

In 2018, SenseTime tripled its valuation. In April, the company received series C funding of $600 million from Alibaba Group Holding Limited, the global Chinese technology company listed on the New York Stock Exchange, as well as the Singaporean sovereign fund Temasek Holdings and the retail chain Suning.[39] The next month, SenseTime raised another $620 million in series C+ funding from major investment companies including Fidelity International, Hopu Capital, Tiger Global, and Qualcomm Ventures.[40]

Tang remained the largest individual shareholder. He retained the title of founder and led SenseTime's 650-person research team (about 20 per cent of whom held PhD degrees), including 18 professors at universities across China.[41] SenseTime created its original libraries of algorithms that could detect, learn, and uncover patterns and attributes in various kinds of images with speed and accuracy.[42] SenseTime's profit-seeking commercial operations were led by Xu, who stated, "We hope our professors would continue to focus on the fundamental research, including our founding professor, so we can continue to have discoveries."[43]

---

[37] Bien Perez, "Meet SenseTime, Hong Kong's First Hi-Tech Unicorn that No One's Heard of," *South China Morning Post*, October 23, 2017, accessed December 21, 2018, www.scmp.com/tech/start-ups/article/2116490/meet-sensetime-hong-kongs-first-hi-tech-unicorn-no-ones-heard.

[38] "Milestones," *op. cit.*

[39] "SenseTime Raises US$600 Million in Series C Funding," SenseTime Group Limited, April 9, 2018.

[40] *Ibid.*

[41] Takeshi Kihara, Michelle Chan, and Nikkei staff writers, "AI Powerhouse SenseTime Shifts Focus to Cars and Medicine," *Nikkei Asian Review*, September 6, 2018, accessed December 21, 2018, https://asia.nikkei.com/Business/Companies/AI-powerhouse-SenseTime-shifts-focus-to-cars-and-medicine.

[42] Eamon Barrett, "In China, Facial Recognition Tech Is Watching You," *Fortune*, October 28, 2018, accessed January 6, 2019, http://fortune.com/2018/10/28/in-china-facial-recognition-tech-is-watching-you.

[43] Shu-Ching Jean Chan, *op. cit.*

CUSTOMERS AND ALLIANCES

SenseTime's strategy to grow its business and create value for its customers had three components: fundamental R&D in AI, the development of customized AI products and solutions, and partnerships with organizations in specific verticals[44] to enhance their operational efficiency and profitability by implementing products and solutions[45] (see Exhibit 3). Yang Fang, co-founder and vice-president of SenseTime, further explained its strategy of vertical penetration: "SenseTime aims to identify early adopters in an industry and explore the way AI can be applied to their projects and products. We would then extend our solutions across the entire industry ecosystem and platformize them."[46]

SenseTime's first commercial success came in the peer-to-peer (P2P) lending applications market in China. China's consumer lending market emerged decades after it had already matured in most Western countries. Starting in 2013, thousands of Chinese P2P lending platforms opened on mobile Internet devices, unimpeded by regulatory oversight and fed by voracious lender and borrower demand. In 2016, SenseTime started providing face recognition services to P2P platforms. The technology used the borrower's mobile phone camera to detect the person's face and compare it to a picture on a previously-photographed personal identification document provided by the borrower. The process saved P2P platforms numerous hours of labor processing time.[47]

Initially, SenseTime sold AI software development kits to its customers. In 2018, however, it changed its operational focus to ongoing partnerships with upstream hardware developers and downstream system integrators. Xu explained the rationale:

> While it's a viable business model to sell software licenses in countries like Japan, Chinese enterprises are not used to spending too much on software. They don't think it's worth it to buy a software package with tens of millions of yuan.... They may demand heavier discounts the second year on the grounds that it seems the suppliers have offered little

[44]A *vertical* business refers to a specific industry, such as public security, banking, or hospitality, whereas a *horizontal* business refers to a specific technology.

[45]Li Xu, *op. cit.*

[46]Tencent Technology, *op. cit.*

[47]Josh Horwitz, *op. cit.*

> service during the first year … this year we are focusing on bringing our upstream and downstream technology to the next level so as to strengthen our competitiveness before it's too late.[48]

SenseTime had three main customer sectors. Chinese non-government entities accounted for about half of all sales. The Chinese domestic government sector accounted directly and indirectly for another 30 per cent.[49] Non-Chinese non-government related revenue accounted for the final 20 per cent.[50]

Chinese Non-government Entities

Chinese non-government entities included smart phone vendors, automakers, Internet service providers, and any company with large volumes of clean data that could use AI to enhance its operations. SenseTime approached potential customers in specific verticals via professional marketing. Rather than using mass media, SenseTime used seminars, events, and conferences to build awareness and explain the value SenseTime could add. For example, if SenseTime could increase profits by 10 per cent, it could split the 10 per cent on an ongoing basis with the companies in the vertical that adopted its technology.[51]

In one case, SenseTime organized a seminar in Shenzhen entitled "AI Application in Real Estate Industry to Create Value and Innovation." Potential customers within the industry were invited to talks by SenseTime and executives from China's leading real estate company Vanke. In the seminar, SenseTime launched its Smart Case Solution Version 1.0, which

---

[48] "$600 Million on Two Things: Interview with SenseTime CEO XU Li, Part (1/2)," *op. cit.*

[49] Josh Horwitz, *op. cit.*

[50] "Chinese AI Start-up SenseTime Snags Alibaba Funding at a Record US$3 Billion Valuation," Bloomberg, April 9, 2018, *South China Morning Post*, accessed January 12, 2019, www.scmp.com/tech/start-ups/article/2140840/chinese-ai-start-sensetime-snags-alibaba-funding-record-us3-billion.

[51] "Shang Tang Technology Xu Bing: Two Paths for Entrepreneurs to Build a Leading Artificial Intelligence Company [in Chinese]," SenseTime Official WeChat Account, accessed January 10, 2019, https://mp.weixin.qq.com/s/slt8845LLGhzSnZxHbRbqw.

provided AI services to the real estate industry, including digital marketing, identification and verification, sales follow-up, and passenger flow statistics.[52]

In another case, several university students approached SenseTime to design a module that would reside on SenseTime's server. The students intended to launch a company that would edit scripted videos taken by customers on their mobile phone. The company would edit the videos in real time by adding augmented reality (AR) special effects. The module on SenseTime's servers would accept streaming videos from the new company's server and use sound and facial features in the videos to determine appropriate timing, nature, and locations for the AR effects provided by the students. Each edited video would be streamed back to the new company's server for onward distribution.

SenseTime focused on four business verticals: smart city, mobile applications, smart phone applications, and automobile applications.[53] In the automobile sector, the company had been collaborating with Honda Motor Company since late 2017 to develop self-driving abilities.[54] SenseTime applied its core technologies in detecting pedestrians, vehicles, driving lanes, traffic signs, and large scenes.[55] It also explored the development of microchips and embedded systems to shorten the R&D cycle for fully-functional AI-enabled automobiles.[56]

In the push for smart city solutions, SenseTime looked at the opportunities to monetize digitization of the physical world by combining profile and personal data.[57] The data could enable AI systems to make

---

[52] SenseTime News, Qian Li, "SenseTime Releases Version 1.0 of the Smart Case Solution: The Trillion Yuan Real Estate Industry Needs AI "Dianzi Shuo," August 14, 2018, accessed April 25, 2020, www.elecfans.com/d/729117.html.

[53] "How to Make Money from the Digitization of the Physical World? Interview with SenseTime CEO XU Li, Part (2/2)," KrAsia, May 4, 2018, accessed December 25, 2018, https://kr-asia.com/how-to-make-money-from-the-digitization-of-the-physical-world-interview-with-sensetime-ceo-xu-li-part-2-2.

[54] "Honda Partners with SenseTime to Accelerate R&D of Smart AI Cars with Autonomous Driving," SenseTime Group Limited, December 7, 2017.

[55] "Autonomous Driving," SenseTime Group Limited, accessed December 25, 2018.

[56] Tencent Technology, *op. cit.*

[57] "How to Make Money from the Digitization of the Physical World? Interview with SenseTime CEO XU Li, Part (2/2)," *op. cit.*

forecasts of future events, such as the passenger flow in a smart city over the next day. The AI system could also provide customized services to individuals based on their personal habits gleaned from daily activities such as shopping and commuting. Data was captured from mobile devices, fixed surveillance cameras, and satellite cameras.[58]

SenseTime provided face comparison and identity recognition services to China Mobile, a publicly listed and centrally controlled SOE. China Mobile was the largest mobile carrier in China. SenseTime's software scanned over 300 million faces of subscribers.[59] SenseTime had contracts with the country's top 10 security surveillance manufacturers.[60] The company's partnerships with numerous camera manufacturers, which had installed 176 million surveillance cameras throughout China,[61] promised to bring a continuous feed of data into SenseTime's deep learning platform. The country's three leading mobile device manufacturers—Huawei Technologies Co. Ltd., Xiaomi Corporation, and Guangdong OPPO Mobile Telecommunications Corp. Ltd. (Oppo)—were eager for product differentiation to compete against each other. All three companies contacted SenseTime to co-develop their software, which would provide SenseTime with even more potential sources of live data.[62]

Chinese Domestic Government Sector

Chinese government sales involved partnering at national, provincial, and municipal levels. These solutions, which were a source of ongoing income for SenseTime, also provided vast amounts of data. Among the most important government business verticals were public transportation and public security agencies. SenseTime worked with 40 local authorities,[63] such as the Chongqing police force, which identified 69 suspects and

---

[58] *Ibid.*

[59] Shu-Ching Jean Chan, *op. cit.*

[60] *Ibid.*

[61] Josh Chin and Liza Lin, "China's All-Seeing Surveillance State Is Reading Its Citizens' Faces," *Straits Times*, July 8, 2017, accessed December 25, 2018, www.straitstimes.com/opinion/chinas-all-seeing-surveillance-state-is-reading-its-citizens-faces.

[62] SenseTime, "About SenseTime".

[63] Shu-Ching Jean Chan, *op. cit.*

detained 14 of them within the first 40 days of using SenseTime systems.[64] At the national government level, the company collaborated with a research institute under the Ministry of Public Security to develop a citizen network identity infrastructure.[65]

Non-Chinese Non-government Partnerships

SenseTime became a strategic partner of Qualcomm Incorporated (Qualcomm), a leading US developer and manufacturer of digital and communications technologies. SenseTime deployed its algorithm modules in face authentication, super resolution, night scenes, and dual camera bokeh (i.e., the aesthetic quality of blur) for Qualcomm's 5G (fifth generation) mobile platform.[66] Analysts commented that Qualcomm's algorithm+chip strategy would lower costs and reduce deployment time.[67] Xu and Keith Kressin, Qualcomm's senior vice-president, expected the collaboration to improve Qualcomm's capabilities of on-device AI for consumers using mobile devices[68] by combining SenseTime's algorithms with Qualcomm's chipsets.[69] Qualcomm also formed partnerships with Chinese mobile phone makers such as Xiaomi Corporation, Vivo Communication Technology Co. Ltd., and Oppo.[70]

---

[64] Josh Chin and Liza, *op. cit.*

[65] Bien Perez, "Meet SenseTime, Hong Kong's First Hi-Tech Unicorn that No One's Heard of," *op. cit.*

[66] "SenseTime Works with Qualcomm to Embrace the Age of 5G Mobile Experience," SenseTime Group Limited, December 6, 2018.

[67] "SenseTime and Qualcomm to Collaborate to Drive On-Device Artificial Intelligence," SenseTime Group Limited, October 20, 2017.

[68] Bien Perez, "Hong Kong's SenseTime Teams up with Qualcomm to Extend AI into More Devices," *South China Morning Post*, accessed January 10, 2019, www.scmp.com/tech/enterprises/article/2116194/hong-kongs-sensetime-teams-qualcomm-extend-ai-more-devices.

[69] "SenseTime Teams with Qualcomm for On-Device AI Push," *Hong Kong Economic Journal*, October 20, 2017, accessed January 1, 2019, www.ejinsight.com/20171020-sensetime-teams-up-with-qualcomm-for-on-device-ai-push.

[70] Panos Mourdoukouras, "The China Trade War Didn't Touch Qualcomm," *Forbes*, accessed January 10, 2019, www.forbes.com/sites/panosmourdoukoutas/2018/11/10/the-china-trade-war-didnt-touch-qualcomm/#47b481347c1.

With Qualcomm's chipsets, SenseTime would be able to capture the faces of a vast number of people, using mobile phones as the input to SenseTime's algorithms. The *South China Morning Post* commented on SenseTime's abilities:

> Backed by Qualcomm, it underscores its status as one of a crop of home-grown firms spearheading Beijing's ambition to become the leader in AI by 2030. And it is a contributor to the world's biggest system of surveillance: if you've ever been photographed with a Chinese-made phone or walked the streets of a Chinese city, chances are your face has been digitally crunched by SenseTime software built into more than 100 million mobile devices.[71]

CONTINUING GLOBAL IMPACT

SenseTime formed strategic alliances with various major academic institutions around the world, including CUHK (its university of origin), Zhejiang University, Tsinghua University, Peking University, and Shanghai Jiao Tong University.[72] In 2018, the company formed the MIT-SenseTime Alliance on AI, a part of MIT's grand scheme of cross-disciplinary research aiming to advance the science of human intelligence and to develop machine-learning algorithms. The alliance planned to fund 27 research projects led by 50 faculty members from various laboratories and all five schools at MIT: Engineering; Science; Architecture and Planning; Management; and Humanities, Arts and Social Sciences.[73]

SenseTime's supercomputing infrastructure was world-class, encompassing 54 million GPU cores over 15,000 GPUs, with an aggregate computing power of 160 petaflops.[74] Its power rivalled the world's top ranked

---

[71] "Chinese AI Start-up SenseTime Snags Alibaba Funding at a Record US$3 Billion Valuation," *op. cit.*

[72] Tencent Technology, *op. cit.*

[73] Meg Murphy, "MIT-SenseTime Alliance Funds Projects from All Five Schools," MIT News, Massachusetts Institute of Technology, August 24, 2018, http://news.mit.edu/2018/mit-sensetime-alliance-funds-projects-human-machine-intelligence-0824.

[74] A petaflop was a measure of a computer's processing speed, expressed as a quadrillion floating point operations per second (FLOPS); "Definition: Petaflop," WhatIs, November 2008, accessed April 10, 2020, https://whatis.techtarget.com/definition/petaflop.

supercomputers, such as the Summit computer at the Oak Ridge National Laboratory in the United States.[75] With one of the largest supercomputing capabilities in China, SenseTime was able to handle large-scale classification with hundreds of billion parameter-level models and hundreds of million categories.[76] Using the $1 billion in funding raised in 2018, SenseTime aimed to build five supercomputers across China that would integrate images from over 100,000 live feeds from remote devices such as traffic cameras, face scanners, and automatic teller machines into a single system.[77]

The burgeoning live data feeds served by SenseTime's AI products and solutions gave SenseTime critical resources to further engage in R&D and optimize its products and solutions. This availability of big data helped SenseTime increase its competitive advantage. By 2018, SenseTime boasted a vast database of images acquired from over 100 million mobile devices embedded with its face recognition software,[78] as well as the authentication services that scanned over 400 million faces when users accessed various online content, retail, and finance services.[79] SenseTime had a proprietary database of over 2 billion images for algorithm training. In comparison, the largest public database—the ImageNet project—had only 13 million images gathered worldwide.[80] SenseTime's core technologies were illustrated in the *Panopto* video, *SenseTime*.[81]

---

[75] Gregory Allan, "Understanding China's AI Strategy: Clues to Chinese Strategic Thinking on Artificial Intelligence and National Security," Center for New American Security, February 6, 2019, accessed December 17, 2021 https://www.cnas.org/publications/reports/understanding-chinas-ai-strategy.

[76] "SenseTime raises US$600 million in Series C funding," *op. cit.*

[77] "China Now Has the Most Valuable AI Startup in the World," Bloomberg, April 9, 2018, accessed December 24, 2018, www.bloomberg.com/news/articles/2018-04-09/sensetime-snags-alibaba-funding-at-a-record-3-billion-valuation.

[78] "The World's Biggest AI Startup Raises $1.2 Billion in Mere Months," *Fortune*, May 31, 2018, accessed December 21, 2018, http://fortune.com/2018/05/30/ai-startup-sensetime-facial-recognition-china.

[79] Shu-Ching Jean Chan, *op. cit.*

[80] Josh Horwitz, *op. cit.*

[81] Howard Pong Yuen Lam and Hugh Thomas, "SenseTime," March 7, 2019, video to accompany Lam, Thomas and Wong, "SenseTime Group Limited: Business Model and Expansion," accessed December 17, 2021 https://youtu.be/VrO7axUSifs.

COMPETITORS

AI competition was asymmetric. Several domestic start-up AI companies were approximately the same size as SenseTime. However, many large domestic and foreign established competitors had substantial AI initiatives. These major global organizations were valued at considerably higher levels than SenseTime and its start-up Chinese competitors (see Exhibit 4).

SenseTime's most direct domestic AI competitor was CloudWalk Technology Co. Ltd. (CloudWalk). The two companies were similar in terms of age, history, valuation, key customers, numbers of external rounds of financing, and business model. Like SenseTime, CloudWalk was founded by a research scientist — Professor Zhou Xi from the Chinese Academy of Sciences. With fellow researchers, Xi started a company in the academy's incubator devoted to commercializing AI facial recognition technology. Funded with state-owned VC, CloudWalk's first business verticals were also in finance, where CloudWalk became the biggest supplier of AI facial recognition to the automated teller machine networks of Chinese banks, including the Agricultural Bank of China and Bank of China (the world's third and fourth largest banks, respectively, by assets).[82] While continuing to pursue core AI proprietary software research and development, and with its strength in serving banks, CloudWalk expanded into public security surveillance and AI related hardware. The company developed and marketed its software development kits to be sold to clients who wanted to monetize their big data through AI.[83] CloudWalk had also recently ventured overseas, providing facial recognition services to security personnel in banks, airports, railways, and bus stations, as well as building a national facial database for the government of Zimbabwe (see Exhibit 5).[84]

---

[82] Iris Deng, "This State-Backed AI Unicorn Has Helped Chinese Police Arrest 10,000 Criminals," *South China Morning Post*, March 28, 2019, accessed January 20, 2020, www.scmp.com/tech/start-ups/article/3003686/state-backed-ai-unicorn-has-helped-chinese-police-arrest-10000.

[83] CloudWalk Technology, *Manual for Facial Recognition SDK* [in Chinese], July 2016.

[84] Amy Hawkins "Beijing's Big Brother Tech Needs African Faces" *Financial Post*, July 24, 2018, accessed January 22, 2020, https://foreignpolicy.com/2018/07/24/beijings-big-brother-tech-needs-african-faces/.

In terms of international competition, SenseTime's research team was similar in size to DeepMind Technologies.[85] The 700-researcher UK laboratory owned by Google was famous for developing the supercomputer AlphaGo. In 2016, AlphaGo had beaten Lee Sedol at the board game Go. Sedol was the world's second-ranked Go master at the time. The event was seen as redefining the relationship between AI and human intelligence.[86]

Generally, the R&D teams of most established Chinese technology firms (including SenseTime) were significantly smaller than most advanced AI technology organizations. Notwithstanding its youth and smaller size, however, SenseTime had been chosen among a group of hand-picked organizations by the national government in Beijing as one of the AI innovation national champions. SenseTime was selected for its intelligent vision, along with Baidu for autonomous driving, Alibaba Group Holding Ltd. for smart city initiatives, Tencent Holdings for computer vision in medical diagnosis, and iFlytek for speech recognition.[87]

China was making rapid strides in its unique AI environment. Early AI research by Western countries had been led by the US Department of Defense.[88] However, by the twenty-first century it was being dominated by high technology companies, universities, and civilian research institutions. Chinese AI, in contrast, originated in private and academic sectors but had become increasingly supported by the government.[89] Since 2006, China had led the world in terms of numbers of academic

---

[85]Gregory Allan, *op. cit*., 7.

[86]Cade Metz, "In Two Moves, AlphaGo and Lee Sedol Redefined the Future," *Wired*, March 16, 2016, accessed January 3, 2020, www.wired.com/2016/03/two-moves-alphago-lee-sedol-redefined-future.

[87]Sarah Dai, *op. cit.*

[88]Oscar Schwartz, "Untold History of AI: The DARPA Dreamer Who Aimed for Cyborg Intelligence", *IEEE Spectrum,* April 8, 2019, accessed December 17, 2021 https://spectrum.ieee.org/untold-history-of-ai-darpa-dream-of-cyborg-intelligence.

[89]Kai-Fu Lee, *AI Superpowers: China, Silicon Valley, and the New World Order*, Houghton Mifflin Harcourt, Boston, 2018.

AI articles published and it was overcoming its reputation for lagging in quality.[90]

In 2010 the Chinese government first recognized AI as a priority industry,[91] a status that was reinforced in the 13th Five Year Plan[92] and confirmed in the 2017 State Council Directive on AI.[93] Although these plans were largely aspirational, they formed the basis on which national and local governments crafted regulations to facilitate AI development, make telecommunications and big data infrastructural investments, increase research funding, and promote AI related projects. In 2018, the Seattle-based Allen Institute for AI predicted that citations of China's research papers on AI would rank among the top 10 per cent by 2020, and

[90]Kumaran and Manoharan looked at over 50,000 English language academic AI research publications from 1996 to 2015 and found that China ranked second to the US but 60% of China's articles were cited by no other article whereas only 46% of US articles were cited by no other article. Kumaran and Manoharan, "Cited and Uncited Publications on Artificial Intelligence Research Output", *Journal of Advances in Library and Information Science* 6:3, July to Sep. 2017, pp.191–195. accessed June 15, 2020, http://jalis.in/pdf/6-3/Kumaran.pdf. Using bibliometrics and data from 2008 to 2018 Gao *et al* looked at the most influential 12,301 articles on AI and showed that 49% of the articles were from researchers in China whereas only 24% were from those in the USA (the second ranked country) and that the Chinese Academy of Sciences was the dominant AI research producing institution globally. See Fang Gao *et al.* "Bibliometric analysis on tendency and topics of artificial intelligence over last decade" *Microsystem Technologies,* March 30, 2019, accessed December 17, 2021. https://www.uscc.gov/research/13th-five-year-plan. Note that, since Chinese researchers also publish articles in Chinese, these numbers (which show only English publications) understate actual Chinese AI research output.

[91]"Decision on Accelerating the Cultivation and Development of Strategic Emerging Industry," State Council of China, October 10, 2010, accessed January 16, 2020, https://chinaenergyportal.org/wp-content/uploads/2017/01/Development-Strategic-Emerging-Industries.pdf.

[92]K. Koleski, "The 13th Five-Year Plan," US-China Economic and Security Review Commission, February 14, 2017, accessed December 17, 2021, https://www.uscc.gov/research/13th-five-year-plan.

[93]"Notice of the State Council Issuing the New Generation of Artificial Intelligence Development Plan," The Foundation for Law and International Affairs, State Council Document [2017] No. 35, July 8 2017, accessed January 16, 2020, https://flia.org/wp-content/uploads/2017/07/A-New-Generation-of-Artificial-Intelligence-Development-Plan-1.pdf.

among the top 1 per cent by 2025, thereby exceeding citations of US research in both cases.[94]

OPPORTUNITIES AND CHALLENGES

Xu expected SenseTime to remain in good shape financially, despite the need for large, ongoing R&D investment. He believed that AI businesses in China would enjoy a natural scale advantage, saying, "The government has the largest data set.... If you have access to them [Baidu, Alibaba, and Tencent] ... you have almost all the data in the world. More importantly, the original data has been encrypted, which means nobody can do reverse engineering to recover the original data."[95]

Xu considered that AI standards were critical for achieving the economies in AI to maximize its social impact, but he did not mind whether the United States or China came up with the standards, as long as global standards could be adapted to suit each country's particular conditions.[96]

SenseTime was one of the AI facial recognition leaders of China, and Xu looked forward to global expansion. He did not want "to create a small company to be acquired." Rather, he wanted to be "an AI platform for global users" that would dominate its market like Google and Facebook Inc. dominated theirs.[97] One barrier to globalization, however, was export controls. Although a company could apply its proprietary AI algorithms in whatever country it was conducting business, the data flows to be analyzed by those algorithms were subject to export controls. For example, no personal data could be exported from China without the explicit authorization of the Cyberspace Administration of China.[98] European countries

---

[94] Asa Fitch, "China Gains on US in Highly Cited AI Research," *The Wall Street Journal*, March 13, 2019, accessed April 10, 2020, www.wsj.com/articles/china-gains-on-u-s-in-highly-cited-ai-research-11552485601.

[95] Josh Horwitz, *op. cit.*

[96] "China Now Has the Most Valuable AI Startup in the World," *op. cit.*

[97] Li Xu, *op. cit.*

[98] Meng Jing, "China Cybersecurity Rule on Exporting Personal Information Seen Raising Compliance Costs for Firms," *South China Morning Post*, June 13, 2019, accessed September 25, 2019, www.scmp.com/tech/policy/article/3014313/china-cybersecurity-rule-exporting-personal-information-seen-raising.

had similar controls, and the United States was becoming increasingly sensitive to strategic cyber threats.[99]

Another concern was privacy. Experts questioned whether the systems in China provided adequate protection to people whose personal data were being collected, stored, and processed.[100] The European Union's General Data Protection Regulation required data users who collected personal data to seek explicit consent from data subjects in advance.[101] While many governments used facial recognition technologies without getting prior consent, the situation in China raised special concerns to non-government organizations such as Privacy International, which stated that "the potentials for abuse [were] even higher than in democratic countries."[102]

Leo Liu, group vice-president of SenseTime, commented that "we don't collect the data or use the data without the permission of users." However, SenseTime had provided AI-powered facial identification to authorities in Guangzhou and Yunnan.[103] SenseTime had also provided scanning and deleting services to the Cyberspace Administration of China to censor online pornography, violence, terrorism, and horror, which prompted *Forbes* magazine to state that the Chinese Internet had thus become the most hygienic on earth.[104]

Certainly, there may have been cases in which SenseTime had not been given explicit permission from people whose faces had been analyzed. For example, if a streaming video was captured using cameras operated by a local public security bureau and then compared with the

---

[99] Zak Doffman, "Cyber Warfare Threat Rises as Iran and China Agree 'United Front' Against US," *Forbes*, July 6, 2019, accessed October 5, 2019, www.forbes.com/sites/zakdoffman/2019/07/06/iranian-cyber-threat-heightened-by-chinas-support-for-its-cyber-war-on-u-s/#2f1fd22e42eb.

[100] James Delaire, "SenseTime: How the World's Most Valuable AI Startup Is Changing China," *NS Tech*, September 28, 2018.

[101] "How Should My Consent Be Requested? Your Guide to Policies, Information and Services," European Commission, accessed December 29, 2018, https://ec.europa.eu/info/law/law-topic/data-protection/reform/rights-citizens/how-my-personal-data-protected/how-should-my-consent-be-requested_en.

[102] James Delaire, *op. cit.*

[103] Andrew Wong, "Everyday Conveniences Will Win over Concerns about Personal Data Collection: A.I. Start-up SenseTime," CNBC, November 30, 2018.

[104] Shu-Ching Jean Chen, *op. cit.*

bureau's file photographs to identify persons of interest, SenseTime would have had no involvement in obtaining permission from any of the people (in videos or photographs) whose images it was processing. In such cases, SenseTime would presumably rely on the provider of the feed or images to ensure that all files were obtained within the law or with permission.

Tang was enthusiastic about global research in AI, in particular about the promising work with the MIT-SenseTime Alliance. "As an MIT alumnus, I'm grateful to have this opportunity to collaborate with my *alma mater*, especially on something that is dear to my heart — to advance research on AI."[105] But MIT was having second thoughts. In April 2019, the university stated that "engagements with … China [including Hong Kong] … merit additional faculty and administrative review beyond the usual evaluations that all international projects receive."[106]

Acting on what alumni believed to be political pressure from the US government,[107] MIT asked its community to exercise vigilance in projects involving faculty, staff, or students working in China or collaborating with Chinese individuals or companies. MIT researchers were especially cautioned in respect to risks related to IP; export controls; data security and access; economic competitiveness; national security; and political, civil, and human rights. As well, any potential impact on the MIT community, consistency with MIT's core values, and alignment with MIT's academic mission were deemed to need to be protected.[108]

---

[105]"MIT and SenseTime Announce Effort to Advance Artificial Intelligence Research: Alliance Will Be Part of New MIT Intelligence Quest," MIT News, Massachusetts Institute of Technology, February 28, 2019, accessed January 12, 2019, http://news.mit.edu/2018/mit-sensetime-announce-effort-advance-artificial-intelligence-research-0228.

[106]Maria T. Zuber, "New Review Process for 'Elevated-Risk' International Proposals," Massachusetts Institute of Technology, April 3, 2019, accessed September 15, 2019, http://orgchart.mit.edu/node/27/letters_to_community/new-review-process-elevated-risk-international-proposals.

[107]Louise Lucas, Nicolle Liu, and Henny Sender, "MIT Cuts Partnerships with China's Huawei and ZTE over Risks: Collaboration with Russia, Saudi Arabia and Hong Kong to Face Stricter Screening Process," *Financial Times*, April 4, 2019, accessed September 15, 2019, www.ft.com/content/0b11d8e0-5689-11e9-a3db-1fe89bedc16e.

[108]*Ibid.*

In its strategy review, SenseTime would have to consider domestic and foreign market opportunities, its competitors, and the evolving global AI environment.

The authors are grateful for the initiation and support provided by Teaching Development and Language Enhancement Grant for 2016–2019 Triennium from The Chinese University of Hong Kong that made the production of this case possible and for the assistance of Professor Huang Rui of The Chinese University of Hong Kong, Shenzhen School of Science and Engineering for discussing with them the current nature and state of ANN.

EXHIBIT 1: AN ARTIFICIAL NEURAL NETWORK (ANN)

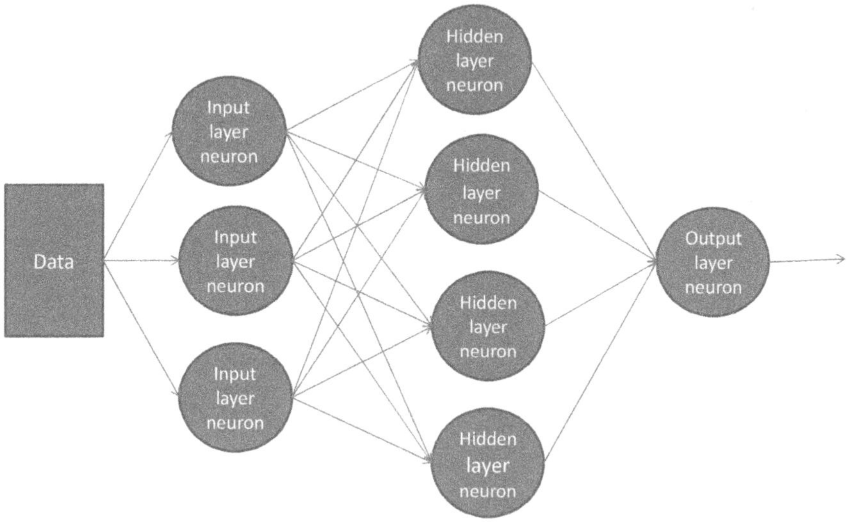

Note: ANNs are analogous to biological networks of neurons that make up the brain. Each ANN has an input layer of neurons that receives data and an output layer of neurons that gives the ANN's numerical conclusion. Each neuron in an ANN transforms input numbers using a non-linear function—such as f(*x*) = (e^*x*) ÷ [(e^*x*) +1)], where *x* is a weighted combination of the neuron's input—into a single numerical output. The output of each neuron not in the output layer is sent to other neurons as input. The ANN is trained by comparing its output with the true state (the "ground truth") and then adjusting each neuron's weight of each input according to an iterative learning function. Designs of ANNs differ by the number of layers, nodes per layer, neuron paths, neuron and learning functions, and the optimization algorithm.

Source: Prepared by the case authors with information from Bill Wilson, "The Machine Learning Dictionary 2012," accessed October 5, 2019, https://web.archive.org/web/20180826151959/ http://www.cse.unsw.edu.au/~billw/mldict.html#activnfn; Simon Haykin, *Neural Networks: A Comprehensive Foundation* (Upper Saddle River, NJ: Prentice Hall, 1999); Francois Chollet, *Deep Learning with Python* (Grand Forks, ND: Manning Publications, 2017), 4–11.

EXHIBIT 2: POTENTIAL IMPACT OF ARTIFICIAL INTELLIGENCE BY INDUSTRY SECTOR

	Personalization	Utility	Time Saved	Data Availability	Average	Percentage of Use Case Adoption within Three Years
Health Care	**3.8**	**3.9**	**2.7**	**4.4**	**3.5**	**37**
Providers and health services	4.1	3.9	3	4.7	3.7	14
Pharmaceuticals and life sciences	3.9	4.2	2.8	4.1	3.6	33
Insurance	3.6	3.8	2.6	4.2	3.3	60
Consumer health	3.4	3.4	2.3	4.8	3.0	50
Automotive	2.5	3.3	2.0	4.4	2.6	46
Aftermarket and repair	4.2	3.6	2.8	4.6	3.5	40
Component suppliers	4.0	3.5	2.0	5.0	3.2	50
Personal mobility as a service	4.0	4.0	3.7	3.7	3.9	67
Original Equipment Manufacturer	4.0	4.0	3.0	3.6	3.7	25
Financing	3.3	3.7	3.0	3.0	3.3	67
Financial services	**2.8**	**3.2**	**2.6**	**4.6**	**2.9**	**41**
Asset & wealth management	2.9	3.7	2.2	4.3	2.9	44
Banking and capital markets	2.5	3.0	2.9	5.0	2.8	31
Insurance	3.1	3.1	2.4	4.4	2.9	50
Transportation and logistics	**3.5**	**3.3**	**2.6**	**3.7**	**3.1**	**42**
Transportation	3.0	3.5	2.8	5.0	3.1	50
Logistics	3.9	3.1	2.5	3.0	3.2	37

Technology, communications, and entertainment	**2.5**	**3.3**	**2.1**	**4.3**	**2.6**	**47**
Technology	2.7	3.6	2.4	4.1	2.9	57
Entertainment, media, and communication	2.5	3.3	2.0	4.4	2.6	46
Retail	**2.8**	**3.3**	**2.1**	**3.8**	**2.7**	**54**
Consumer products	3.0	3.3	2.3	3.8	2.9	67
Retail	2.6	3.3	2.0	3.7	2.6	42
Energy	**2.6**	**3.3**	**2.0**	**3.7**	**2.6**	**42**
Oil and gas	4.0	2.9	2.1	3.0	3.0	43
Power and utilities	2.0	3.3	2.1	3.2	2.5	37
Manufacturing	**2.0**	**3.7**	**1.2**	**3.8**	**2.3**	**14**
Industrial manufacturing	2.0	3.7	1.4	3.9	2.4	18
Industrial products or raw materials	0.0	3.6	1.0	3.7	1.5	8

Note: Four Artificial Intelligence Impact Index scores were determined by PricewaterhouseCoopers in co-operation with Fraunhofer to identify and evaluate use cases across four criteria: potential to enhance personalization (Personalization), potential to enhance quality (Utility), Potential to save time for consumers (Time Saved), and availability of data to make these gains possible (Data Availability). The Average column displays the simple average of the four scores. The final column is the percentage of use cases that are predicted to be adopted within three years.

Source: Prepared by the case authors with information from PricewaterhouseCoopers, *Sizing the Prize: What's the Real Value of AI for Your Business and How Can You Capitalise?*, accessed December 17, 2021, https://www.pwc.com/gx/en/issues/analytics/assets/pwc-ai-analysis-sizing-the-prize-report.pdf.

EXHIBIT 3: SENSETIME GROUP LIMITED BUSINESS VERTICALS

Industry	Solutions Provided	Selected Clients
Banking and finance	• Face identification • Identify verification • Identification card and credit card recognition to speed up and secure credit application processes	• Rong 360 • Huanbei • UnionPay • JD Finance • China Merchants Bank
Online entertainment	• Face effects • Beautification • Gesture recognition • Background segmentation	• Sina Weibo • Bigo Live • Meitu Inc.
Mobile device	• Dual camera photo taking • Image processing • Face grouping • Intelligent photo albums • Face unlocking	• Guangdong OPPO Mobile Telecommunications Corp. Ltd. • Vivo Communication Technology Co. Ltd • QiKU • Huawei Technologies Co. Ltd. • Xiaomi Corporation
Retail shopping	• Face identification in unmanned shopping and membership management • Use of big data in analyzing sales and optimizing operation efficiency	• Suning
Public transportation	• Identity verification systems for boarding trains or airplanes to replace payment systems	• HNA Group Co., Ltd. • Shanghai Metro
Public security	• Video detection systems that identify and compare facial captures with criminal databases to assist crime prevention and investigation	• Public security bureaus at municipal and provincial levels, including in Guangzhou, Shenzhen, and Yunnan

Source: "Intelligent Finance," SenseTime Group Limited, accessed December 25, 2018, www.sensetime.com/cases#3; "Internet Entertainment," SenseTime Group Limited, James Delaire, "SenseTime: How the World's Most Valuable AI Startup Is Changing China," *NS Tech*, September 28, 2018, "Intelligent Terminal," SenseTime Group Limited, "Intelligent Business," SenseTime Group Limited, "Mobile Operator," SenseTime Group Limited, "Intelligent Security," SenseTime Group Limited.

EXHIBIT 4: SENSETIME GROUP LIMITED COMPETITORS

Leading Chinese AI Start-ups Focusing on Facial or Identity Recognition Solutions	Year Founded	Core Technologies or Solutions	Key Customers	Major Investors	Raised Funds / Valuation (in US$)
Cloudwalk	2015	Facial recognition, voice recognition, public security	Agricultural Bank, Bank of China, China Construction Bank, China Merchants Bank	Shunwei Capital, Oriza Holdings, Puhua Capital, Bohai Capital Holding Co., China Reform Fund Management, Guangdong Technology Financial Group	509 million vs. 3.25 billion
Yitu Technology	2012	Facial recognition, public security, traffic management, medical imaging, intelligent terminal	China Merchants Bank, Huawei, Shanghai Pudong Development Bank	Sequoia, Banyan, Yunfeng, Hillhouse, Zhen, China Industrial, ICBC, Shanghai Pudong DB	416 million/ vs. 2.2 billion
Megvii Technology (Face++)	2011	Facial recognition, identity verification, video detection, public security	Alibaba, Huawei, Lenovo, Foxconn, Xiaomi, CITIC Bank, Bank of Beijing, public security bureaus, Fresh Your Life	Foxconn, Sunshine, State-Owned Assets Venture Investment, Ant Financial, Russia-China Investment, SK, Alibaba, Boyu	607 million vs. 2 billion
Mobvoi	2012	Voice recognition, natural language processing, wearables, audio, automobile	Volkswagen	ZhenFund, Sequoia Capital China, SIG China, Google, Volkswagen	253 million vs. undisclosed

Source: Compiled by case authors with information from “China AI Top 50,” China Money Network, September 2018, accessed January 12, 2019, https://assets.chinamoneynetwork.com/wp-content/uploads/20180921201850/China-AI-Top-50-2018-EN1.pdf; “Fundraising Activities,” CloudWalk Technology, Crunchbase, accessed January 11, 2019; “Fundraising Activities,” Yitu Technology, Crunchbase, accessed January 11, 2019; “Fundraising Activities,” Megvii Technology, Crunchbase, accessed January 11, 2019; “Fundraising Activities,” Mobvoi, Crunchbase, accessed January 11, 2019: “Our Products [in Chinese],” CloudWalk Technology, accessed January 11, 2019, www.cloudwalk.cn; “Our Products [in Chinese],” Yitu Technology, accessed January 11, 2019, www.yitutech.com; “Our Products [in Chinese],” Megvii Technology, accessed January 11, 2019, www.megvii.com; “Our Products [in Chinese],” CloudWalk Technology.

EXHIBIT 4: (*Continued*)

Leading Chinese Technology Companies with Artificial Intelligence Initiatives

Company	Business Focus	Artificial Intelligence Focus	Year Founded	Annual R&D Budget (US$ billion)	Company Valuation (US$ billion)	Listing or Financing
Alibaba	E-commerce, payments	Search, shopping recommendations, data analystics, image analysis, speech recognition, artificial intelligence speaker	1999	1.82	357	NYSE, HKSE
Tencent	Gaming, payments	WeChat assist, game playing, content recommendation, machine translation	1998	3.65	380	HKSE
Baidu	Internet search, advertising	Self-driving, speech recognition, voice assist, text input improvement, user recommendations, video generation, advertising	2000	2.29	162	HKSE
Meituan Dianping	Food delivery	Intelligent Delivery Dispatching	2010	1.12	32	HKSE
NetEase	Gaming, music and content	Gaming (e.g., augmented reality and role-playing game enhancement)	1997	1.23	237	NASDAQ
Bytedance	Tic-tok and toutiao business-to-business artificial intelligence video distribution	Video aggregation, editing	2012	NA	75	VC backed
Xiaomi	Cell phone design, distribution	Voice recognition, Internet of Things applications, smart home, mobile phone personal assistant	2010	0.91		HKSE
JD.Com	E-commerce	Voice recognition, chat service, advertising optimization, personalized recommendation, stock-keeping unit selection	1998	1.77	22	NASDAQ
Didi Chuxing	Ride hailing	driver routing and scheduling Smart transportation in co-operation with municipal traffic authorities	2012	NA	56	VC backed

Note: NYSE = New York Stock Exchange; HKSE = Hong Kong Stock Exchange; NASDAQ = US National Association of Securities Dealers Automatic Quotation Exchange; NA = not available.

Source: Alibaba Group Holding, "Annual and Transition Report (foreign private issuer) filed with the United States Securities and Exchange Commission (Form 20-F)," June 5, 2019, accessed April 23, 2020, https://otp.investis.com/clients/us/alibaba/SEC/sec-show.aspx?FilingId=12879202&Cik=0001577552&Type=PDF&hasPdf=1; Tencent Holdings Limited, "2018 Annual Report," March 21, 2019, accessed April 23, 2020, http://cdc-tencent-com-1258344706.image.myqcloud.com/storage/uploads/2019/11/09/da62661e976ea6cf64551dc5cdf079ea.pdf; Baidu Inc.; "Annual and Transition Report (foreign private issuer) filed with the United States Securities and Exchange Commission (Form 20-F)," March 15, 2019, accessed April 23, 2020, http://ir.baidu.com/static-files/4ce88b07-60fe-4561-9cc9-2b0e0ec9dfd6; Meituan Dianping, *Annual Report 2018*, April 11, 2019, accessed April 23, 2020, http://meituan.todayir.com/attachment/2019041121050100033461369_en.pdf; Netease, Inc., "Annual and Transition Report (foreign private issuer) filed with the United States Securities and Exchange Commission (Form 20-F)," April 26, 2019, accessed April 23, 2020, http://ir.netease.com/static-files/ed2a1743-a797-43b7-a81f-7cfaf40a0867; Bytedance, "About Us," Bytedance, accessed April 23, 2020, /www.bytedance.com/en/; Xiaomi Corporation, *2018 Annual Report,* April 8, 2019, accessed April 23, 2020, http://cnbj1.fds.api.xiaomi.com/company/results/en-us/2018%20AR.pdf; JD.com, "Annual and Transition Report (foreign private issuer) filed with the United States Securities and Exchange Commission (Form 20-F)," April 15, 2019, accessed April 25, 2020, http://ir.jd.com/static-files/d4d1ee39-164d-4adb-9805-39f105d91eae; Didi Chuxing, "About Us," accessed April 23, 2020, www.didiglobal.com/about-didi/about-us; Cai Fangyu, "Chinese Gaming Giant NetEase Leverages AI to Create 3D Game Characters from Selfies," Synced, accessed January 16, 2020, https://syncedreview.com/2019/09/10/chinese-gaming-giant-netease-leverages-ai-to-create-3d-game-characters-from-selfies/; Sam Byford, "TikTok Owner Bytedance Is Now the World's Most Valuable Startup," The Verge, October 26, 2018, accessed January 15, 2020, www.theverge.com/2018/10/26/18026250/bytedance-china-tiktok-valuation-highest-toutiao; Sarah Dai, "China's Biggest Ride-Hailing Platform Didi Now Wants to Help Cities Solve Traffic Jams," *South China Morning Post*, July 10, 2018, accessed January 15, 2020, www.scmp.com/tech/china-tech/article/2154027/chinas-biggest-ride-hailing-platform-wants-crunch-its-data-improve; CNBC, "China's Ride-Hailing App Didi Gets $500 Million Funding from the Parent of Booking.com," July 17, 2018.

EXHIBIT 4: (*Continued*)

Leading US Technology Companies with Artificial Intelligence Initiatives

Company	Areas of Artificial Intelligence Focus	Notable Applications	Investment in Artificial Intelligence Acquisitions, 2006–17 (in US$ Million)	Artificial Intelligence Patents, 2009–2017	Company Valuation (in US$ Billion)
Google LLC.	Natural language search, image recognition, machine learning	Google Assistant, Cloud Auto ML, DeepMind, TensorFlow	3,900	295	737.59
Amazon.com, Inc.	Natural language processing, automatic speech recognition, shipping prediction, voice recognition, image analysis	Alexa, Polly, Rekognition, Comprehend, Lex	871	75	802.18
Facebook, Inc.	Natural language processing, image recognition, facial recognition	DeepText	60	76	413.85
Apple Inc.	Facial recognition, voice recognition	Siri, FaceID	786	23	720.3
Microsoft Corporation	Machine learning, virtual assistant	Cortana	690	268	794.53

Source: Oliver Krauth, "The 10 Tech Companies that Have Invested the Most Money in AI," TechRepublic, January 12, 2018, accessed January 12, 2019, www.techrepublic.com/article/the-10-tech-companies-that-have-invested-the-most-money-in-ai; "The Race for AI: Google, Intel, Apple in a Rush to Grab Artificial Intelligence Startups," CB Insights, February 27, 2018, accessed January 12, 2019, www.cbinsights.com/research/top-acquirers-ai-startups-ma-timeline; "Artificial Intelligence," Index by TNW, accessed January 12, 2019, https://index.co/market/artificial-intelligence/acquisitions; Jenny Scribani, "These US Tech Giants Have the Most AI-Related Patents," World Economic Forum, September 17, 2018, accessed January 12, 2019, www.weforum.org/agenda/2018/09/the-ai-mazing-patent-race; Bloomberg.

EXHIBIT 5: CLOUDWALK TECHNOLOGY CO. LTD.

Comparison of CloudWalk Technology and SenseTime Group Limited

Item	CloudWalk	SenseTime
Year Founded	2015	2014
Headquarters	Guangzhou	Beijing
Other Offices	Beijing, Chengdu, Chongqing, Shanghai, Tianjin, Xi'an	Chengdu, Hangzhou, Hong Kong, Kyoto, Shenzhen, Singapore, Tokyo
Total External Financing Raised (in US$ Billion)	0.24	2.87
2018 Post-Money Valuation (in US$ Billion)	3.60	7.60
Investors	Chinese investors including Bohai, China Reform, Galaxy, Guangdong Technology, Guocheng Oriza, Puhua, Sensegain, Shenzhen Qianhai, Shunwei, Wangtai, and YueXiu	Global investors include Alpha Intelligence, Fidelity, Glade Brook, IDG, Qualcomm, Singtel, Softbank, and Temasak, and Chinese investors including Alibaba, Bank of China, Huaxing Fund, Silver Lake, Tiger Global Management, Hopu Investment Management
Description	Develops an artificial intelligence facial recognition technology designed for financial, public security and aviation sectors in China. The company's products include facial recognition terminals, facial scanning door entry and infrared binoculars scanning machines. It also develops big-data platforms for public security to collect and recognize airline passengers and their ticket information, and a facial-recognition platform that connects with data base from the police department.	Provides artificial intelligence solutions used in computer vision and visual technology. The company specializes in developing artificial intelligence driven facial recognition platforms and deep learning systems used in smart city development, mobile security, automobiles, finance and education, aiming to create artificial intelligence technologies that positively contribute to economies, society and humanity.

EXHIBIT 5: (*Continued*)

Business Model Canvas

Key Partners
- Companies providing artificial intelligence and information technology solutions to the customer segments
- Strategic investors, including central government and provincial funds
- China National Development and Reform Commission (artificial intelligence standards setting)
- Chinese Academy of Sciences
- Universities in mainland China

Key Activities
- Develop artificial intelligence solutions from operating system to applications
- Research and development in face, human action, voice, pedestrian, vehicle and document (eg., bank card) recognition
- Research and development in natural language processing and human-machine conversation in Chinese
- Risk assessment technology

Key Resources
- Highly trained specialists in designing artificial intelligence foundation platform and artificial intelligence application platform, chip platform and Software Development Kits (SDKs)

Value Proposition
- Provide customers with custom made intelligent solution for different contexts
- Provide solutions with core proprietary technologies -- not US open standard

Customer Relationships
- Customer service hotline
- Artificial intelligence open platform support email
- Partnership development email
- Direct sale of SDKs
- Consulting / partnering to providers of artificial intelligence and information technology

Channels
- Potential customers submit enquiries via website to indicate area of interest
- Offices in ten Chinese cities: Beijing, Chengdu, Chongqing, Guangzhou, Nanjing, Shanghai, Suzhou , Tianjin, Urumqi, Xian

Customer Segments
- Finance
- Public security
- Airport security
- Universities
- Retail

Cost Structure
- Human resources costs for research and development Computing hardware amortization
- Sales force

Revenue Streams
- Total artificial intelligence solution sales to customers within each segment
- Revenue sharing of artificial intelligence / information technology solution providing partners in offering services to customer segments
- SDK sales

Source: "Cloudwalk Technology Private Company Profile," Pitchbook Database, accessed December 12, 2019; "SenseTime Private Company Profile," Pitchbook Database, accessed January 22, 2020; Alexander Osterwalder, "A Better Way to Think about Your Business Model," *Harvard Business Review*, May 6, 2013, accessed September 26, 2019, https://hbr.org/2013/05/a-better-way-to-think-about-yo; "Contact Platform [in Chinese]," CloudWalk Technologies, accessed January 19, 2020, https://ai.cloudwalk.cn/cloudwalk/#/about; Iris Deng, "This State-Backed AI Unicorn Has Helped Chinese Police Arrest 10,000 Criminals," *South China Morning Post*, March 28, 2019.

Chapter 11

Redhill Capital: Strategy in a Pandemic

Introduction

Financing is critical for a company taking innovation to market. The money can be generated from operations or asset sales, personal funds, friends and family, angel capital, supplier and buyer credit, commercial bank loans, and public equity and debt. VC, however, is a unique institutional source of equity risk capital for new ventures. The ventures that turn to VC need more funds than they themselves, family or friends can provide. The ventures are not mature enough and their project structures are not safe enough to attract bank debt. Banks are traditionally interested in lending against collateral. They want near-certainty of repayment on time and in full. The ventures using VC are too young to approach public markets. The ventures may be able to tap angel funds, but angels are hard to find and typically do not have much money to invest. The figure on the next page shows venture capital relative to alternative sources of finance in two-dimensional investment stage-risk space.

Stages of Development, Risk and Sources of Finance

The vast majority of start-ups — in China and in the rest of the world — are not eligible for VC financing. The VC wants a good chance of a multiple return on investment (2×, 3× even 10×), rather than a small

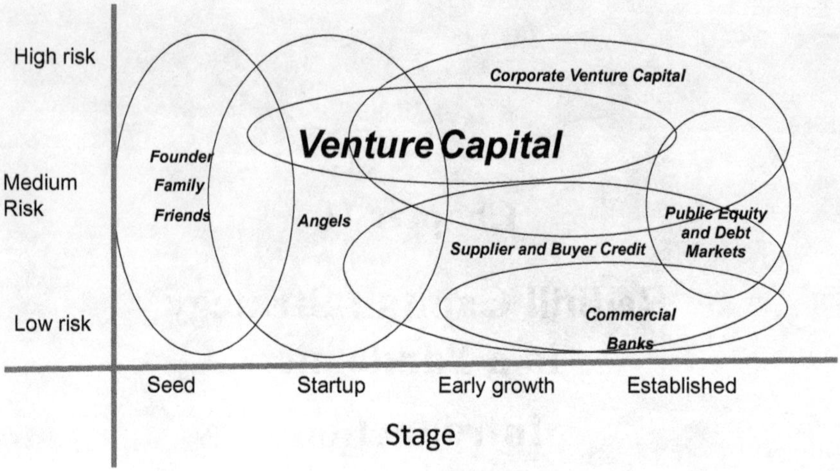

percentage return. So the innovation of the venture must be attractive and impactful enough to yield many times the initial investment, assuming it succeeds. The need for high returns drives VC investing toward very innovative young companies. There must be a good match: the venture's team must be attractive to the VC and the VC must be able to add value to the venture. Adding value is much more than simply investing money: the VC's monitoring, professionalism, industry expertise, introductions, etc. should make the investee more valuable than if the VC simply invested money. Finally, only investments above a minimum size — say ¥10 million — are worth the trouble for the VC. There are scale economies in employing trained financial specialists to run the fund, work with investors in the fund, and monitor the investee companies.[1]

Redhill Capital is a start-up VC firm. As a case concerning a start-up, Redhill Capital continues the theme of Chapters 9 and 10 where ofo and SenseTime, respectively, grew their companies to become unicorns — i.e., startups whose values each exceed US$1 billion — thanks to the VC financing. Chapter 11, however, shifts perspective from investee to investor. The protagonists in Redhill are Cherry Lu Qingchao, Redhill's

[1]For a discussion of the economic functions of VC in a Chinese context, an overview of the market and recommendations for improving it, see Lin William Cong, Charles M. C. Lee, Yuanyu Qu, and Tao Shen, "Financing Entrepreneurship and Innovation in China: A Public Policy Perspective", SSRN August 20, 2018. https://papers.ssrn.com/sol3/papers.cfm?abstract_id=3249278 (accessed April 25, 2021).

founding and managing partner and her co-founder and partner, Frank Su Zhenbo. Redhill is facing the coronavirus disease of 2019 (COVID-19) pandemic.

We wrote the case to illustrate how VC functions in China and give an example of how the interface between government policy and private markets works.

The case starts with the famous quote from the 20th century, Austro-Hungarian, economic historian, Karl Paul Polanyi:

> *The road to the free market was opened and kept open by an enormous increase in continuous, centrally organized and controlled interventionism.*[2]

Although easy to ignore, both in the West and in China, government-sponsored institutions have played a decisive role in setting and keeping the rules of the game necessary for social order and market operation. These rules include property rights, protection of capital, and contracting norms that allow capitalism to exist.[3] The intervention of the government to direct society in China, and to indirectly stimulate innovation, was discussed in Chapters 1 and 2. When the West invaded China, it was through government-sponsored policies of colonization and imperialism.

As Chapter 12 will discuss, government-sponsored central and commercial banking provides critical liquidity to the economy. Central banking is an SOE innovation developed in the West. China has largely adopted that innovation. Most recently, in the West, government involvement in central banking and commercial banking has been deepened through the great recession of 2008–2009[4] and the COVID-19 pandemic.

---

[2]Karl Polanyi, *The Great Transformation: The Political and Economic Origins of Our Time*, Beacon Press, Boston, 2002 (first published, 1944) p. 146. https://inctpped.ie.ufrj.br/spiderweb/pdf_4/Great_Transformation.pdf (accessed June 10, 2020). Polanyi is most famous for the Polanyi paradox, the idea that we know more than we can tell, because humans have a tremendous wealth of tacit knowledge that we cannot verbalize.

[3]This definition allows one to characterize China today as capitalist. It also allowed some scholars to date the innovation of capitalism to the medieval middle east and China. See Jürgen Kocka, *Capitalism*, Princeton University Press, Princeton NJ., 2016, https://muse.jhu.edu/book/64498 (accessed April 23, 2021).

[4]Paul Kellogg, "Gods outside the Market: Central Banks, China and the Emergence of Neoliberal State Capitalism", *World Review of Political Economy* 8:1 (2017).

Finance is too important for any country to leave finance exclusively to *laissez faire.*

The innovation of VC as a set of financial institutions also shows how government policy shapes private markets, be they in the West or in China. Government decision makers — CPC members in China — set the rules of the VC game. The case shows how China copied the U.S. VC model. VC's rise in China, starting from zero in the 1980s, has been rapid and volatile. It has produced a market that, as the Redhill Capital case shows, has recently, sporadically, exceeded the U.S. market. Scholars have documented this rise, and its macroeconomic Granger-causes[5]: GDP and export growth, monetary expansion, increased patenting, and roller-coaster stock market performance.[6]

The rise of VC in China to global leadership has led to considerable attention among instructors and case writers in international business and finance. Some cases provide background information about the market.[7] Others look at investees seeking VC funds, allowing students to take roles of VCs or ventures seeking VC funds.[8] But recent cases on start-up VCs are rare.[9]

Redhill Capital is focused on early stage medical technologies and biotechnology investment in the Greater Bay Area of Guangdong Province in Southeast China. As Chapter 2 mentioned, med- and biotech are also are high on the priority list of technologies the CPC desires to develop in

---

[5]Grainger causation involves the ability to forecast an outcome in a time-series regression from previous realizations of a (set of) variable(s).

[6]Ning Yixi, Xu Gubo and Long Ziwu, "What Drives the Venture Capital Investments in China?", *Chinese Management Studies* 13:3 (2019).

[7]Wee Kiat Lim and Jeremy Chen, "China's Venture Capital and Tech Startup Landscape", Nanyang Technical University Asian Business Case Center, Harvard Business Publishing, 2016.

[8]Jeremy B. Dann, Katherine Bennett, Andrew Ogden, "Xiaomi: Designing an Ecosystem For the 'Internet of Things'", Harvard Business Publishing, July 2017; Vincent Chang, Liman Zhao, S. Ramakrishna Velamur, "Chasm Security: Facing the Technology Startup's Dilemmas (A) (B) and (C)", CEIBS Harvard Business Publishing, August 2020. For a disguised simulation exercise involving social enterprise issues, see Byron Lee and Liman Zhao, "Smart Health (A) and (B): Negotiation with a Social Purpose", CEIBS, Harvard Business Publishing, 2020.

[9]A popular exception, giving the viewpoint of an SOE (government backed fund manager) VC confronting rapid changes, is Paul A. Gompers, Shaohui Chen, Jessie Lin, Shelley Ling, "Shenzhen Capital Group", Harvard Business Publishing, 2010.

China. In the 14th Five-Year Plan, the CPC ranks life and health as #4, brain science as #5 and biological breeding as #6, just after AI (#1), quantum information (#2) and integrated circuits (#3).[10] The official prioritizing is helpful for a VC, but the reader should note that Cherry Lu, Frank Su and their company are private: they do not act as conduits of CPC directives.

Med- and Bio-Tech, *Shanzhai* and BGI

In the last chapter, we spoke of the openness of AI research environments when discussing SenseTime. Although medical and bio-technology typically can support highly defensible patents and are not known for openness of IP, there are aspects of the Chinese industry, especially in Shenzhen, that break the Western norms with a spirit better known in the electronics industry as *shanzhai.*[11]

We introduced *shanzhai* in Chapter 3. *Shanzhai* is a copycat, "Robin Hood" ethos. Fast, fun, nimble, flexible, open, incrementally innovative, with rapid design, prototyping, and production, enabled by cooperation between suppliers, buyers, designers, and production units in a shifting, informal supply network. *Shanzhai* brings to mind the shifting platforms of Haier's *rendanheyi* in Chapter 7. And one can use it to describe the largest genomics sequencing company in the world, the Shenzhen-based BGI.

Only 18 years have gone by since the sequencing of the human genome. It was a massive international project, that lasted over a decade, received funding from over a dozen countries and employing thousands of expert researchers all with one objective: determining the base pairs that make up human DNA and mapping all genes in the human genome. In 2003, ahead of schedule and under budget, the global project was completed.

---

[10] AI is the first technology mentioned in the 14th Five-Year Plan. "Proposals of the Central Committee of the Communist Party of China on the formulation of the 14th Five-Year Plan and the 2035-year long-term goals", [中共中央關於制定十四五規劃和二〇三五年遠景目標的建議], The People's Net, November 4, 2020. Section 3 Clause 7.

[11] Hallam Stevens, "Starting Up Biology in China: Performances of Life at BGI", Osiris University of Chicago Press, 33:1 (2018). https://www.journals.uchicago.edu/doi/10.1086/699235?mobileUi=0 (accessed September 21, 2020).

One of the teams in the project was from the Chinese Academy of Sciences Institute of Genetics. After the project ended, the team members left their government positions to start their own company Beijing Genomics Institute or BGI.[12] But as the innovative, regulatory and meteorological climates of Shenzhen proved more attractive than Beijing, the team moved south, retaining their acronym, BGI. They entered a disruptive space in global genetic research: outsourced sequencing. Using Illumina sequencers,[13] the painstaking work of sequencing genes was becoming less expensive[14] but BGI radically cut costs, made a business of it and supplied highly efficient, accurate sequencing services to researchers throughout the world, globalizing the research supply chain.

BGI receives biological samples from the client, extracts the genetic material from the sample, reproduces it millions of times, prepares the sample, feed the Illumina sequencers, analyzes the output and sends the digital sequences back to the client. Depending on the project, BGI received for its services either cash or academic credit or a combination of both. Co-publishing credit in *Science*[15] or *Nature*[16] for example, might lead BGI to provide the sequencing services for free. As BGI becomes more efficient, the degree to which it becomes a more senior partner in research teams increases. And BGI makes a show of its openness. If you visit their facility, you can look through glass windows into their labs — row after row of DNA-sequencing machines attended to by trained researchers and robots. BGI supports a concept of open source of gene sequencing data, allowing access to its big data bioinformatics resource center. It opens to the world the ability to read, write, and store massive biological resources. BGI runs, in cooperation with Oxford University

---

[12]BGI, "Whole Genome Sequencing", BGI [华大] Website: https://www.bgi.com/us/sequencing-services/plant-animal-microbial-dna-sequencing/plant-animal-and-microbe-whole-genome-resequencing/ (accessed December 17, 2021).

[13]Illumina was a company started in 1998 to make machines to sequence DNA. See Illumina Website: https://www.illumina.com (accessed April 25, 2021).

[14]Matthew Herper, "Flatley's Law: The Company Speeding A Genetic Revolution", *Forbes*, Aug 20, 2014. https://www.forbes.com/sites/matthewherper/2014/08/20/flatleys-law-how-one-company-became-the-force-behind-medicines-genetic-revolution/#77e6f84076bd (accessed April 25, 2021).

[15]*Science* is a leading weekly magazine first published in 1880. See *Science* Website: https://www.sciencemag.org/journals (accessed April 25, 2021).

[16]*Nature* is "… the leading international weekly journal of science first published in 1869". See "About Us", *Nature* Website: https://www.nature.com (accessed April 25, 2021).

Press, a rapid research online peer reviewed journal, *Gigascience Journal*, whose principles are:

> to make all articles freely and permanently accessible online immediately upon publication, without subscription charges or registration barriers. All software is published under Open Source Initiative (OSI)-approved open source licences, and supporting data presented under a public domain.[17]

Shanzhai in genetics is fast, fun, nimble, flexible and open. And BGI's logo? The DNA molecule: a symbol of both life and the copy; copying is necessary for life and for pursuing life itself.[18]

The Issues in Redhill Capital

Readers take the role of Cherry Lu and Frank Su in May 2020 while they review the portfolio companies in Redhill's ¥505 million first fund. Redhill is also in the midst of raising a second RMB onshore fund and a first United States dollar offshore fund, both of similar size to its first RMB fund. The plans of Redhill, however, are being impacted by the collapse of the Chinese VC market and the onset of the pandemic.

We researched the case in the early, uncertain, days of the pandemic when China seemed most at risk from COVID-19. In retrospect, China was far less impacted by the pandemic than the rest of the world. The world, China, and Redhill have changed and students analyzing the case must think through the changes that its top management faces.

---

[17] *Gigascience*: https://academic.oup.com/gigascience (accessed April 25, 2021).

[18] Hallam Stevens, "Starting up Biology in China: Performances of Life at BGI", Osiris University of Chicago Press, 33:1 (2018), 106. https://www.journals.uchicago.edu/doi/10.1086/699235?mobileUi=0 (accessed September 21, 2020).

REDHILL CAPITAL: STRATEGY IN A PANDEMIC

Kevin Au and Hugh Thomas wrote this case solely to provide material for class discussion. The authors do not intend to illustrate either effective or ineffective handling of a managerial situation.

> The road to the free market was opened and kept open by an enormous increase in continuous, centrally organized and controlled interventionism.
>
> Karl Paul Polanyi[1]

Cherry Lu Qinchao, Founding and Managing Partner of Redhill Capital (Redhill), looked from the window of her office on the 35th floor of the Chow Tai Fook Financial Center in the Pearl River New City district towards the old center of Guangzhou. It was late May 2020. The year was developing differently from what she, her partner Frank Su Zhenbo, their eleven employees at their two year-old VC firm, their fund's limited partners (LPs) and investees, China, and the world had expected. Earlier that year, the genome of a new virus, Severe Acute Respiratory Syndrome

[1]Karl Polanyi, *The Great Transformation: The Political and Economic Origins of Our Time* Beacon Press, Boston, 2002 (first published, 1944) page 146, accessed June 10, 2020, https://inctpped.ie.ufrj.br/spiderweb/pdf_4/Great_Transformation.pdf.

Coronavirus 2 (SARS-CoV-2), had been sequenced, identifying the source of rapidly spreading outbreaks of flu-like pneumonia first diagnosed in Wuhan, Hubei. Since then, millions of people from every corner of the world had contracted COVID-19. Hundreds of thousands had died. Countries had locked down. The world had plunged into recession. Lu and Su considered how their start-up, biotechnology- and medical technology-themed, VC company should adjust its strategy to survive the crisis and take advantage of opportunities in the rapidly changing world.

VENTURE CAPITAL

VC was patient, professionally managed, equity, risk capital, invested in recently-formed, potentially high-growth, companies. Risk capital was as old as capital itself, but the modern VC industry was started in 1946 in the United States, when Massachusetts Institute of Technology (MIT) President Karl Compton and Harvard University Professor, General George Doriot joined with local business leaders to form the publicly listed fund, American Research and Development (ARD), to commercialize government-funded military technologies that had been developed at MIT during World War II.[2] The innovative elements ARD combined in its new business model were high tech, blind, investment pooling. Money was ***pooled*** into a fund from otherwise unrelated investors. The investors were largely ***blind*** to the investees — i.e., the fund manager, legally, was given control over the investments. And ARD said — but was not legally required to — pursue an investment strategy of buying substantial equity stakes in small startup ***high technology and other high growth potential*** companies.[3]

By the late 1970s, the preferred vehicle for VC investment became the limited partnership[4] (see Exhibit 1). Most fund investments failed to live up to the VC firm's hopes, but even if only one in 10 investment was highly successful, the success could offset lackluster performance from the all others, thus making the entire fund successful.[5]

---

[2]Paul Gompers and Josh Lerner, "The venture capital revolution", *Journal of Economic Perspectives*, Nashville 15:2, Spring 2001, pages 145–168.

[3]Spencer Ante *Creative Capital: George Doriot and the Birth of Venture Capital*, Boston, Harvard Business Press, 2008.

[4]Paul Gompers and Josh Lerner. *The Venture Capital Cycle*. MIT Press, 1999, pp. 7–9.

[5]ARD was a case in point: one investment, US$ 70,000 in the mini-computer start-up Digital Equipment Corporation (DEC) in 1957 made the difference between ARD's

Aggregate capital invested VC funds grew cyclically in the United States. Boom years when investors piled into VC funds were followed by bust years when new money dried up but on balance VC's role in the economy increased . By the end of 2019, the five largest publicly traded companies in the U.S. by market capitalization — Apple Inc., Microsoft Corporation, Alphabet Inc., Amazon.com Inc., and Facebook Inc. — all had been VC-backed, and 42 per cent of drugs recently approved by the United States Food and Drug Administration had originated with VC funding.[6] Moreover, the VC industry had become global.[7]

VENTURE CAPITAL IN CHINA

In 1978, the CPC began its *reform and opening up* policy to restructure its formerly centrally planned economy and to increase contacts with the rest of the world.[8] Over the next forty years, China's real GDP growth was over 7 per cent per year,[9] and China became the second largest economy in the world by GDP and the largest by real GDP.[10]

---

respectable 14.7 per cent annual return on investment and a sub-market 7.4 per cent had ARD not made the investment in DEC, a company that grew to dominate global mini-computing from the 1960s through the 1980s, Spencer Ante, *Creative Capital: George Doriot and the Birth of Venture Capital* Boston, Harvard Business Press, 2008.

[6]*North American Venture Capital Association 2020 Annual Report* PitchBook Data, Inc. 2020, Page 11, accessed May 29, 2020, https://nvca.org/wp-content/uploads/2020/03/NVCA-2020-Yearbook.pdf.

[7]Robyn Klingler-Vidra, *The Venture Capital State: The Silicon Valley Model in East Asia*, Cornell University Press, Ithaca, 2018.

[8]CPC Central Committee "The Report of the Third Plenum of the 18th Party Congress" December 22, 1978, accessed June 24, 2020, http://cpc.people.com.cn/GB/64162/64168/64563/65371/4441902.html.

[9]The growth rates from the early 1950s to 2018 are based on the US Federal Reserve data base FRED. Real growth rates subtract off the inflation rate. Typically, GDP growth uses nominal, not real growth. Inflation varies from year to year and country to country but using USD, one could add roughly 3 per cent to the numbers quoted to get nominal GDP growth.

[10]International Monetary Fund, "World Economic Outlook Database" October 11, 2019 accessed 31 March, 2020, https://www.imf.org/en/Publications/SPROLLs/world-economic-outlook-databases#sort=percent40imfdatepercent20descending.

Financial reform was part of the reform and opening up. China's state-owned, bank-led, financial system was inefficient and fragile,[11] so the Chinese government encouraged the development of public capital markets and independent financial institutions, among them, VC.[12] In March 1985, the Central Committee of the CPC decided to expand the technology market and change the situation in which too many research institutions were separated from enterprises, research, design, education, and production. The intention was to support high technology with rapidly evolving, high risk endeavors and VC.[13]

The direction was clear; however, in 1985, there was neither the institutional infrastructure nor the expertise for VC. Many years were required. China would have to wait five years for the Shanghai Stock Exchange to re-open,[14] nine years before a company law came into force[15] and 17 years before the large state-owned banks began to list their shares,

---

[11] See for example Carl Walter and Fraser Howie, *Red Capitalism: The Fragile Financial Foundation of China's Extraordinary Rise*, Wiley, Singapore, March 6, 2012.

[12] Jun Li, "Government-Backed Venture Capital as a Science, Technology and Innovation Policy Instrument: A Chinese Perspective", *STI Policy Review* 7:1, 2016, accessed March 31, 2020, https://www.researchgate.net/profile/Jun_Li184/publication/303944715_Government-backed_venture_capital_as_a_science_technology_and_innovation_STI_policy_instrument_A_Chinese_perspective/links/575fdc2708ae9a9c9560fe77/Government-backed-venture-capital-as-a-science-technology-and-innovation-STI-policy-instrument-A-Chinese-perspective.pdf; Jun Wen Xiu-yun Yang, Gen-fu Feng, Bo Sui, Chun-ping Chang, "The comovement between venture capital and innovation in China: what are the implications?", *Quality and Quantity* 51:6 (November 2017); Richard Kozul-Wright and Daniel Poon, "Learning from China's Industrial Strategy", *Project Syndicate,* Prague, April 28, 2017.

[13] "Decision" is an understatement, as it was co-published with over 40 separate directives, and impacted over 50 current cases at the national government level and was a point of departure for similar "decisions" at regional and local levels. See CPC Central Committee, "Decision of the Central Committee of the Communist Party of China on the Reform of the Science and Technology System" March 13, 1985 listed on Peking University *Love of Law has a Future,* accessed June 22, 2020, http://www.pkulaw.cn/fulltext_form.aspx?Gid=2323.

[14] Shanghai Stock Exchange, "History and Development", *SSE Website: About,* accessed June 20, 2020, http://english.sse.com.cn/aboutsse/overview/.

[15] Chang Wang, *Inside China's legal system,* Nathan Maddison, Oxford, 2013.

marking the beginning of the commercialization of lending markets.[16] And it was only in 2009 and 2019, respectively, that ChiNext in Shenzhen and the Science and Technology Innovation Board (STAR) Market in Shanghai were set up as growth enterprise stock exchanges modeled on the United States' Nasdaq Stock Market to provide initial public offering (IPO) exits for VC firms.[17]

In 1986, the Chinese State Science and Technology Commission and the Ministry of Finance co-founded China's first VC company, the China New Technology Venture Investment Corporation (CNTVIC). CNTVIC was followed by a plethora of regional and local government copies of CNTVIC. They were mainly commercial failures, plagued by inexperience in high technology investment, lack of property rights and relevant laws, and the fatal attraction of real estate and finance schemes.[18] Yet even as CNTVIC went bankrupt in 1997, a growing number of commercially viable VCs were ushering in the second VC phase.[19]

Legal reforms in the late 1990s clarified the status of VC.[20] De-nationalization of large numbers of SOEs released millions of employees as state planning was replaced by the market economy.[21] Waves of Chinese returned after studies abroad, and entry of China into the WTO in

---

[16]Hugh Thomas, "The Bank of China Hong Kong 's Initial Public Offering" *Journal of Financial Education* 30, pp. 87–111, 2004.

[17]Chinext was established at the Shenzhen Stock Exchange in 2009 "Shenzhen Stock Exchange Chinext Market Overview" *Hong Kong Exchange Website,* Accessed June 24, 2020, https://www.hkex.com.hk/Mutual-Market/Stock-Connect/Getting-Started/Information-Booklet-and-FAQ/ChiNext-Market-Overview?sc_lang=en and a decade later the Sci-Tech Innovation Board (STAR Market) was established at the Shanghai Stock Exchange. Shanghai Stock Exchange, "SSE Star Market Debuts", *News Release* June 13, 2019, accessed July 22, 2020.

[18]Jo-Ann Suchard, "The Chinese Private Equity Market and the Impact of Foreign Venture Capitalists", *The World Scientific Reference on Entrepreneurship (in Four Volumes)* Chapter 11.

[19]Steven White, Jian Gao and Wei Zhang, "China's venture capital industry: Institutional trajectories and system structure" INSEAD Working Paper, International Conference on Financial Systems, Corporate Investment in Innovation and Venture Capital, Brussels, November, 2002, accessed June 22, 2020, https://flora.insead.edu/fichiersti_wp/inseadwp2002/2002-122.pdf.

[20]*Ibid.*, page 25.

[21]National People's Congress, "The "Ninth Five-Year Plan" of the National Economic and Social Development of the People's Republic of China and the Outline of the 2010 Vision",

2001 confirmed that 20-year old reform and opening up policy was permanent.[22] Non-local VC firms and private equity (PE) companies[23] took advantage of the opportunities. Starting with IDG (a VC firm based in Boston, United States) in 1992,[24] a steady stream of non-Chinese VCs and PEs, including Barings LLC, Draper Laboratory, Softbank Group Corp and Warburg Pincus LLC, structured the mainland Chinese investments of their LPs as offshore US dollar JVs whose equity could be transferred in offshore industry sales or IPOs (in foreign exchanges such as the Nasdaq Stock Exchange).[25] These VC firms successfully financed start-ups who flipped business models to China, which was referred to as having *copied to China*, from Western countries. Examples of these start-ups included the search engine Baidu, the Internet portal Sina.com, the email and news service Sohu, and the gaming company NetEase.[26] Following the dot-com

---

March 19, 1996, accessed June 24, 2020, http://www.npc.gov.cn/wxzl/gongbao/2001-01/02/content_5003506.htm.

[22] David Zweig, "Competing for talent: China's strategies to reverse the brain drain" *International Labour Review*, Geneva 145: 1/2, 2006, pp. 65–90. accessed December 17, 2021, https://www.researchgate.net/publication/229519904_Competing_for_talent_China%27s_strategies_to_reverse_the_brain_drain.

[23] A PE firm is like a VC, setting up successive limited partnership funds to make blind (to the pooled LPs) investments in companies, but while VCs typically focus on early, growth or late stage newly formed companies, PEs focus on leveraged buyouts, distressed capital, growth capital, mezzanine capital and other opportunities. The "private" of private equity refers to equity investments that are not in publicly traded equity markets and, hence are "private" equity. Because VC can be considered a type of "private" equity investments many consider VC to be a subset of PE. Note that the blind nature of the LP agreements with the fund allow a PE fund legally to invest in VC opportunities and vice versa. However making such investments could, if they proved unsuccessful, tarnish the VC's reputation, hindering his or her ability to enter the markets for subsequent funds. See Josh Lerner, Felda Hardymon and Ann Leamon, *Venture Capital and Private Equity: a casebook*, 5th edition, Wiley, New York, 2012.

[24] IDG Capital "About Us" https://www.idgcapital.com.

[25] Mark Humphery-Jenner and Jo-Ann Suchard, "Foreign venture capitalists and the internationalization of entrepreneurial companies: Evidence from China", *Journal of International Business Studies,* 44, 607–621, show that the presence of a foreign VC among the investors in a Chinese company that received VC or PE investment and is recorded in the *ChinaVentures* database, if the investee IPOs, reduces the likelihood of a domestic IPO (i.e., increases the likelihood of an international IPO).

[26] Jame DiBiasio, "PRC Internet IPO pipeline emerges", *Emerging Markets Week* New York, 7: 29, July 19, 1999; Leslie Chang, "Chinese Internet Portals Are Set to List On

bust of 2001, local Chinese, private, *renminbi*[27] (RMB) VC firms began to challenge the foreign players.

In 2009 the ChiNext Market opened after 10 years of planning, providing VC with a new RMB IPO exit alternative. RMB liquidity released by the People's Bank of China (PBOC) to mitigate the effects of the 2008 global financial crisis flowed into new, local, private VC funds. Confidence increased through mid-year 2010, with more funds chasing deals, before the ChiNext Market went into a correction, deflating the bubble.[28] The subsequent recovery ushered in an unprecedented VC boom.[29] Investor optimism, entrepreneurial acumen, increasing innovation, regulatory reform, and government support[30] led China's share of global VC fundraising to displace the traditional front-runner, the United States, in 2016 and 2017, before the Chinese VC boom slackened in 2018 and then steeply declined in 2019 (See Exhibit 2).

Internet, telecommunications and IT took up over half of Chinese VC deals, far exceeding biotechnology and healthcare.[31] According to Nisa Leung, VC industry pioneer and partner of Qiming Venture Capital, India was initially better placed than China to attract overseas players to biotechnology.[32] Yet in 2000, the number of VC investments in biotechnology and medical technology in China passed those in India and exceeded them for the next 20 years thanks to greater investment in medical

---

Nasdaq Market", *Wall Street Journal*, New York, NY. June 28, 2000; Robert Weisman, "Chinese IPO rockets in 1st trading day", *Knight Ridder Tribune Business News*, Washington, August 6, 2005.

[27]The Chinese yuan (¥) or *renminbi* (RMB) was the currency of China. As of the end of May, 2020, US$1.00 = ¥7.13.

[28]Mark Cannice and Ling Ding, "China Venture Capitalist Confidence Index", San Francisco, First Quarter 2011.

[29]Investment Web [ed] *Venture Capital — Private Equity* [in Chinese], "中国创投简史" (2017) 人民邮电出版社, People's Post Press, Beijing, 2017.

[30]Zhaojun Huang and Xuan Tian "China's Venture Capital Market" *The Handbook on China's Financial System*" Tsinghua University People's Bank of China School of Finance, July 22, 2019 accessed March 31, 2020, https://papers.ssrn.com/sol3/Papers.cfm?abstract_id=3423553;

[31]"Greater China Information Technology-Focused Private Equity & Venture Capital Assets under Management" Preqin Markets in Focus: Private Equity and Venture Capital in Greater China — China's Innovation Economy July 2019.

[32]Nisa Leung (梁頴宇), *Adventures: My days in China Venture Capital* "奇遇: 我在中國創投的日子". 巴士的報 (978-988-14485-1-4), 2016 [full cite] page 191.

research from both government and private funding.[33] Moreover, biotech and medical technology investors were encouraged by China's faster convergence to international IP norms than India's, despite India's earlier accession to the WTO in 1994.[34]

As the second decade of the 21 century drew to a close, the medical technology, biotechnology and healthcare ecosystem in China was maturing. Under cost pressures, major global pharmaceutical companies increasingly used foreign contract research organizations to handle research, clinical trials, and reporting. In this outsourcing of big pharma's supply chains, China enjoyed a comparative advantage.[35] A new generation of companies ushered in what Redhill called the era of *China Healthcare Innovation 3.0*. In the new era, Lu and Su targeted early stage companies with best-in-class strategy and cross-border innovation focus for their VC investments (see Exhibit 3). And good news for exits was coming from the 10-month old STAR Market. With an aggregate ¥1.3 trillion capitalization, STAR Market logged its 100th company listing in late April, 2020. High technology medical companies made up 14 of the listings, just behind software at 12 and ahead of semiconductors at 13 and AI at 12.[36]

LU, SU AND REDHILL

Lu was a native of Hubei province in China. In 1996, Lu graduated from the Tongji Medical College of Huazhong Science & Technology University in Wuhan with BSc in clinical medicine. After working for six years marketing medical equipment, Lu moved to Hong Kong to take an MBA at CUHK where she worked with a leading CUHK professor commercializing diabetes research. Lu then joined Sequoia Capital China where she spent the next decade as a VC pursuing opportunities in healthcare and biotechnology. During those years, Sequoia China, under

---

[33] Justin Chakma, Stephen M Sammut and Ajay Agrawal, "Life sciences venture capital in emerging markets", *Nature Biotechnology* 31: 3, March 2013.

[34] Christine Greenhalgh, "Science, technology, innovation and IP in India: new directions and prospects", *Economic Change and Restructuring* 49: 2–3, 2016, pp. 113–138.

[35] Laura Wood, "China Contract Research Organization (CRO) Industry Report 2017" *NASDAQ OMX's News Release Distribution Channel*, New York, October 23, 2017.

[36] Shanghai Stock Exchange, "SSE STAR Market Scores First Century of Listed Companies", *News Release*, April 29, 2020, accessed July 22, 2020.

Managing Partner Neil Shen, a graduate of Shanghai Jiaotong University in China and Yale University in the United States, became one of the most successful VC firms in China[37] investing in 49 of China's 209 unicorns.[38]

Lu became a partner in Sequoia Capital China investing funds in and developing several leading companies. Most notably, Jafron Biomedical was a blood purification company[39] and Shenzhen New Industries Biomedical Engineering Company was a researcher and manufacturer in clinical lab instruments and in vitro diagnostic reagents. Both companies were listed on the Shenzhen Stock Exchange.[40] Lu also invested in ARMO, a developer of pancreatic cancer therapy drugs based in California and listed on the Nasdaq Stock Exchange which was subsequently acquired by Eli Lilly and Company.[41] She also invested in Winner Medical, a medical dressing manufacturer, owning the consumer brand Purcotton and passed IPO review on the Shenzhen Stock Exchange. Two other notable investees of Lu were Shanghai Iray, a developer and manufacturer of X-ray components, which filed for an IPO on the Shanghai STAR Market[42] and Shenzhen XtalPi, a US-China AI based drug development company.[43]

---

[37] Tao Li, "Sequoia Capital China's Neil Shen tops the list of China venture capital investors according to CB Insights ranking", *South China Morning Post*, Hong Kong, April 3, 2019, page B3.

[38] A unicorn is a privately owned, recently formed, VC-backed company valued at more than US$ 1 billion. The unicorn count and ranking of Sequoia Capital China comes from Rupert Hoogewerf, "The Hurun Global Unicorn List 2019". Hoogewerf reports that China had the largest country share of the world's 494 unicorns and Sequoia Capital China worldwide rose was the greatest creator of unicorns.

[39] Jafron Website, accessed March 30, 2020, http://www.jafron.com/index.php?m=content&c=index&a=lists&catid=10.

[40] SNIBE website, accessed March 30, 2020, Chinese Internet Portals Are Set to List On Nasdaq Market, Pleasing Rivals. By Leslie Chang. *Wall Street Journal*, Eastern edition; New York, NY. 28 June 2000.

[41] Eli Lilly and Company 2018 annual report, accessed March 30, 2020, https://investor.lilly.com/static-files/9a86e5d8-705c-4315-a3b2-56bfc208d1ca.

[42] Iray website, accessed March 30, 2020, http://www.iraygroup.com/site/company?lang=EN.

[43] "US-China biotech startup XtalPi lands $15M from Google, Tencent and Sequoia Capital China", *Global Data Point*, January 25, 2018.

Lu also obtained an executive MBA degree from the Cheung Kong Graduate School of Business in Beijing. She developed her network among the companies, universities, research centers and incubators devoted to furthering bioscience and healthcare research development and commercialization. She had been highly successful at locating, investing in and guiding (through her appointments to the boards of directors of investee companies) a steady flow of bio- and med-tech enterprises. However, Lu felt she had reached her peak at Sequoia Capital China. As a partner, she enjoyed a comfortable salary,[44] but Sequoia Capital China was a VC firm that invested across the full spectrum of high growth potential companies while Lu was interested in early stage biotechnology and medical technology. She wanted to grow.[45] Therefore, in 2018, Lu left Sequoia Capital China to found Redhill and asked fellow Guangzhou native, Su, to join her as a co-founder.

Trained as both a medical doctor and a lawyer, Su worked for over four years at the Johnson & Johnson medical device division marketing to both the United States and China. He left Johnson & Johnson to co-found Techlink Medical, a surgical products company in Beijing, with ex-Johnson & Johnson colleagues and with angel capital from their former manager. After successfully launching and selling the company, he transferred his role from entrepreneur to VC investor. He worked for five years as a Managing Partner at Share Capital Medical, a VC firm based in Shenzhen, China. Su had extensive experience in developing startups into leading, publicly listed companies. Notable companies included Gentron Health, a companion diagnosis company listed on the Nasdaq Stock Market,[46] Medprin, a neuro-surgery company that filed for an IPO on the

---

[44]At top VC firms, associates typically make \$120,000 to \$150,000 per year; junior VCs make \$500,000 per year and general partners make in excess of \$1,000,000 per year. Gary Rivlin, *Becoming a Venture Capitalist*, Simon and Schuster, New York, 2019, p. 28.

[45]Emily Chang, *Brotopia: Breaking Up the Boys' Club of Silicon Valley*, Portfolio-Penguin Random House, New York, 2018. Chang, in her expose of sexual discrimination in Silicon Valley, notes that "Sequoia Capital did not hire a single female US investor in the firm's first 45 years", page 138. Sequoia Capital was founded in 1972.

[46]Gentron Health, *Form F-1 Registration Statement under the Securities Act of 1933: Genetron Holdings Limited*, October 11, 2019, accessed August 4, 2020, https://ir.genetronhealth.com/node/6401/html.

ChiNext Market[47] and TCRCure, a US-China based cell therapy company,[48] among over a dozen others.

Lu and Su were the only members of Redhill's investment committee. Lu focused on finance and human resources; Su headed post-management and compliance. Commenting on the division of tasks at Redhill, Lu stated that "if we had some LP or external advisors that liked gathering and other social activities ... Frank [Su] would be the right person to do that. I do not like that. He is good at this."

Su provided a summary of his essential social activities as a VC investor:

> I am more comfortable with social situations. I think that the networking is necessary for the VC. We are positioning ourselves as very unique in the early stage medical technology area. We need not only deep understanding in science and the healthcare industry, but also very good deal sourcing capability and a very good reputation and our reputation and chemistry with the [investee] company and our resources to add value to our portfolios are all very important. All that requires very strong connections with the industry. This does not mean that we just go for a dinner or useless gatherings. We will spend a lot of time very closely with academics. Like on oncology, I attend ASCO [the American Society for Clinical Oncology] conference every year in Chicago and also CSCO [Chinese Society of Clinical Oncology] conference in Xiamen [China] every year to meet with the academic and industry players there. Our team attends different meetings like AI, biotechnology, and cardiovascular intervention conferences regularly to keep up with the industry developments and expand our network. Actually, networking is more about building the connections there and building very professional mechanisms.

47 "About MEDPRIN", *Medprin Website*, accessed August 4, 2020.

48 "About us: on the way to curing cancer", *TCRCure Website* accessed August 4, 2020 http://en.tcrcure.com/ and "TCRCure Company Profile: Valuation & Investor" *Pitchbook*, accessed August 4, 2020, https://pitchbook.com/profiles/company/235287-73.

REDHILL RMB FUND 1: FUND RAISING AND LPS

Redhill's first task was raising commitments for RMB Fund 1, a seven year (extendable to nine years) limited partnership fund focused on early-stage deals. Fees payable by RMB Fund 1 to Redhill were 2 per cent per year of funds under management for the first seven years and 0 per cent per year for any extendable period. Carried interest was 20 per cent of all disbursements following repayment of the limited partnership's principal.

Lu mentioned that, had she and Su started Redhill two years earlier, they would have entered the China VC market at the peak, rather than during a down-turn. Nonetheless, fundraising for RMB Fund 1 proceeded smoothly. In July 2018, they did a first close of the fund and started to invest in deals. By early 2019, they had fully closed the fund, exceeding by ¥5 million their target of ¥500 million.

Redhill took pride in managing its LPs very carefully, identifying four different types of investors: (1) investors of significance (2) industry investors (3) financial investors and (4) government funds (see Exhibit 4).

Lu described the first type, investors of significance:

> Investors of significance including famous VCs or PEs or asset management companies like Sequoia China, Everbright, Wens Capital … are general funds or more focused on the growing stage or late capital, but we are early stage and healthcare focused. For them, we are a bit like a partnership …. They trust our experience and judgement on healthcare deals and ability on the deal sourcing and execution, so they prefer spending time with us discussing possible investment opportunities, the next round or the round after that …. They have their expectations besides financial return…. We are pre-A or A round focused. Maybe for, or after the B round we will help the portfolio companies to raise new money from investors like Sequoia China or Wens Capital or Everbright…. Early stage new investment in medical technology or biotech, costs a lot of money. Actually, those startup companies burn a lot of money before they have their revenue, so the partners for later stage investment are very important.

Industry investors were existing non-financial corporations in the same sector — i.e., healthcare — as Redhill was targeting. In RMB Fund I,

By-Health, China's biggest nutritional product company, entered as an LP. Su explained:

> ...these companies, besides financial return, also have industry considerations and investment requirements.... Given the China market dynamics where competition is increasing fiercely, ... a successful deal depends not only on a good technology, but also on how you manage execution and the resources and the capital market and so on. So this kind of LP can be a potential partner for us. [They] seldom *buy* a young company but they will *invest* in the young company. And when the young company has stable cash flow then they partner. ... Actually these companies ... are more open to [other alternatives beyond] whether the portfolio IPOs or merges. ... They can be very flexible for a business development strategy... like I can invest in you, I can help you develop the business and I can have some royalties here.

Financial investors were professionally managed funds that had no particular VC or industry expertise. A financial investor could be a fund of funds, a family office for a wealthy individual or a trust fund. "They normally have very good governance and can help us to manage our fund better, for example, on related transaction or DPI[49] strategy," explained Lu. "They are experienced and can see many different traps in governance. It helps."

Government funds were also keen to be LPs. Su was particularly enthusiastic about the Chinese city of Guangzhou:

> The local government funds are a bit like industry players. They are more focused on promoting the local economy.... China has over 200 local governments who have investment funds. Different government funds have different negotiating power. Guangzhou government funds welcome us because we are based in Guangzhou in the Greater Bay Area where they have very good medical schools and engineering schools — a bit like Boston 20 years ago.

---

[49]A DPI strategy is a strategy that affects the distributions to paid in capital ratio, calculated as (cumulative distributions)/(cumulative paid in capital). The DPI is a simple metric often used by LPs in evaluating VC and PE fund performance.

Su recognized the needs, strengths and weaknesses of government funds.

> We are very focused on financial returns. However, they are not.... They generally cannot tell which company is more promising, so they need a good VC [firm], a good general partner, to help them... They may invest in you but require you to invest in local companies with a multiple of the amount they invest. We can calculate how many local companies are in our pipeline.... and negotiate with them.... Some local government funds are very flexible. They say, "hey, you do not have to invest in local companies. But you need to contribute some influence in the local industry, ... to hold healthcare conferences, to help build our reputation and attract new startups here." ... Some local government funds require investment committee membership but it is our principle that there is no external investment committee member.... We will give them observation seats.... They can join the investment committee discussion, but they do not have voting rights.

REDHILL RMB FUND 1: INVESTEES

At the same time as Lu and Su were raising capital for RMB Fund 1, they and their growing team were researching potential investees. The strategy for RMB Fund 1 was to invest 70 per cent in medical technologies and 30 per cent in innovative pharmaceuticals and healthcare services. As Su noted:

> Most Chinese medical technology companies are very focused on the China market. Basically from 70 per cent to 90 per cent.... They have some overseas sales but they don't sell directly to the [overseas] hospitals. They sell to the dealers and distributors.... They focus on catching the China opportunity: that's enough.... It's a little bit like the U.S. market maybe 50 years ago. The U.S. companies did not start globalization until after World War II. Before that, they grew their local market.

In identifying investees, Redhill relied on its contacts, its top-down research, and four partners: He Weiwu, Zhang Mingdong, Wang Ping and

Sun Jianguo. All four were based both in the United States and in Asia and all four had worked with Lu and Xu prior to Redhill's founding. He Weiwu was an oncology, molecular biotechnologist with a PhD degree from Baylor College of Medicine and an MBA from Wharton Business School. Zhang Mingdong also a PhD from Baylor and did post-doctoral research at Harvard. He then worked for several years as a reviewer in clinical trials of cardio-vascular devices at the United States Food and Drug Administration. Wang Ping, a PhD from California Institute of Technology and a professor at the University of Southern California was an expert in wireless bio-engineering. And Sun Jianguo, a biomedical sciences PhD from Tufts University was a medical device entrepreneur who had founded Curative Medical, a manufacture of respirators that was acquired by the United States company ResMed.

By the end of 2019, RMB Fund 1 had invested in 13 companies. The average investment was ¥30 million (just under US$5 million), each representing an equity stake of 1 percent to 30 per cent of the investee company. Of the original ¥505 million only slightly more than 10 per cent remained uncommitted: essentially there was no dry powder[50] left. No exits had occurred; however, subsequent rounds of investments in investee companies had increased the recorded book values of some of the RMB Fund 1 investments. Redhill calculated that, if the portfolio had been liquidated for book value as of July 18, 2019, investors would have received an annualized 31 per cent rate of return (See Exhibit 5).

RMB FUND 2, USD FUND 1, AND THE PANDEMIC

In late 2019, Redhill began preparing two new funds: RMB Fund 2 and USD Fund 1, with target sizes of ¥500 million and US$100 million respectively. The strategy was a gamble. Although both Lu and Su were well known in the industry, Redhill was new. As Exhibit 6 shows, VCs were judged overwhelmingly on past performance. RMB Fund 1, had performed well, yet the performance was short in duration and based on accounting (not cash). The lifespan, fee structure and philosophies of the two new funds were to replicate RMB Fund 1. But while RMB Fund 2 was

[50]"Dry powder" refers to undrawn and unallocated commitments of the investors in a fund.

to follow the same investee focus as RMB Fund 1, USD Fund 1 was to increase exposure to the global market. Thus, RMB Fund 2 would predominantly target domestic Chinese investors, whereas USD Fund 1 would be marketed to global investors.

As Redhill started fund raising, the global environment deteriorated. But Su was sanguine about the US-China trade war's effect on Chinese medical technology and biotechnology:

> …Health care is unlike [computer] chips …. Those are very sensitive because they might be related to the military.… [and] for biotechnology and medical technology… people are more important. The China market is very important. Some [overseas Chinese] people come back here, and they can separate it.… Their US company focuses on United States operations. Their Chinese company focuses on Chinese operations. Their IP is already separated. So, the [trade war] influence is minimized for them. And finally, … [the Chinese players] have their headquarters in mainland China … [and] for the next 10 years … [they] won't focus on the developed markets. …. So even if there is a trade war with the United States, it's not very important for the Chinese local players.

Through 2019, notwithstanding the decline of new funding for Chinese VC, Lu and Su found that interest in early stage, medical technology and biotechnology remained strong, as did investors' confidence in the Redhill team. Prospective LPs' informal commitments to the two new funds steadily increased. And Redhill signed letters of intent with potential investees, committing equity subject to the anticipated successful closing the two new funds. In short, the team looked forward to a highly successful 2020.

But in late December 2019, rumors began circulating of a spate of atypical pneumonia cases in Wuhan. By the end of January 2020, Hubei was in extreme lockdown and Guangzhou was taking serious precautions to prevent COVID-19 from spreading. Most of Redhill's employees began working from home. Visits to existing and prospective investees and LPs were cancelled. Conferences were delayed. Roadshows for the new funds were scrapped. Socializing ended. However, when the two week Chinese New Year holiday ended on February 10, Redhill resumed work as usual.

Before the outbreak of the COVID-19 pandemic, Redhill's employees had been required to meet face-to-face at the office only once a week, on Mondays. They travelled on their own schedules and frequently used web conferencing software such as Zoom or Tencent VooV Meeting. After the pandemic struck, masks were required during the Monday meetings and web conferencing became a daily occurrence. Lu improved Redhill's internal systems (including enterprise resource planning, performance assessment with KPIs, investee company due diligence, reports and employee training). To help fight the pandemics, Redhill and two partners donated more than ¥300,000 cash and preventive materials to NGOs, doctors and nurses. Redhill's RMB Fund 1 investee companies also took part in the anti-pandemic activities. Sales of those companies related to the prevention or treatment of COVID-19 increased, whereas those unrelated to COVID-19 experienced reduction or delay as healthcare resources shifted into the fight against COVID-19.

Fundraising for USD Fund 1 continued only fitfully due to the interruption of travel to Hong Kong and overseas.[51] Closing USD Fund 1 would require travelling outside of mainland China to at least Hong Kong. Yet only Hong Kong residents were being allowed into Hong Kong, subject to a 14-day quarantine. So even if the prospective LPs in USD Fund 1 kept their commitments, travel restrictions could prevent fund closing.

Fundraising for RMB Fund 2 continued without interruption. In March, Lu resumed travel to Beijing and Shanghai to meet with potential LPs with whom Redhill was in ongoing discussions. Most of them expressed continued commitment. And two local government funds were still competing to attract Redhill RMB Fund 2 to register in their different jurisdictions. Redhill had received expressions of interest for nearly ¥300 million. Lu and Su considered holding a "first close" of RMB Fund 2, notwithstanding that it would be for less than the initial target amount. After the first close, Redhill could hold a subsequent close when more of the funds were committed, as Lu explained:

> We are currently in the process registering our first close which would be around ¥200 million. Besides that, we have signed term sheets for another ¥100 million.... Competing government funds are committing 20 per cent of the total amount of RMB Fund 2. So we have strong

[51] Faye Moore, "Will Covid-19 trigger a force majeure clause?", *Out-Law Guide*, Pinsent Masons, 26 March 2020, accessed May 30, 2020, https://www.pinsentmasons.com/out-law/guides/covid-19-force-majeure-clause.

> confidence that we can successfully close the fundraising of RMB Fund 2.

As an early stage VC firm, Redhill relied on other VCs to pick up the financing for subsequent rounds as Lu noted:

> Seven of the 14 portfolio companies from our RMB Fund 1 have raised the next round financing successfully by July 2020. Although the environment is tough, we believe that good quality portfolio companies will still have good opportunities.

Yet the collapse of the Chinese VC boom and the subsequent pandemic had shown that financing for promising investees was not a sure thing. And rapidly evolving conditions necessitated a clear evaluation of Redhill's evolving strategy.

EXHIBIT 1: THE LIMITED PARTNERSHIP STRUCTURE OF VC FUNDS

(a) Cash Call During Investment Period

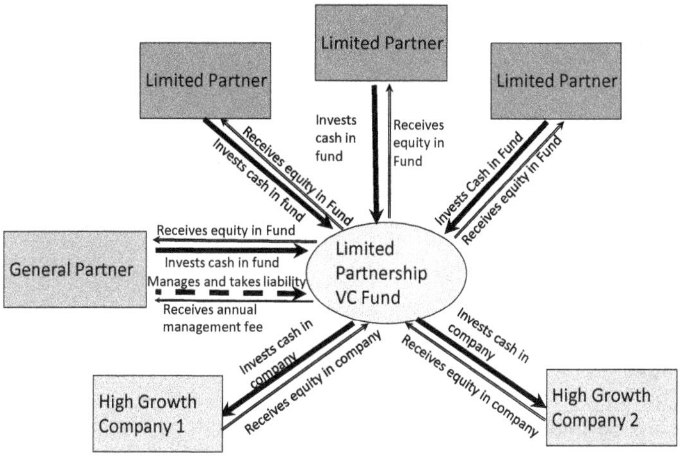

(b) Exit by Initial Public Offering: Part 1 – Listing

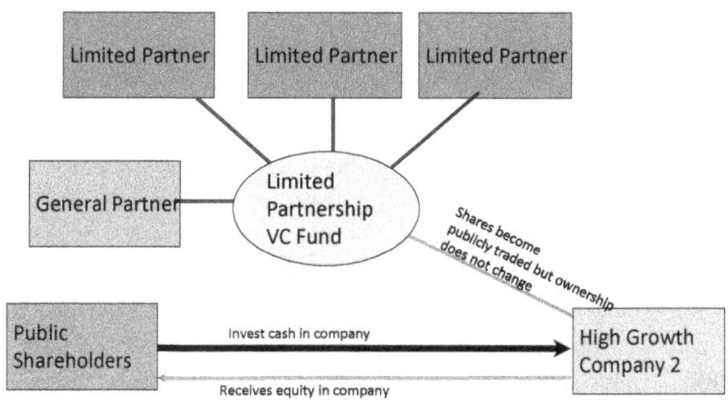

(c) Exit by Initial Public Offering: Part 2 – Distribution of Listed Shares

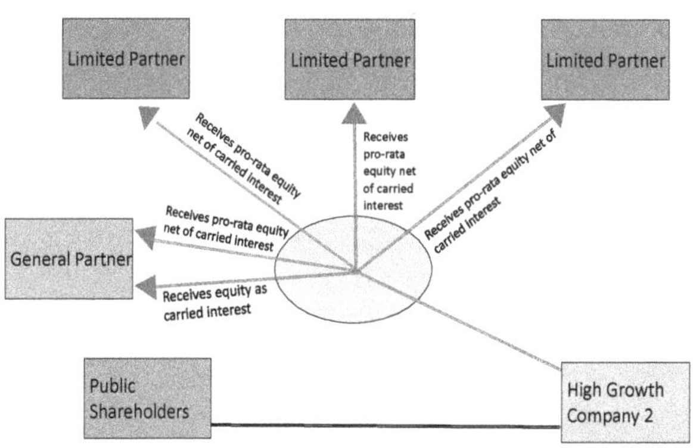

EXHIBIT 1: (*Continued*)

Note: Each fund has one general partner (GP) and several LPs. The GP is the investment manager, who is legally liable for the partnership's actions. The LPs are fund investors, not liable for the partnership's actions, so the maximum amount that they could lose is limited to their original investment. Each VC limited partnership is also limited in a lifespan specified in the fund documentation. The fund is not "funded" by the LPs at closing (the date when all documentation is signed). LPs and the GP, regarding its own investment in the fund (known as "skin in the game") give commitments at closing to remit their contributions when the GP requires it. Panel A above shows cash calls to the investors to pay investee companies and annual management fees, which are typically 2 per cent per year of the total fund with a range of 0.75 per cent to 3 per cent. Conditions to investment, in addition to equity held by the fund, usually include a seat on the investee company's board and a veto over important investment and financing decisions. GPs provide not only money but market expertise, administrative guidance, technical knowhow, contacts, introductions and monitoring, including staged investment, conditional on meeting milestones.[52]
Panel B shows the effect of an investee's IPO. The IPO changes the nature of the shares from private to publicly listed. Panel C shows the shares being distributed from the fund to investors as shares, not sold for cash. Share distribution avoids violating a lock-up period (typically a half a year but could be longer[53]) and has no effect on the market price of the shares. The value of the distribution is valued based on the prices of shares at the date of distribution (not the IPO price). Distributions are allocated pro-rata to each investor's investment percentage in the fund after carried interest. Carried interest, which forms the successful VC's main source of profit, is a percentage of distributions (cash plus shares) before distribution to fund investors (LPs and GP's investment). Carried interest (typically from 20 to 30 per cent of the distribution) is paid to the GP only after the fund has returned to LPs 100 per cent of contributed capital.
Source: Prepared by the case authors with information from Ning Jia and Dan Wang, "Skin in the Game: General Partner Capital Commitment, Investment Behavior and Venture Capital Fund Performance," *Journal of Corporate Finance* 47 (2017); Asher Bearman, "How VC Funds Work: Capital Commitments and Closings," *Investors*, November 8, 2010, https://www.theventurealley.com/2010/11/raising-a-fund-capital-commitments-and-closings; W. A. Sahlman, "The Structure and Governance of Venture Capital Organizations" *Journal of Financial Economics* 27 (1990): 473–524; Karen Weise, "Explaining Facebook's Epically Complex Stock Lockup," *Bloomberg*, August 22, 2012, https://www.bloomberg.com/news/articles/2012-08-22/explaining-facebooks-epically-complex-stock-lockup; There are signalling and potential wealth transfer implications of venture capital share distributions to limited partners; Paul Gompers and Josh Lerner, "Venture Capital Distributions: Short-Run and Long-Run Reactions," *The Journal of Finance* 53, no. 6 (1998): 2161–83.

---

[52]W. A. Sahlman, "The Structure and Governance of Venture Capital Organizations" *Journal of Financial Economics* 27 1990, pp. 473–524.

[53]Karen Weise, "Explaining Facebook's Epically Complex Stock Lockup" *Bloomberg* August 22, 2012, accessed June 10, 2020, https://www.bloomberg.com/news/articles/2012-08-22/explaining-facebooks-epically-complex-stock-lockup.

EXHIBIT 2: VC FUND RAISING IN THE US AND CHINA

(a) Number of Funds Closed in US and China 2015-2019

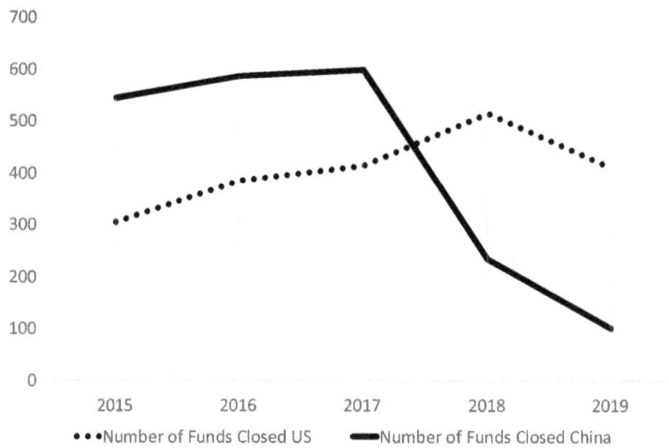

(b) Value of Capital Raised in US and China 2015–2019

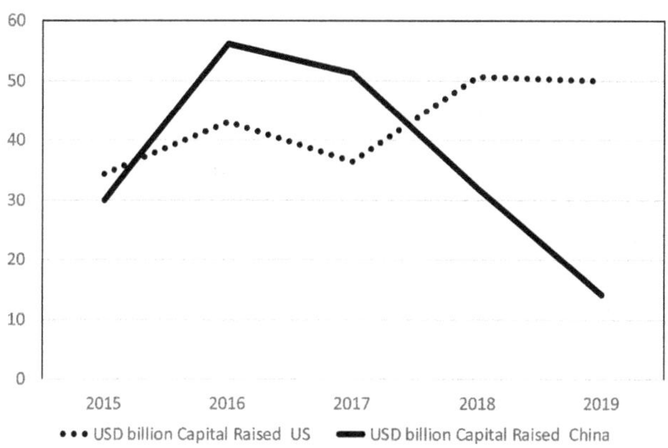

Source: Preqin, *Preqin Markets in Focus: Private Equity and Venture Capital in Greater China's Innovation Economy*, December 2019, https://docs.preqin.com/reports/Preqin-Markets-in-Focus-Private-Equity-and-Venture-Capital-in-Greater-Chinas-Innovation-Economy-December-2019.pdf.

EXHIBIT 3: EVOLUTION OF CHINESE BIO-TECHNOLOGY, MEDICAL TECHNOLOGY AND HEALTHCARE

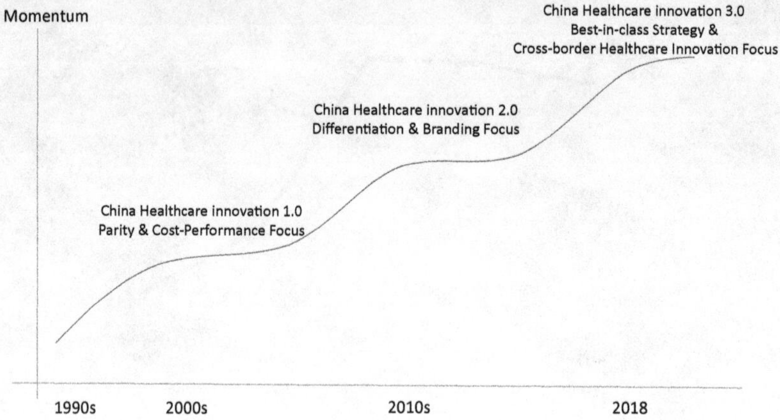

Note: Redhill Capital believes that entrepreneurs in the Chinese healthcare industry like other industries, started from "copy to China" and have progressed to "copy from China". Reflecting the increase in innovation Redhill Capital describes the progress of the Chinese healthcare sector from 1.0 to 2.0 to 3.0. In 1.0, leading entrepreneurs focused on parity with foreign companies and cost-performance. In 2.0 leading entrepreneurs focused on differentiation and branding. In 3.0 leading entrepreneurs focused on a best-in-class strategy and cross-border healthcare innovation. From 2000 to 2008, most healthcare investors found most profitable pre-IPO and growth stage opportunities in 1.0 companies aiming for IPO on stock exchanges' main boards and small and medium sized enterprise/ growth enterprise market boards. From 2010 to 2017, most healthcare investors pursued those companies which had branded products or service and strong capability and market potential replacing imported products, largely 2.0 companies. From 2018, profits of good, private, healthcare companies have declined. Chinese government policies to encourage innovation and entrepreneurship have increased. Well-educated and experienced Chinese returning from overseas and locally educated, strong entrepreneurs have also increased. The newly launched STAR Market and new rules for listing in Hong Kong Stock Exchange encourage new ventures with innovative technologies to get listed. All those changes stimulate healthcare investors to finance innovation, which Redhill Capital sees as the beginning of 3.0. "We are committed to be a preferred capital partner for bio-technology and medical technology startups in the coming age of cross-border healthcare innovation."
Source: Company documents.

EXHIBIT 4: INVESTORS IN RMB FUND 1

Investor Type	Holdings in Millions of RMB
(1) Investors of Significance	110
(2) Industry player	60
(3) Financial Investors	150
(4) Local Government Funds	145
(5) Redhill Capital's Own and Related capital	40
Total	505

Note: Investors of significance included a Sequoia Capital JV, two funds of the Hong Kong based financial group, Everbright and Wens Capital of Guangzhou. The industry player was By-Health, a vitamin and health supplements producer. Financial investors included Starquest Capital, one of the largest PE companies in China, and local government funds included funds from the State Development and Investment Corp, the largest state-owned investment company in China, and two Guangzhou development funds.
Source: Redhill Capital.

EXHIBIT 5: INVESTEE COMPANIES IN RMB FUND 1 AS OF JULY 18, 2019

	Company	Location	Type	Year established
1	Hamesh	Guangzhou	Surgical robots R&D, sales and marketing (1)	2017
2	Vistel	Beijing	Medical Artificial Intelligence — diabetic retinopathy (3)	2016
3	Liangyihui	Suzhou	Oncology doctors platform (6)	2015
4	Sinos	Shenzhen	Electrophysiology device for atrial fibrillation ablation R&D, sales and marketing (1)	2017
5	Mingyitang	Chongqing	Chongqing focused Traditional Chinese Medicine hospital & clinics chain (4)	1958
6	Vita Vitro	Shenzhen	Egg flushing Fluid Fertilizer fluid embryo transplantation tube (1)	2015
7	Juventas	Tianjin	CAR-T (genetically engineered T cells to attack cancer cells) (7)	2018
8	PandaMed	Changzhou	Gastro volume reduction balloon (4)	2017
9	Meyer	Shenzhen	Functional Special medical food R&D, sales and marketing (5)	2017
10	Cofoe	Changsha	Home Care Devices — blood pressure (2)	2005
11	Yichenyun	Guangzhou	Infection Control Products (1)	2016
12	Manteia	Xiamen	AI big data based precision adaptive radiation therapy (ART) system. (3)	2017
13	Breocare	Shenzhen	Portable hand massagers R&D, production and sales (2)	2000

(*Continued*)

EXHIBIT 5: (*Continued*)

Note: As of July 18, 2019, ¥385.9 million had been invested in the above companies. In addition to the ¥385.9 million invested, approximately ¥65 million had been committed to be invested, leaving slightly over 10 per cent of the fund uncommitted. RMB Fund 1's investments in the above companies ranged from ¥11 million to ¥60 million. Six of the companies had received investments from other investors subsequent to RMB Fund 1's investment. Each of the subsequent investments valued the shares of the investee company higher than the price per share at which RMB Fund 1 had invested. Increasing the values of RMB Fund 1's holdings in these six companies led to a total invested portfolio value on the books of RMB Fund 1 of ¥448.7 million. Taking the timing of each of the investments in each investee company into consideration, the total annualized rate of return for investors in RMB Fund 1 from the closing of the fund until July 18, 2019 was estimated by Redhill to be approximately 31 per cent. Investees can be classified by type as follows: (1) equipment and consumables (¥125.6 m); (2) home medical equipment (¥ 71.3 m); (3) medical AI (¥ 51 m); (4) medical services (¥48 m); (5) nutrients (¥ 30 m); (6) Internet pharmacy (¥ 30 m); and (7) new pharmaceuticals (¥ 30 m).
Source: Redhill Capital,

EXHIBIT 6: FACTORS TO CONSIDER WHEN SELECTING A VENTURE CAPITAL FUND MANAGER

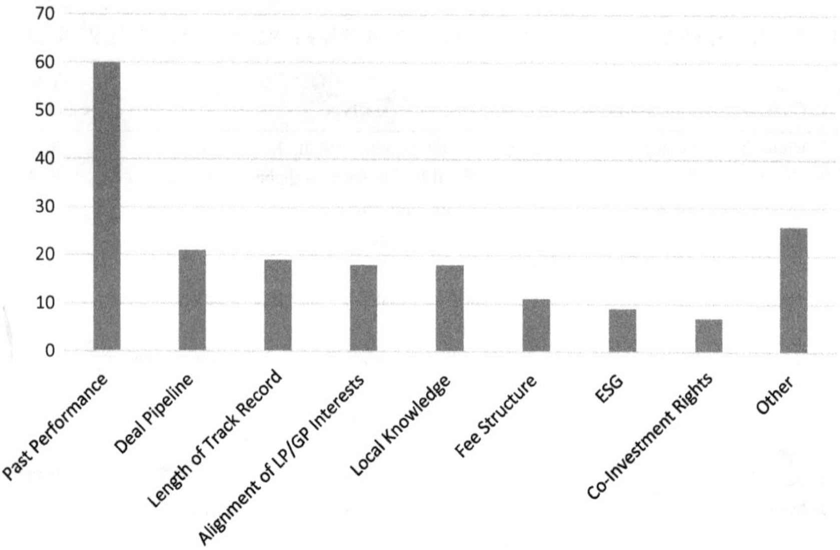

Note: LP = limited partner; GP = general partner; ESG = environmental, social, and governance. Histograms show the percentages of respondents from a survey of over 50 global investors conducted by Preqin in August 2019. Each investor was asked to identify the key factors they consider when selecting a private equity and venture capital fund manager.
Source: Preqin, *Preqin Markets in Focus: Private Equity and Venture Capital in China's Innovation Economy*, December 2019, https://docs.preqin.com/reports/Preqin-Markets-in-Focus-Private-Equity-and-Venture-Capital-in-Greater-Chinas-Innovation-Economy-December-2019.pdf.

Chapter 12

China Merchants Bank: Light Banking, Payments, and Blockchain

Introduction

The final chapter in this casebook introduces how China Merchants Bank (CMB) stimulates innovation in a controversial technology, blockchain.

Innovation in Retail Mobile Payments

The case lets students play the role of Tian Huiyu, President of CMB. CMB is an SOE. So Tian is a member of the CPC and his appointment is made through the COD. Yet, even so, he faces the same market dilemma as the chief executive officer of a privately owned enterprise: to provide better, more cost-effective services to customers than the competition or to be defeated. Banks must provide attractive financial products to maximize return on risk capital while meeting regulatory constraints.

CMB has been restructuring away from traditional, balance-sheet-oriented banking since the days of its former CMB president, Ma Weihua.[1] President Tian's strategy of light banking is a continuation that strategy

[1] For a case detailing the first and second transformation of CMB, see Mingkang Liu, Hugh Thomas, and Gang Du, "China Merchants Bank: Business Model Transformation", Ivey Publishing/Harvard Business Publishing, 2014. The case also has an accompanying video, Hugh Thomas, "China Merchants Bank: Business Model Transformation", YouTube video, CUHK SLI, 2013 https://www.youtube.com/watch?v=uAsLBtkJx4k (accessed December 17, 2021).

for the digital age. Banking in China is a crowded, changing industry. Competitors include the four largest commercial banks in the world, dwarfing CMB in asset size and income. Another five banks, each roughly the same size as CMB, have unique ownership structures, histories and competitive strengths. A greater challenge, however, comes from non-bank financial technology (fintech) companies.

Two second-generation entrepreneurs who were introduced in Chapter 9, Jack Ma Yun and Pony Ma Huateng, present threats not only to Tian, but also to traditional banking in general. Alibaba (and its affiliate, Ant Financial, which operates Alipay) and Tencent (which operates WeChat Pay), unleashed a revolution in payments to which the case refers. Anyone who has spent any time in China over the last five years knows that China is largely a cashless society where retail payments are overwhelmingly made using mobile phones. The case does not dwell on this obvious innovation, but it's worth reviewing in this chapter's introduction.

The success of Alipay and WeChat Pay (who jointly share 90% of the Chinese mobile payments market) is striking because neither company began as a fintech. Alibaba was an e-commerce platform and WeChat was a video game and social apps company. Now each has about 1 billion users, meaning that, since China has a smart-phone penetration rate of over 60%,[2] mobile payment users typically have both Alipay and WeChat Pay accounts. Alipay and WeChat Pay made three interlocking innovations to implement mobile payments: (1) the QR code that identifies the merchant and its bank account, (2) placing digital connectivity in the hands of the purchaser through his or her mobile phone and (3) connecting the digital wallets with the purchaser and merchant bank accounts. These innovations allow the purchaser to push payment from the purchaser's bank account (or a stored value fintech account) into the merchant's bank account. The purchaser can make payment to the merchant as long as the purchaser's cellphone has a mobile signal and the merchant has an account-identifying QR code. Neither the purchaser nor the merchant pay fees. Alipay and WeChat Pay recoup their costs through interest on the float of wallet accounts, ancillary financial services and, more importantly, using the highly granular information about the purchasing habits of customers to sell other products and services.[3] The Chinese retail

[2]Newzoo, *Global Market Report 2019*.

[3]Aaron Klein, "China's Digital Payments Revolution", *Global China*, April 2020. http://euro.ecom.cmu.edu/resources/elibrary/epay/ChinaPaymentRevolution2020.pdf (accessed

mobile payments system revolution is well catalogued in several cases distributed by Harvard.[4]

The payments revolution, however, adversely affects banks like CMB by reducing the stickiness of banker-customer relationships. The new payments system does not actually disintermediate the banks. Funds still flow from the bank account of the purchaser to the bank account of the merchant. Yet customers are in closer digital contact with the fintechs, and their direct contract with the banks is reduced. So consumers are more likely to buy ancillary financial services from or through the fintechs rather than going to the banks. And because the fintechs, not the banks, possess the newly generated, highly granular, consumer-specific data on spending habits, the fintechs, and not the banks, become more able to sell their services effectively to consumers.

The retail digital payments revolution was effected by private companies, Alibaba and Tencent, who successfully challenged SOE banks in a socialist economy. Similar challenges have occurred in other industries since the reform and opening boom started in the 1980s. But for such a revolution to occur in the critical activities of banking, money and payments is striking!

Today, central governments of most countries agree that money and payments systems are too systemically important to be left to the private sector: they should be public utilities. From Afghanistan to Zimbabwe, SOEs and government departments control the issuance of bills and coins. Central banks, through which high power money is cleared to effect final payment, are all government-owned. Governments strictly regulate — and often own parts of — the banking systems whose liabilities (bank deposits) make up with bulk of the money supply of today's world. And governments take pains to assure that all aspects of their financial systems

---

April 26, 2021).

[4]For example, Feng Zhu, Ying Zhang, Krishna Palepu, Anthony Wu, and Nancy Dai, "Ant Financial (A)", Harvard Business Publishing, 2019 starts with the global record breaking online sales on singles day (November 11) and reviews financial services of Alibaba's providing retail asset management, automatic credit granting, rural and international trade credit, insurance, etc. Ning Su, Yulin Fang, Yukun Yang, "Tencent: The WeChat Red Envelope Initiative", Ivey Publishing/Harvard Business Publishing, 2015 describe an early success in WeChat Pay with Chinese New Year red envelopes delivering digital cash. For an international comparison of models, see also Eduard Calvo, "Mobile Payments: the keys to success", *IESE Insight*, Harvard Business Publishing, 2016.

serve the interests of society in general and those parts of society that keep them in power in particular. China is no exception.

The Chinese regulators saw and allowed Alibaba and Tencent to implement their revolution. Without such an accommodative regulatory environment and without regulators courageous enough to take the risk of innovation, the fintechs could never have succeeded. This innovation can be viewed as yet one more instance of crossing the river by feeling the stones. The final word on payments and money innovation has not been uttered. As this book is going to press, the regulators have changed course.

Ant Financial's IPO was cancelled in late 2020 and subsequently Alibaba was fined for anti-competitive behavior.[5] This is certainly not the end of private sector fintech innovation in China. But it does mean that the rules of the game are being (re)written to allow an alternate platform design and allocation of access to customers and their data between the SOEs, banks, the central bank and the privately owned fintechs. Retail digital payments was a massive and successful innovation. It was not planned by central authorities. It was simply allowed to unfold over a decade. Regulatory flexibility encouraged innovation.

Today, debates and lobbying over the next steps are undoubtably raging. As the rules of the game become clearer, one can expect a steady flow of well written cases business cases, inviting readers to analyze this globally significant financial system innovation.

Blockchain, Bitcoin, and Banking

We wrote the CMB case partly to introduce students to the dynamic of financial innovation surrounding a controversial technology: blockchain.

---

[5]The last minute cancellation of the US$37 billion IPO of Ant Financial in November 2020 was followed by anti-trust fines of US$2.8 billion. See Tom Mitchell, "Ant Financial in China's Central Bank Fights Jack Ma's Ant Group over Control of Data", *Financial Times*, April 23, 2021 and "Robert Olsen Jack Ma's Alibaba Hit with $2.8 Billion Fine for Abusing Its Dominant Market Position", *Forbes*, April 10, 2021 https://www.forbes.com/sites/robertolsen/2021/04/10/jack-mas-alibaba-hit-with-28-billion-fine-for-abusing-its-dominant-market-position/?sh=1403b51437d1 (accessed April 25, 2021). For a video with Jack Ma discussing his innovations, see "Steve Forbes Interviews Jack Ma at Forbes Global CEO Conference", *YouTube Video*, October 18, 2019. https://www.youtube.com/watch?v=AqMdrgmd39s (accessed May 4, 2021).

Blockchain is not a single invention. It is a set of constantly evolving technologies. The core technologies of blockchain are distributed ledgers, public private keys for encryption,[6] hashing,[7] and Byzantine fault tolerance.[8] None of blockchain's core technologies are defensibly patentable although some aspects have been patented.[9] Some of the technologies are very old. Distributed ledgers are as old as off-site computer backups or, before the computer age, keeping copies of key documents. Public-private keys for encryption are at least 45 years old and hashing is at least 40 years old. Bitcoin, the payment innovation from Satoshi Nakomoto[10] that launched blockchain, is 12 years old. Nakomoto's innovation was to solve the Byzantine fault tolerance problem through proof of work[11] and voting by computing power. But Nakomoto's innovation is actually not used in CMB's cross border payments blockchain system (CBPBS), the subject of this chapter's case.

Bitcoin's explosion into global financial consciousness 12 years ago opened possibilities. The fact that the cryptocurrency itself has not lived up to its promise as a workable, peer-to-peer payments system, usable as international, uncontrolled, money — it's too volatile, too slow, too wasteful to mint, too subject to criminal use, too beholden to periodic branching, too much a hostage to unregulated exchanges[12] — has not stopped

---

[6] Encryption allows a private message to be sent along a public telecommunications channel, allowing decoding only by the holder of the private key.

[7] The hashing algorithm of most blockchains, including bitcoin is Sha-256. Online tools for Sha256 are found at *Online Tools*. https://emn178.github.io/online-tools/sha256.html (accessed April 26, 2021). Hashing is the technique for generating the unique digital signature of each block and chaining the blocks together.

[8] Byzantine fault tolerance allows the introduction of false data in the distributed ledger, either by accident or fraudulent design of one or more nodes without endangering the integrity of the distributed data set.

[9] Chapter 3 introduced the concept difference between an invention being patentable and the patent being defensible.

[10] Satoshi Nakomoto, *Bitcoin: A Peer-to-Peer Electronic Cash System*, white paper, 2008. https://bitcoin.org/bitcoin.pdf (accessed June 16, 2019).

[11] Proof of work involves the solving of a difficult to solve but easy to verify problem. Bitcoin's problem involves setting the hashed Sha256 output of the new block to an arbitrarily low number (e.g., 32 leading zeros in the 64 hex number output) by introducing a nonce (a number used once). The problem has to be solved iteratively, using tremendous amounts of computing power.

[12] Bank for International Settlements, Annual Economic Report: V. Cryptocurrencies: looking beyond the hype, June 24, 2018, 91–114. www.bis.org/publ/arpdf/ar2018e.htm (accessed April 24, 2021).

bitcoin from becoming a frothy, new-age, speculative asset. But more than that, bitcoin has drawn tremendous attention to currency- and token-related innovations. And it has inspired innovators to investigate blockchain's scope for solving distributed ledger problems in a host of industries with no relation to cryptocurrencies.

Even as China became the undisputed leader in producing bitcoin mining tools — specially designed computers to run the algorithms to mint coin — and Chinese private computer engineers became the world's keenest miners of new bitcoin, the CPC made it abundantly clear that it would tolerate no challenge to its control through the PBOC's money supply. So trading in crypto currencies and initial coin offers in China was strictly forbidden. Yet the official attitude to blockchain technologies in China is highly welcoming.

The case describe how CMB's blockchain team has been set up within its information technology department to undertake both internal and external projects sponsored by line units of the bank (i.e., units of the bank producing value for customers). The case focuses on the CBPBS. Although it is somewhat technical, the readers of the case should note what CBPBS does — it is a payments advisory — whom it competes with — its competitor is the Society for Worldwide Interbank Financial Telecommunication (SWIFT) — and in what niches it can successfully compete.

The blockchain team at CMB also works on projects which essentially design blockchains for corporate bank customers' own distributed ledger needs. Students may debate the benefits versus costs of free blockchain consulting for CMB's customers. And they may also comment on the high-tech glamour of blockchain that may bring prestige to CMB through closely working with customers on blockchain even if the consulting projects are not fully successful. As a marketing tool, the blockchain team initiative seems effective.

Central Bank Digital Currencies and the People's Bank of China

The CMB blockchain team, however, is completely allergic to any involvement in cryptocurrencies. Yet a key component of the excitement of blockchain is precisely bitcoin, cryptocurrencies and the future of money.

The case raises very obliquely central bank digital currencies (CBDC)[13] in the Venn Diagram of Exhibit 3.[14] The diagram shows four binary characteristics by which one can classify all currencies: (1) access: widely or narrowly accessible (2) form: digital or physical (3) issuer: central bank or non-central bank and (4) technology: token based or accounting entry. While bitcoin occupies the region labeled "J" (widely accessible, digital, non-central bank, token), a more relevant innovation from the point of view of China's currency is labeled "G" (widely accessible, digital, central bank, token).

Bitcoin's launch in 2009 caught Chinese central bankers' attention. Five years later, the PBOC set up a unit to research CBDC and in 2016 the PBOC became the first large central bank in the world to announce it would issue CBDC. This is not a race. The Federal Reserve Board in the United States has been uniformly cautious about CBDC. And it has challenged the efforts of Facebook to launch its own digital coin, Libra (now Diem).[15] As of late 2020, PBOC had conducted CBDC pilot tests in Suzhou and Shenzhen of several million transactions involving "airdropping" more than ¥2 billion into test subjects CBDC wallets. The regulators have demonstrated a positive zest for testing new financial innovation models.[16] CBDC, if it becomes the dominant money in the Chinese economy, will provide a degree of monetary policy control that central bankers elsewhere can only dream of.

There is another dimension: the internationalization of the RMB. Financially, China is partially closed. It is open on current account — one can obtain foreign exchange to purchase imports but one must apply first. One can sell products and services overseas to obtain foreign currency,

---

[13] In Chinese, 数字货币电子支付 or simply 数字人民币 E-CNY.

[14] The Venn Diagram is based on the more attractive "money flower" in Morten Bech and Rodney Garratt, *Central Bank Cryptocurrencies*, Bank for International Settlements, 2017. https://papers.ssrn.com/sol3/papers.cfm?abstract_id=3041906 (accessed January 29, 2021).

[15] James T Areddy, "China Creates Its Own Digital Currency, a First for Major Economy; A Cyber Yuan Stands to Give Beijing Power to Track Spending in Real Time, Plus Money That Isn't Linked to the Dollar-Dominated Global Financial System", *Wall Street Journal*, New York, NY, April 21, 2021.

[16] Martin Chorzempa, "China, the United States, and Central Bank Digital Currencies: How Important Is It to Be First?", Peterson Institute for International Economics, January 13, 2021. https://doi.org/10.1080/17538963.2020.1870278 (accessed April 26, 2021).

but one must declare it and apply for its conversion into RMB. Yet there is no "openness on capital account". Foreigners cannot freely buy or sell RMB for foreign currency. Chinese cannot freely buy or sell foreign currency for RMB. The RMB is not a global financial asset.

To become a fully functional international currency, to challenge the dominance of the U.S. dollar, the RMB must be opened on capital account. Yet the CPC is loath to open the RMB if by doing so it cedes control over its currency to the whims of Chinese and foreign investors and speculators. So far, it has been keener to extend reliance on the U.S. dollar than put the RMB at risk of a run following internationalization. So China does not get either the financial gains of seigneurage[17] or the political power to deny foreigners access to its international payments system through sanctions. The United States enjoys both.

CBDC could present a route to careful entry of the RMB as a global asset class. If it were restricted to individuals and with ceilings on total balances and transaction amounts per day, it could enter first the retail wallets of foreigners. In the same way that one can easily make payment in digital currency of Ali Pay or WeChat Pay over the internet regardless of location, holders of CBDC RMB would be able to make payment regardless of where they were located in the world. Payment would be instantaneous and free of charge. Restrictions could be steadily relaxed if and when the system proved popular. Identities of the holders of accounts would be automatically available to the PBOC. Loss of anonymity would be the price paid as every payment crossed the books of the PBOC.

This innovation is likely to occur. And it will highlight the tremendous difference between attitudes to financial innovation in the United States on one hand and China on the other. A major reason for this is the difference is the attitude of an incumbent with much to lose versus a challenger with much to gain.

How to Stimulate Innovation in a Bank

Although we wrote the CMB case to introduce blockchain, the issue that President Tian Huiyu confronts and that students analyze in the case is how to manage innovation. The competitive environment of banking makes innovation necessary. Yet SOEs in general and banks in particular,

---

[17] Seigniorage is the ability to make money and spend by minting money.

the world over, have a tradition of conservatism. Tian has chosen to stimulate innovation through an incubation fund. Unlike the incubators discussed in Chapter 5, CMB's fund is purely internal. Those outside CMB need not apply. Unlike the *rendanheyi* approach of Haier discussed in Chapter 7, each project approved by the innovation fund must be sponsored by an existing line (i.e., revenue generating) unit of the bank. The applicants apply for funds to implement projects. They do not propose new stand-alone business models of micro-enterprises. Readers should assess projects of the blockchain group and the types of innovations that are likely result from this structure.

CHINA MERCHANTS BANK: LIGHT BANKING, PAYMENTS, AND BLOCKCHAIN

Mingkang Liu, Hugh Thomas, and Gang Du wrote this case solely to provide material for class discussion. The authors do not intend to illustrate either effective or ineffective handling of a managerial situation.

Imagine a world with no out-of-sync ledgers. No need for reconciliations. No fragmented or hidden data that create multiple versions of the truth. This world is coming, and its name is blockchain.

KPMG, *Blockchain and the Future of Finance*[1]

Blockchain is not only crappy technology but a bad vision for the future. Its failure to achieve adoption to date is because systems built on trust, norms, and institutions inherently function better than the type of no-need-for-trusted-parties systems blockchain envisions. That's

[1]KPMG, *Blockchain and the Future of Finance: A Potential New World for CFOs — and How to Prepare*, 1, accessed May 5, 2020, https://advisory.kpmg.us/content/dam/advisory/en/pdfs/blockchain-future-finance.pdf.

permanent: no matter how much blockchain improves it is still headed in the wrong direction.

Kai Stinchcombe, chief executive officer and founder of True Link Financial[2]

In 2017, Tian Huiyu, president of CMB, was convinced that the centuries-old traditional banking model was nearing the end of its useful life. Tian concluded that fintech would reorder financial services, blurring boundaries, rebalancing the business ecology, and presenting CMB with both opportunities and threats. Yet, CMB's commercial bank culture focused on financial indicators and relied on legacy IT systems. Believing that such a culture could delay CMB's business units' responses to the fintech challenge, Tian set up the CMB incubation fund for new projects, using 1 per cent of annual profits, or ¥700 million.[3] One set of CMB incubation fund projects came from a team that was engaged in applying blockchain technology to resolve various IT problems for CMB and for its customers. However, by mid-year 2018, the blockchain team's cross-border payments project matured and CMB's top management reassessed its views of the usefulness of the technology. CMB had to decide whether to reduce, maintain, or increase its financing of the incubation fund in general, and of the blockchain team's projects in particular.

BACKGROUND AND STRATEGY

After the founding of the People's Republic of China, the CPC led government consolidated commercial and central banking into a single institution, the PBOC.[4] From the early 1950s until 1978, all domestic deposits

---

[2]Kai Stinchcombe, "Blockchain Is Not Only Crappy Technology but a Bad Vision for the Future," *Medium Cryptocurrency*, April 5, 2018, accessed October 18, 2018, https://medium.com/@kaistinchcombe/decentralized-and-trustless-crypto-paradise-is-actually-a-medieval-hellhole-c1ca122efdec.

[3]¥ = CNY = Chinese yuan renminbi; US$1 = ¥6.62 on June 29, 2018.

[4]The history of the People's Bank of China can be traced to the founding of the Chinese Soviet Republic National Bank in 1931 in Jiangxi. Its founding, under the current name, occurred in Shijiazhuang in 1948. Since then, through the founding of the People's

held by private individuals, government units, non-government organizations, and companies were the liabilities of the PBOC.[5] As the reform and opening of China accelerated, during the 1980s, commercial banking was separated from central banking with the establishment of the Industrial and Commercial Bank of China (ICBC), which took over the commercial operations of PBOC in 1984.[6] Increasingly, during the 1990s, the government defined legal and market-oriented principles of finance as differentiated from government policy considerations. The China Development Bank was founded in 1994, leaving the Construction Bank of China (established in 1954 as a government development finance entity) to pursue commercial banking.[7] Bank of China, formerly restricted to international operations, developed domestic business,[8] and the Agricultural Bank of China, established as a nationwide agricultural credit co-operative in 1950, also embraced commercial banking.[9]

To encourage competition and innovation in banking, starting in the late 1980s, the government chartered several new banks. By the end of

---

Republic of China in October 1949 and through to 1953, which was the inaugural year of the first national Five-Year Plan, its functions in the national banking system have been consolidated; "History of the People's Bank of China," People's Bank of China [in Chinese], accessed February 20, 2020, www.pbc.gov.cn/rmyh/105226/105433/index.html and brief introduction to the history of banking in the People's Republic of China [in English] at Franklin Allen, Xian Gu, Jun Qian, "People's Bank of China: History, Current Operations and Future Outlook," SSRN working paper, October 10, 2017, accessed February 20, 2020, https://papers.ssrn.com/sol3/papers.cfm?abstract_id=3018506; history and prospectus of each bank listed on the Stock Exchange of Hong Kong available on the Hong Kong Exchanges and Clearing Market website (www.hkex.com.hk/?sc_lang=en).

[5]Agricultural Bank of China, *Industry Overview: History and Development*, 70, June 30, 2010, accessed February 20, 2020, www1.hkexnews.hk/listedco/listconews/sehk/2010/0630/ltn20100630147.

[6]Industrial and Commercial Bank of China, *Banking Industry in China*, 47, accessed February 20, 2020, www1.hkexnews.hk/listedco/listconews/sehk/2006/1016/01398/ewp111.pdf.

[7]*Ibid.*, p. 45.

[8]Bank of China Limited, *Industry Overview*, May 18, 2006, accessed February 20, 2020, www1.hkexnews.hk/listedco/listconews/sehk/2006/0518/3988/f114_e.pdf.

[9]Agricultural Bank of China, *Our History, Restructuring and Operational Reform*, 111, June 30, 2010, accessed February 20, 2020, www1.hkexnews.hk/listedco/listconews/sehk/2010/0630/ltn20100630015.htm.

2017, there were over 9,000 commercial banks in China,[10] but the country was dominated by the Big Four: ICBC, Bank of China, Construction Bank of China, and Agricultural Bank of China. With average assets totalling over ¥23 trillion, the Big Four were not only the largest banks in China but also the largest banks in the world.[11] All of the Big Four were majority owned and effectively controlled by Central Huijin Investment Ltd., a national government-owned investment company that reported directly to the Ministry of Finance[12] but all had minority public floats of their shares (H-shares) listed on the Stock Exchange of Hong Kong.[13]

CMB was one of the six next-largest banks in China, alongside the Bank of Communications, CITIC Bank, the Industrial Bank, Minsheng Bank, and Pudong Development Bank (see Exhibit 1 and Exhibit 2). Each of these "smaller banks" was among the largest 50 banks in the world, and each had a unique history and shareholding structure.[14]

CMB was established in 1987 as China's first joint-stock commercial bank subsidiary of a corporate entity.[15] CMB's main shareholder, the China Merchants Group (CMG), was a shipping-based diversified conglomerate owned by SASAC, a state-owned commission under the State Council of China. During the closed years of Chinese central planning, from 1950 to 1978, CMG was primarily focused on international shipping and was open to the world.[16] China's first export processing zone, established by CMG in Shekou, Guangdong (bordering Hong

---

[10]"Banking Regulatory Quarterly Statistics," China Banking Regulatory Commission, February 9, 2018.

[11]"TOP 20 Largest World Banks in 2019 by Total Assets," FXSSI, January 13, 2019, accessed June 12, 2019, https://fxssi.com/top-20-largest-world-banks-in-current-year.

[12]"About Us," Central Huijin Investment Limited, accessed January 20, 2020, www.huijin-inv.cn/huijineng/About_Us/index.shtml.

[13]Prospectuses and all subsequent publicly disclosed information about the Big Four can be found on the website of the Stock Exchange of Hong Kong (www.hkex.com.hk/?sc_lang=en).

[14]"TOP 20 Largest World Banks in 2019 by Total Assets," *op. cit.*

[15]China Merchants Bank, *Our History and Corporate Structure*, September 8, 2006, accessed February 20, 2020, www1.hkexnews.hk/listedco/listconews/sehk/2006/0908/03968/ewp113.pdf.

[16]"About Us: Introduction," China Merchants Group, accessed February 20, 2020, www.cmhk.com/main/a/2016/a26/a30448_30530.shtml.

Kong) was the forerunner of the Shenzhen SEZ.[17] CMB listed its A-shares on the Shanghai Stock Exchange in 2002 and its H-shares on the Hong Kong Stock Exchange in 2006. By the end of 2017, CMG owned 29.97 per cent of CMB, compared to other Chinese SOEs, which owned 22.5 per cent. The remainder of shares were widely held. CMB seemed proud of its history of innovation and of its brand, and focused on its customers, with the English slogan, "We are here, just for you." However, the Chinese, "We are changing for you," seemed to place more emphasis on the future.[18]

As Tian took over the presidency of CMB from Ma Weihua in 2013, China was changing, entering a new normal: gross domestic product growth dropped to below 8 per cent; PBOC cancelled the lower limit on loan interest of 70 per cent of the benchmark rate;[19] total social financing exceeded ¥2 trillion;[20] investments in the Alibaba Group Holding Limited (Alibaba) money market fund Yu'e Bao[21] exceeded ¥180 billion, six

---

[17] *Ibid.*

[18] The slogan in Chinese is 招商银行,因您而變; China Merchants Bank, *2017 Annual Report*, accessed January 20, 2017, http://file.cmbimg.com/cmbir/20180424/d0fe62f9-3db1-4835-90cf-8ed64d7c0ab7.pdf; China Merchants Bank, *2017 Annual Report* [in Chinese], accessed January 20, 2017, http://file.cmbimg.com/cmbir/20180424/d83541b1-4019-46fc-b456-330c4dc15ad3.pdf.

[19] The cancellation was part of a decades-long gradual process of reforming bank lending from rationing to a market-led process.

[20] Also known as "total social financing" or "aggregate financing to the real economy," it was calculated on a year-on-year basis, including all new net lending (i.e., bonds, bank, non-bank financial institutions, non-financial institutions) to the non-financial sector; "Total Social Financing," *China Banking News*, accessed October 31, 2019, www.chinabankingnews.com/total-social-financing; Beijing Monitoring Desk, "China Total Social Financing Rises to 2.21 Trillion Yuan in September," *Reuters*, October 17, 2018, accessed October 31, 2019, www.reuters.com/article/us-china-economy-social-financing/china-total-social-financing-rises-to-221-trillion-yuan-in-september-idUSKCN1MR0YT.

[21] By 2017, Yu'e Bao was the largest money market mutual fund in both China and the world, with over 300 million account holders and US$200 billion in assets. It was started as a short-term investment vehicle available to those using AliPay, the third-party mobile payment platform owned by Ant Financial, a company in the Alibaba Group that was set up to provide escrow services for payments for goods transacted on Alibaba's Taobao and Tmall sites; Yifan Xie and Chuin-wei Yap, "Meet Earth's Largest Money-Market Fund," *The Wall Street Journal*, September 13, 2017, accessed April 29, 2020, www.wsj.com/

months after its launch, as it rose to become the world's largest mutual fund; and Tencent Holdings Ltd. (Tencent) and Alibaba together controlled over 90 per cent of mobile payments.[22] Tian continued Ma's "second transformation" to aim for improving capital use, pricing, cost control, customer value, and risk management.[23] Tian summarized CMB's strategic positioning with the metaphors of "light banking" and "one body; two wings," in which "one body" referred to retail finance and the "two wings" were corporate finance and financial institutions (FI). CMB had seven key businesses where it enjoyed a competitive advantage. In retail finance, it excelled in retail wealth management, small and micro business finance, and consumer finance. CMB had increased its competitive strength in corporate finance transaction banking and corporate finance investment banking. And in providing financial services to other FIs, Tian saw CMB's strength in interbank asset management and interbank financial markets.

CMB had established its "one body" in upmarket retail banking in the 1990s, before the Big Four state-owned banks entered the retail customer market and before the other five smaller and newer banks caught up. Retail income from loans and other operating income accounted for over 50 per cent of CMB's profit in 2017. CMB's private banking, wealth management, and credit card businesses ranked first in China.[24] In terms of its "two wings," CMB successfully caught-up with the Big Four. By 2018, its asset management scale and assets under management were the largest in

---

articles/how-an-alibaba-spinoff-created-the-worlds-largest-money-market-fund-1505295000.

[22] Adam Lashinsky, "Alibaba v. Tencent: The Battle for Supremacy in China," *Fortune*, June 21, 2018, accessed January 14, 2019, http://fortune.com/longform/alibaba-tencent-china-internet/.

[23] Mingkang Liu, Hugh Thomas, and Gang Du, *China Merchants Bank: Business Model Transformation* (London, ON: Ivey Publishing, 2014). Available from Ivey Publishing, product no. 9B14N016.

[24] "About Credit Cards," China Merchants Bank, accessed October 30, 2019, http://english.cmbchina.com/CreditCard/DetailInfo.aspx?guid=9a75f179-db66-4295-8072-9d4804f5ea5f.

China.[25] In bills and financial markets, CMB often ranked first.[26] And in investment banking, it was establishing a solid reputation.[27]

CMB pursued the strategy of "one body; two wings" through light banking, which referred to light assets, light business, light management, and light culture. *Light assets* involved booking loans and other securities whose low risk weighting would require less risk capital and less regulatory capital.[28] Interbank loans, credit card assets, housing mortgage loans, small and medium enterprise loans, money market investments, and some fixed income trading assets would be preferred over corporate lending, while asset securitization would shift risk assets off CMB's balance sheet into special purpose vehicles whose securities could be sold to CMB's wealth management customers. *Light business* involved reducing the human and physical resources involved in delivering financial services to customers. CMB would strive to reduce its reliance on large branch networks staffed by many employees and to also increase the digital banking contribution to revenue. *Light management* was a plan to reduce bureaucratic drag to present customers with friendly, client-oriented interfaces and enjoyable experiences, reducing barriers between departments by streamlining internal processes. *Light*

---

[25]"China 2018 AUM League Table," Asia Private Banker.

[26]China Merchants Bank, *2018 Annual Report: We Are Here Just for You*, 56, accessed June 15, 2020, http://file.cmbimg.com/cmbir/201904/476b7790-2259-4f08-a457-f1437d92620b.pdf.

[27]"Euromoney," Global Capital, accessed October 23, 2019, www.globalcapital.com/data/bank-profiles/china-merchants-bank-co-ltd.

[28]Risk capital was the amount of equity that internal analysts of the bank believe is required to cushion a bank's position against the maximum probable losses of that position. Regulatory capital was the amount of liquid equity that (i.e., easily sold securities) that must be held in relation to a certain level of assets. Capital adequacy standards referred to the Basel capital adequacy framework, an accord agreed to by bank regulators of major countries through which assets, off-balance-sheet positions, and other business activities were quantified and subject to risk weighting to convert them into risk weighted assets for use in computing a capital adequacy ratio (risk assets/capital). Each bank was required by regulators to exceed specific levels of capital adequacy; Basel Committee on Banking Supervision, *Basel III: International Regulatory Framework for Banks* (Basel: Bank for International Settlements, 2011–2014), accessed October 16, 2017, www.bis.org/bcbs/basel3.htm.

culture was a philosophy of simplicity and practicality, whether meeting customer needs or assessing employee performance. Tian championed a "common goal, one direction, simple evaluation criteria, and few implied rules."

In developing light banking, CMB sought to differentiate itself from its main banking competitors. Light banking for retail customers was exemplified by CMB's App 6.0 customer interface, which used AI to address customer problems. Launched in 2017, App 6.0 achieved 50 million downloads, and more than 70 per cent of CMB's retail banking transactions migrated to it in the year after its launch.

CMB implemented light banking to compete not only with other commercial banks but also with the fintech companies, led by Alibaba and Tencent. In 2017, CMB's retail customers exceeded 100 million for the first time. That milestone had been reached through 30 years of hard work since CMB's founding. But as Tian commented, "WeChat[29] went from zero to 100 million users in only 433 days."

PAYMENTS

Payments were at the core of banking, spanning the businesses of retail, wholesale, corporate, FI, domestic, and international. Final settlement[30] in renminbi occurred in clearing[31] bank accounts at PBOC. However, in China, as in most countries of the world, many small banks and

[29] In 2017, WeChat was China's leading messaging service, with over 900 million active monthly users. Starting in 2014, Tencent began allowing for retail payments through its WeChat service, with users exchanging red envelopes (small cash gifts). It grew rapidly to a 37 per cent market share of the US$5.5 trillion Chinese mobile payments market (against 54 per cent for Alipay), a market approximately 50 times the size of the U.S. mobile payments market; Louise Lucas, "Race for China's $5.5tn Mobile Payment Market Hots Up," *Financial Times*, May 1, 2017, accessed October 31, 2019, www.ft.com/content/e3477778-2969-11e7-bc4b-5528796fe35c.

[30] Settlement was the discharge of an obligation in accordance with the terms of the underlying contract. Final settlement was a legally defined moment describing the irrevocable and unconditional transfer of an asset or financial instrument or the discharge of an obligation by a financial institution in accordance with the terms of the underlying contract.

[31] Clearing was the process of transmitting, reconciling, and in some cases, confirming transactions prior to settlement, potentially including the netting of transactions and the establishment of final positions for settlement.

non-bank FIs as well as all non-FI private individuals and companies did not have PBOC bank clearing accounts. They accepted the liabilities of commercial banks, non-bank FIs and non-FI payment agents such as Alibaba and Tencent as money. This fostered payment systems not only at the PBOC, but also on intra-FI, inter-FI, and FI-non-FI payment agent platforms.[32]

The mobile payment platforms of Tencent's WeChat and Alibaba's AliPay (the main Chinese payment fintech companies) offered user-friendly and high-frequency customer interaction, which reduced bank contact, weakened bank–customer relationships, changed bank–customer behaviour, and depleted bank data accumulation. These changes could have potentially adverse effects on wealth management, credit, and other opportunities for business development (see Exhibit 3).[33] Although fintech companies were winning the mobile payment battle, CMB maintained its lead in payments made through credit cards and in international payments agency business, where it was second only to Bank of China.[34]

In 2017, CMB had over 50 million credit cards in circulation, for an increase of over 10 per cent compared to the previous year. Its credit card platform Life App was AI-powered to analyze customer data and boasted daily activity above 4 million transactions. The app provided customers with temporary increases in credit lines, fixed-credit invitations, and assistance to cardholders outside China with credit card difficulties. By 2017, more than half of the consumer credit card activity took place through the Life App. Annual transaction volume reached ¥24 billion and an annual growth rate of 46 per cent. Over 500,000 enquiries per day came through the Life App, of which 95 per cent were handled by

---

[32] Dietrich Domanski, Leonardo Gambacorta, and Cristina Picillo, "Central Clearing: Trends and Current Issues," *BIS Quarterly Review*, December 2015, 59–76, accessed February 20, 2020, www.bis.org/publ/qtrpdf/r_qt1512g.pdf.

[33] Fern Wang, "Tech Disruption in Retail Banking: China's Banks Are Playing Catch-Up to Big Tech," *S&P Global*, May 14, 2019, accessed February 20, 2020, www.spglobal.com/en/research-insights/articles/tech-disruption-in-retail-banking-china-s-banks-are-playing-catch-up-to-big-tech.

[34] In international payment agency businesses, China Merchants Bank acted as agent for small- and medium-sized Chinese banks in transacting their ¥ payments through the cross-border interbank payment system. These rankings and subsequent information in this section were provided by the China Merchants Bank.

machine intelligent matching. Between 2010 and 2016, the number of CMB credit card customers tripled and their purchases increased fivefold, while customer service staff was reduced by 61 people. CMB's credit card fraud rate dropped nearly 10-fold and customer transaction approval rates rose from 91 per cent to 96 per cent, maintaining first place in the industry. CMB was effectively controlling risk while enhancing customer experience.

International Payments

To make international payments[35] on behalf of their clients, banks set up mutual correspondent accounts with other banks based in different currencies to be debited and credited for the benefit of client accounts at correspondent banks (Exhibit 4). Because each bank typically had correspondent banking accounts with only a limited set of other banks, an international payment from a bank client to the payee designated by the bank client often relied on passage between several correspondent banks. This relay model in cross-border payments could take days, introducing liquidity and credit risk. Several fees (known as "lifting fees") were charged by any or all of the payer's bank, beneficiary's bank, and intermediary correspondent bank(s). The delay between debiting the payer's account and crediting the beneficiary's account (known as the "float") could also affect the value of the payment.

In 1973, to facilitate communication among banks and FIs, a secure telecommunications system had been set up called SWIFT.[36] SWIFT was not a payment system; it was a communications medium among FIs. It standardized the FI messaging format for a variety of instructions. For payment instructions the same "SWIFT MT 103" format (see Exhibit 5) was used by over 11,000 FIs using SWIFT, and each was verified through a business identifier code (SWIFT Code). SWIFT rapidly rose to dominate global messaging for payments (see Exhibit 6), with almost 15 million messages passing through its network each day. However, critics pointed out that it was a centralized private ledger run by a company in Brussels

---

[35] G.A. Walker, "Financial Technology Law—A New Beginning and a New Future," *International Lawyer* 50 (2017): 137–215.

[36] "History," Society for Worldwide Interbank Financial Telecommunications, accessed October 23, 2019, www.swift.com/about-us/history.

and vulnerable to cyberattacks. For example, in 2016, the Central Bank of Bangladesh was hacked and lost $81 million.[37] Eventually, delays and security vulnerabilities in the SWIFT system led CMB's blockchain team to challenge its dominance in China and Hong Kong.

BLOCKCHAIN

After more than 40 years in development, blockchain emerged in the second decade of the 21st century as a highly promising but contentious database technology (see Exhibit 7). A blockchain was a single ledger identically shared among multiple nodes of a network, in which transactions from time to time were cryptographically bundled in blocks and immutably bound into a chain.[38] The key characteristics of blockchain were public–private keys and hashing. Public–private keys consisted of private cryptographic keys that allowed data to be securely transmitted over a public channel.[39] Hashing was a cryptographic function that accepted in each case a string of data of arbitrary length as an input and returned a string of data of a specific (but short) length. Minor changes in the input string resulted in major changes in the output string, and the output string could not be reversed to obtain the input string.[40] In addition, some blockchains incorporated Byzantine fault tolerance. This meant that, in the absence of a trusted intermediary, the system would tolerate, without loss of data integrity, the failure (either random or intentional) of nodes storing the data proof of work. Miners in network nodes competed by solving computationally difficult to solve, but easy to verify, problems

---

[37]Reuters, "Bangladesh Probes 2013 Hack for Links to SWIFT-Linked Central Bank Heist," *CNBC*, May 25, 2016.

[38]Luon-Chang Lin and Tzu-Chun Liao, "A Survey of Blockchain Securities Issues and Challenges" *International Journal of Network Security* 19, no. 5 (September 2017): 653–659.

[39]Whitfield Diffie and Martin E. Hellman, "New Directions in Cryptography," *IEEE Transactions on Information Theory* 22, no. 6, (1976): 644–654, accessed October 27, 2019, https://ee.stanford.edu/~hellman/publications/24.pdf.

[40]United States Patent and Trademark Office, *Ralph C. Merkle*: *Method of Providing Digital Signatures*, U.S. Patent 4,309,569, Filed September 5, 1979, and Issued January 5, 1982, accessed October 27, 2019, http://patft.uspto.gov/netacgi/nph-Parser?Sect1=PTO1&Sect2=HITOFF&d=PALL&p=1&u=%2Fnetahtml%2FPTO%2Fsrchnum.htm&r=1&f=G&l=50&s1=4309569.PN.&OS=PN/4309569&RS=PN/4309569.

to authorize each new block in the chain. Anonymity ensured that the ultimate identity of the participating node was known only by an electronic address. It was not associated with a physical or legal person.[41]

Blockchains differed in their level of exposure to the public. Public blockchains allowed anyone with an Internet address and sufficient capacity to view and participate as a node in the blockchain. Private open blockchains allowed ledger contents to be seen by all, but the right to transact in the ledger was limited to select nodes. Private closed blockchains restricted both viewing and transacting in the ledger. Blockchain's major drawback was its computational intensity, but analysts considered that it could provide IT solutions for users of shared ledgers in real time, especially where a trusted intermediary was absent.[42] Use cases included real estate, medical, and supply chain ledgers. However, by far the most famous and controversial application of blockchain was with cryptocurrencies. Cryptocurrencies were digital payment devices that could also be free from central bank control. First introduced in 1989,[43] cryptocurrencies burst into public awareness in 2009 with the launch of bitcoin.[44] As of the end of 2019, there were over 3,000 different bitcoin-inspired cryptocurrencies[45] available.[46]

Bitcoin's development was both promoted and hampered in China. Chinese private entrepreneurs formed early and active cryptocurrency

---

[41] Leslie Lamport, Robert Shostak, and Marshall Pease, "The Byzantine Generals Problem" *ACM Transactions on Programming Languages and Systems* 4, no. 3, (July 1982): 382–401, accessed December 17, 2021 https://lamport.azurewebsites.net/pubs/byz.pdf.

[42] R. Jesse McWaters, *The Future of Financial Infrastructure: An Ambitious Look at How Blockchain Can Reshape Financial Services*, report for the World Economic Forum, 2016, accessed October 30, 2019, www.weforum.org/reports/the-future-of-financial-infrastructure-an-ambitious-look-at-how-blockchain-can-reshape-financial-services.

[43] Julie Pitta, "Requiem for a Bright Idea," *Forbes,* November 1, 1999, accessed October 27, 2019, www.forbes.com/forbes/1999/1101/6411390a.html#5ce20b66715f.

[44] Satoshi Nakamoto, *Bitcoin*: *A Peer-to-Peer Electronic Cash System*, white paper, 2008, accessed June 16, 2019, https://bitcoin.org/bitcoin.pdf.

[45] Bank for International Settlements, *Annual Economic Report,* 91–114, accessed October 26, 2019, www.bis.org/publ/arpdf/ar2018e5.pdf.

[46] Cryptocurrency List, Coinlore, accessed December 15, 2019, www.coinlore.com/all_coins.

exchanges.[47] China's electronics industry became the leading producer of computer components dedicated to bitcoin mining. And its mining pools rose to mint 60 to 70 per cent of cryptocurrency tokens in the world by 2018.[48] All of this occurred while the PBOC, protective of its payments monopoly and concerned about financial security, imposed a ban on initial coin offerings (ICOs) in September 2017. It then issued regular advisories and took steps to deter the use of cryptocurrency in the country.[49] The CMB blockchain team, however, focused not on cryptocurrencies or other tokens, but on non-token-related distributed ledger applications.

CMB Blockchain Team and Cross-Border Payments

In 2018, CMB's blockchain team comprised 20 of the 3,000 people within its IT department. The blockchain team was dedicated to serving the business departments of CMB using blockchain solutions. The team had started using open-source IBM Hyperledger Fabric[50] in August 2016. Its goal was to develop a platform for delivering messages for direct payments, in both Hong Kong dollars and US dollars, among all CMB branches, including Mainland branches, the CMB Hong Kong Branch, and CMB's 100 per cent subsidiary in Hong Kong, Wing Lung Bank. The team developed the blockchain application for CMB's interbank customers, which were approximately 200 small and medium domestic Chinese banks.

On December 20, 2017, the platform was launched. CMB booked its first blockchain cross-border payment between Wing Lung Bank in Hong Kong as the remitting bank and Wing Lung Bank in Shenzhen as the receiving bank, with CMB as the agent bank. CMB's blockchain platform

---

[47] Sue Liu, "Fortune Telling," *International Financial Law Review* 36, no. 1 (2017); Chao Deng, "China Quietly Orders Closing of Bitcoin Mining Operations," *The Wall Street Journal*, January 11, 2018, accessed December 27, 2018, www.wsj.com/articles/china-quietly-orders-closing-of-bitcoin-mining-operations-1515594021.

[48] Jordan Tuwiner, "Bitcoin Mining in China," Buy Bitcoin Worldwide, accessed December 27, 2018, www.buybitcoinworldwide.com/mining/china/.

[49] Kenneth Rapoza, "Cryptocurrency Exchanges Officially Dead In China," *Forbes*, November 2, 2017, accessed October 27, 2019, www.forbes.com/sites/kenrapoza/2017/11/02/cryptocurrency-exchanges-officially-dead-in-china/#1d9050cb2a83.

[50] "A Blockchain Platform for the Enterprise," Hyperledger Fabric, accessed October 31, 2019, https://hyperledger-fabric.readthedocs.io/en/release-1.4.

replaced SWIFT's MT103 message on the payment. The ultimate payer and payee were corporate customers using Wing Lung. However, if the customer used another bank in Hong Kong, that bank could use Wing Lung as its correspondent. The correspondent payment could be sent through Hong Kong's real-time gross settlement system, with advising done through SWIFT. In the eight months after the launch of the system, more than 51,000 transactions were booked. Most transactions involved two-bank, cross-border advice. Initially, the nodes of the blockchain were only CMB, CMB Hong Kong, and Wing Lung. However, any computer with a link to the Internet and verification from CMB could join as a node.

After the successful replacement of SWIFT messages in three-party cross-border US dollar and Hong Kong dollar payments, the team applied for financing from CMB's new incubation fund. The team hoped to use funding to improve the blockchain platform by implementing a cross-border payments blockchain system (CBPBS). The CMB committee that considered applications for funding required each applicant to be a CMB business unit. Unlike staff units, such as the IT department, business units generated revenue from customers and served as a cost centre. Therefore, to become eligible for funding, the team joined forces with CMB payments units, including the Hong Kong Branch and Wing Lung Bank, who believed in the team's ability to address real business issues.

Hou Tingwei, head of the public team management design office of CMB's IT department, explained the proposed innovation:

> The first 2017 model was a step-by-step relay model. We wanted to change that relay model into a contracting model (i.e., the CBPBS). [The CBPBS] was our second system. The payer puts the contract on the blockchain. Others look at the contract, and if it's workable, they sign it and implement it. In the signing process, each party is independent.... In the SWIFT model, the bank has to worry about the bank from which it receives the money and the bank to which it pays. With blockchain, you just have to be concerned about yourself. Then everyone does what he contracts to do. If, on implementing, one party does not implement, then the process is immediately reversed. [The CBPBS] reduces steps. ... In a foreign remittance, the more the steps, the greater the time, the greater the cost and the greater the chance of non-fulfillment. Typically, in international remittances, banks use intermediary banks because the

> banks dealing with the customers are both local banks ... They need to work with an intermediary correspondent bank.... In the old system, each bank based its decision on what the bank ahead of it would do.... Now, we can control the risk.

The team was based in Shenzhen and had to comply with the PBOC (both locally and nationally) concerning changes to international payment advice. In Hong Kong, through Wing Lung Bank, the team sought guidance from the Hong Kong Monetary Authority (HKMA), who placed the testing of CBPBS under its regulatory oversight. HKMA constraints differed in some respects from those of the PBOC. For example, Wing Lung had to give advance notice to HKMA of all customers affected and HKMA would then limit the amount for each customer. However, the PBOC just required that it be kept fully informed.

The team believed that the CBPBS would save time and fees. As Hou explained:

> It can reduce clearing time by about 50 per cent, reduce clearing costs by about 80 per cent and reduce query and recovery work by about 90 per cent.... The whole process is transparent to the funds remitter, receiver, and agent (s) because it is broadcast to all parties through the blockchain. It is a cryptographically protected, internet-residing platform and can be accessed by a time-limited 2-D barcode available to both the remitter and the beneficiary, but not to the nodes.

A major advantage of CBPBS was that all customers and their bankers could see the entire remittance process, but the node banks were restricted from seeing it due to encryption. The nodes could only have access to their own customers, even though the entire blockchain file resided on their computers, and the keys for encryption were held by each customer's bank.

In the test phase of the CBPBS, every transaction had its own block. However, the team anticipated that in the near future, as transactions increased, several transactions would be bundled in each block. The blockchain being tested in mid-2018 was small: only 4 kilobytes. And although it would expand over time as the number of transactions per block and the number of blocks chained together increased, the file would still remain relatively small. The CBPBS did not employ proof of work because it was run by CMB — a trusted intermediary — and it was housed on other trusted banks' computers.

During the tests, only one bank outside of the CMB system was involved as a node sharing the blockchain. In the future, however, the team planned to have from 40 to 60 banks directly participating as nodes. The number of nodes would be restricted to preserve efficiency, because latency in updating the blockchain increased with the number of nodes. The team saw no need to increase the number of nodal banks beyond 60 because the nodal banks would establish their credibility based on which of the hundreds of smaller banks could participate on a correspondent bank basis.

As of 2018, the CBPBS was free to use, as Hou explained:

> We are building a system for our own needs. If it is valuable, then there may be no need to charge. CMB is working with several other banks … but as it's in the testing stage and nobody knows its value, it's difficult to consider fees. This system is useful to CMB. From an operations point of view, we are already saving money.

Other Projects of the CMB Blockchain Team

The team did not limit its blockchain projects to payments. It welcomed any business department of CMB to bring its project proposals for discussion. Hou stated that "We think of what we want to do, and then we talk it over with the business unit. This involves us thinking through what is feasible, making a demo, and if it has value, discussing how to use it with the business department." If the discussion was successful, the business unit would apply to CMB's incubation fund committee for project approval, as Hou explained:

> If it's a pure IT project without any business unit background, we cannot actually do it. We could only do a demo.… To implement it, of course we need the business unit.… Usage relies on the existing system. It has to be in accord with regulations, the workflow of the business unit, the tellers, and the accounting unit.

By mid-2018, the team was working on 10 projects. Over half of them (including CBPBS, a digital signature project, and a project on supply chain financing) were highly related to banking. The remainder were implemented to increase strategic partnering with corporate customers, as Hou explained:

> We're essentially giving the corporate customer a blockchain for free. Then we can bring the customer into our banking services. For example, we are doing a project for the records of a medical services company. Then the company is brought closer into the bank's customer base. This is part of the business department's expansion strategy to improve the banking ecosystem.

However, Hou stated that none of the blockchain projects involved ICOs, cryptocurrencies, or other tokens:

> CMB cannot even touch them. ... There is no point in going into cryptocurrencies. Cryptocurrencies bring in issues of KYC [know your customer]. Proving the legitimacy of the origins of the cryptocurrency is difficult — hard to meet the regulatory requirements. What is the origin of your cryptocurrency? Is it money laundering?

Competitors in Blockchain

The team was acutely aware that it was working on an extremely important technology. Its competitors were also looking for better ways to serve their customers with blockchain. According to Hou, each of the Big Four had contracted fintech companies to pursue blockchain-related projects. As far as the team knew, however, none involved in-house teams, none involved cross-border payment advice, and none had been fully implemented.

In 2017, SWIFT had launched global payments innovation (GPI) to further improve its payment messaging.[51] GPI provided end-to-end transparency to participating banks — 270 of them around the world, including CMB, and around 70 other banks from China. GPI was designed to improve SWIFT's user experience, lower fees, and increase

[51]"SWIFT GPI: Cross-Border Payments, Transformed," Society for Worldwide Interbank Financial Transactions, accessed October 26, 2019, www.swift.com/our-solutions/swift-gpi.

capacity. It also had a blockchain component.[52] That component was tested in the regulatory oversight of the UK Financial Conduct Authority by SWIFT and 34 global banks (including China Construction Bank and China Minsheng Bank, but not CMB).[53] It focused on optimizing real-time liquidity management in the Nostro accounts (i.e., the account that a bank had with a correspondent bank) of SWIFT members.[54] Following the successful test, however, no implementation plans were reported.

CMB's model was comparable to San Francisco-based Ripple's xCurrent, which also used existing bank infrastructures, payment instructions for conventional currencies, and pre-validation and post-validation (confirmation of completion) for each transaction. It was financed by Google, Santander Bank, Standard Chartered, and others. Ripple boasted over 50 FI customers worldwide. However Ripple also offered the xRapid System, which used the cryptocurrency XRP on the public ledger to enhance user liquidity. And Ripple was not available in China.[55]

Hou considered that CMB's closest competitors in blockchain were Alibaba and Tencent. Both companies had blockchain development teams about four times the size of CMBs. Hou described their initiatives:

> Ali has a payment platform. But they are a third-party payment solution provider, not an FI. They are trying to solve their own international

---

[52] "GPI Real-Time Nostro Proof of Concept. Final Report," Society for Worldwide Interbank Financial Transactions, February 2018, accessed October 26, 2019, www.google.com/url?sa=t&rct=j&q=&esrc=s&source=web&cd=1&ved=2ahUKEwiC3ez30rnlAhVbA4gKHYO8BMUQFjAAegQIAxAC&url=https%3A%2F%2Fwww.swift.com%2Fresource%2Fgpi-real-time-nostro-proof-concept&usg=AOvVaw2rHv8T3u-S5b1MRRvtN1Bk.

[53] "SWIFT Completes Landmark DLT Proof of Concept," Society for Worldwide Interbank Financial Transactions, March 8, 2018, accessed February 20, 2020, www.swift.com/news-events/news/swift-completes-landmark-dlt-proof-of-concept.

[54] Lower fees were achieved through requiring banks participating in GPI to sign a service level agreement ensuring fee standards, which prohibited intermediary banks from charging lifting fees not already disclosed to the payer when the payer arranged the payment with its bank.

[55] "Product Overview: A Technical Overview of xCurrent," Ripple, accessed January 14, 2019, https://ripple.com/files/ripple_product_overview.pdf.

> payment problems. They are not a bank trying to solve customer problems.... Even though they use blockchain, they are more interested in solving problems of payments for *Zhifubao*.... Tencent has Weibank. But they are an internet bank. Weibank has P2P lending and are doing blockchain research for making payments to their customers, but it does not do international payments. And Weibank does not have a branch network.

THE ASSESSMENT

CMB had to decide whether it should increase its support in blockchain development. However, as Tian explained, the decision involved an assessment of its fit with CMB's strategy:

> Strategy is a choice. Without giving up something, there is no strategy. Strategic positioning means to make a choice.... CMB's size and scale mean that we can't do everything. We decided to focus on seven businesses, giving up others and daring to determine our own character.... The choice of one body, two wings was not made by sitting in the office and fantasizing. It was built on much research and analysis.

As top management analyzed CMB's foray into blockchain, it examined the technology. Blockchain was a system developed for networks lacking trust. Yet trust was fundamental to banking in general, and CMB did not want to signal otherwise and jeopardize its brand.[56] Could CMB's blockchain project compete successfully against those of Alibaba and Tencent, the Big Four Chinese banks, SWIFT, and the hundreds of other banks around the world? As part of the Made in China 2025 initiative by the central government, state-owned enterprises like CMB had to increase expenditures in research and development.[57] Did the CMB incubation

---

[56]"China Merchants Bank," Ranking the Brands, accessed October 23, 2019, www.rankingthebrands.com/Brand-detail.aspx?brandID=346.

[57]Government of China, *Notice of the State Council on Printing and Distributing: Made in China 2025*, May 8, 2015.

fund in general, and the blockchain project in particular, signal the right direction for that increased expenditure?

The authors sincerely thank Professor Marlene Amstad for her patient reading, in-depth discussions and many suggestions that helped this case to its successful completion.

EXHIBIT 1: CMB'S BANK COMPETITORS

Bank (Headquarters)	Background (Year Founded)	Largest Shareholder (and Stake)	*Forbes* Description of Sectors (*Forbes* World Rank)	Total Assets in US$ Billion (GFM World Rank by Assets)	Share Listing
Industrial and Commercial Bank of China (Beijing)	Assumed all commercial banking activities of People's Bank of China, with separation of central from commercial banking in the reform and opening of China (1984)	Huijin (34.7%)	Commercial and investment banking, insurance, and investment (8)	4,006 (1)	A and H
Construction Bank (Beijing)	Initially, a financial institution under the Ministry of Finance to distribute funds for infrastructure projects; since late 1970s, evolved commercial banking functions; reformed in 1994 into a commercial bank following establishment of China Development Bank (1954)	Huijin (57.1%)	Financial and banking services (3)	3,398 (2)	A and H

(*Continued*)

EXHIBIT 1: (*Continued*)

Bank (Headquarters)	Background (Year Founded)	Largest Shareholder (and Stake)	*Forbes* Description of Sectors (*Forbes* World Rank)	Total Assets in US$ Billion (GFM World Rank by Assets)	Share Listing
Agricultural Bank of China (Beijing)	Set up as the Agricultural Cooperative Bank; since late 1970s, evolved commercial bank functions; in 2010, became joint-stock commercial bank (1951)	Huijin (40.0%)	Commercial banking and financial services (4)	3,233 (3)	A and H
Bank of China (Beijing)	Initially the "Great Qing Bank" under the Qing Dynasty; renamed Bank of China in 1912; restricted to international banking after 1950; reorganized as commercial bank in 2003 (1903)	Huijin (64.0%)	Banking and related financial services (8)	2,990 (4)	A and H
Bank of Communications (Shanghai)	In the Qing Dynasty, the first commercial note issuing bank; following China's reform and opening, reopened as first nationwide state-owned joint-stock commercial bank in China (1908/1987)	Various entities of State Council (34.6%)	Commercial banking, securities, trust, leasing, fund management, insurance (39)	1,338 (21)	A and H

China Industrial Bank (Fuzhou)	One of the first national joint-stock banks approved by the State Council (1988)	Financial Bureau of Fujian Province (18.8%)	Corporate and personal banking services, financial lease, asset custody services, and conducting treasury business (55)	985 (29)	A and H
Shanghai Pudong Development Bank (Shanghai)	Set up in Shanghai's new financial district to serve China and world as full financial group; China Mobile is 18.2% strategic investor (1993)	Shanghai International Group Co. (21.6%)	Commercial, personal, and investment banking (65)	942 (32)	A
Minsheng Bank of China (Beijing)	First national joint-stock commercial bank founded and owned (mostly) by non-SOE (1996)	Anbang Insurance (16.8%)	Corporate and personal banking, treasury business, finance leasing, asset management, and other financial services (67)	906 (36)	A and H
China CITIC Bank (Hong Kong)	Formerly a Hong Kong family-owned commercial bank, Ka Wah Bank; controlling stake acquired by CITIC in 1986 (1922)	CITIC International Financial Holdings (75.0%)	Corporate and personal banking, treasury and asset management, leasing (93)	871 (37)	H

(*Continued*)

EXHIBIT 1: (*Continued*)

Note: GFM = global financial market; CITIC = China International Trust and Investment Corporation (set up in 1979, at the beginning of the reform and opening period, as the first market-oriented state-owned investment company and investment bank in China) Huijin = China Huijin Investment Company (the sovereign wealth fund for financial institutions directly under the State Council of the Chinese Government; A = A common stock (listed on the Shanghai Stock Exchange); H = H common stock (listed on the Stock Exchange of Hong Kong).

Sources: The *Forbes* ranking is from Kurt Badenhausen, "The World's Best Banks 2019," *Forbes*, February 28, 2019, accessed January 29, 2020, www.forbes.com/worlds-best-banks/; Total assets in billions US$ (GFM world rank by assets) are taken from David Sanders, "Biggest Banks In the World 2018," *Global Finance*, November 1, 2018, accessed February 24, 2020, www.gfmag.com/magazine/november-2018/biggest-banks-world-2018; Huijin share holdings as of December 31, 2017 in each of the Big Four are taken from China Construction Bank Corporation, *Annual Report 2017: Exploring the Blue Ocean*, 85, accessed February 24, 2020, www.bankcomm.com/BankCommSite/fileDownload.do?fileId=f377730d06954435b2a37ccc7ec0344a; Headquarters, Year Founded, Background, and non-Huijin share holdings are taken from bank websites, as follows: "ICBC History (1984–2014)," Industrial and Commercial Bank of China, accessed February 24, 2020, www.icbc-ltd.com/ICBCLtd/About%20Us/ICBC%20History; "Investor Relations Corporate Profile, Overview," China Construction Bank, accessed February 24, 2020, http://en.ccb.com/en/investorv3/corporateoverview/overview.html; "Company Overview," Agricultural Bank of China, accessed February 24, 2020, www.abchina.com/en/investor-relations/company-overview/; "About Us, History," Bank of China, accessed February 24, 2020, www.boc.cn/aboutboc/ab7/200809/t20080926_6931.html; "Our Values: Overview," Bank of Communications, accessed February 24, 2020, www.bankcomm.com/BankCommSite/shtml/jyjr/en/2600223/2600240/2600344/list.shtml?channelId=2600223; "Company Introduction," China Industrial Bank, accessed February 24, 2020, www.cib.com.cn/cn/aboutCIB/investor/profile; "About CMB," China Merchants Bank, accessed February 24, 2020, http://english.cmbchina.com/CmbInfo/About/DetailInfo.aspx?guid=ce1230c5-de69-441a-8861-d520fe3d287c; "Shanghai Pudong Development Bank Co., Ltd., Introduction," Shanghai Pudong Development Bank, accessed February 24, 2020, https://news.spdb.com.cn/about_spd/implementation; "Introduction to China Minsheng Bank," China Minsheng Bank, accessed February 24, 2020, http://en.cmbc.com.cn/CMBCToday/AboutCMBC/IntroductiontoCMBC/index.htm; "About Us: Our Heritage," China CITIC Bank International, accessed February 24, 2020, www.cncbinternational.com/about-us/our-heritage/en/index.jsp.

EXHIBIT 2: CHINA MERCHANTS BANK RELATIVE FINANCIAL PERFORMANCE

Item	CMB	Average of Big Four Banks	Average of Next Five Banks
Absolute Magnitude			
Assets (in ¥ billion)	6,298	22,183	6,634
Assets CAGR 2014–2017 (%)	10.00	8.97	12.94
Operating income (in ¥ billion)	221	592	161
Operating income CAGR 2014–2017 (%)	10.02	2.39	5.52
Profit after tax (in ¥ billion)	70	223	55
Profit after tax CAGR 2014–2017 (%)	7.77	1.24	3.39
Assets under custody (in ¥ billion)	11,970	11,716	9,107
Assets under custody CAGR 2014–2017 (%)	50.05	29.71	35.06
Assets under management (in ¥ billion)	2,178	2,094	1,383
Assets under management CAGR 2014–2017 (%)	33.86	17.72	26.40
Employees (in thousands)	72,530	401,027	63,432
Employees CAGR 2014–2017 (%)	−1.16	−0.53	4.43
Domestic branches and sub-branches	1,830	16,431	2,306
Domestic branches and sub-branches CAGR 2014–2017 (%)	8.72	−0.28	14.09
Ratios			
Return on equity (%)	16.54	13.99	13.38
Net interest margin (%)	2.43	2.14	1.69
Non-interest income as percent of operating income	34.43	25.76	36.97
Cost to operating income (%)	30.23	28.18	29.09
Non-performing loans/total loans (%)	1.61	1.58	1.72
Loan loss provisions/non-performing loans (%)	2.62	1.73	1.64
Total capital adequacy (%)	15.48	14.64	12.34
Price-to-earnings ratio	11.79	7.53	6.81
Price-to-book ratio	1.67	1.01	0.87

(Continued)

EXHIBIT 2: (*Continued*)

Note: CAGR = Compound annual growth rate; CMB = China Merchants Bank; ¥ = CNY = Chinese yuan renminbi; US$1 = ¥6.62 on June 29, 2018; Big Four = Agricultural Bank of China, Bank of China, Construction Bank of China, and Industrial and Commercial Bank of China; next five banks = Bank of Communications, CITIC Bank, Industrial Bank, Minsheng Bank, and Pudong Development Bank; operating income includes interest income, fee and commission income, and other income (changes in value of securities, investment income, exchange gains and losses, insurance income, rental income) after deduction of interest expenses but prior to deducting operating expenses, loan loss provisions, and taxes; custody = holding securities where purchase and sale of the securities remains at the sole discretion of the owner; management = holding of securities where the purchase and sale of the securities are carried out by the manager on behalf of and in the interest of the owner; total capital adequacy = Basel III definition of the ratio of total equity capital to risk-adjusted assets.

Source: The authors, compiled from company annual reports as follows: "ICBC Annual Reports 1984–2014," Industrial and Commercial Bank of China, accessed February 24, 2020, www.icbc-ltd.com/ICBCLtd/Investor%20Relations/Download%20Center; "Investor Relations, Corporate Profile, Overview," China Construction Bank, accessed April 29, 2020, http://en.ccb.com/en/investorv3/corporateoverview/overview.html; "Annual Reports 2015–2017," Agricultural Bank of China, accessed February 24, 2020, www.abchina.com/en/investor-relations/performance-reports/annual-reports; "Annual Reports 2015–2017," Bank of China, accessed February 24, 2020, www.boc.cn/en/investor; "Annual Reports 2015–2017," Bank of Communications, accessed February 24, 2020, www.bankcomm.com/BankCommSite/shtml/jyjr/en/2600223/2600236/list.shtml?channelId=2600223; "Company Annual Reports 2015–2017," China Industrial Bank, accessed February 24, 2020, www.cib.com.cn/en/aboutCIB/investor/reports; "Annual Reports 2015–2017," China Merchants Bank, accessed February 24, 2020, http://english.cmbchina.com/CmbIR/intro.aspx?type=report; "Shanghai Annual Reports 2015–2017 [in Chinese]," Shanghai Pudong Development Bank, accessed February 24, 2020, https://news.spdb.com.cn/investor_relation/periodic_report; "Annual Reports 2015–2017," China Minsheng Bank, accessed February 24, 2020, http://en.cmbc.com.cn/CMBCToday/InvestorRelations/AnnouncementsandDisclosures/Hshare/index2.htm; "Annual Reports 2015–2017," China CITIC Bank International, accessed February 24, 2020, www.cncbinternational.com/about-us/investor-relations/interim-and-annual-reports/en/index.jsp

EXHIBIT 3: FOUR BINARY CHARACTERISTICS OF MONEY

Venn Diagram

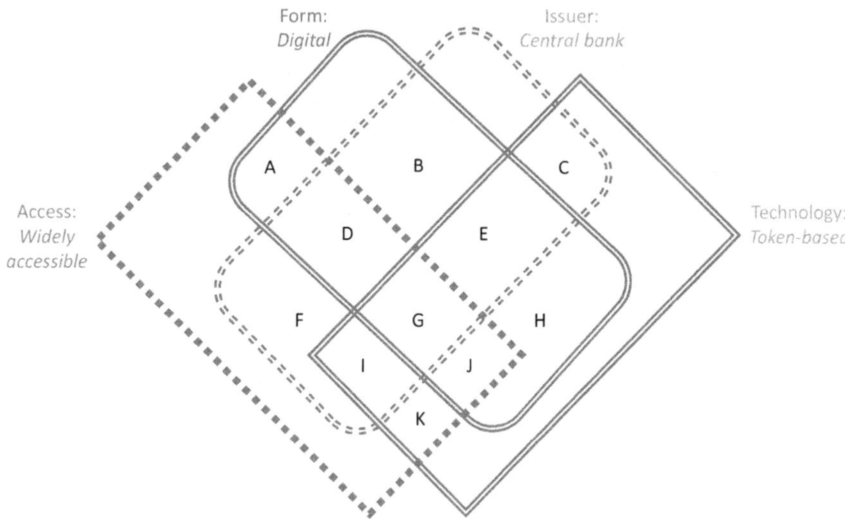

The Venn diagram above classifies money into four binary characteristics. Clockwise, from the left, (1) Access: whether it is widely accessible to the general public or restricted to a small class of institutions/individuals, (2) Form: whether it is in digital form (i.e., electronically recorded and transacted) or physical, (3) Issuer: whether it is issued by a central bank or by another institution/individual, and (4) Technology: whether it is token-based or an accounting entry.

EXHIBIT 3: (*Continued*)

Characteristic Intersections			
Item	Intersection	Example	Payment System
A	Widely accessible, digital	Bank deposits	If payer and payee have a common bank, bank debits payer and credits payee. If not, but payer's and payee's banks are correspondents, payer's bank debits payer's deposit and credits correspondent's deposit; correspondent accepts payer's correspondent deposit and credits payee's deposit.
B	Digital, central bank issued	Central bank electronically registered reserves and settlement accounts	The payer bank instructs the central bank to debit its account and credit the account of the payee bank. It allows final settlement in currency defined by central bank.
C	Central bank issued, token-based	Central bank wholesale bearer notes (e.g., Bank of England consul bonds)	Physical handling of the bonds from the payer to the payee or transferral of ownership by change of ownership of bonds is held at depository.
D	Widely accessible, digital, central bank issued	Central bank computerized retail deposits (e.g., last years of PBOC 1950-84 unitary banking)	The payer requests the central bank to debit the payer's deposit with central bank and credit the payee's deposit with central bank. Entries are done through a computerized IT system.
E	Digital, central bank issued, token-based	No examples, but central banks are currently researching feasibility of wholesale CBDCs	Private, closed, double-spend protected distributed ledger may use blockchain technologies.
F	Widely accessible, central bank issued	Central bank manual book entry retail deposits (e.g., PBOC 1950-84 unitary banking)	The payer requests the central bank to debit payer's deposit with the central bank and credit payee's deposit with central bank. Entries are done through manual bookkeeping.

G	Widely accessible, digital, central bank issued , token-based	No examples, but central banks are currently researching feasibility of retail CBDCs	Private, open, double-spend protected distributed ledger may use blockchain technologies.
H	Digital, token-based	Wholesale cryptocurrencies	Private, open, double-spend protected distributed ledger may use blockchain technologies.
I	Widely accessible, central bank issued, token-based	Coins and central bank notes	Physical handing of notes and coins is done from payer to payee.
J	Widely accessible, digital, token-based	Retail cryptocurrencies such as bitcoins	Blockchain is public open.
K	Widely accessible, token-based	Private bartering of physical tokens such as cowry shells, miniature knives, and privately minted coins	Physical handing of tokens is done from payer to payee.

Note: CBDC = Central bank digital currencies; IT = information technology.

Source: Created by the authors based on the "Money Flower" in Morten Bech and Rodney Garratt, *Central Bank Cryptocurrencies*, (Bank for International Settlements, 2017), accessed January 29, 2020. https://papers.ssrn.com/sol3/papers.cfm?abstract_id=3041906.

EXHIBIT 4: CORRESPONDENT BANK SYSTEM FOR CROSS-BORDER PAYMENTS

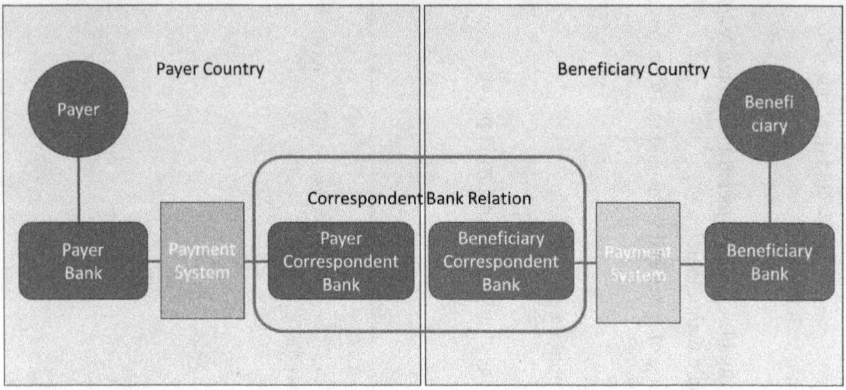

Five Payment Steps:

1. Payer instructs the payer bank (who is not a member of the beneficiary country's payment system and has no corresponding bank in the beneficiary country's payment system) to debit its account and make payment to the beneficiary's bank account.
2. The payer bank makes the payment to the payer correspondent bank through the payer country payment system.
3. The payer correspondent bank instructs the beneficiary correspondent bank to debit its nostro account and credit the account of the beneficiary bank.
4. The beneficiary correspondent bank makes the payment to the beneficiary bank through the beneficiary country payment system.
5. The beneficiary bank advises the beneficiary that it has received the payment and has credited the beneficiary's account.

Note: nostro = account (particularly in foreign exchange transactions) that a bank owns in and owes to its correspondent bank; nostro account from the bank's perspective = vostro account from the correspondent's perspective (from the Latin "ours" and "yours" respectively).
Source: Created by the authors.

EXHIBIT 5: SOCIETY FOR WORLDWIDE INTERBANK FINANCIAL TELECOMMUNICATIONS MT 103 FIELDS

Field / Tag	Field and Tag Name
:20	Transaction reference number
:23B	Bank operation code
:32A	Value date/currency/interbank settled
:33B	Currency/original ordered amount
:50A, F, or K	Ordering customer (payer) or address of the remitter
:52A or D	Ordering institution (payer's bank)
:53A, B, or D	Sender's correspondent (bank)
:54A, B, or D	Receiver's correspondent (bank)
:56A, C, or D	Intermediary (bank)
:57A, B, C, or D	Account with institution (beneficiary's bank)
:59 or 59A	Beneficiary
:70	Remittance information
:71A	Details of charges (OUR/SHA/BEN)
:72	Sender to receiver information
:77B	Regulatory reporting

Source: "What Is an MT103?" Money Mover, accessed February 5, 2019, www.moneymover.com/about/faqs/what-mt103.

EXHIBIT 6: SOCIETY FOR WORLDWIDE INTERBANK FINANCIAL TELECOMMUNICATIONS

Item	Content
Ownership and membership	Over 11,000 banks, securities firms, and other financial institutions and corporations
Countries and territories served	Over 200
Messages per year	7.1 billion
Maximum messages recorded per day	32.8 million (as of November 2016)
Annual revenue (2017)	US$357.2 million
Annual profit (2017)	US$45.1 million
Most recent systems update	Global payments initiative to increase speed and transparency, allowing end-to-end payment tracking and facilitating application process interfaces
Use of blockchain	Proof of concept of optimizing time liquidity management in nostro accounts with 34 international (including three Chinese) banks, using hyperlink fabric

Source: "2017 Annual Review: Moving Fast Efficiency without Compromise," Society for Worldwide Interbank Financial Telecommunications, May 2018, accessed May 5, 2020, www.swift.com/file/51966/download?token=0UogFJo6.

EXHIBIT 7: BLOCKCHAIN HISTORY

Year	Event	*Source*
1976	A method is described whereby private cryptographic keys can be securely exchanged over a public channel: public–private key technology.	Whitfield Diffie and Martin E. Hellman, "New Directions in Cryptography," *IEEE Transactions on Information Theory* 22, no. 6, (1976): 644–654, accessed October 27, 2019, https://ee.stanford.edu/~hellman/publications/24.pdf.
1977	A method is described as a cryptographic system to transmit a computationally secure cryptogram over an insecure communication channel without prearrangement of a cipher key.	United States Patent and Trademark Office, *Martin E. Hellman, Bailey Whitfield Diffie, and Ralph C. Merkle*: *Cryptographic Apparatus and Method*, U.S. Patent 4200770, Filed September 6, 1977, and Issued April 29, 1980, accessed October 27, 2019, http://patft.uspto.gov/netacgi/nph-Parser?Sect1=PTO2&Sect2=HITOFF&p=1&u=%2Fnetahtml%2FPTO%2Fsearch-bool.html&r=1&f=G&l=50&co1=AND&d=PTXT&s1=4200770. PN.&OS=PN/4200770&RS=PN/4200770.
1979	A hash (or Merkle) tree is described that recursively hashes each block of data and the hash of the blocks of the previous hashes in the tree, allowing verification of transmitted or stored data of data without a prearranged key resulting in a viable digital signature.	United States Patent and Trademark Office, *Ralph C. Merkle: Method of Providing Digital Signatures*, U.S. Patent 4309569, Filed September 5, 1979, and Issued January 5, 1982, accessed October 27, 2019, http://patft.uspto.gov/netacgi/nph-Parser?Sect1=PTO2&Sect2=HITOFF&p=1&u=%2Fnetahtml%2FPTO%2Fsearch-bool.html&r=1&f=G&l=50&co1=AND&d=PTXT&s1=4309569.PN.&OS=PN/4309569&RS=PN/4309569.
1980	Conditions are specified for Byzantine fault tolerance for network security where nodes evidence the Byzantine Generals' Problem due to nodal failure or fraud.	Leslie Lamport, Robert Shostak, and Marshall Pease, "The Byzantine Generals Problem" *ACM Transactions on Programming Languages and Systems* 4, no. 3, (July 1982): 382–401, accessed December 17, 2021 https://lamport.azurewebsites.net/pubs/byz.pdf.

1982	Details the use of private–public keys for blind signatures in an anonymous cryptocurrency payment system.	David Chaum "Blind Signatures for Untraceable Payments," in David Chaum, Ronald L. Rivest, and Alan T. Sherman, *Advances in Cryptology* (Boston, MA: Springer, 1983): 199–203.
1989	DigiCash Inc. set up as world's first cryptocurrency company, providing anonymous payments of DigiCash.	Julie Pitta, "Requiem for a Bright Idea," *Forbes* (November 1, 1999), accessed October 27, 2019, www.forbes.com/forbes/1999/1101/6411390a.html#5ce20b66715f.
1992	Cyberpunk Manifesto sets out principles for privacy in the electronic age: "Privacy is necessary for an open society in the electronic age. Privacy is not secrecy. A private matter is something one doesn't want the whole world to know, but a secret matter is something one doesn't want anybody to know. Privacy is the power to selectively reveal oneself to the world."	Eric Hughes, "A Cypherpunk's Manifesto," *Activism.net*, 1992, accessed October 27, 2019, www.activism.net/cypherpunk/manifesto.html.
1992	A method is described for requiring users to compute a difficult function to access a shared resource, like email, aimed at preventing spamming and other abuses.	Cynthia Dwork and Moni Naor, "Pricing via Processing or Combatting Junk Mail," conference paper presented at Crypto '92, accessed October 27, 2019, www.wisdom.weizmann.ac.il/~naor/PAPERS/pvp.pdf.
1993	Secure Hash Algorithm (or SHA-0) is developed as a collision-resistant hashing algorithm able to convert data blocks of arbitrary lengths into an output string of a specified length.	National Institute for Standards and Technology, *FIPS 180: Secure Hash Standard*, May 1993, accessed October 27, 2019, https://csrc.nist.gov/publications/detail/fips/180/1/archive/1995-04-17.

EXHIBIT 7: (*Continued*)

1996	E-gold is set up as the first anonymously traded cryptocurrency backed by gold and held in trust.	Douglas Jackson and Barry K. Downey, "e-Gold: Transnational e-Money," e-gold, accessed October 27, 2019, www.e-gold.com/unsecure/homepage.htm.
1997	Hashcash proof of work system is described as computing a token to reduce spam. The hash function resides on the headers in the email with a nonce value determined by the sender to give an arbitrarily low hash value. Only emails with hashes less than the determined value are accepted. The lower the accepted value, the greater the amount of the sender's work that is proven.	Adam Back, "Hashcash — A Denial of Service Counter-Measure," Cypherspace.org, August 2002, accessed October 27, 1919, www.hashcash.org/hashcash.pdf.
1998	Characteristics of a cryptocurrency are described in a cyberpunk online post.	Dai Wei, "b-money, an anonymous, distributed electronic cash system," WeiDai, accessed October 27, 2019, www.weidai.com/bmoney.txt.
1999	Platforms to exchange digital gold and other cryptocurrencies are set up.	"e-gold Ltd. Assumes Responsibility for e-Gold Family of Currencies," e-gold blog, accessed October 27, 2019, https://blog.e-gold.com/2000/01/e-gold-ltd-assu.html.
2002	A set of improved hash functions, including SHA-2 and SHA-256, is published.	Roger A. Grimes, "All You Need to Know about the Move from SHA-1 to SHA-2 Encryption" *CSO*, July 6, 2017, accessed October 27, 2019, www.csoonline.com/article/2879073/all-you-need-to-know-about-the-move-from-sha1-to-sha2-encryption.html; "SHA256 Hash Generator Online," National Institute of Standards and Technology, 2018, accessed June 16, 2019, https://passwordsgenerator.net/sha256-hash-generator/.

(*Continued*)

EXHIBIT 7: (*Continued*)

2007	Magic: The Gathering Online Exchange (Mt. Gox) is set up to trade points from the former Magic card game's online game Magic: The Gathering Online.	Jed McCaleb, 2014 Mt. Gox Interview, accessed October 27, 2019, www.gwern.net/docs/bitcoin/2014-mccaleb.
2008	The peer-to-peer network bitcoin is proposed, which can provide secure payments without the need for a trusted intermediary by using a Merkle tree, Hashcash, and a Byzantine fault tolerance system where non-co-operative nodes in the network accept the longest chain of blocks as authoritative.	Satoshi Nakamoto, *Bitcoin: A Peer-to-Peer Electronic Cash System*, white paper, 2008, accessed June 16, 2019, https://bitcoin.org/bitcoin.pdf.
2009	Bitcoin software implementing Nakamoto's 2008 paper using public–private key technology to authenticate participating nodes and the SHA-256 hashing function is published on the Internet. Bitcoin is launched by Nakamoto mining the first block.	"Bitcoin Is an Innovative Payment Network and a New Kind of Money," Bitcoin, accessed October 27, 2019, www.bitcoin.org.
2011	2011 Silk Road, a black market for illegal drugs, adopts bitcoin as its sole means of payment.	Jose Pagliery, "FBI Shuts Down Online Drug Market Silk Road," *CNN Business*, October 2, 2013, accessed October 27, 2019, https://money.cnn.com/2013/10/02/technology/silk-road-shut-down/index.html.

EXHIBIT 7: (*Continued*)

2013	U.S. Federal Bureau of Investigation shuts down Silk Road website for narcotics trafficking, computer hacking, and money laundering.	Jose Pagliery "FBI Shuts Down Online Drug Market Silk Road," *CNN Business*, October 2, 2013 accessed October 27, 2019, https://money.cnn.com/2013/10/02/technology/silk-road-shut-down/index.html.
2014	Etherium, an open-source blockchain-based digital computing platform enabling smart contracts, raises US$2.3 million worth of bitcoins in a 12-hour crowdfunding to support Ether, in the world's first initial coin offering.	Armand Tanzarian, "Ethereum Raises 3,700 BTC in First 12 Hours of Ether Presale," *Cointelegraph*, July 23, 2014, accessed October 27, 2019, https://cointelegraph.com/news/ethereum-raises-3700-btc-in-first-12-hours-of-ether-presale.
2014	2014 Mt. Gox, the world's main cryptocurrency exchange for Bitcoin, collapses	Takashi Mochizuki, "Mt. Gox Files for Liquidation," *The Wall Street Journal*, April 16, 2014, accessed October 27, 2019, www.wsj.com/articles/mt-gox-files-for-liquidation-1397625896.
2014	People's Bank of China instructs all banks and payment processors to close bitcoin trading accounts.	Alex Hern, "Chinese Bitcoin Exchange Closes Deposits after Central Bank Clampdown," *The Guardian*, April 3, 2014, accessed October 27, 2019, www.theguardian.com/technology/2014/apr/03/chinese-bitcoin-exchange-closes-after-central-bank-clampdown.
2015	Linux Foundation starts Hyperledger Project, an umbrella organization for open-source blockchain related tools.	"The Linux Foundation Projects," Hyperledger Organization, accessed October 27, 2019, www.hyperledger.org.
2016	IBM launches Fabric in the Hyperledger.	"Hyperledger: Blockchain Collaboration Changing the Business World," IBM, accessed October 27, 2019, www.ibm.com/blockchain/hyperledger.

(*Continued*)

EXHIBIT 7: (*Continued*)

2016	China Merchants Bank starts blockchain initiative.	China Merchants Bank's blockchain team, in conversation with the case authors.
2017	Royal Bank of Canada announces use of Hyperledger for U.S.–Canada interbank settlements.	Matt Scuffham, "Exclusive: Royal Bank of Canada Using Blockchain for US/Canada Payments — Executive," September 27, 2017, Reuters, accessed October 27, 2019, www.reuters.com/article/us-rbc-blockchain/exclusive-royal-bank-of-canada-using-blockchain-for-u-s-canada-payments-executive-idUSKCN1C237N.
2017	Bitcoin value on cryptocurrency exchanges reaches US$17,500.	*Coindesk.*
2017	People's Bank of China bans all initial coin offerings.	Kenneth Rapoza, "Cryptocurrency Exchanges Officially Dead In China," *Forbes*, November 2, 2017, accessed October 27, 2019, www.forbes.com/sites/kenrapoza/2017/11/02/cryptocurrency-exchanges-officially-dead-in-china/#1d9050cb2a83.

Note: patent year = year of filing; *source* of patents = year of publishing; year of articles = year of first submission or proposal (if known); *source* of articles = year of publishing

Source: Created by the case authors.

EXHIBIT 8: CHINA MERCHANTS BANK CROSS-BORDER PAYMENT BLOCKCHAIN SYSTEM

Step 1:
The remitting bank sends its intention to remit with full information similar to SWIFT MT103. The system simultaneously informs the correspondent bank and beneficiary bank and requests their confirmation of undertaking to take receipt or make payment, or both.

Step 2.
The beneficiary bank and the correspondent bank confirm that they will take or make payment.

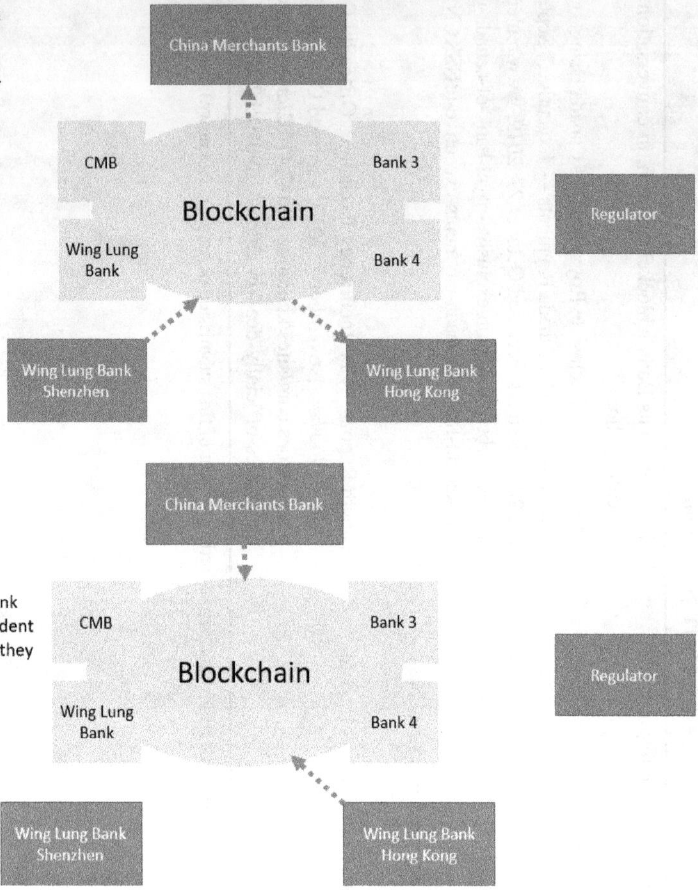

EXHIBIT 8: (*Continued*)

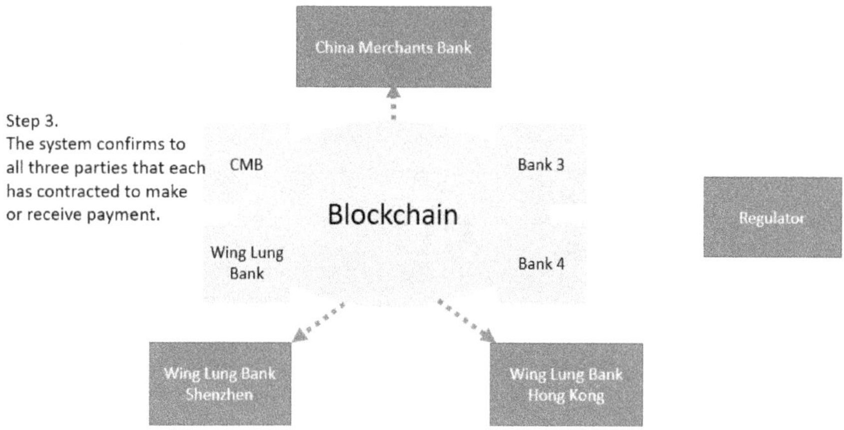

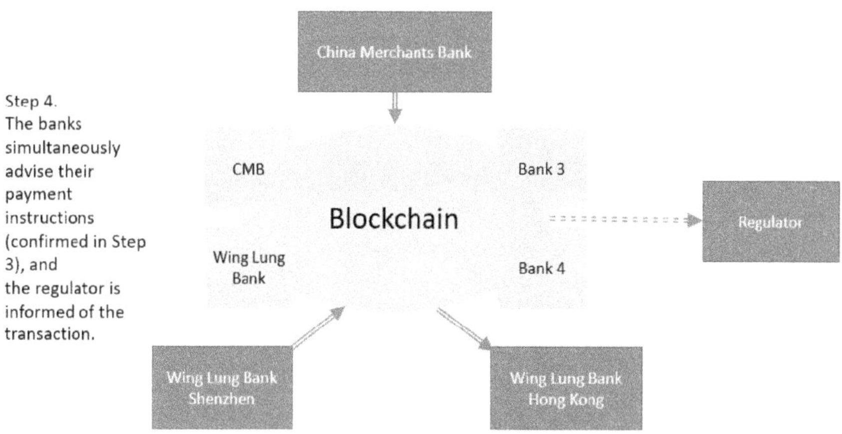

Note: SWIFT = Society for Worldwide Interbank Financial Telecommunications; CMB = China Merchants Bank.

Source: Created by the authors based on Company files.

Concluding Words

Cases — teaching cases used in the business school — often contain a bare-faced lie. Repeated over and over again, typically at the top of a case, we find the words:

> The authors do not intend to illustrate either effective or ineffective handling of a managerial situation.

which is, of course, exactly the opposite of the truth. The main reason for writing cases is *precisely* to illustrate either effective or ineffective handling of managerial situations.

It is true to say that there is no right answer in a case. All analyses involve assessing the future and God (only) knows what the future will bring. But each case has *conditionally* right answers, *conditionally* wrong answers, and likelihoods of conditions prevailing such that there are effective or ineffective management actions. Those of us who use the case method believe that students and instructors can fruitfully analyze and debate correct or incorrect handling of situations. We think that through debate, students are likely to remember what they learn by placing analyses in actual business situations, and to apply their learning more effectively.

This book has presented only a few of the examples of management of innovation in China. I hope that, through reading it, you have come to appreciate a little more not just how innovation is managed in China, but about China itself. I have enjoyed a lifetime of learning real Chinese stories.

China, as the cases in this book show, is NOT monolithic. "China" does not think or do anything. Individual residents of China think and act, as indeed do individuals the world over. We are all seven or eight billion individuals, trying to make our ways in the world and to make the world a little better in the process.

Wherever we live, innovation will shape our futures. Innovation is managed by the rules of the game of human interaction. People in the most powerful countries of the world tend to write the rules of the game. As the second decade of the 21st century closed, the economies in real terms of China, the United States, and Europe were roughly the same size. China is growing faster. If it continues to grow just over two percent per year faster than the United States and Europe, China will exceed the combined economies of the United States and Europe by 2049, the 100th anniversary of People's Republic of China. Can we thrive in a world in which Chinese write rules? At least we must try. Understanding is the first step.

Index

E

F

O

CPSIA information can be obtained
at www.ICGtesting.com
Printed in the USA
JSHW051140020522
25176JS00001B/4

9 789811 245886